freedom's frontier

freedom's frontier

California and the Struggle
over Unfree Labor, Emancipation,
and Reconstruction

Stacey L. Smith

THE UNIVERSITY OF NORTH CAROLINA PRESS
Chapel Hill

© 2013 THE UNIVERSITY OF NORTH CAROLINA PRESS

All rights reserved
Designed by Sally Scruggs
Set in Quadraat by codeMantra
Manufactured in the United States of America

The paper in this book meets the guidelines for permanence
and durability of the Committee on Production Guidelines for
Book Longevity of the Council on Library Resources.

The University of North Carolina Press has been
a member of the Green Press Initiative since 2003.

Library of Congress Cataloging-in-Publication Data
Smith, Stacey L.
Freedom's frontier : California and the struggle over unfree labor,
emancipation, and reconstruction / Stacey L. Smith.
pages cm
Includes bibliographical references and index.
ISBN 978-1-4696-0768-9 (cloth : alk. paper)
ISBN 978-1-4696-2653-6 (pbk.: alk. paper)
1. Forced labor—California—History—19th century. 2. Slave labor—
California—History—19th century. 3. California—Social conditions—
19th century. 4. California—Economic conditions—19th century. 5. Slavery—
California—History—19th century. 6. Labor—California—History—
19th century. 7. California—Gold discoveries—Social aspects. I. Title.
HD4875.U5S525 2013
331.11'730979409034—dc23
2013001365

Portions of this work appeared earlier, in somewhat different form, as
"Remaking Slavery in a Free State: Masters and Slaves in Gold Rush California,"
Pacific Historical Review 80, no. 1 (February 2011): 28–63. © 2011
by the Pacific Coast Branch, American Historical Association,
and the Regents of the University of California.

THIS BOOK WAS DIGITALLY PRINTED.

for David

Contents

Illustrations and Tables

Illustrations

Tables

Acknowledgments

Writing a book can often be a solitary venture. I am fortunate, however, to have had the support and encouragement of many people, who have made the research and writing process far less lonely and far more rewarding than I would have ever imagined.

My greatest debts, intellectual and personal, are to Susan Lee Johnson. I first met Susan when I was an undergraduate at the University of Colorado–Boulder. In a serendipitous turn of events, she ended up taking a job at the University of Wisconsin–Madison shortly after I began my graduate career there. I am thankful every day for the twist of fate that caused our paths to cross again. Susan read earlier versions of this work over and over again, always with an eye for detail and story, and always with excellent advice, encouragement, and praise. Susan is a dogged researcher, a fantastic writer, a generous scholar, an amazing editor, and a dedicated teacher. Her guidance over the past decade has made me a better writer and a better historian. I could not have asked for a more engaged and helpful mentor.

I owe a great deal to several other Wisconsin faculty who have shaped this project along the way. My earliest graduate adviser, Stephen Kantrowitz, guided me through my first years of the program. His unfailing faith in my abilities, his spirit and smarts, and his boundless enthusiasm for history helped me make it through those first angst-filled years of graduate school. Whenever my confidence faltered, Steve was always there to remind me of the significance of this project and the important work yet to be done. Bill Cronon, Arthur McEvoy, and Ned Blackhawk also played critical roles in shaping this text. Bill is a model of how to be a generous and engaged scholar and teacher, and I am indebted to him for all the time he has invested in my career. Art has been of invaluable help in teaching me to navigate the treacherous waters of U.S. legal history. Ned's teaching and scholarship have greatly enhanced my understanding of the history of North American indigenous peoples, and he has been a great influence on this work.

As an undergraduate and later as a graduate student, I have been fortunate to work with many other wonderful scholars, teachers, and fellow students. I am grateful to Fred Anderson, Virginia Anderson, Julie Greene, and Martha Hanna at the University of Colorado–Boulder for encouraging me to go on to graduate school and for keeping in touch with me long after. At Wisconsin, I had the good fortune to work with the late Jeanne Boydston, as well as with Cindy I-Fen Cheng, Colleen Dunlavy, Florencia Mallon, Tony Michels, Francisco Scarano, and Steve Stern. A number of gifted fellow graduate students also helped my career, and this book, come to fruition. Many thanks to Catherine Burns, Sarah Costello, Suzanne Danks, Jerome Dotson, Jim Feldman, Mark Goldberg, Kori Graves, Rob Harper, Michel Hogue, Jennifer Holland, Sarah King, Abigail Markwyn, Gladys McCormick, Michelle Morgan, Haley Pollack, Gil Ribak, Kelly Roark, Kendra Smith-Howard, and Tyina Steptoe for support, friendship, food, and fun over these many years.

My colleagues at Oregon State University, where I arrived in 2008, have aided immensely in the production of this book. As chairs of the History Department, Paul Farber, Jonathan Katz, David Luft, and Ben Mutschler guided me through the hiring and tenure process and made sure I had time and resources to complete the book manuscript. Very special thanks go to Jeffrey Sklansky for his enthusiastic support of my research and the many hours he spent helping to get me settled in at Oregon State. Fellow Americanists Mina Carson, Marisa Chappell, and Christopher Nichols and fellow western historian Bill Robbins have been generous with their time and help. I have also benefited from many conversations with colleagues in other fields, including Gary Ferngren, Anita Guerrini, Jake Hamblin, Bill Husband, Hung-Yok Ip, Paul Kopperman, Bob Nye, Mary Jo Nye, Mike Osborne, Stephen Rubert, Lisa Sarasohn, and Nicole von Germeten.

Beyond my own institution, I have been fortunate to receive help from many generous and talented scholars. Michael Magliari has shared his scholarship on Indian slavery with me, commented on the entire book manuscript, and helped me to tackle the vast California manuscript collections at the Huntington Library. He has my eternal thanks for his generous spirit and for his help correcting many mistakes. Thanks, too, to the editors of the *Pacific Historical Review*, Carl Abbott, David Johnson, and Susan Wladaver-Morgan, as well as to Amy S. Greenberg and several anonymous readers who helped me develop an earlier article related to this book. Thanks also to Stephen Aron, Alicia Chávez, Lauren Cole, William Deverell, Robert Dykstra, Joseph Genetin-Pilawa, Deena González, Kelly Sisson Lessens, Joshua Paddison, Heather Cox Richardson, Steven Rosales, Allison Tirres, and Richard White for reading and commenting on portions of this work at various conferences and workshops over the years.

A number of institutions also made my writing and research possible. Funding from the Horning Endowment and the Center for the Humanities at Oregon State University provided me with much-needed leave time to finish the book revisions. As a graduate student, I also benefited from funding by the Doris G. Quinn Dissertation Fellowship, sponsored by the University of Wisconsin–Madison Department of History and the Doris G. Quinn Foundation, as well as the Dana-Allen Dissertator Fellowship at the University of Wisconsin–Madison Institute for Research in the Humanities and the American Historical Association's Albert J. Beveridge Grant. The Western History Association–Huntington Library Martin Ridge Fellowship and the Annaley Naegle Redd Award in Western Women's History from the Charles Redd Center for Western Studies at Brigham Young University allowed me to travel to crucial archives.

This project would not have been possible without the expertise and untiring help of the dozens of librarians and archivists whom I have met during my research travels. Peter Blodgett, curator of western history collections at the Huntington Library, has spent many hours talking with me about my project, helping me to make my way through the Huntington Library collections, and recommending secondary literature. He is also a great friend and has always made the Huntington feel like home. I also appreciate the help of Chris Adde, Jill Cogen, Bill Frank, and Kate Henningsen of the Huntington Library; Walter Brem, Iris Donovan, David Kessler, and Theresa Salazar of the Bancroft Library; Pat Johnson of the Center for Sacramento History; and Linda Johnson of the California State Archives. All of them patiently answered my numerous questions and tolerated my unending manuscript retrieval requests.

This book would not have come together (literally) without the unflagging efforts of the editorial team at the University of North Carolina Press. Mark Simpson-Vos, my acquiring editor, took an interest in the project very early on and has encouraged me every step of the way. He has answered endless first-time author questions, helped me manage the review and editorial process, and made many helpful suggestions that focused and tightened my arguments. Ron Maner, Zachary Read, Jay Mazzocchi, and Dorothea Anderson have provided much-needed assistance with matters of presentation, style, and organization. They have helped me create a much more polished final product.

My parents, George and Cindy Smith, and my in-laws, David and Eve Bishop, have long supported my pursuit of higher education and eagerly read my work. Many thanks to all of them for standing by my history dreams these many years. My grandmother, Edna Mae Bly Clark, never had the chance to earn a high school education. She was, nonetheless, an avid reader and a great lover of history. I likely owe my lifelong engagement with the past to her. This project would almost certainly never have come to fruition without the love and encouragement of my husband, David Bishop. David, a historian-turned-academic administrator, has read and commented on many of these pages. More important, his unfaltering faith in me as a teacher, as a scholar, as a historian, and as a person has kept me going with the project during my greatest moments of uncertainty and frustration. I am forever grateful to him.

freedom's frontier

Introduction

California, Free and Unfree

In December 1856, more than six years after California entered the Union as a free state, an African American woman named Charlotte Sophie Gomez appeared before San Francisco's Fourth District Court on charges of kidnapping. Gomez's accuser, a prominent white physician named Oliver Wozencraft, testified that she had taken a nine-year-old girl named Shasta from his home and concealed her for nearly three years. Gomez belonged to a small network of African American abolitionists who aided enslaved people brought to California in violation of the state's antislavery constitution. Shasta's "abduction" had all the trappings of a fugitive slave case. After Gomez took Shasta from Wozencraft's home, she changed the girl's name and eventually cut her hair so that she could pass as a boy. When Wozencraft caught wind of Shasta's whereabouts, Gomez spirited her out of the city to live with a free black family in the countryside. To all appearances, Shasta was a fugitive slave on free soil.[1]

But Shasta differed from other California runaways in a critical regard: she was a Yuki Indian child. Wozencraft, a former federal Indian commissioner, had captured her during a punitive campaign against her people in northwestern California in 1851.[2] He then bound her as his ward under the provisions of California's 1850 Act for the Government and Protection of Indians. This law allowed whites to keep Indian children and profit from their labor until they reached adulthood. Gomez had, in effect, used the same underground networks developed to smuggle African American slaves out of bondage to liberate an Indian child from long-term servitude in a white household. Gomez appeared before the court and, supported by "a large delegation of the colored population, both male and female," refused to disclose the child's whereabouts. These efforts to conceal the young girl failed. A private detective finally tracked Shasta to her hiding place. Wozencraft reclaimed the

Shasta's master, Oliver Wozencraft (seated center), served as a special Indian commissioner and negotiated several treaties with northern California bands. Wozencraft met with these Maidu headmen in July 1851, three months before he and his entourage clashed with Yuki Indians and took the infant, Shasta, prisoner. Unknown photographer, *Maidu Indians and Treaty Commissioners*, 1851. Courtesy of George Eastman House, International Museum of Photography and Film, Rochester, N.Y.

child, and she remained with his family as a domestic servant until at least the 1880s.[3]

In unearthing stories of people like Shasta and Charlotte Sophie Gomez, this book seeks to recast the narrative of the sectional crisis, emancipation, and Reconstruction in the United States by geographically recentering it in the Far West. It contends that California's struggle over slavery did not end with its entrance into the Union as a free state as part of the Compromise of 1850. Instead, as Shasta's case shows, California's free soil was far less solid, its contests over human bondage far more complicated, contentious, and protracted, than historians have usually imagined. Across the antebellum and Civil War decades, Californians saw the rise of a dense tangle of unfree labor systems—most real, some imagined—that undermined and unsettled free-state status. The development of African American slavery, diverse forms of American Indian servitude, sexual trafficking in bound women, and contract labor arrangements involving Latin Americans, Asians, and Pacific Islanders all kept the slavery question alive in California during the 1850s. The rise of the Republican Party and national slave liberation in the 1860s eroded the state's coercive labor systems, emancipating California alongside the rest of the nation. By Reconstruction, California's struggles over slavery became narrowly focused on the growing perils that allegedly unfree Chinese, "coolie" contract laborers and bound prostitutes, posed to the accomplishments of emancipation. Deftly fusing the anti-Chinese cause with the antislavery cause, California's legislators formulated immigration restriction laws that excluded Chinese "slaves" without explicitly violating new Reconstruction prohibitions on race-based civil and legal discrimination. California politicians eventually carried these anti-Chinese antislavery laws beyond California's borders to Congress, where, despite recent efforts to liberate and enfranchise African Americans, they became the blueprints for the nation's most racially exclusive immigration statutes to that date. Once we set our sights on the Pacific Coast, it becomes clear not only that the struggle over slavery was a truly national story, encompassing North, South, and West, but that the Far West played a critical role in remaking the post–Civil War nation.

Moving the crisis over slavery, emancipation, and Reconstruction to California upends familiar narratives of regional and national history. First, the presence and persistence of unfree labor in California seems at odds with much of western history. In popular mythology, the American West stands as a kind of ultimate free-labor landscape, a place where autonomous, mobile individuals were at perfect liberty to pursue their economic interests and raise their social status. Historical scholarship, too, has often linked the West's destiny with that of free labor. Frederick Jackson Turner's 1893 frontier thesis depicted the West as a space of freedom characterized by individual autonomy, geographic mobility, and social and economic fluidity. Starting in the 1920s, historians of the American South also naturalized free labor in the West by arguing that western geography and climate were incompatible with plantation agriculture, thus placing "natural limits" on slavery's expansion. Social and political historians working in the latter half of the twentieth century took a different approach, documenting how the militantly free-labor, antiblack, and antimonopoly politics of many western whites, rather than geography alone, precluded slavery. Taken together, these works present the region's history as incompatible with—even antithetical to—slavery. The triumph of free labor in the West appears, if not predetermined, then at least overdetermined.[4]

The persistence of the slavery question in California also challenges us to rethink the broader narrative of nineteenth-century U.S. history. Histories of the sectional crisis invariably focus on politics east of the Mississippi River and treat the Far West as an imagined space, a place onto which northerners and southerners projected their hopes and fears about slavery's future. Pro- and antislavery advocates, North and South, argued over whether the region would be opened to slaves and slaveholders, or whether it would be preserved for prospective free white laborers. Once California adopted an antislavery constitution and gained admission as a free state under the Compromise of 1850, it promptly disappears from most discussions of the sectional crisis and the Civil War.[5] As a result, we lose sight of how slavery became an issue of long-term social and economic importance within western communities. California, and, by extension, the rest of the Far West, seems an isolated, peripheral region, disconnected from the monumental conflict over slavery and freedom that rocked the nation after 1850.

Freedom's Frontier addresses the absence of slavery in western regional history and the absence of the Far West in the broader history of American slavery and emancipation by bringing the two fields into dialogue with each other. It both integrates California into the history of the Civil War and Reconstruction eras and suggests that California's story can enhance our understanding of U.S. national history in fundamental ways. A multiracial society with multiple systems of bound and semibound labor, California complicates familiar black-white, slave-free binaries at the heart of most histories of the era. There, categories like "free" and "slave" often adhered to racially marked bodies in unfamiliar or unpredictable ways. In the legal and political struggles over the state's multitude of labor systems, white Californians were just as likely to express concern about American Indian, Mexican, Chilean, and Chinese "slaves" as they were to discuss the fate of African American bondpeople. Politicians, reformers, and lawyers refashioned the language of antislavery in new and surprising ways to contest labor systems ranging from peonage to contract labor to prostitution. California, then, opens new insights into the instability and fluidity of racial categories, particularly the ideological linkages between slavery and race. It also shows that "slavery" and "free labor" were not rigid oppositional categories but fluid concepts that could each be reimagined to encompass a wide range of waged, unwaged, voluntary, and involuntary work.[6]

California's freedom struggles not only give scholars a more complete, complex understanding of this transformative period in American politics, law, and race relations. They also help to explain a critical paradox of the postwar era: how Reconstruction, a period focused on the breakdown of race-based civil and legal inequalities, also witnessed the nation's most virulent anti-Chinese immigration laws. This book suggests that the re-racialization of slavery in California—the association of Chinese with forms of degraded servitude that threatened the United States' new birth of freedom—helped shape national debates over race and liberty in the wake of emancipation. California politicians, both Democrats and Republicans, framed Chinese immigration restriction as an antislavery measure that advanced the emancipatory principles of the Thirteenth Amendment rather than as a racially exclusive policy. In doing so, they evaded the guarantees of due process and equal protection, regardless of race, embedded in the Civil Rights Act of 1866, the Fourteenth Amendment, and the Ku Klux Klan Acts and made anti-Chinese laws appear wholly consistent with the national Republican Party's emerging Reconstruction policy on race, slavery, and civil rights.[7] This strategy hastened the federal march toward Chinese immigration restriction, inspiring both the Page Law of 1875 and the general exclusion of most Chinese in 1882. California's internal slavery debate reached eastward to shape national Reconstruction policy in crucial, but overlooked, ways.[8]

This story of California's contest over unfree labor builds on the work of other historians who have begun to narrow the chasm between the history of the American West and the history of American slavery. In the past three decades, scholars of western North America have problematized free labor in the region. In a pathbreaking 1985 essay, "From Bondage to Contract," Howard Lamar challenged Frederick Jackson Turner's assertion that in the West "free land meant free people and a democratic society." Instead, slavery, debt bondage, contract labor, and indentured servitude were critical to the development of western colonial economies. The American West was, in fact, "more properly a symbol of bondage than freedom when it comes to labor systems," and scholars would do well to explore the connections between western labor history and the broader national history of slavery.[9]

Many western historians have heeded the call. The burgeoning field of western borderlands history has done much to dispel the myth that the West was a landscape of liberty. Borderlands scholars have documented the importance of captive raiding and slavery to the social, cultural, economic, and biological reproduction of both Native and European borderlands communities. Scholars of transnational labor migrations across the West have also demonstrated how the region's vast geography and seemingly limitless opportunities restricted rather than enhanced workers' freedom. Reliant on employers and labor contractors to move them to and across the West's wide-open spaces, immigrant workers often became enmeshed in debt peonage and contract labor.[10] Historians of California have contributed a great deal to this growing literature. They have documented the journeys of slaves to the goldfields, California's systems of forced Indian labor, the lives of Chinese women bound in the sex trade, and the debates over imagined Chinese "coolie" slavery on the Pacific Coast.[11] In light of this research, the idea that western environments, economies, or social structures were somehow incompatible with bound labor is gradually losing its force.

This book weaves together these histories of California's bound workers into a common narrative about western unfreedom. It takes stories that have often been told separately and along racially segmented lines—of westward-bound African American slaves, of northward-bound Mexican and Chilean contract workers, of eastward-bound Chinese credit-ticket laborers and prostitutes, of Native American apprentices—and puts them next to and up against each other. Once integrated into the same story, it becomes clear that California's diverse labor systems and the debates over them did not stand in isolation from each other. Instead, they were each different facets of a common struggle over the meaning of freedom in California, and their simultaneous rise and fall collectively illustrate the West's tortuous, and torturous, transition through the era of emancipation.

In addition to helping lay the groundwork for a history of the unfree West, this study also builds on the findings of scholars who have worked to construct a truly national narrative of the sectional crisis, the Civil War, and Reconstruction that encompasses North, South, and West. Western scholars such as Eugene Berwanger, Elliott West, Alvin M. Josephy Jr., and Joshua Paddison have proposed West-centered histories of the Civil War and Reconstruction eras, while scholars of western Native America have analyzed the complex transition from slavery to freedom in the Indian Territory. Together, these works not only demonstrate that federal policies regarding slavery, emancipation, and Reconstruction extended westward to shape the region's law and politics. They also illuminate how the West's multiracial populations, together with its position at the leading edge of U.S. empire, gave the region a prominent role in national discussions about race, freedom, religion, and the republic's future.[12] Historians of the Civil War and Reconstruction have also begun to reframe the contest over slavery and freedom as a three-sided struggle fought on northern, southern, and western fronts. This project initially focused on integrating the North more fully into the story of emancipation and Reconstruction. Eric Foner, Amy Dru Stanley, and Heather Cox Richardson made compelling arguments that the end of slavery transformed the industrializing North along with the South, embroiling northerners in conflicts over the unfreedoms of wage labor and marriage.[13] Recent works bring this analytical frame westward. Leonard L. Richards, Heather Cox Richardson, and Adam Arenson show that the national politics of the Civil War and Reconstruction were intimately bound up with the politics of westward imperial expansion, western economic development, and the complexity of western race relations. Nation transformed region, and region, in turn, transformed nation.[14] Following the lead of works that break the North-South binary, this book contributes to the construction of a new national history that treats the Far West as an equal participant in the crisis over slavery and emancipation rather than as an isolated outpost of frontier freedom.

IN 1850, FEW CALIFORNIANS anticipated that their state would become the stage for a long-term struggle over slavery. For most of the nineteenth century, California was (at least nominally) free soil. Mexico outlawed slavery in its territorial possessions in 1829. Twenty years later, the U.S. conquest of California and the discovery of gold in the Sierra Nevada foothills created a national crisis over slavery's status in the West. The free-soil movement emerged in the Northeast and the Midwest, dedicated to keeping slavery out of California and other former Mexican territories. Free-soilers argued that the West should be preserved as a haven for white workers, free from competition with slaveholders and slaves. Between 1846 and 1850, they pressed for federal legislation, including the unsuccessful Wilmot Proviso (1846), to ban slavery from the entire Mexican cession. Their efforts soon locked Congress into a stalemate over slavery's westward expansion that stalled California's bid for territorial organization.[15]

In the meantime, thousands of goldseekers crushed into the diggings. Californians, desperate for government, called their own constitutional convention in 1849 and made plans to apply for immediate statehood. California's free-soilers took advantage of this lawmaking opportunity, as well as the absence of formal party organization in the region, to secure free-state status. They quickly proposed an antislavery provision for the new state constitution. Proslavery, southern-born California politicians, wary of losing support among their miner constituents or delaying statehood, chose not to press the question. In the fall of 1849, delegates to the constitutional convention voted, unanimously and without discussion, that "neither slavery, nor involuntary servitude, unless for the punishment of crimes, shall ever be tolerated in this State." After a long struggle, Congress finally granted California statehood and approved its antislavery constitution as part of the Compromise of 1850.

Foes of slavery rejoiced that the Golden State would remain forever a "wonderland open to free labor."[16]

Even as free-soilers congratulated themselves on rescuing California from the Slave Power, they confronted a rapidly changing political scene and a confusing array of labor relations, which shook their confidence in free-state status. The most obvious challenge to free soil came from the thousands of white southerners who migrated to California. In 1850, roughly 36 percent of California's U.S.-born residents hailed from the slave South. Many of these migrants had owned slaves in their home states; several hundred brought their bondpeople with them to work in the mines.[17] White southerners may have been a minority and California masters may have been a minuscule group, but they had clout. Southern whites avidly sought political and legal office in the early 1850s and were vastly overrepresented in the state legislature and judiciary. As one California abolitionist remembered, "The southern element was exceedingly strong, and especially at [the state capital of] Sacramento, and anybody who had any tincture of abolitionism or sympathy with antislavery, was practically an outcast."[18] When Californians organized formal political parties in 1850–51, these southerners flocked to the Democratic Party. They created a well-oiled political machine under the leadership of Mississippi slaveholder-turned-U.S. senator William M. Gwin. Nicknamed the "Chivalry" (or "Chivs") for their aristocratic pretensions and the elite backgrounds of their planter leaders, California's southern-born Democrats emerged as strident voices for slaveholding rights in the Far West.[19]

Meanwhile, northerners who had been Democrats back east also gravitated to the Democratic Party of California. They constructed their own powerful political machine under New Yorker David C. Broderick. Broderick's branch of the Democratic Party appealed to urban working-class whites and became popularly known as the "Shovelry," in opposition to the southern Chivalry. Many Broderick Democrats, including Broderick himself, embraced free soil and chafed at the power of the southern "slaveocracy" at home and in national politics. Hoping to maintain the West as a refuge for humble white workers, free from slaveholder land monopolies, the Shovelry supported free homesteads on public lands and strongly opposed the federal Kansas-Nebraska Act (1854), which threatened to open up new western territories to slavery. They also posed the primary antislavery challenge to California's proslavery Chivs.[20] This was because the Whig Party, the main rival to the Democrats at the national level, was weak in California and its members were lukewarm (or outright hostile) to free soil. The state's Whigs ranged from middle-class, commercially oriented urbanites to adamant proslavery southerners. Few were outspoken opponents of slavery, and a great many even sided with the Chivalry Democrats on the issues of fugitive slaves and the Kansas-Nebraska Act. Only when a state branch of the Republican Party gathered force in the late 1850s would the Chivs face a major external antislavery threat to their power.[21] Before then, California's struggle over slavery happened mainly within political parties rather than between them.

The contest between California's free-soilers and proslavery Chivs went far beyond the abstract question of whether slavery should expand westward. The presence of several hundred enslaved African Americans in the state forced California politicians to confront the question of slaves' and slaveholders' rights on free soil. Slaves played a central role in bringing the issue to the forefront of political debate. Once in California, they ran away, used the threat of escape to extract concessions from their masters, and petitioned the courts for their freedom. Their actions compelled anxious slaveholders to seek new legal strategies to enforce their mastery and protect their rights to slave property. Masters found sympathetic advocates among southern politicians and judges who, though they had no slaves in California themselves, were eager to press the issue of slaveholding rights in the West. Echoing a central proslavery legal argument of the sectional crisis, Chivs insisted that the U.S. Constitution gave southerners equal rights with northerners to carry their property into the federal territories.[22] California's antislavery constitution thus could not suddenly deprive masters of slave property that they had legally transported into the region during the pre-statehood era. Proslavery forces proposed a state fugitive slave law that allowed masters to claim any slaves that they had brought before California's official statehood in September 1850. The new law also committed the state government to capturing and returning resistant slaves to the South. Free-soilers fought the bill by contending that the antislavery constitution immediately liberated every slave who set foot in California. The proslavery faction had the votes, and in 1852 the fugitive slave bill became law. Renewed twice by the state legislature and upheld by a proslavery state supreme court, the California fugitive slave law vitiated the antislavery constitution and carved out a foothold for slavery on free soil.[23]

At the same moment that enslaved African Americans occupied the attention of the legislature, other, ambiguously free laborers generated a new set of social and political conflicts. Gold rush California lay at a global labor crossroads. The expansion of capitalism into northern Mexico, Chile, the Pacific Islands, and East Asia created new disruptions and new opportunities that impelled many people to seek their fortunes in California's goldfields. A number of these new arrivals financed their goldseeking journeys through intricate relations of debt and credit by which they pledged to pay off their passage money by working in the California diggings. Poorer Sonorans and Chilean contract workers, sometimes known as *peones*, bound themselves to work for wealthy *patrones* in exchange for transportation to the mines. Native Hawaiian workers left their island homeland for California under long-term contracts with British and American employers. Hopeful goldseekers from southern China made similar arrangements with American and British entrepreneurs or borrowed their passage money from Chinese merchants and committed to pay back the loans, with heavy interest, by working in California.[24]

The labor arrangements that brought many Sonorans, Chileans, Hawaiians, and Chinese to California bore key hallmarks of free labor: workers voluntarily entered into contracts, and they frequently received wages. And yet free-soilers railed that these "foreign miners" were not free laborers at all but peons and coolies, little different than slaves. Among foreign miners, contracts were not symbols of freedom but markers of bondage. Foreign employers used these legal instruments to bind otherwise free workers to toil for years on end and to accept nonmonetary compensation—passage, food, clothing, and goods—in lieu of meaningful cash wages. Workers' debts to employers made them powerless to resist abuse and severely limited their autonomy and mobility. On one level, peons and coolies threatened to destroy the free-labor refuge that free-soilers hoped to create with the antislavery constitution. Allegedly trapped in semislavery, they would be a cheap, tractable workforce that would reduce wages, compete with independent white miners, and eventually drive whites out of the mines. On another level, peons and coolies highlighted and magnified free-soilers' own anxieties about the emerging capitalist economy and American imperial dominance on the Pacific Coast. In their utter servility and dependence on their employers, both groups portended the fate that might await free white men if they became trapped in permanent wage labor. The pawns of wealthy employers who carried off California's wealth to distant lands, they also challenged white supremacy and U.S. imperial control over the West and its resources. Prohibiting the immigration of alleged peons and coolies and expelling both groups from the state remained leading free-soil preoccupations long into the Reconstruction era.[25]

The debate over slaves, coolies, and peons centered on mining, work that white Americans invariably constructed as a male sphere of labor. Free-soilers emphasized that mining needed to be preserved for free, white, U.S.-born men and protected against men who were unfree, nonwhite, foreign-born, and degraded. This incessant focus on male gold diggers often obscured crucial ties between bound labor and domestic work in California. Amid the overwhelmingly male population of goldseekers, domestic work that whites customarily associated with women—cleaning, cooking, child care, laundering, and nursing—commanded a high price. Sometimes white, American Indian, African American, and Chinese men made lucrative careers providing these services to fellow goldseekers. But demand for domestic labor also fueled a market in bound women and children who worked in private households as wards, apprentices, debt-bound servants, and slaves. For women and girls, labor exploitation and sexual exploitation frequently went hand in hand. Diverse Californians bought and sold women as domestic servants and as forced sexual partners, prostitutes, concubines, and wives. The struggle over free-state status, then, often moved out of the mines and into the intimate labor and sexual relations of California households.[26]

One front of this battle focused on children who, like the Yuki girl Shasta, spent their youths as bound domestic servants. White Californians and elite Mexican Californians (Californios) were often desperate for household help, and they turned to the state's guardianship laws to procure youthful domestic servants. The most important of these laws was the 1850 Act for the Government and Protection of Indians, section three of which allowed non-Indian families to claim Native American children as wards. The children's new guardians enjoyed their labor and their earnings until they reached adulthood. The law ultimately fueled a statewide traffic in kidnapped or captive Native children, bought and sold as domestic servants. African American children of enslaved parents suffered similar fates, although on a much smaller scale. Southern slaveholders eager to hold onto the children of slaves that they had brought to California used the state's general guardianship laws. These statutes authorized state probate courts to assign new guardians for orphans and children of impoverished or "unsuitable" parents. Slaveholders often succeeded in obtaining guardianship by arguing that enslaved children were parentless or that slave mothers were too poor or immoral to care for them.[27]

Once the courts transformed children into wards and masters into guardians, the compulsive nature of children's household labor—and the labor itself—became culturally invisible. Male heads of household simply commanded the labor of bound children just as they did that of their other domestic dependents, their wives and children. For this reason, legal and political officials generally failed to see bound children's labor or hesitated to intervene lest they disrupt white men's mastery over their household dependents. The status of unfree child laborers thus remained relatively uncontroversial until the late 1850s, when a small cadre of politicians from southern California proposed a formal program of forced apprenticeship for both Indian and black children. Free-soilers defeated these efforts but failed to block a later, larger campaign to add an expansive apprenticeship provision to the Act for the Government and Protection of Indians. Passed in 1860, the new amendment allowed the binding out of Indian children and Indian adults convicted of vagrancy or captured in war. The apprenticeship provision expanded the Indian slave trade in northern California and kept the question of compulsive Indian labor alive into the Civil War era.[28]

Like children, bound women also played crucial roles as domestic laborers in California households. But there, as in the rest of the nation, control over women's labor could seldom be separated from mastery over women's bodies, sexuality, and reproduction. Just as cultural understandings of domestic labor as a female endeavor generated demand for bound women as household laborers, social constructions of male desire also generated sexual commerce in captive and enslaved women. During the 1850s and 1860s, California became the site of two such enduring trades. One involved captive American Indian women and girls whom rural whites bought and sold as domestic servants, concubines, and wives. The other centered on bound and indentured Chinese women who arrived in California to work in the urban sex trade or to be sold as wives, secondary wives, concubines, and domestic servants to Chinese men. Both traffics raised profound moral and political dilemmas for free-soilers, who perceived them as dangerous intrusions of the market into the home. The sale of women's bodies—both sexual commerce and the literal sale of female persons—rendered intimate family and household relations such as domestic labor, sex, marriage, and childbearing mere matters of bargain and sale. These transactions turned women into slaves and upended the normative gender and sexual relations of free society. Whether the victims of unscrupulous white "squaw men" on the northwestern California frontier or of tyrannical Chinese husbands and brothel keepers, bound women (according to free-soilers) fell prey to defective gender and sexual relations born of inferior class and ethnic cultures. Free-soilers strove to eliminate both forms of woman slavery by suppressing interracial sex between whites and Indians and by excluding both Chinese men and Chinese women from the state.[29]

The 1860s brought the struggle over unfree labor in California to a head. National slave emancipation, heralded by the Emancipation Proclamation (1863) and the Thirteenth Amendment (1865), inspired Californians to assail a variety of local compulsive labor systems. Republicans took the lead in these efforts. First organized by free-soilers in 1856, the Republican Party of California rose to power when the state Democratic Party, like its national counterpart, fractured completely along sectional lines during the election of 1860. Republicans took the governorship in 1861 and swept state legislative elections in 1862 by merging with former free-soil Democrats to form a new Union Party.[30] The short-lived Union coalition ousted the Chivs and dismantled much of the proslavery, antiblack legislation that had long made the state's African Americans vulnerable to exploitation and reenslavement. It repealed the apprenticeship provisions of the Act for the Government and Protection of Indians that had once fueled the state's Indian slave trade. Finally, it moved to suppress woman trafficking in rural northwestern California and in urban brothels. But the Union Party was a diverse and fractured coalition of true Republicans and former Democrats, and there were limits to both its unity and its antislavery ideology. None but the most radical Republicans embraced full suffrage and civil rights as the end point of African American emancipation. Most Union Party members hoped to integrate American Indians into the state labor market and balked at completely eliminating compulsive work for Native people. Emancipation and Reconstruction would be uneven and incomplete processes for the state's diverse peoples.[31]

California's Chinese residents felt the contradictions of the state's Reconstruction politics most acutely. A handful of Radical Republicans in the Union coalition advocated the extension of legal and civil rights to Chinese alongside African Americans. Most Unionists worried, however, that expanded rights for black Americans would pave the way for the enfranchisement, naturalization, and unrestricted immigration of Chinese. They invoked the threat of Chinese "slavery," the twin specters of coolie labor and prostitution, to justify the continued exclusion, disfranchisement, taxation, and harassment of Chinese nationals. Eventually, the intertwined Negro, Chinese, and coolie questions split the coalition entirely. Increasingly uncomfortable with Radical Republican Reconstruction, erstwhile free-soil Democrats fled the Union Party and rejoined their former Chivalry allies on a party platform pledging "no Negro or Chinese suffrage."[32] They turned emancipation back on the Republicans and warned that equal rights for Chinese encouraged coolie emigration and revived slavery in the United States. Taking up the cause of working-class whites, they also predicted that coolies would convert California's free-labor paradise into a dreary landscape of capitalist masters and degraded hirelings. Democrats ultimately swept the 1867 state elections, and California became one of a handful of nonsouthern states to lose its Republican majority that year. Once they regained control of the governor's office and the legislature, Democrats engineered the state's rejection of the Fourteenth and Fifteenth amendments. California did not ratify either of these core planks of Reconstruction until the civil rights movement of the 1950s and 1960s.[33]

The shift in California politics prompted many Republicans to take up the banner of Chinese exclusion. In 1870, some California Republicans united with Democrats to pass two new state laws restricting Chinese immigration. One barred immigration by "coolies," and another prohibited the entrance of imported Chinese prostitutes.[34] California Republican proponents of this kind of anti-Chinese legislation evaded Reconstruction civil rights legislation, and their own party's ostensible dedication to equal protection, by framing restriction statutes as antislavery laws. Restricting Chinese immigration was crucial to defeating the dual threats of Chinese coolie slavery and Chinese woman slavery and was essential to upholding the Republican accomplishments of emancipation and the Thirteenth Amendment, they argued. When federal courts overturned California's 1870 restriction laws on Fourteenth Amendment grounds, California Republicans took their crusade to Congress. Their mixture of anti-Chinese, antislavery arguments successfully persuaded fellow Republicans to pass the federal Page Law of 1875. The Page Law masqueraded as an antislavery law. It purported merely to prohibit the entrance of imported Asian coolies and prostitutes, not all people of Asian descent. In actuality, it stood as the harshest and most racially exclusive U.S. immigration law to that date and severely curtailed the immigration of Chinese women.[35] It also became the model for the general Chinese Exclusion Act of 1882, a law that circumvented Reconstruction civil rights legislation by purporting to bar entry only to Chinese *laborers* (as a group of servile and undesirable working people), rather than to all Chinese (as a racial or national group). California's internal struggle over the meaning of slavery, freedom, and race thus helped to shape the contours and contradictions of national Reconstruction law.[36]

California's complex, multiracial world of labor enriches our understanding of race and resistance, sex and slavery, manhood and mastery, in the era of emancipation. Once we reframe the struggle over slavery as a western problem, we can see a new story about the transition from bondage to freedom begin to emerge, one in which categories like black and white, free and slave, lose their coherence and in which ideas about freedom, race, gender, and sexuality often intersect in confusing and unfamiliar ways. But California's story presents us with more than just an interesting or aberrant regional counterpoint. The importance of California's antislavery struggle to shaping postwar racial and immigration policy suggests that the Pacific West is more crucial to understanding the national history of slavery, emancipation, and Reconstruction than we have recognized. Looking west of north and south, a new narrative of national history, one more attuned to the complexity and diversity of race and labor across the entire United States, starts to take shape.

CHAPTER ONE

California Bound

Robert Baylor Semple made an odd spokesman for free labor. A tall and lanky frontiersman who frequently donned a backward coonskin cap, "Long Bob" was famous for his leading role in the 1846 Bear Flag Revolt, which helped topple California's Mexican government. He also came from an old and distinguished family of Kentucky slaveholders. In the fall of 1849, the residents of Sonoma, California, sent Semple as their delegate to the state constitutional convention in Monterey. His admiring American colleagues quickly elected him as the convention president.[1] Only nine days after the convention voted unanimously to prohibit slavery in the state, Semple proclaimed that California's free white men still faced a threat from slave labor. He warned that enterprising southern slaveholders, lured by the same promises of fast fortune that drew other Americans to the goldfields, plotted to circumvent California's ban on slavery. They would bring their slaves west under contracts and indentures, hold them in the state and profit from their labor, and then set them free. The presence of these degraded slave-hirelings threatened to drive down wages, promote land monopolies, and deprive the free white man "of all that encourages him to industry and makes labor profitable." Semple insisted that the only way to protect free white labor would be to prohibit all black Americans, free or slave, from migrating into the state. "In God's name, I say, let us make California a place where free white men can live," he implored.[2]

Semple's condemnation of slavery and his plea to preserve California as a haven for free white men rested on a series of assumptions: that white men were free, that most blacks were slaves, and that a ban on all African Americans provided the most effective prohibition against slavery. Others shared his logic. A majority of the convention delegates initially voted for a constitutional provision barring all future black migration; they reasoned that it would keep slavery from gaining a foothold in the new state. The debates over the measure revealed, however, that Semple's division of the world into black and white, slave and free, inadequately described California's emerging labor landscape. One delegate who supported banning black migration argued that this exclusion did not go far enough. Protecting free white labor from the degrading effects of slavery also required outlawing "the peons of Mexico, or any class of that kind; I care not whether they be free or bond." Alternately, opponents of antiblack legislation contended that "foreigners" were primarily responsible for bringing slavish and degraded labor into the state. The proposed constitution did nothing to restrict the migration of "the miserable natives that come from the Sandwich Islands and other Islands of the Pacific" or "the refuse of population from Chili, Peru, Mexico, and other parts of the world." These people were "as bad as any of the free negroes of the North, or the worst slaves of the South." Prohibiting black laborers made little sense if these foreign slaves were allowed to migrate freely into California.[3]

The convention delegates eventually reconsidered and voted down the black exclusion law, amid growing fears that it would provoke controversy in Congress and hold up California's bid for statehood.[4] The discursive wrangling over black exclusion was, nevertheless, instructive about the instability of racial and labor categories on the eve of statehood. When delegates condemned Mexican peons who were neither clearly "free or bond" and Pacific Islanders who were worse than black slaves, they tried to make sense of a complex gold rush environment in which familiar racial and labor designations—black and white, free and slave—no longer adhered to bodies or labor systems in predictable ways. It was a world where there were not just slaves and free people but also "peons." It was also a world where there were not just whites and "negroes" but also Pacific Islanders, Mexicans, and Chileans. Most important, it was a world in which people perceived to be "slaves" were not exclusively black and where antislavery measures would not necessarily preserve the state for labor that was "free" and "white." California, in short, exploded dichotomous, binary conceptions of both race and labor and forced delegates to embrace new categories—like "peon"—and attach new meanings to old categories—like "slave." Political and legal struggles over the content of these categories fueled a decade-long debate about how to defend California's free-state status from the incursions of bound, semibound, and quasibound labor.[5]

The complexity of California's gold rush labor relations drove this debate. A conquered land only recently carved out of the national territory of the Republic of Mexico and a region poised on the leading edge of global capitalism, California was an international labor borderlands in the 1840s and

1850s. As diverse peoples congregated in the mines, divergent ways of orga-
nizing, managing, binding, and disciplining labor converged there as well.
The qualities that made California a desirable place for "free white men to
live"—the low capital investment required for placer mining, the scarcity of
workers, and the relatively high monetary rewards for work—also made it an
attractive sphere for different forms of bound and semibound labor. Speculators, including merchants, landowners, and slaveholders, recognized that
they could profit from the rush by transporting people to the gold country to
labor for them. And yet California held out so many opportunities for lucrative employment and presented so many temptations for desertion that these
speculators had to devise elaborate methods of binding and holding labor.
As a result, California witnessed the emergence of multiple labor systems
that relied on physical coercion, long-term contracts, debt servitude, or ties
of personal obligation to enforce labor discipline and limit worker mobility.
The gold rush California that Semple envisioned as the last best hope for free
white labor became, at the same time, a profitable area for the expansion
of competing labor systems that neither he nor his colleagues would have
recognized as free.

What follows is an effort to trace the routes of people and capital across
and between nations in order to reconstruct the social and economic contours of bound labor in gold rush California. On the eve of the gold discoveries, California was a transnational space where work relations that originated
in Mexico and the United States overlapped each other. With the conquest
of California, free-state northerners and slaveholding southerners replicated
familiar systems of waged labor and slavery in the region. These labor systems existed alongside Spanish-Mexican labor traditions that bound Indian
workers to large ranchos through a mixture of wage labor, captivity, and
debt peonage. As the local gold rush of 1848 expanded into a global rush
in 1849, this borderland became far more complicated. California was the
locus of migrations from North America, South America, Asia, and the Pacific Islands. Peoples from the United States, Mexico, Chile, Peru, China,
and Hawai'i brought regionally and temporally distinctive renditions of wage
labor, slavery, contract labor, debt bondage, peonage, and indentured servitude to the gold country. As these people crowded into the mines, labor
systems ran up against and intersected with each other. They also changed
dramatically as employers and employees, *patrones* and *peones*, masters and
slaves, creditors and debtors, abandoned, renegotiated, or reinvented their
relationships. Making sense of California's crisis over the boundaries of free
and unfree labor during the antebellum era requires us first to follow people,

money, and work relations over deserts, across seas, and into the Sierra Nevada foothills.

California's Indigenous Labor Systems and the Gold Rush

Eight months after the first discovery of gold on the American River, a party of thirty goldseekers set out from the village of Los Angeles for the diggings in the north. Six prominent Californios, including a young ranchero named Antonio Francisco Coronel, headed up the expedition. The Californios' success rested on the backs of dozens of Indian men whom they transported north to work in the mines. Coronel's personal retinue included two men whom he described as mute Indians (indios mudos). One of them, seventeen-year-old Augustín, was a genízaro, a detribalized Indian captive from New Mexico. Coronel had obtained Augustín as a child several years earlier when New Mexican traders agreed to part with the boy in exchange for a set of fine California horses. The young man became a valuable worker on Coronel's rancho, and now the Californio sought to make use of his labor in the gold-fields.⁶ Coronel was not alone. His traveling companion Ramón Carillo had "at his disposal twenty or more Indians," whom he put to work in the mines. After traveling several hundred miles to the north, the party settled in the Southern Mines, the southernmost region of the gold country drained by the San Joaquin River. The fall of 1848 proved profitable, and after a brief winter hiatus, Coronel and his party headed out to the dry diggings along Weber's Creek. There they fell in with a heterogeneous "population of Chileans, Peruvians, Californians [Californios], Mexicans, and many Americans, Germans, etc." All of the miners worked peacefully until the Americans, determined that no "foreigners" should benefit from the gold rush, threatened to expel all but U.S. citizens. The party left for new diggings in the Northern Mines, the northern end of the gold country adjacent to the Sacramento River, only to be run off of a second claim. A dismayed Coronel took his Indian servants back to Los Angeles, never to return to the mines.⁷

The journey of Augustín and the other Native workers who traveled north with their Californio masters helps to illuminate the complexity of labor relations that existed in California long before the gold rush. With the conquest of the Mexican North in the 1840s, the United States absorbed a distinctive set of Spanish-Mexican labor practices that had no direct American analogues. The rancho system under which Augustín and other Native people labored rested on paternalistic ties of mutual obligation and involved elements of captivity, slavery, debt peonage, and wage labor. Born of secularization in the 1830s, it provided the rising Californio ranchero class with a semipermanent Indian workforce. Once this Mexican territory became American, U.S. officials were quick to label the rancho system a backward and undesirable form of slavery. U.S. authorities' desire to maintain a stable Indian workforce finally prevailed over these concerns, and much of the old rancho system survived into the American era and traveled into the mining country, intact. Indian workers continued to enrich rancheros in the goldfields until new American emigrants, insistent that both groups threatened the economic interests of white U.S. citizens, expelled them from the mines. The persecution of Indian miners presaged a broader assault on Native peoples and cultures, which came to fruition in California's 1850 Act for the Government and Protection of Indians.[8]

The rancho system that the United States inherited in 1848 grew out of the Mexican government's secularization of California's Catholic missions during the 1830s. Prior to secularization, many Indians who lived in Spanish-speaking communities were neophytes who labored under the supervision of Franciscan missionaries. They worked and lived on lands that adjoined mission churches—partly from necessity, partly from physical compulsion—and they received religious instruction. Following independence in 1821 and the adoption of a liberal constitution in 1824, Mexican authorities eventually secularized the missions by breaking up their large landholdings and liberating neophytes from Franciscan control. Emancipated neophytes became eligible for Mexican citizenship and grants of former mission land. In actuality, mission Indians benefited little from secularization. Eager to develop and fortify the far northern frontier, the Mexican government granted enormous parcels of former mission lands—lands on which Indian people had lived and labored for generations—to its own citizens who promised to settle, improve, and defend them. This new landed class consisted of both Mexican-born Californios and American and European immigrants who adopted Mexican citizenship. They converted their land grants into massive ranchos where they raised thousands of cattle to supply a burgeoning demand for beef tallow and cowhides in New England tanneries. Dispossessed and landless, former neophytes became a "windfall of cheap Indian labor" essential to rancheros' participation in this global trade.[9]

Rancheros gradually tied Indian workers to the ranchos through an intricate labor system that historians have variously described as slavery, peonage, feudalism, seigneurialism, or paternalism. Rancheros themselves insisted that only familial ties of mutual affection and obligation bound Indians to their employ. Salvador Vallejo, brother of the famous Sonoma ranchero General Mariano Guadalupe Vallejo, remembered fondly that "many of the rich men of the country had from twenty to sixty Indian servants whom they dressed and fed." The Californios considered Indians "as members of our families[,] we loved them and they loved us." Francisca Benicia Carrillo de Vallejo, Salvador's sister-in-law, affirmed that Indian servants "do not ask for money, nor do they have a fixed wage; we give them all they need and if they are ill we care for them like members of the family."[10]

Rancheros' claims of benevolent paternalism and their depictions of Indians as dependent children obscured a much more complex and coercive set of labor exchanges. Most rancho Indians labored for little more than weekly rations, two sets of clothing per year, and the right to establish villages on rancho land. The most skilled Indian vaqueros might also earn monthly wages or cash payments for each cow they killed and skinned.[11] Rancheros used both of these waged and nonwaged exchanges to lock Indians into debt servitude. They advanced food, goods, or cash to their workers and demanded repayment in future labor. Local laws upheld these claims by prohibiting Indian debtors from leaving the ranchos, requiring all Indians to obtain the approval of their ranchero before securing employment elsewhere, and punishing those who "enticed" away Indian workers. Rancheros relied on local alcaldes to enforce these measures. American John Bidwell, the magistrate for San Luis Rey during the U.S.-Mexico War, remembered that "owners of ranches came to reclaim Indians, asking me to command them to return to their service, generally on the ground of indebtedness." Mexican law and custom, they alleged, gave them the "right to make the demand." Bidwell refused to return the workers, but at least some American alcaldes honored these requests.[12]

Californios also bound Indians into the rancho system through captivity and slavery. In southern California, Californios purchased captive Indian children from the Great Basin. Like Antonio Coronel's servant Augustín, these captives arrived with New Mexican and Ute traders, who exchanged them for California horses. Californios justified these transactions by claiming that they had adopted the poor waifs into their families and educated them in the Catholic faith. These relationships were usually embedded in Catholic traditions of compadrazgo (godparenthood). Rancheros stood as padrinos (godfathers) and madrinas (godmothers) to young Indian captives or orphans or the children of their rancho laborers at their baptisms. Then they took charge of the children until adulthood. Coronel raised Augustín in just such a manner, and he averred that purchasing captives had "great benefits to the Indians," who were "educated and treated as members of the family."[13]

Other methods of obtaining captives involved more overt violence. Parties of Mexicans and their Indian allies raided villages in the California interior and took captives whom they held as long- and short-term laborers. This slave raiding often went hand in hand with punitive expeditions against so-called horse thief Indians accused of stealing livestock from Mexican coastal settlements. U.S. naval officer Joseph Warren Revere reported, for instance, that an 1840s campaign against Coast Miwok horse raiders near present-day Marin County netted dozens of captives. "The prisoners thus pressed into our service were divided equally among our party," he noted. Rancheros compelled the captives to make adobe bricks before finally releasing them. Sometimes retribution played no part in the raiding; obtaining lifelong captives was the goal. Well-armed rancheros in need of servants would "club together," attack an unsuspecting village, kill any resistant Indians, and carry off "to the settlements such as they thought best suited for servants."[14] Kidnapping became so prevalent by the 1840s that, according to one historian's estimate, nearly one-fifth of California's Indian population suffered captivity and enslavement.[15]

Californios seized Native people of all descriptions, but women and girls were especially desirable captives. Female prisoners made valuable domestic laborers on the ranchos. Around the time that he purchased Augustín, Antonio Coronel brought another captive child, a teenaged girl, into his household. She arrived in Los Angeles with a Sonoran who had kidnapped or purchased several children on his way to the pueblo. Coronel "acquired her as a houseservant," baptized her, and renamed her Encarnación. On another occasion, an Angelino official obtained three captive Indian girls, "the oldest not more than thirteen years old," from a visiting Ute delegation. After proclaiming that "in California such traffic was not tolerated," he paid the Utes with goods and horses and placed the girls "in the care of respectable families so that they would raise and educate them." The girls probably became house servants like Encarnación.[16] Female captives thus pressed into labor as domestic servants often suffered sexual exploitation as well. John Sutter, the German-born Swiss proprietor of New Helvetia, frequently engaged in captive raiding. One observer accused him of habitually trafficking in Indian women and girls, whom he held in his compound as coerced sexual partners. Some of these rape victims included very young girls, including a ten-year-old child who reportedly died of injuries sustained during one of Sutter's attacks. Sutter's sexual assaults have never been well substantiated, but the stories cast light on the potential perils of captivity for Native women and girls.[17]

The rancho system, with its distinctive mix of debt bondage, wage work, captivity, slavery, and sexual exploitation, persisted long into the era of American rule. After the U.S. invasion and occupation of California in 1846–47,

American military officials did make overtures toward curbing the abuses of rancheros. Steeped in free-slave binaries that prevailed on the East Coast, U.S. military commander John B. Montgomery charged rancheros with treating Indians like "slaves." He ordered the release of all Indians held "against their will, and without any legal contract, and without a due regard to their rights as freemen when not under legal contract for service." Montgomery's desire to keep Indians in the labor market, where they might become civilized and useful, tempered his declaration that they were freemen with free will and contract rights. He declared that Indians would "not be permitted to wander about the country in [an] idle and dissolute manner." They must "obtain service," and, after choosing their "own master and employer," they had to stay put and work. Unemployed Indians could be arrested and compelled to labor on the public works. Montgomery's successors eventually required all Indians to carry passes verifying their employment or face arrest as suspected horse thieves.[18] Foreshadowing later California Indian policy, U.S. military officials envisioned a system of quasi–bound labor in which Native people were entitled to compensation and some choice in their employer but were not free to live outside the labor market altogether.

Military officials' ambivalence about the freedom of Indian workers kept the rancho system intact into the gold rush era. In fact, rancho Indians played a crucial part in the early development of California's gold country. The earliest reports from the diggings indicate that rancheros quickly and successfully adapted older labor practices to gold extraction. During 1848, when the gold rush remained largely local, Indians may have made up nearly half of the 4,000 miners in the diggings. Hundreds of these Native people mined independently and traded their gold for goods and food. Hundreds more were rancho laborers like Augustín who accompanied their employers to the goldfields.[19] Around 1,300 Californios traveled to the gold country. With this migration, according to historian James Rawls, "the Hispanic system of Indian labor exploitation was transferred from the ranchos to the mines" as Californios gave their rancho laborers food and clothing in exchange for the gold they dug.[20] In August 1848, an American observer found wealthy ranchero Antonio María Suñol supervising thirty Indian hands along the American River. Suñol and his partners paid the Indian laborers "principally in merchandise of various kinds." Farther north, American ranchero Pierson B. Reading worked the Trinity River with sixty "domesticated Indians" from his rancho. The group took out around $80,000 in gold dust in a matter of weeks.[21] For a time, Mexican systems of Indian labor control helped rancheros to build new gold rush fortunes under the U.S. flag.

But rancheros' golden dreams soon turned to dust. California's local gold rush went global in early 1849, and rancheros and their Indian laborers came under attack from newly arrived white Americans. Many of these belligerents were white Oregonians recently embroiled in their own bitter Indian wars. Most had "no prior contact with the Hispanic system of Indian labor exploitation." They viewed Indians as threats to their personal security and contended that Native workers were slaves who enriched their rancho masters at the expense of new white arrivals.[22] One Oregonian justified assaults on rancheros and Indians as a necessary evil to dissolve "the old California system." It purged the state of an outmoded "system of inequality—of proprietors and peons" and replaced it with "the system of free labor."[23] Oregonians expelled and slaughtered hundreds of Indians in the mines during 1848 and 1849. Pierson Reading reported that he had been at work for only six weeks before white Oregonians arrived and "at once protested against my Indian labor." Reading quickly decamped. The following year, Oregonians attacked a large group of rancho Indians who were digging gold for their employer, American ranchero William Daylor, along the American River. They murdered two of the men on the spot and drove the rest off the river. They followed the survivors to the vicinity of Daylor's rancho and massacred dozens more. As many as eighty-three Indians may have lost their lives in the attacks.[24] Around the same time, Californio employers of rancho laborers suffered ejection from lucrative claims in the Northern Mines. Antipathy toward Indian labor grew so pronounced on the American River in 1849 that white miners in the region debated whether large companies "should have the privilege of employing Indians." The same miners eventually passed informal mining codes that forbade Indian hiring altogether.[25]

Expulsion campaigns deprived rancheros of gold. They cost many Native people their means of survival and, sometimes, their lives. In their wake, hundreds of Indians fled the diggings or were indiscriminately murdered during makeshift vigilante and militia "Indian-hunting" expeditions. The violence, disease, and malnutrition bred by the gold rush invasion of Indian homelands took a horrendous toll on indigenous communities. A pre–gold rush population of roughly 150,000 Indian people dropped to around 25,000 or 30,000 by 1865.[26] Cut off from access to gold and commercial opportunities that had once mitigated the destruction of food resources, Native people developed new survival strategies. They retreated farther into the interior, worked for wages in cities and on farms, or moved to treaty lands temporarily reserved for them by federal Indian agents. All the while, they confronted an emerging legal assault on their autonomy, the California legislature's 1850

Act for the Government and Protection of Indians.[27] Reproducing the coercions of Mexican ranchos, the law constructed a formal system of bound Indian labor that confounded free-state status for more than a decade.

Patrones, Peones, and the Journey al Norte

When Augustín and his fellow *indio mudo* traveled north with Antonio Coronel in 1848, they worked alongside other people who were bound to their Californio employer in different ways. A man named Benito Pérez and his wife also joined the expedition to the diggings. The couple were recent arrivals from the northern Mexican state of Sonora. Like many of their poorer compatriots, they made their way to the diggings by attaching themselves to a *patrón*, a wealthy Mexican or Californio employer. *Patrones* valued both the labor power and the considerable mining skill of their Sonoran employees. They paid the Sonorans' way to the mines and recouped their investment by taking a share of their indebted workers' earnings. Sonorans who paid off their debts could then strike out on their own. Once in the mines, the Pérezes set to work to secure their liberty. Benito Pérez worked alongside Coronel and dug gold to pay back the couple's debts.[28] Señora Pérez may have been more successful than her husband. She washed and cooked for the party, and Coronel paid (or credited) her half an ounce of gold per day for these services. She also made extra servings of beans and tortillas and sold the leftovers to neighboring miners. "This business reached such proportions that she made three or four ounces of gold a day," Coronel remembered. The Pérezes returned to Los Angeles in early 1849 with nearly $4,000 in gold, more than enough to pay off Coronel and leave his service.[29]

It made sense that the Pérezes and their fellow Sonorans would be among the first to venture to California's mines in 1848. Sonora was one of the closest Mexican states to the goldfields. It lay just south of the new national border, and its capital city, Hermosillo, was but 550 miles from Los Angeles. The state's vast, rugged, desert terrain was also dotted with rich silver deposits, which many Sonorans had mined for generations. Long accustomed to pushing northward in search of new opportunities, Sonoran miners moved with relative ease into what had been, until just a few months before, their national territory. They quickly gained renown for their mining skill, and hundreds of Californio and white American miners relied on their expertise. Antonio Coronel recalled, for instance, that Benito Pérez was "experienced in gold mining" and that he depended on the Sonoran's know-how at almost every turn. English miner William Kelly reported that new American arrivals also turned to "the Chilians and Mexicans for instruction and information, which they gave them with cheerful alacrity."[30] Americans would have had ample teachers. Alarmed Mexican officials estimated that from 4,000 to 6,000 Sonorans left for California between the fall of 1848 and the fall of 1849. In all, around 10,000 Sonorans made their way to the gold country in the first two years of the rush.[31]

Gold in California's rivers lured thousands of northern Mexicans across the new national border, but deteriorating conditions in Sonora also explained and constrained these migrations. Mining was always a precarious endeavor in the far north. Decades of raiding by and warfare with powerful Apache peoples forced Sonorans to abandon isolated mines and villages. Wars over imperial control and national territory compounded these troubles. For more than a century, Sonorans' prosperity hinged on the Spanish Crown's efforts to stave off Indian raiding and to promote trade. The chaos of the Mexican War for Independence (1810–21), followed by the withdrawal of royal troops from the north, plunged the region into turmoil and economic decline. Revolts and raids by Yaqui, Mayo, and Apache Indian peoples severely disrupted the Sonoran mining economy. The U.S. War with Mexico in 1846 further destabilized Mexican-Apache diplomacy in the north. By mid-century, fewer Sonoran families were eking out tenuous livings in poorly defended mining villages and ranchos. A large number moved to the region's cities or took up agricultural work for hacendados, large landholders. Some of the latter became peones, landless laborers who—much like rancho Indians in California—were bound to large estates by social custom and debt.[32] Poverty, indebtedness, and displacement impelled Sonorans northward just as surely as golden dreams.

Sonorans made their way to California under a diverse array of labor arrangements that reflected the complex processes under way in their homeland. Sonorans of modest means went to the goldfields as gambusinos, independent miners and prospectors traveling on their own hook. Gambusinos usually went north in large parties made up of people related to each other by blood and marriage. Many included women and children. During their time in the Southern Mines, Antonio Coronel and his companions camped near one such party. It included "one of the most famous gambusinos among the Sonorans, known by the nickname of 'Chino Tirador.'" Coronel reported—half in annoyance, half in awe—that Chino Tirador gathered seventeen ounces of gold in two hours armed with nothing but a horn spoon, a wooden bowl, and his hat. The man used his earnings to set up a gaming table, quickly lost all his money, and then went off to prospect richer diggings. In the meantime, Coronel, Benito Pérez, and the two indios mudos pulled only a paltry six ounces from their own claim.[33]

Chino Tirador's freewheeling independence, entrepreneurialism, and freedom of movement stood in stark contrast to the condition of other Sonorans in the mines. *Gambusinos* could pay their own way north and spend gold as they pleased, but their less fortunate compatriots enjoyed far less autonomy. Some, like the Pérezes, bound themselves to Californios or wealthy Sonorans who agreed to outfit and convey them to the mines. In what amounted to short-term debt servitude, they worked for these *patrones* in the diggings to pay off the cost of their equipment and transportation. The Pérezes discharged these debts quickly, but other Sonorans may have found it much more difficult to secure their independence. Coronel's fellow Angelino, Andrés Pico, outfitted a large party of Sonorans and took them to the Stanislaus diggings. They were to work off the cost of their journey, and "in order to insure the payment of his money, he [Pico] had them working together under the supervision and care of a Spaniard." Satisfying these debts was no mean feat. Many of these Sonorans were still in Pico's service in March 1849, seven months after their initial departure for the goldfields.[34] Still, Pico's workers may have enjoyed more liberty than other Sonorans. Wealthy northern Mexicans sometimes led or sent large parties of *peones* to the California mines to labor in exchange for their upkeep and a portion of their earnings. Tied by custom and debt to their *patrones* and, presumably, bound to return to Sonora, these migrants had less mobility and autonomy.[35] Sonoran miners, in short, ranged from those completely free to pursue their own interests, to those temporarily limited in mobility, to those who went north under more rigid forms of debt servitude.

Just as Antonio Coronel and the Pérezes left the diggings for good in early 1849, other groups of Spanish-speaking goldseekers were making their way north. In February, twenty-two-year-old Ramón Gil Navarro set out from the Chilean city of Concepción for San Francisco. Son of a middle-class Argentine family that had been exiled to Chile four years earlier, Navarro hoped to improve his fortunes by leading an expedition to the California goldfields. Before sailing from Talcahuano, Concepción's commercial port, Navarro contracted thirty men to work for two years in the diggings. Had Navarro left from Valparaíso, the larger port city to the north, he might have been able to recruit experienced miners from Chile's rugged *norte chico*. It is more likely, however, that his men came from the ranks of landless rural poor from Chile's central valley. Many such people flocked to the nation's major cities in the middle of the nineteenth century. If they were like other Chilean workers who contracted to go to California, the men probably agreed to work out their terms in exchange for a set wage, passage money, food, board, and (perhaps) a share of the expedition's profits.[36]

Like Sonorans, migrants from Chile were among the earliest arrivals in the goldfields. The rapidity of ocean travel allowed news of gold discoveries to spread quickly to the Pacific Coast of South America. Rumors of big strikes swirled around Chilean ports as early as August 1848, and the first shiploads of goldseekers left Valparaíso in September of that year. Altogether, around 8,000 Chileans traveled to the goldfields before 1853. These new arrivals fanned out all over the mining country, but a very large number, including Ramón Gil Navarro and his party, settled in the Southern Mines alongside other Spanish speakers. There they, like the Sonorans who lived nearby, gained reputations as skilled and successful miners.[37]

Like Sonorans, Chileans made their way north under labor arrangements that reflected the economic and political changes afoot in their homelands. For many of these goldseekers, the journey to California was structured by the long-standing social and economic hierarchies of the Chilean countryside. Chile was predominantly rural, and its economy was focused on agricultural production. The country's fertile central valley had a similar climate to the central valley of California, making it an ideal place for viticulture, fruit and grain production, and ranching. *Hacendados*, wealthy hereditary proprietors, owned around 80 percent of this fertile land. They commanded the labor of two classes of landless workers: *inquilinos* and *peones*. Both groups were tied to landholders, their *patrones*, through webs of mutual obligation and economic exchange. *Inquilinos*, service tenants, performed a weekly quota of labor in exchange for the right to farm on their *patrones*' estates.[38] A much larger "floating population" of poor, mobile, and landless *peones* worked for large landholders on a seasonal basis. Some earned cash wages for their work. Most merely received food, drink, or goods. While scarce land and abundant labor gave *patrones* little incentive to bind these laborers permanently, they sometimes used debts and long-term contracts to keep *inquilinos* or *peones* on their estates.[39]

Independence from Spain in the 1820s and the shift to a republican government did little to improve the lives of Chile's rural poor. Growing foreign demand for Chilean grain and the new government's interest in promoting large-scale agricultural production for the global market precluded land reform. Moreover, ramping up grain production encouraged the consolidation of landholding, subjected rural workers to greater labor exploitation, and eliminated opportunities for tenant farming. Both *inquilinos* and *peones* suffered deteriorating working and living conditions by mid-century. One Chilean journalist railed that large rural landholders treated their "peons and tenants" no better than "raw Negro slaves." These unfortunates "never escape their lot because they have no time to work for themselves; they do not have enough even to care for their own families. So, having nothing and constantly in debt, they go to jail, or they turn to crime." Others flocked to urban centers, especially the burgeoning cities of Valparaíso, Talcahuano, and Concepción, which reflected Chile's interconnectedness to the global market. In these cities, many displaced rural workers heard about gold in California and decided to try their fortunes in the north.[40]

Would-be migrants depended on entrepreneurial rural landholders and urban merchants like Ramón Gil Navarro who also hoped to profit from California gold discoveries. During the last months of 1848, dozens of these speculators organized mining and trading expeditions to the gold country. These men had the capital and commercial connections necessary to get to the goldfields. They needed able-bodied men accustomed to hard labor to do the actual digging. They found willing recruits among the *peones* who crushed into the cities. The challenge lay in transporting these men north and hanging onto them once the party arrived in California. Unlike Sonoran and Californio proprietors, who mainly relied on informal relationships of dependence and debt to bind their workers, Chilean entrepreneurs turned to a relatively new feature of the emerging capitalist economy: the labor contract. Employers and employees bound themselves to each other in formulaic documents drafted before legal officials. Each agreed that they would be subject to prosecution and economic penalties if they neglected their obligations. Impersonal documents that relied on formal legal structures for their enforcement, these labor contracts would be of limited use in gold rush California, where courts and law operated erratically.[41]

Chilean labor contracts embedded in customary rural relationships of power and deference best survived the trip to California. Wealthy landholders who went to the goldfields often recruited small groups of *peones* and *inquilinos* to go with them under contracts that approximated familiar relationships of the Chilean countryside. Rural *patrones* generally paid for the transportation and upkeep of their men and gave them a small portion of the party's mining profits. *Peones* and *inquilinos* agreed to labor faithfully for their *patrones* for a period of years. Once in California, family ties, common geographic origin, shared history, and *patrón* paternalism seem to have bound these rural parties close together and mitigated the problem of contract breaking. A wealthy *patrón* who led one such group reflected fondly on the cohesiveness of his small "society" of goldseekers. His *peones* remained loyal despite the excitement and temptations of California. More than that, they were unfailingly attentive to the needs of their *patrones*, welcoming them home every winter day with a warm kitchen and hot drinks.[42]

Urban middle-class proprietors like Navarro who hired strangers in the cities could not depend on familiarity and long-standing relationships of mutual obligation to keep workers loyal. They relied on contracts to replicate the hierarchies of customary *patrón-peón* relationships and the impersonal forces of the law and the market to enforce them.[43] Unable to command personal deference from *peones*, urban *patrones* tried to compel worker obedience by building severe economic sanctions into their contracts. Many contracts denied workers any wages until they had completed their full terms. A good number also threatened unfaithful laborers with *multas*, impossibly high fines that were double or triple a worker's annual wage and that could only be paid off with future labor. Not all of these contractual safeguards were negative. Embracing a capitalist ethos, some employers tried to secure loyalty from workers by promising them a share of the expedition profits or offering bonuses to those who dug substantial amounts of gold for the company.[44]

In spite of all their efforts, urban entrepreneurs found it difficult to stave off desertions once they arrived in California. Lost wages, *multas*, and prosecution were nearly meaningless in a land where economic opportunities were bountiful and law enforcement was informal, haphazard, or nonexistent. Many disappointed Chilean employers found that their workers abandoned them as soon as they dropped anchor in California and that they had no legal recourse to stop them. Several of Ramón Gil Navarro's men jumped ship once the party arrived in San Francisco. Navarro's business partner warned the runaways that they could "flee if they want, but if they do they should be prepared to work in jail." The risk of legal punishment did little to deter the men. "Since they know that his threats cannot be backed up, they say that they will go whenever they want," Navarro lamented. After losing nearly a third of his workers (and all their passage money), Navarro finally departed for the Southern Mines with the remainder of his men.[45] Of these, he lost all but a handful to desertion. By October 1849, the few remaining men, discontented by illness, exhausting work, cold weather, and declining prospects, demanded that Navarro dissolve their contracts and allow them to return to Chile. He had little choice but to disband the company and send the men on their way.[46]

For ambitious Chilean entrepreneurs like Navarro, reaping the golden promises of California required commanding and controlling the labor of others. California's numerous opportunities and inducements for escape endangered the substantial capital that entrepreneurs invested in transporting workers to the mines. Chilean employers eager to protect these investments developed complex hybrid labor systems. They merged older relations of rural peonage common to the Spanish Americas with newer forms of contract labor and wage labor that accompanied the expansion of the global capitalist market economy. These labor systems rarely survived the journey to the mines. Workers often broke their contracts, and employers, lacking established legal structures to prosecute them, frequently lost their investments. Despite Chilean employers' incomplete power over their workers, white Americans insisted that the bulk of Chilean workingmen in California were peons, a class of degraded, subservient laborers little different from slaves. The struggle to identify and exclude peons drove debates over the status of slavery, wage labor, and the foreign-born in California across the gold rush era.

Contracts and Credit: Making a Transpacific Labor Force

Mexicans and Chileans looked north to California for gold, trade, work, and investment opportunities. Other peoples looked east. The discovery of gold in California transformed the region into a major locus of transpacific journeys that shuttled people, goods, and capital between western North America, the Pacific Islands, and East Asia. Few people were positioned to profit from this trade better than U.S.-born California merchants Thomas O. Larkin and Jacob Primer Leese. Larkin, the former U.S. consul to California, played an integral role in seizing the territory from Mexico. Leese was a naturalized Mexican citizen who married into the prominent Vallejo family and owned a large Mexican rancho. Both arrived on the gold rush scene early, and both acquired substantial amounts of dust in 1848. Anticipating high demand for luxury goods in the mines, the men each reinvested 1,500 "troy ounces of placer gold," worth approximately $24,000, into a trading expedition to China.[47] Leese planned to sail to Hong Kong and bring back Chinese goods to sell at inflated prices. The partners had another goal in mind: recruiting laborers to work in their various California enterprises. On the way to China, Leese stopped for supplies in the Kingdom of Hawai'i, known to English speakers as the Sandwich Islands. There he contracted a youth named Kiopaa to work for him for three years in California. When Leese reached Hong Kong in the fall of 1849 he not only stocked his ship; he also entered into labor contracts with at least seven Chinese men who also agreed to work for him in California.[48]

Leese's Hawaiian and Chinese workers followed well-worn paths of trade and migration that had been building a transnational Pacific World since the sixteenth century. Although they lay more than 5,000 miles apart, the homelands of Kiopaa and the seven men from Hong Kong were linked together in a far-flung web of economic exchanges that accompanied the spread of global capitalism and colonialism. When he sailed west in 1849 from California to the Hawaiian Islands to Hong Kong, Jacob Leese followed in the wake of British and American merchants who had made similar journeys for decades. English and U.S. ships traded for furs along the Pacific Coast of North America and brought stores of otter pelts to China. They exchanged them for luxury goods—teas, silks, and tableware—that sold for high prices in distant metropolises. China initially enjoyed a powerful position in these exchanges. Chinese imperial laws confined foreign trade to a handful of cities and restricted the entrance of foreign goods into China's markets. Still, the increasing presence of foreign merchants eroded Chinese imperial power. The first Opium War (1839–42), a bloody conflict with the British, forced China to open its markets to English, French, and American trade.[49]

The Hawaiian Islands, also the subjects of British imperial interest, played an important part in the expanding China trade. Ships that traversed the vast expanse of water between the Pacific Coasts of Asia and North America stopped in the Islands to replenish their stores and crews. Merchants and missionaries from Britain and the United States soon followed in large numbers. Despite Hawai'i's status as an independent monarchy, these newcomers exerted strong control over the Islands' economy and politics. They worked to transform an island economy based on subsistence agriculture into one focused on the production of tropical luxury goods to ship to East Asian, American, and European markets. This transpacific circuit of goods coincided with a movement of people. Chinese and Hawaiians took passage aboard British, American, and Russian ships to work as sailors and cooks. Some traveled to colonial outposts abroad to work in agriculture, mining, and the fur, hide, and tallow trades. The gold rush that brought both Chinese and Hawaiian workers to California only accelerated patterns of economic exchange and transnational labor migrations that had long been knitting together a Pacific World.[50]

We know little about Kiopaa, the Hawaiian youth whom Jacob Leese bound to accompany him to Hong Kong and back to California in 1849. The two made their labor contract in Honolulu, which suggests that the young man was probably from the bustling town. The primary port city of the Hawaiian Kingdom, Honolulu was home to hundreds of foreign merchants and traders and served as a key resupply point between the Americas and East Asia. It also became a major labor entrepôt as thousands of Hawaiians—nearly 3,500 annually by the 1840s—left the Islands under contracts to work for Russians, English, and Americans as sailors, domestic servants, fur trappers, and general laborers. Most non-Hawaiians called these workers "kanakas," a term derived from "Kānaka Maoli," the name that native Hawaiians called themselves in their own language. Honolulu's trade in goods and kanaka laborers skyrocketed when news of California gold discoveries reached there in 1848. Honolulu merchants outfitted expeditions to the goldfields, and dozens of ships stopped over in the Hawaiian Islands as they brought goods and passengers to the placers. Hundreds of native Hawaiians entered into contracts to work aboard these California-bound vessels. They labored as ship cooks and sailors on the way to California; after arriving, many stayed to take up work as miners, fishermen, and domestic servants. Kanwa, Kiopaa's father, apparently hoped to acquire similar opportunities for his son. On March 23, 1849, Kanwa bound the young man over to Leese for a three-year term. Leese promised that he would "take as good care of him as if he were his own Son" and to return him to the Islands at the end of the term.[51]

Historically, Hawaiian laborers had little power to negotiate their own contracts. The feudalistic social structure of the Islands placed legal and political power into the hands of the ali'i, a ruling class made up of hereditary chiefs and their families. The ali'i commanded the obedience, labor, and loyalty of Hawaiian commoners. A set of strict taboos and laws, the kapus, reinforced these hierarchies by requiring commoners' acquiescence to local ali'i and reverence for the deities they represented.[52] With the arrival of foreign merchants seeking laborers, the ali'i, especially the Islands' governors, acted as labor brokers for Hawaiian common people. They determined who could leave the Islands on what terms and negotiated all contracts with foreign employers. These contracts, which became fairly standardized across the Islands by the 1840s, often bound workers for three-year terms at wages of ten dollars per month. Ali'i brokers took a percentage of each worker's earnings, usually in the form of a cash advance that employers paid out to the ali'i before leaving the Islands. They also stipulated that employers had to bring all workers back to the Islands at the end of their terms or face hefty fines for every man and woman lost.[53]

These contracted Hawaiians played a critical role in California's economic development both before and after 1848. John Sutter relied heavily on them. Ten years before the gold rush, Sutter passed through Honolulu on his first trip to California and contracted eight Hawaiians to work under the standard arrangement of ten dollars per month for a three-year term. Once in California, the men helped establish Sutter's farms at New Helvetia, while their wives washed, sewed, and taught American Indian women to perform similar duties. The discovery of gold at New Helvetia in 1848 hurled Sutter's

Hawaiian employees into the maelstrom of the rush and exposed them to an additional set of coercive labor relations. That year, Sutter headed for the mines with a party of one hundred Indians and Hawaiians, including a group of fifty newly arrived laborers from the Hawaiian Islands. In a few months, Sutter entangled all the men and women in relations of debt bondage. He advanced them food and goods and required them to pay back the debts with their mining earnings. The Hawaiians and Indians never succeeded in repaying these loans. Sutter alleged that they spent all their gold in sprees at "traveling grogshops" that left them too sick to work. They consequently had to keep mining for him to pay off their debts.[54]

Other American and European employers may have profited from similar tactics. By 1850, just over 300 Hawaiians, organized into large mining parties and numbering as many as sixty men, were living in the Calaveras diggings, along the Trinity River, and on the North and Middle Forks of the American River. Some mined independently, but probably most worked for wealthy employers. Miner William Kelly reported the formation of "large associated companies with considerable capital, employed in turning branches of the [American] river, having several Indians and Kanakas at work." When not helping to dam and turn rivers, Hawaiians used their considerable swimming skills to aid their employers. "The most expert divers in the world," they scoured the bottoms of riverbeds, gathering as much as twenty dollars in gold per day.[55]

The Hawaiians that William Kelly found on the American River not only worked alongside American Indians; they also labored with other transpacific migrants whose histories and homelands were intertwined with their own. In September 1850, a California census taker found a group of fifty-nine Hawaiians working on Lacy's Bar on the North Fork of the American River. These miners, listed only as anonymous and undifferentiated "Kanakas" in the census reports, lived close to fifty-four "Chinamen," whom the census taker also failed to identify with names and ages.[56]

Like their Hawaiian neighbors, the anonymous Chinese men on Lacy's Bar embarked on journeys to California that reflected the growing webs of capital that bound the eastern and western edges of the Pacific Basin together. The men likely came from Guangdong Province in South China. The location of the thriving Pearl River delta and the bustling commercial center of Guangzhou (Canton), Guangdong boasted "China's oldest, best-developed, and most aggressive market economies." Guangzhou's forward-looking merchant class avidly pursued trade with Southeast Asia for centuries, and the city became a major hub of Chinese trade with Europe by the sixteenth century. Peasants in the densely populated Guangdong countryside shared this commercial orientation. Many produced fish, cloth, and cash crops for regional and international markets and journeyed abroad in search of work. Thousands of people from South China migrated to Thailand, Malaysia, Indonesia, the Philippines, Mexico, and Peru to labor in mining and agriculture. Guangzhou merchants served as labor brokers in these overseas transactions, loaning migrants passage money, to be repaid at high interest. Overseas migration became so common that most poor Guangdong families sent at least one son to labor in foreign lands every generation.[57]

By the middle of the nineteenth century, political and economic crisis in China stimulated these overseas journeys. A series of costly imperial wars with Great Britain ended in Chinese defeat. By the 1840s, the British forced open the empire's markets to foreign trade and compelled it to pay massive indemnities. Imperial tax hikes and competition with cheap foreign goods wrecked the peasant economy and left thousands hungry, homeless, and landless. Domestic unrest and a series of bloody civil wars ensued. The desire to escape from poverty, famine, warfare, and political upheaval combined with a long tradition of overseas commerce and migration to create the Chinese rush to California.[58]

The earliest Chinese migrants traveled to the diggings under conditions that resembled those of early Hawaiian arrivals. When Jacob Leese returned from his Chinese trading expedition in late 1849, he not only brought the Hawaiian youth Kiopaa under contract. He was also accompanied by at least seven Chinese men, bound under contracts to work for him for three years in California. In a series of preprinted contracts provided by Hong Kong authorities, Leese and the Chinese men spelled out the terms of their future working arrangements. Monq qui and Ahine, described as "coolies" (denoting their status as common laborers), pledged to work at the rates of fifteen and twelve dollars per month, respectively. Atu, Achue, and Affon, who were to labor as cooks in California, would earn between fourteen and fifteen dollars per month. Finally, Leese engaged Awye and 'Ai to work as tailors at fifteen dollars per month. All of the men pledged to stay with Leese for three years after their arrival and to provide their own tools and clothing. Leese promised, in turn, to supply the men with decent lodging and food and to pay their wages on a monthly basis. He also guaranteed them return passage to China and a fifteen-dollar severance if he terminated the contract early.[59]

Leese was probably the first of several American and European employers who recruited Chinese contract workers during the earliest years of the rush. Most of these entrepreneurs hoped to get around California's chronic

ARTICLES OF AGREEMENT made, entered into and concluded this 28 ͭ ͪ day of July , in the Year of Our Lord, One thousand Eight hundred and Forty nine Between Jacob. P. Leese Esq. of Monterey - of the one part and 'Ai a Chinaman of the other part, Witness that for the consideration hereinafter contained on the part of the said Jacob. P. Leese Esq. he the said 'Ai doth hereby covenant, promise and agree with, and to the said Jacob. P. Leese Esq. that he the said 'Ai will proceed in and on board of a certain Brig or Vessel called the Eveline whereof Cooper is Master now lying in the Harbour of Hongkong, and about to proceed on a voyage to San Francisco Port or Ports, on the West Coast of America, and that he will any where in that Country, for the space or period of (3) three Years from the date of his arrival at the Port of destination, work as a Tailor or otherwise to the best of his knowledge and ability, under the orders and directions, of the said Jacob P Leese Esq. or any other person holding this Contract. And that he the said 'Ai will keep and provide himself with all the necessary, and proper tools of his trade, and will also find, and provide his own clothing. And that he will not do or assist to do or direct or aid in any manner whatsoever any work or business, other than, that ordered or directed by the said Jacob P. Leese Esq. or any other persons to whom this contract may be transferred. And these presents further witness that in consideration of the covenants herein before contained on the part of the said 'Ai he the said Jacob P Leese Esq. doth hereby for himself his Heirs Executors, and Administrators covenant promise, and agree with, and to the said 'Ai that he his Survivors or Substitutes shall and will afford to him a passage in the above mentioned Vessel, to the West Coast of America, and shall, and will as soon as he shall have entered upon such work or trade of a Tailor as aforesaid furnish and provide him with lodgings, and suitable provisions, and food for, and during the said space or period of (3) three Years, and that the said 'Ai is to be paid for his work at the rate of ($15 ͤ) Fifteen Dollars per month payable monthly in the due, and proper fulfilment, and completion of their said agreement, and covenants herein before contained, the said wages to be computed for the period of (3) three Years from the date the said 'Ai shall arrive at the Port of destination. And it is hereby agreed by and between the said parties hereto that the said 'Ai shall not receive any wages until, and after the Sum of Thirty ($30 ͤ) Dollars advanced to the said 'Ai shall have been paid off, and satisfied, and the said 'Ai doth hereby acknowledge the receipt of the said advance so made to him by the said Jacob P Leese Esq. And it is hereby further agreed, that in case the said Jacob P. Leese Esq. or his substitute *not requiring* the services of the said 'Ai at any time during the said period of (3) three Years he the said Jacob P Leese Esq. or his substitute shall be at liberty to cancell this Contract on giving to said 'Ai One Month's notice, and from and after the expiration of such one Month's notice, this contract shall be null and void.

In Witness whereof the said parties to the presents have hereunto set their Hands and affixed their Seals at Victoria, Hongkong aforesaid the Day and Year first before written.

Signed Sealed and delivered after being first duly explained in the presence of 阿 Shue 書

Brinley

Henry Anthon Jr
acting Vice Consul
United States of America

亞
Ai
叔
告

J P Leese

('ai)

labor shortages by binding Chinese workers for long terms at low wages. But before they could profit from Chinese labor, each of these employers had to make a substantial preliminary investment in paying workers' transportation to California. A transpacific voyage usually cost between forty and fifty dollars per person.[60] Whenever a worker ran away or refused to labor, his employer lost all the advantages of a long-term contract and his initial investment to boot.

Canny employers anticipated these problems and went to great lengths to prevent contract breaking. Some included entire performance clauses in their contracts that required workers to serve out the whole contract term before receiving any wages. Bernard Peyton Jr., an American businessman who engaged twenty Chinese men in Hong Kong in 1852, made wages completely contingent on contractual compliance. The men promised to work for Peyton in California for three months in exchange for their passage money and a dollar per day. Peyton would pay them at the end of their terms, and they would get nothing if they left before the three months were up or failed to render "utmost service in any labor." Jacob Leese made similar arrangements. None of his seven workers received any wages until they had worked off the thirty-dollar advance he had paid for their passage to California.[61] In a gold rush world where few workers had incentive to stay with one employer for any length of time, employers of Chinese struggled to balance risk with reward.

Even these harsh measures failed to hold Chinese contract workers to their employers. Eager for mobility and better opportunities in the goldfields, Chinese frequently broke their contracts and ran away. In 1850, the Stockton Times reported that four Englishmen arrived in the city with several tons of provisions and thirty-five Chinese men "hired to work in the mines for 2 years at stipulated wages, and [who] gave bonds for the fulfillment of the contract." The men found losing the bonds preferable to performing their contracts. Once in the diggings, the Chinese employees "determined on leaving the place," and with their departure "the golden dreams of their employers vanished."[62] Another unlucky Englishman told of a similar revolt among the "fifteen coolies" he brought to San Francisco under contracts to work for two years. The men were "no sooner ashore than they resisted their contract, and each turned his own separate way." The Englishmen could expect little help from the courts. When a San Francisco employer brought criminal charges against six Chinese who refused to serve out their contracts and fled without paying back their passage money, a judge ruled that contract breaking was a civil matter, not a criminal offense. Even a civil suit was unlikely to succeed because few jurists agreed about whether labor contracts made in foreign countries were valid and binding on U.S. soil. In this climate of uncertainty, Chinese desertions became so commonplace that the editor of the *Alta California* recommended state laws enforcing labor agreements made in China. Only then could American employers eliminate "the ease with which all contracts made for labor with these people have been broken through."[63]

Chinese migrants' resistance to fixed, long-term contracts and their desires for mobility may have quashed American and European employers' efforts to recruit and bind them directly. It appears that after 1851 few non-Chinese employers brought Chinese to work in California under contracts.[64] This may be because California-bound Chinese preferred to rely upon their own countrymen and new types of contractual arrangements to get them to California. A group of several such migrants left Shanghai for San Francisco in 1849. The men, mostly "mechanics and labourers," entered into an agreement with Tseang Sing Hong, a Chinese merchant house. The merchants hired an American ship to transport the workers to California and advanced each man $125 for passage and travel expenses. They also contracted with an English merchant to take charge of the men upon arrival and to "search out and recommend employment" for them. Once the workers settled into new jobs, the merchant house would arrange with their employers to deduct a "moiety of their wages" each month. This money would be sent back to China "until the debt is absorbed." Afterward, the men retained all their wages and, presumably, were free to go where they pleased.[65]

The contract between the Tseang Sing Hong and the party of Shanghai workers reflected the growing importance of the credit-ticket system in California. Long a part of Chinese migrations across the Pacific Basin, the credit-ticket system more closely resembled debt bondage than contract labor. Since passage to California cost four or five times what an average Chinese man earned in China per year, would-be migrants usually borrowed their passage money from Chinese brokers and merchant houses like the Tseang Sing Hong. The merchants hoped to profit from migrants' California labors by charging them heavy interest on these loans—between 4 and 8 percent per month.[66] Instead of being bound to labor for the merchants for a set number of months or years, the migrants sent regular remittances from their California earnings back to China. As a guarantee against default or abandonment, migrants put up their property as collateral or asked their relatives in China to stand as security on the loans. Once they got to California, migrants relied on the Chinese Six Companies (*huigans*), mutual aid societies made up of Chinese from a particular province, for help finding housing and work. As soon as they paid back their debts, Chinese migrants were free from any further obligation and worked entirely for themselves.[67]

Nearly all Chinese migrants who arrived by the credit-ticket system in the 1850s were men. Chinese women made the journey to California as well, but they came in smaller numbers and were often bound laborers in a commercialized sex trade that presented far fewer opportunities for mobility. Chinese women who worked in California's earliest urban sex trade did enjoy relative autonomy as independent agents. The most famous of these women, Ah Toy, came to San Francisco at the age of twenty in 1849. By her own account, she was a single woman who lived with her widowed mother in Guangzhou and migrated to California "for the purpose of bettering her condition." One of only a tiny handful of Chinese women in the city, she supported herself and made a healthy profit by selling companionship and sex to a multiracial clientele.[68] The young woman eventually controlled the labor of other Chinese women who sold sex for cash. In 1852, a San Francisco newspaper noted that a number of Chinese women "under the guardianship of Miss Atoy" lived in a brothel on Dupont Street. A sensationalized 1855 report claimed that she imported from China "six or eight women, whom she had purchased at $40 each." She employed the women in her brothel and then sold them off for $1,000 to $1,500 each to "Chinese merchants and gamblers."[69]

Newspaper accounts of Ah Toy buying and selling her countrywomen may have been exaggerated, but they nonetheless reflected important changes in the urban commercial sex trade. After 1854, independent Chinese prostitutes like Ah Toy began to disappear. Chinese tongs, secret societies that controlled the urban vice economy in Chinese communities, took over the business of prostitution. Women who worked in these tong-operated brothels had little control over their labor or their lives. Kidnapped in Chinese port cities, acquired from impoverished families, or lured with false promises of high-paying work in California, many of these young women wound up in a harsh, exploitative form of debt bondage. Procurers in China generally paid a woman's passage to California and held her accountable for paying back the fare and all of her living expenses. They then sold and transferred the woman's debt (and, effectively, the woman herself) to Chinese in California. Some of these women became the wives, secondary wives, concubines, or domestic servants of the people who bought their debts. Less fortunate women ended up in tong-operated brothels, where their employers forced them to pay off their debts by working as prostitutes. Securing freedom was difficult. Brothel keepers charged the women heavy interest, refused to credit them for days of work lost to menstruation and illness, and required them to repay the expense of their room, board, and clothing. Hundreds of women escaped the system by marrying Chinese men who spirited them away from the *tongs* or paid off their debts. Others died young from sexually transmitted diseases, suicide, drug addiction, and violence.[70] Debt bondage, then, was much more likely to become a permanent condition for Chinese women in California than it was for Chinese men.

Across the 1850s, the relationships of contract and debt that brought Chinese men and women to California came under scrutiny from politicians like Robert Semple who insisted that the state should remain a haven for free white labor. Equating the Chinese credit-ticket system and prostitution with chattel bondage, these politicians waged a battle against "coolie slavery" and "woman slavery" that they pronounced to be menaces to California's free-state status. This antislavery, anti-Chinese campaign spurred a variety of anti-coolie bills and prohibitory taxes aimed at suppressing Chinese immigration. Ironically, these efforts to exclude Chinese "slaves" coincided and overlapped with a struggle over the fate of actual chattel slaves whom Semple's own countrymen brought west. Before most Chinese set foot in California and before the constitutional convention banned slavery in the new state, slaveholding southern whites attempted to transplant the peculiar institution to the Pacific Coast. As Robert Semple predicted, writing an antislavery constitution and declaring California a free state did not completely deter eager slaveholders who looked to press the boundaries of slavery westward.

The Slave South Goes West

When word of the California gold discoveries reached Missouri in 1848, Reuben and Elizabeth Knox imagined the possibilities that the new territory held for slave labor. The Knoxes, like many residents of the Border South, were accustomed to moving west in pursuit of prosperity. The family had migrated from North Carolina to St. Louis with several slaves in the early 1840s, participating in a decades-long migration that expanded the frontier of slavery westward. In St. Louis, the Knoxes followed the lead of fellow urban slaveholders. They hired out their bondpeople to other city dwellers and collected their wages. By the time of the gold rush, the Knoxes' profits from slave hiring had started to decline. They looked west again.[71]

In the spring of 1849, Reuben Knox set out for California with a group of family slaves. These included four men—Bill Hunter, Romeo, Lewis, and George—as well as two adolescents—thirteen-year-old Sarah and nine-year-old Fred. "I propose now to free them," Knox wrote of his bondpeople, on the "condition that they work for me one year in the gold mines of California."[72] Knox hoped that the promise of emancipation would keep the enslaved people loyal on the journey. When the party arrived in Sacramento, Knox found that the familiar practice of urban slave hiring promised higher returns than taking the bondpeople with him to the goldfields. Before leaving for the mines, he hired out each slave to city residents. Bill Hunter and Romeo brought in at least eight dollars a day working as carpenters, and Lewis worked for three or four dollars a day as a brick maker. Sarah, hired out as a domestic servant, fetched ten dollars per week. After an eight-month absence in the mining country, Knox returned to find that, despite promises of freedom, three of the six enslaved people had run away.[73]

The saga of these Missouri migrants was hardly unique. Thousands of white southerners rushed to California during the 1840s and 1850s. Almost 25,000 southern-born whites made it to the goldfields by 1850 and together made up roughly 36 percent of the state's U.S.-born population.[74] Of these thousands, several hundred brought their bondpeople west with them. Early state censuses, though frustratingly incomplete, recorded around 381 enslaved African Americans living with their masters. Another historian has speculated that somewhere between 500 and 600 slaves worked in the goldfields across the 1850s. Contemporary accounts suggest that slave numbers may have been higher, perhaps even reaching around 1,500 in the first two years of statehood.[75] Free-state status clearly did not preclude the extension of slavery into California.

Slaveholders who transported their bondpeople west reenacted familiar migrations that had long sustained the southern slave economy. With the start of the cotton boom in the early nineteenth century, thousands of whites moved west in search of land. Successive waves of migration brought masters and enslaved people into the Old Southwest and Texas, pressing the boundaries of slavery westward. Many slaveholding families saw migration as an opportunity to ensure economic security for their children. Older family members lent younger people money and slaves to help them journey west and establish their own farms. Westward migration was a familiar way of transferring capital to the next generation—in the form of cash, land, or slaves—that financed future comfort and independence.[76]

Although only temporary, white southerners' journeys to the Pacific Coast served similar purposes. A substantial number of California slaveholders were young men without slaves or land of their own. They relied on older slaveholding kinsmen to finance their California journeys and to lend them slaves to make mining more profitable. With help from their family's slaves, they hoped to dig enough gold to return home and buy land (and slaves) of their own. Kentuckian George Murrell traveled to California with Rheubin, one of the twenty-seven bondpeople who belonged to his father. With Rheubin's help, Murrell wanted to earn a "comfortable independence" and "acquire enough in a few years to settle me comfortably in old Ky." George P. Dodson went to California from North Carolina with four of his father-in-law's bondpeople. He later returned to buy a farm with the profits of his mining.[77] Murrell and Dodson never intended to stay in California. Nonetheless, their journeys, like those of their fathers and brothers before them, helped them live out a particular vision of white southern manhood that included independent landownership and mastery over a household and slaves.

Once they arrived in California, slaveholders adapted older practices of slavery to the gold rush economy. Some made the transition to gold mining with relative ease. As many as 200 goldseeking masters and slaves came from Burke and McDowell counties in western North Carolina.[78] The Burke area was rich in gold and had been the site of one of the half-dozen gold rushes that cropped up across the American South during the early nineteenth century. Most North Carolina slaveholders who traveled west in the 1850s had employed slaves in placer mining for decades before going to California. Imitating work relations in the North Carolina placers, they brought large numbers of young enslaved men to the diggings, pooled them into large gangs, and set them to work under an overseer. For these particular masters and slaves, daily work in California bore striking similarities to that in the slave South.[79]

Masters from the Border and Upper South—mainly Missourians, Kentuckians, and Tennesseans—approached slavery in California differently. In their home states, most had been small slaveholders engaged in diversified commercial agriculture. They tended to take only one or two slaves to California, and, replicating labor patterns common on Missouri's small farms, they worked alongside their bondpeople on modest claims. These small slaveholders were also more likely to engage in slave hiring. Hiring out, whereby masters temporarily rented slaves to other whites, enhanced the flexibility and profitability of chattel slavery. Southern farmers hired out their slaves during lulls in the agricultural cycle, and urban slaveholders, like Reuben and Elizabeth Knox, rented unneeded bondpeople to fellow city dwellers.[80] The demand for hired laborers in mining, personal service, and domestic work encouraged some of these small slaveholders to pull slaves off their own claims and hire them out on a permanent basis. Some reported hiring out enslaved men as mining laborers at $65 or $75 per month, a spectacular rate that far exceeded the $175 to $300 per year that a hired enslaved man might bring in Missouri during the 1850s.[81] Domestic and personal service work brought even higher returns. Kentuckian George Murrell did poorly in California until he hired out his father's slave, Rheubin, as a hotel cook at the rate of $10 per day. "Foolish I was that [I] did not have him hired all the time," Murrell confided to a friend; "I might have been a great deal better off. $10.00 a day is big wages and but few hands can get it now."[82] Hiring practices originally designed to mitigate the fluctuating labor demands of the southern slave economy could be reworked to capitalize on gold rush markets for mining and domestic labor.[83]

Many slaveholders successfully transplanted the labor practices that underpinned slavery in the American South to California soil. Maintaining mastery over slaves was a more difficult proposition. The vast geographic expanse of California, the isolation and anonymity of the mines, and the presence of antislavery northerners meant that slaveholders constantly confronted the dangers of slave flight and slave rescue. Constructing slavery in California required more than transporting familiar labor relations to the West. It necessitated social and cultural adaptations designed to enforce labor discipline and extend surveillance over bondpeople.

Goldseeking slaveholders tried to combat the fluidity, anonymity, and uncertainty of gold rush society by reconstructing familiar ties of kinship and community. Men who took slaves to California frequently journeyed west with and settled alongside other men related to them by blood or marriage. When Burke County, North Carolina, resident Thomas Lenoir Avery embarked for California with twelve enslaved men belonging to his father and brother, he traveled with his uncle, Alexander Hamilton Erwin, who brought along seven slaves of his own. At least four other Avery and Erwin relatives from Burke County brought slaves to California. They eventually settled next to Thomas and Alexander in the Wood's Creek Diggings, located in Tuolumne County in the Southern Mines.[84] Their choice of location was significant. The Southern Mines lay closer to the end of the southern overland trail to the Pacific and became the destination of large numbers of slaveholders. Three counties in the Southern Mines—Mariposa, Tuolumne, and Calaveras—were home to more than 35 percent of the state's enslaved black population. Slaveholding whites were so numerous in the region that one Kentuckian, Robert Givens, assured his father that the antislavery constitution posed no obstacles to bringing slaves there. "No one will put themselves to the trouble of investigating the matter," he explained.[85]

As Givens pointed out, slaveholders who settled in groups with family and neighbors established de facto slaveholding communities in California.

Party of white miners and black miners working on Spanish Flat, El Dorado County, Calif., 1852. This interracial mining company may have included masters and slaves, as El Dorado County had the highest number of slaveholding households in the Northern Mines in the 1850 census. Joseph Blaney Starkweather, *Spanish Flat*, 1852. Courtesy of the California History Room, California State Library, Sacramento, Calif.

These communities insulated master-slave relationships from interference and allowed greater surveillance over slaves. In Wood's Diggings, the home of the many Burke County parties, angry North Carolinians banded together against a local "abolishness" who was "prejudice[d] against . . . every one that has negroes here." They ruined the man's business by boycotting his store.[86] Slaveholders also joined forces to supervise, punish, and intimidate slaves so that no wily "abolishness" would tempt them to run away. They formed informal posses that chased down runaways, shot and beat recalcitrant slaves, and helped masters return their bondpeople to the slave states.[87] They also watched over each other's slaves. When Thomas Lenoir Avery and several of his slaves died of cholera in 1855, Alexander Hamilton Erwin took charge of his nephew's surviving bondpeople. He promised Avery's father that he would keep the men "safe from the influence of abolitionists" by dividing them into small gangs, "an honest one in each," and setting them to work on nearby mining claims where he could monitor them.[88] The transplantation of social networks to the Pacific Coast proved a vital way of sustaining servitude on free soil.

As slaveholders cast about for ways to make slavery work, enslaved people made their own calculations and adjustments. The journey to California that promised independence and wealth to young slaveholding white men brought familiar terrors for enslaved people, who had endured forced migration and relocation for generations. With each wave of slaveholder movement into the Old Southwest, slaves suffered separation from families and communities farther east, harrowing overland journeys, exposure to disease, and unrelenting toil under rough frontier conditions. The journey to California—a trip of more than 1,500 miles from the closest slave state—and the prospect of constant employment in placer mining posed similar hardships. California-bound slaves might have taken heart that these privations would be temporary. Few masters wanted to stay in California, and most planned to take their bondpeople back to the South after a few years. Still, the dangers of the trip and the enormous distance between the Pacific Coast and the slave states could shatter these hopes. Fatal mining accidents and deadly diseases took enslaved people's lives and prevented the reunion of families. A master's death in the mines or his inability to pay for slaves' passage home resulted in abandonment and separation from loved ones.[89] As in the slave South, masters' ambitions rested on suffering and uncertainty for slaves.

New opportunities for freedom and autonomy both complicated and mitigated California's hardships. Like Chileans and Chinese who arrived under contracts, slaves were often quick to see that the insatiable demand for labor in California, coupled with the vast spaces and anonymity of the mines, gave them many prospects to leave their masters and strike out on their own. But enslaved African Americans who considered running away faced impossible choices between liberating themselves and maintaining ties with loved ones. Slaves who took their freedom in California faced permanent separation from their families thousands of miles away in the slave states. Factors such as gender, age, and family status often shaped individual decisions to remain with masters or to seize freedom. Running away was rarely an obvious, easy, or even desirable option for most.[90]

The stories of the enslaved people whom Missourian Reuben Knox left hired out in Sacramento give rare insight into these complexities. Recall that after an absence of eight months, Reuben Knox returned to Sacramento in the fall of 1850 to discover that three of his six bondpeople had fled the city. Romeo and George, both young men, took passage on outbound ships. Thirteen-year-old Sarah, the only female member of the party, married a free black man and apparently ran away to live with her new husband. The remaining slaves, Bill Hunter, Fred, and Lewis, rejoined Reuben Knox and continued to work for their freedom.[91]

Whether staying or fleeing, the six enslaved people made difficult choices based on their family lives and personal experiences. Romeo's and George's decisions to run away may have been shaped by their status as young, mobile, unmarried men who could easily jump aboard a ship and find employment elsewhere in the mines. Sarah's method of flight likely intersected with considerations of age and gender. A teenaged African American girl living in a predominantly male society, she might have looked to an early marriage as a way to obtain economic security and protection from her master. Bill Hunter may have concluded that appeasing Knox was the only way to ensure his reunion with his family. Hunter's wife, Harriet, was still a Knox slave back in Missouri. Lewis, another of the "faithful" slaves, had already paid Knox a portion of his purchase price. Staying for a few more months probably seemed the best way to secure permanent freedom. Finally, Fred, who was only nine years old, likely had few chances to escape the control of Knox or his hirers.[92] In the end, the slaves who ran away may have been more successful at getting their freedom than those who stayed. Knox's halfhearted attempts to track down the runaways were cut short by his sudden death in the spring of 1851. It is unclear whether Knox's sons, who had also accompanied the party to California, honored their father's promise to emancipate Bill Hunter, Lewis, and Fred. They may have taken them back to Missouri as slaves. Staying with masters could be as fraught with difficulty as escaping from them.[93]

The dilemmas of runaway slaves, as well as those of slaveless masters, came into greater focus after statehood. After months of wrangling and negotiation, Congress hammered out the Compromise of 1850 and approved California's entrance into the Union as a free state. California masters and their proslavery allies countered new free-state status with laws of their own. Arguing that California could not deprive masters of slave property that they brought in during the pre-statehood period, proslavery forces successfully passed a state fugitive slave law in 1852. The law stipulated that any enslaved people transported to California before statehood—like all of the Knox slaves—could be taken back to the South. People who resisted leaving California or who ran away—like Romeo, George, and Sarah—would be arrested by state officials, remanded to their owners, and sent back to the slave states. On the books until 1855, California's fugitive slave law authorized the enslavement of African Americans who had been on free soil for half a decade. When the state supreme court upheld the law, black and white antislavery activists alike lamented that California was a free state in name only.[94]

The fugitive slave question exposed the cracks in California's free-soil foundation. The constitutional provision banning slavery and involuntary servitude did not, and could not, speak to the sheer diversity of California's peoples and labor systems. Most whites who arrived in California understood the world in black and white terms; they imagined the United States as a nation of "negroes" and white people, slaves and free people. A land inhabited by a diverse array of Native and Spanish-speaking peoples before the U.S. conquest, and a place where the world rushed in quickly afterward, California unsettled these assumptions. Blacks and whites, Indians and Californios, Sonorans and Chileans, Hawaiians and Chinese made their way into the gold country under myriad labor relationships that crossed and blurred boundaries between free and slave. Not only did the constitutional convention struggle to imagine or account for this intricate web of race and labor relationships. In an ironic turn, it failed to shut out the familiar labor system that most appeared to menace "free white labor": African American slavery. In the hands of determined proslavery southerners, the antislavery constitution that the convention constructed proved exceedingly malleable and open to contestation. Working to carve out a legal niche for slave property on free soil, slaveholding whites ensured that California continued to be a battleground over slavery's westward expansion across the 1850s.

CHAPTER TWO

Planting Slavery on Free Soil

As the fiftieth anniversary of California statehood loomed in 1900, Edwin Allen Sherman reflected on California's birth as a free state. A Massachusetts-born antislavery journalist who had once worked with William Lloyd Garrison, Sherman argued that California's free-soil destiny had been fixed long before it entered the Union in September 1850. With the gold discoveries of 1848, independent white miners, the friends of free labor and free soil, flooded to the mines and turned back the grasping hand of the Slave Power. Sherman claimed to have witnessed the ultimate showdown between freedom and slavery at Rose's Bar, a mining community on the Yuba River, during the summer of 1849. In July, a large party of well-armed Texans settled on the bar. They traveled under the leadership of Thomas Jefferson Green, a war-hardened veteran of the Texas Revolution and an outspoken defender of slavery. They also had fifteen enslaved black men under their control. Within days of their arrival, the white Texans fanned out along the Yuba, staked claims for themselves and their slaves, and threatened to shoot anyone who protested the incursion. Angered by slaveholder monopoly on the bar, Sherman and his fellow white miners held a mass meeting. They declared that "no slaves or negroes should own claims or even work in the mines." When the miners resolved to eject all violators, Green and his followers fled with their bondpeople. The incident galvanized the entire district in favor of the immediate prohibition of slavery. Miners there elected William Shannon, an antislavery lawyer-turned-miner, to represent their cause at the upcoming state constitutional convention in Monterey. Shannon then proposed a constitutional provision barring slavery and involuntary servitude. The convention passed it unanimously, "to the great satisfaction of everybody," Sherman remembered. The next year, Congress admitted California into the Union as a free state.[1]

Sherman's tale of vigilant white miners, ferociously protecting the interests of free labor from the incursions of slavery, has become California's standard free-soil creation story. Like Sherman, historians often point to Rose's Bar as the turning point at which free-soil interests coalesced in the mines and determined California's future as a free state. White American miners wanted to preserve California for free labor. They envisioned the state as a place where equal access to land and resources would allow white U.S.-born men of humble origins to achieve comfortable economic independence, or, with luck, spectacular wealth. Fearful of slaveholder land monopoly and competition from bound labor, they shunned both masters and slaves. The unity of white free-soil sentiment in California virtually guaranteed that the state would have a free constitution. The Compromise of 1850, the congressional omnibus bill that brokered California's entrance into the Union as a free state, merely ratified overwhelming local sentiment in favor of freedom. With the status of slavery settled, once and for all, California did not suffer from the same internal struggle over slavery and emancipation that tore North from South.[2]

As compelling as this origin myth is, it crowds out other stories that reveal that California's free soil was shaky and that its domestic battle over African American slavery extended long past 1850. In the spring of 1852, almost three years after the events on Rose's Bar and a year and a half after California officially became a free state, the state assembly heard an unusual petition. In a lengthy memorial, twenty-three slaveholders from South Carolina and Florida requested permission to establish a permanent slave colony in the state. Led by James Gadsden, later famous for engineering the Gadsden Purchase, the petitioners complained that they were unfairly excluded from sharing in California's bounty. Slaveholding southerners had sacrificed "their blood and their treasure" to acquire the new territory for the United States, but California shut them out by prohibiting slavery. The petitioners urged state legislators to redress this injustice by granting several dozen slaveholding families the "privilege of emigrating with *their household*, and *domestics* reared under their roofs and bound to them by many endearing associations, and sympathies." They insisted that California was particularly well suited to slave labor. Mining in the rainy season and tilling fertile valleys in drier weather, slaves would make the "wilderness . . . blossom like the Rose." Lawmakers had a duty to ensure "the permanent and future prosperity of California," and, in Gadsden's words, "Negro Slavery, under Educated and Intelligent Masters can alone accomplish this." Rather than throwing out the petition altogether, assemblymen referred it to the Committee on Federal Relations.[3]

Gadsden and his followers never got their California slave colony. But the request itself and the confidence with which slaveholders addressed the legislature shows that white southerners contested free-state status long after statehood. California's new constitution declared that the state would never tolerate slavery or involuntary servitude, except in punishment for a crime. Antislavery northerners like Edwin Allen Sherman assumed that California was literally free soil—once a slave stepped inside its boundaries, he or she, unless a fugitive from another state, was forever free. This understanding of free-state status clashed with that of proslavery and southern-born whites who, since the earliest days of the gold rush, imagined the possibilities that California held for slave labor. Arriving in the thousands with hundreds of bondpeople, they had established slavery in the state months before the constitutional convention met. Just as free-soilers insisted that slavery ceased to exist on free soil, goldseeking masters and proslavery politicians were adamant that California should preserve "southern rights." This might include individual mastery over particular slaves, state aid in recovering runaways, and, most important, validation of slaveholders' rights to bring slaves into the western territories and work them there without interference. In many ways, the Compromise of 1850 marked the beginning, rather than the end, of a fierce contest over African American slavery in the Pacific West.

This struggle began in the day-to-day conflicts between masters and slaves and eventually expanded to the highest levels of the state government to involve questions of national importance. Masters who traveled to the gold country with their bondpeople worked hard to transplant the economic and social relationships of southern slavery in California. But enslaved people soon found new opportunities for resistance and negotiation that eroded slaveholder authority and destabilized bondage. They found allies among antislavery white northerners and free African Americans who used the courts and extralegal action to aid bondpeople in their quest for freedom. Slaveholders hoped to counter this resistance and evade California's ban on slavery by formulating emancipation contracts and manumission bargains that compelled slaves to work in exchange for their freedom. These relations, too, drew the anger of free-soil and antislavery northerners who advocated anti–black exclusion laws to rid the state of slaveholders, slaves, and manumitted hirelings. The debate over manumission and black migration subsided, only to be replaced by a contest over another, more vital, issue: whether slaveholders who brought their bondpeople to California were entitled to keep them and take them back to the slave states. At stake were monumental national questions about slaveholding rights in the federal territories, the status of enslaved people taken into free states, and masters' ability to recover fugitive slaves. Although geographically distant from both the slave South and the free North, California became a theater of the sectional crisis, a place where Americans reworked and remade the boundaries of freedom and slavery in the antebellum era.

Undermining Mastery

When he first heard news of California gold in 1848, William Marmaduke was on the verge of bankruptcy. A loan to a friend had gone badly. He stood to lose his small Missouri farm, the only support for his family of six, if he did not make back the money quickly. Like a number of other young white southern men, Marmaduke looked to California and family capital to improve his fortunes. He planned to join the overland rush of goldseekers, and his brother, James Marmaduke, loaned him an enslaved man named Bob to help him dig gold. Before William and Bob headed west, the brothers and the enslaved man reached an understanding. Bob would work faithfully for William in California, and if he earned $1,000 toward his purchase price, James would set him free. Soon after the two men arrived in the goldfields in late 1849, Bob fell ill. Instead of earning a steady income for the Marmadukes, he lay idle and racked up debts to the local doctor. William suspected that Bob was malingering and gave him an ultimatum. He hired out the enslaved man as a hotel cook and told him that he "never shall have his freedom" if he did not earn enough money to pay for himself. Bob's promises to work hard and faithfully failed to set William at ease. The enslaved man seemed honest enough, but he might forget his promises if "put estray by some of these mean Yankeys [with which] the country abounds."[4]

Like William Marmaduke, many white southerners who hoped to profit from slavery in California soon worried that the institution might unravel before their eyes. California was a wide-open terrain where opportunities for escape and resistance abounded, where nonslaveholding and antislavery northerners were numerous, and where, after 1850, the constitution banned slavery. Far from home and traditional mechanisms of surveillance and discipline, enslaved people might become far less compliant. A seemingly trustworthy man like Bob could feign illness, refuse to work, or run off with "mean Yankeys." The presence of these Yankees themselves presented unfamiliar challenges. Slavery's survival in the South required the tacit cooperation of all free white men, slaveholding and nonslaveholding alike, to police slave behavior and put down slave resistance.[5] Slaveholders who came to California in large groups might count on close family, friends, and neighbors to perform these duties. But a large number of California slaveholders lived among white northerners who were, at best, ambivalent toward slavery and, at worst, downright hostile to it. Few of these new neighbors could be depended on to discipline slaves or to recover runaways; many might encourage slave flight or protest slaveholders' presence in the diggings. Before it reached California's courts or legislative halls, the contest over slavery began in the daily life of the diggings.

William Marmaduke's worries that Bob might shirk his duties or fly into the arms of northern abolitionists spoke to a growing reality. Slaves behaved differently in California than they did back home. Slaves often recognized that conditions in the goldfields disrupted familiar power relations and presented new opportunities for flight, negotiation, and economic reward. A few used the chaos, anonymity, and new economic opportunities in the mines to emancipate themselves. Many others, caught between desires for freedom and the reality that their masters remained their only connection with their loved ones thousands of miles away, refashioned master-slave relationships in smaller ways. Turning slaveholders' anxieties to their own advantage, they renegotiated the conditions of their labor, pressed masters to honor their ties with distant family members, and demanded a share of California's wealth. These types of resistance and negotiation rarely ended in full freedom. They nonetheless allowed enslaved people to challenge slaveholder mastery and create new kinds of lives for themselves within slavery.

Running away was the most obvious and powerful way that enslaved people might resist bondage. Masters saw opportunities for escape almost everywhere they looked. One Tennessean pointed out that many parts of the diggings were so "hidden and retired" that slaves could escape without fear of recapture. A Kentuckian speculated that each slave had so many "facilities and temptations presented to him to run away that he would be worth very little money to his owner."[6] Enslaved people were just as quick to recognize these chances for escape. One correspondent reported that some slaves stayed with their masters but many found "it as easy to dig gold for themselves as for others and leave for 'parts unknown' soon after arrival."[7] Dozens of men and women secured their freedom by fleeing into remote mining areas or cities. Jack Varney, an enslaved man from Missouri, dug more than $1,000 in gold for his master before running away and finding shelter among a company of New Yorkers. His master never found him, and he stayed with his new companions for several months. Two anonymous enslaved men from Missouri lived with their master in one of the few parts of Mariposa

County where "Yankees abounded." They soon caught "the Spirit of Liberty" from their neighbors and fled with all of their master's livestock.[8]

For slaves who feared permanent separation from their families in the slave states, short-term escape could wrest significant concessions from masters. An enslaved man named Andrew Jackson ran away after his master died in the mines. Jackson wrote to the slaveholder's widow in Tennessee and promised to return to her service if she allowed him to come back to his family and purchase his freedom. "I would like to know the least money you will take for me and if your price is a reasonable one I will come home and pay for myself as I had rather live in that country than this," he explained. The widow, who probably feared losing Jackson altogether, agreed to free him in exchange for $1,500.[9]

Running away was only one of the ways that enslaved people undermined slaveholders' tenuous authority in the mines. They also renegotiated the terms and conditions of their labor by refusing to work. An enslaved man named Scipio may have used his master's concerns about his faithfulness to fashion a more palatable working life. Scipio's master wrote home that the man seemed loyal and hardworking. Yet when he tried to hire Scipio out to a stranger, the enslaved man protested the arrangement. Scipio declared that he could make more money for himself by remaining with his master and argued that separation might endanger his chances of returning home. The slaveholder capitulated. In Sacramento, an anonymous enslaved man reshaped the terms of his labor by refusing to work for his hirers. In 1849, Thomas Eads, the man's master, filed suit against two local merchants who hired the slave's services but failed to pay for them. The merchants argued that they owed Eads nothing because the "Negro refused to render service as stipulated in the contract . . . and did not at any time comply with any part of said agreement but on the contrary wholly refused to do so."[10] The outcome in court is unknown, but Eads eventually reclaimed the enslaved man from his hirers. Refusal to work, whether to escape distasteful hirers or to protest hiring altogether, could mold master-slave relationships into a new shape.

For most slaves, running away or refusing to work were far less common strategies of resistance than economic negotiation. Slaves who dug gold out of riverbeds or worked for wages in hotels saw, in a very direct way, the wealth that their labor produced. They pushed masters for time and opportunities to earn money for themselves. This pressure resulted in an innovation called the "Sunday claim," which drew inspiration from older patterns of bondage. Across the South, many masters granted their slaves small pieces of land where they cultivated gardens during their time off on evenings and Sundays.

African American miner working in Auburn Ravine, Placer County, Calif., 1852. Joseph Blaney Starkweather [attributed], *Auburn Ravine*, 1852. Courtesy of the California History Room, California State Library, Sacramento, Calif.

Enslaved people sold this produce for cash or used it to supplement meager plantation provisions. Many slaves viewed access to garden plots as one of the central rights their masters owed them.[11] In the mines, the Sunday claim served the same purpose as the garden plot. Slaveholders permitted slaves to stake their own mining claims and to keep the gold they dug on Sundays and during the evenings. Leonard Noyes lived beside a large party of slaveholders in Calaveras County and observed that "the Negroes worked all the week for their masters and on Sundays they had claims wher[e] they worked for themselves." Similarly, Burke County slaveholder Robert McElrath promised his four slaves that they could work their own claims on the weekends and keep their earnings. Working under this system, each man returned to North Carolina with several hundred dollars in gold.[12]

While slaveholders viewed Sunday claims and access to cash as privileges, many slaves regarded them as fundamental entitlements. Enslaved people defended rights to their own time, the fruits of their weekend labor, and the ability to spend their California earnings as they saw fit. A perturbed Isaac T. Avery complained that his slaves demanded to have the entire weekend off for leisure and to work for themselves. The incident led Avery to despair that "Negroes in California are not the same that they are at home by a long gap." Albert McDowell, stranded in California by the departure of his master's son, subtly asserted his right to a portion of his time and his California earnings. He sent his master $400 in gold, but he informed him that he had reserved another $200 for himself.[13] Once they had established their entitlement to California gold, enslaved people also asserted the right to spend their money according to their own goals and values. A few fortunate men and women used their earnings to buy their freedom from their masters or to purchase their family members.[14] Many more chose to redistribute California funds to enslaved family members in the South. Albert McDowell sent his $200 of gold dust to his wife in North Carolina. The four enslaved men belonging to Robert McElrath instructed their master to mint their gold and distribute it to their loved ones.[15] Claiming California gold and the ability to control how it would be spent, enslaved people financed new lives for themselves and their families both inside and outside of slavery.

Through running away, refusing to work, and insisting on a share of the gold rush's wealth, enslaved people remade the contours of slavery in California. Slaves' actions shifted familiar dynamics of power and undermined slaveholders' efforts to reproduce familiar master-slave relationships in the mines. Accustomed to commanding slaves, masters now found that they had to negotiate with them. Isaac T. Avery's lament that "Negroes in California are not the same that they are at home" captured an important truth: the journey west transformed the conditions of servitude, creating a regional variation of slavery in which power relations between slaveholders and the enslaved were remarkably fluid, ambiguous, and unstable.

Part of what made slave resistance so effective and so troubling for masters was that slaveholders could rarely depend on fellow whites to suppress it. Once outside of southern enclaves, enslaved people often found allies among northern-born whites. Hostile toward slavery, or at least unsympathetic to slaveholding rights in a free state, these northern neighbors seemed to present slaves with "numerous facilities and temptations" for escape. Some, like the New Yorkers who harbored Jack Varney, helped runaways elude their masters. Others used the courts to defend enslaved people. When Missourian James Brown captured Richard and Lucy, two runaway slaves, a solicitous white neighbor named Lewis Kethley appealed to the Sacramento courts.

He asked a judge to issue a writ of habeas corpus, a document that forced Brown to bring the enslaved people before the court to determine whether he unlawfully detained them. This intervention did little good. The judge absolved Brown of any wrongdoing, and the master had Kethley prosecuted for perjury. John Purdy, a Los Angeles policeman, made a similar intervention with a similar result. In 1850, a party of Texans led by Colonel Thomas Thorn brought more than two dozen slaves to the town. When the masters beat and shot at several slaves who tried to run away, Purdy charged them with assault. The Texans evaded the charges by threatening Purdy's life and running him out of town.[16]

While individual acts often failed to thwart determined slaveholders, large-scale, organized efforts to drive masters out of the mines had more success. These campaigns usually started among white miners who wanted to stamp out slavery but who were ambivalent or hostile toward slaves themselves. Merging free-soil and antiblack arguments, they protested that slaveholders employed gangs of degraded enslaved laborers to monopolize gold claims and push out independent white proprietors. Rather than seeking to emancipate slaves, they hoped to drive both masters and slaves out of the diggings. Recall that the miners who ejected Thomas Jefferson Green from Rose's Bar during the summer of 1849 also ran off his bondpeople, proclaiming that no African Americans, free or enslaved, "should own claims or even work in the mines." Even in Mariposa County, a major slaveholding refuge in the Southern Mines, simmering anxieties about slaveholder monopoly boiled over into expulsion campaigns that targeted both white and black southerners. Thomas Thorn, fresh from his altercation with John Purdy in Los Angeles, moved on to Mariposa with his huge party of slaves. Disgruntled white miners promptly "stampeded" his bondpeople out of the district. Hostility to slavery, which might erupt into violence against enslaved people themselves, made life in the diggings precarious for masters and slaves alike.[17]

Slaveholders may have imagined California's antislavery population as traitorous whites—"mean Yankeys"—but enslaved people got more help from California's small free black community. United through loose social networks and religious organizations, free black Californians regularly spread news about masters who illegally detained slaves, encouraged enslaved people to flee, and harbored runaways. James Williams, a black Sacramento resident who had fled slavery in Maryland thirteen years earlier, engineered the escape of an enslaved woman from her master's home. He later enlisted the aid of white lawyers when the master threatened to kill him if he did not reveal her whereabouts. In Stockton, a well-armed group of free black men—some of whom had been active in New England abolitionist circles—made covert trips into the rural countryside of San Joaquin County, where masters and slaves lived in great numbers. They urged enslaved people to run away and hid them from their owners.[18]

Free black Californians also presented the most concerted legal challenge to slaveholder power. They launched almost every slave case that reached the California courts in the 1850s. When slaveholders captured fugitives or tried to carry slaves out of the state, free black residents petitioned for writs of habeas corpus, recruited sympathetic white lawyers, and paid for enslaved people's defense. In San Francisco, free African Americans harbored a runaway named Frank and hired four of the city's leading white lawyers to defend him. Similarly, the Perkins case, California's most famous fugitive slave incident, began when African Americans in Sacramento brought the case to the attention of local merchant and future railroad mogul Mark Hopkins and attorney Cornelius Cole, two well-known antislavery advocates who later played leading roles in California's Republican Party. The city's black residents managed to raise several hundred dollars for the enslaved men's defense. Much of this money went to one of Cornelius Cole's reluctant white colleagues, who was unwilling "to take hold of the dark side of these cases without a handsome fee being paid in advance."[19]

African Americans had to pay such steep prices for white allies because California law restricted their ability to mount a case in the courts on their own. Many early California legislators were southerners or midwesterners who came from states with harsh black codes. In 1850, these lawmakers passed statutes barring black testimony against whites in criminal cases. The legislature extended these prohibitions to civil cases in 1851.[20] At first it seemed that these laws would bar African Americans from even bringing complaints against slaveholders. Shortly after they passed, a free black man petitioned a Sacramento judge for a writ of habeas corpus aimed at freeing his wife from her master. The judge denied the request because he doubted that a black man could "obtain such a writ to the detriment of the claims of a white person." The woman remained in slavery. Only later did the courts loosen these restrictions by permitting African Americans to swear out complaints against whites but not to testify against them in open court.[21]

California's ban on African American testimony stayed on the statute books until the middle of the Civil War. Until then, California's free black residents continued to use the few legal avenues open to them—as well as a few extralegal ones—to aid slaves and thwart slaveholders.[22] They often found allies among urban, northern-born whites, the "mean Yankees" of slaveholder nightmares, who opposed slavery on humanitarian and political grounds. Working together, both groups disrupted the everyday relations of slavery in California, and they brought the plight of enslaved people before the courts and to the forefront of political debate. In a place where there was little white unity behind slavery and black resistance cropped up at every turn, slaveholders scrambled to secure bondpeople's loyalty and compel their obedience. They cast about for new legal strategies to plant slavery more firmly on free soil.

Bargaining for Freedom: The Struggle over Slave Contracts and Black Migration

California masters eager to suppress slave resistance and antislavery interference initially turned to a surprising remedy: contracts. Slaveholders tried to hold onto their slaves without directly violating the antislavery constitution by binding them under contracts that resembled those between free laborers and their employers. Masters' turn to contracts seems unusual, at least at first. Nineteenth-century Americans typically defined slavery by its lack of contractual relations. Antislavery and free-soil critiques of slavery held that the right of voluntary contract, the ability to sell one's labor to employers on terms of one's own choosing, was a crucial distinction that set the free worker apart from the slave. As property, slaves were incapable of making contracts. They rendered up their labor to their masters not by choice but by force.[23]

But contracts were not completely absent from slavery. Masters occasionally made formal manumission agreements with their slaves in which they agreed to free bondpeople in exchange for a future term of service or a sum of money. Southern courts upheld these contracts because they preserved the rights of masters to dispose of their slave property as they saw fit. These kinds of arrangements proved especially important when masters hoped to hold and extract labor from enslaved people in places where slavery was illegal. Masters in Illinois Territory evaded the 1787 Northwest Ordinance's ban on slavery (and the antislavery Illinois state constitution of 1818) by binding their slaves to work under long-term contracts. Proslavery forces passed laws that validated these contracts and forced slaves to complete them. Southern migrants into Mexican Texas bypassed that nation's antislavery law by compelling their slaves to work under similar arrangements.[24] Contracting with slaves, a concept that initially seemed at odds with the institution of slavery, actually became a long-standing slaveholder strategy of perpetuating master-slave relationships on free soil. Transplanted to California, these contracts blurred sharp dichotomies between free labor and slavery, which had already softened when masters and slaves arrived in the mines.

Contracts between California-bound masters and slaves established the reciprocal obligations that would govern their relationships in the diggings. Enslaved people ostensibly agreed to work for a period of months or years in the mines or to make a sum of money equivalent to their purchase prices. Masters, in turn, promised to emancipate slaves once they served their terms or earned the cash. The specifics of these contracts varied. In Stockton, a hired-out enslaved man named Nathaniel signed a contract promising his master that he would "well and truly serve" his hirer for nine months. After that time, he would get his freedom. Taylor Barton vowed to free his slave, Bob, on Christmas, a traditional day of paternalist goodwill on plantations. Barton spelled out that this promise was good only so long as Bob agreed to "remain with me as my slave, faithful and obedient unto me" until that day arrived. Peter Green, one of the few slaves who remained with Thomas Thorn after he was "stampeded" out of Mariposa County, promised to labor for one year or to earn his master $1,000 before getting his free papers.[25] Despite these individual differences, slave contracts served similar purposes. They gave enslaved people with many opportunities to run an incentive to continue laboring for their masters. Slaveholders could also continue to profit from their bondpeople's labor without directly violating state law. If eventually forced to comply with the constitution, they could free their slaves without losing their full market value. Contracts mitigated the threats of flight, rescue, and confiscation that vexed California masters.

Contracting with slaves also served a more complicated, insidious purpose. Many slaveholders brazenly appeared before county and city authorities to request that their contracts be documented in official record books.[26] That slaveholders—who, presumably, would have been reluctant to call attention to their relationships with their bondpeople—were so eager to put these agreements into writing suggests a deeper motive behind them. When slaveholders transformed slaves into workers laboring under contractual arrangements and then officially recorded those transactions, they may have sought to put the power of the state behind enforcing them. They not only hoped that state authorities would fail to identify their relationships with slaves as slavery, but they also expected that officials would intervene in master-slave relationships to uphold contracts and to punish slaves who broke them. Slaveholders, in short, hoped that they had devised a way to commit a free state to enforcing slavery and disciplining slaves.

At least one case of slave contract breaking, *People of California v. Richard and Lucy Brown*, suggests that some California legal officials forced bondpeople to abide by these agreements. Richard, aged twenty-one, and Lucy, aged fourteen, migrated from Missouri to California in 1849 with their master, James Brown. Brown had the young people sign contracts in which they agreed to either work for him for three years or earn $1,800 in exchange for their emancipation. Two years into the contract, Richard and Lucy fled to San Francisco. They made their escape with their clothing and a few personal items, all of which James Brown claimed as his own property when he filed a criminal complaint for theft. Police brought the enslaved people back to Brown's house, and he chained them up in a back bedroom. At their hearing, held in Brown's own front parlor, a Sacramento County justice of the peace dismissed the theft charges against the bondpeople on the condition that they return to Brown and fulfill their contracts. To punish them, he extended their terms. They would have to serve Brown another eighteen months or pay him an additional $1,500 to get their freedom.[27] These shady proceedings drew protest from Lewis Kethley, the abolitionist who later faced perjury charges, but the judge never removed Richard and Lucy from Brown's control or overturned their contracts. In fact, the slaves' legal travails continued for another two years. After Lucy finally got her freedom in 1853, James Brown's son tried to force her to go back to Missouri as a slave. Police arrested Lucy, and she only narrowly avoided reenslavement when her lawyer came forward with her free papers.[28] Slaves who fulfilled their contracts could not necessarily rely on masters to do the same.

Enslaved people working under contracts often realized that they could not depend on masters' professions of paternal benevolence. Slaveholders like Brown could break, ignore, or renegotiate contracts with ease. For this reason, slaves, like their masters, looked to the courts to enforce slave contracts. Once they earned their freedom, many hurried to justices of the peace and county clerks to have manumission proceedings and free papers copied into county record books. They likely hoped that these official documents would protect them from masters who went back on their promises. In 1853, a justice of the peace in San Joaquin County transcribed a set of manumission papers that verified that Jacob Christmas, a former slave, had completed a contract in which he had agreed to pay his master $500 for his freedom. He noted that he had recorded the transaction at "the request of Jacob." Lewis Taylor also took pains to make his freedom a matter of public record. Taylor's master stipulated that the enslaved man could have his freedom after working for a year or paying $500. When Taylor chose to purchase his freedom, he

To Families.

FOR SALE—A valuable NEGRO
GIRL, aged eighteen, bound by indentures for two years. Said girl is of an amia-
ble disposition, a good washer, ironer and
cook. For particulars inquire at the *Van-
dorn Hotel*, of [ap1-tf] J. H. HARPER.

Advertisement for an indentured slave, 1850. A California slaveholder, J. H. Harper, bound a young African American woman under a two-year indenture and then attempted to sell her to a third party as a domestic servant. His brazen advertisement, which came six months after Californians adopted an antislavery constitution, underscored the unsettled status of slavery and slave contracts in the early 1850s. *Sacramento Transcript*, April 1, 1850.

enlisted a white man, A. G. Simpson, to manage the transaction. Simpson collected the money from Taylor, paid it to the master, and then requested the Butte County clerk to record the affair. Taylor not only ensured that he had a formal record of his manumission, but he also gained a white witness to testify to his freedom.[29]

As masters and slaves struggled over the terms of freedom, slave contracts sparked debate at the highest levels of state government. Free-soilers immediately denounced slave contracting as a scheme to foist bondage on the state and flood it with degraded free black workers. Delegates at the 1849 constitutional convention had barely approved the antislavery provision when they started to debate the evils of slave manumission. Several delegates warned that slaveholders either planned to, or already had, brought hundreds of slaves into California under contracts for their freedom. One reported that many "gentlemen prominent in the state of Maryland" intended to journey to California "with a large number of negroes, to be emancipated on the condition of serving them six or twelve months in the mines."[30] Another invoked predictable free-soil arguments and warned that masters would use their slave-hirelings to monopolize mining lands and push out independent white miners. Competition from black workers, free or enslaved, would deprive the white miner of "his freedom and render him a slave in the strongest sense of the term." Adding to these troubles, manumitted slaves, inherently idle and dissolute, threatened to fill California's jails and poorhouses.[31]

A vocal core of delegates argued that the convention could only avert the miseries of slaveholder monopoly and a free black population by banning all future African American immigration, free or slave. That way, masters could neither bring their slaves in under contracts nor manumit them in the southern states and work them in California. Delegates initially approved a constitutional provision to block black immigration but later changed their minds and rescinded it. Many worried that such a discriminatory measure would provoke controversy in Congress and hold up statehood for yet another year. As one free-soil delegate put it, no U.S. congressman sympathetic to "free soil and free speech" and "the universal liberty of mankind" would ever approve a constitution "that bears upon its face this darkest stigma."[32] Statehood came without any restrictions on African American migration.

The linked questions of slave manumission and black migration continued to shape early statehood politics. Just a month after voters approved the antislavery constitution, the state's first governor, Peter Burnett, urged the legislature to pick up where the convention left off. A Border State Democrat suspicious of free blacks, Burnett congratulated the convention for drafting a constitution that "wisely prohibited slavery within the state" and made California "once and for ever free from this great social and political evil." Still, California had not yet escaped the clutches of clever slaveholders who looked to evade the law. "If measures are not early taken by this State," Burnett advised, "slaves will be manumitted in the slave States, and contracts made with them to labor as hirelings for a given number of years, and they will be brought to California in great numbers." Masters would do more than introduce slavery to California. They would also bequeath to it a noxious free black population. Closed off from all "moral or intellectual improvement," new black migrants would become "teachers in all the schools of ignorance, vice, and idleness." As a sovereign state, California had both the power and the obligation to exclude a class of people so injurious to its constitution, its domestic happiness, and its moral welfare.[33]

The state's first legislature responded to Burnett with two measures regarding manumitted slaves and free blacks. The first, a Bill for an Act Prohibiting the Immigration of Free Negroes and Persons of Colour to this State, barred all future black immigration into California. New African American arrivals, free or enslaved, would face deportation. Blacks already resident in California had to obtain licenses verifying their "good character and behavior" to avoid expulsion. At the same time that it constructed African Americans as a criminal and undesirable class, the law also struck at slaveholders. It prohibited manumitted slaves from staying in California and prescribed harsh fines and jail time for anyone convicted of transporting African Americans into the state.[34]

The second measure was far more complex. An Act Relative to Free Negroes, Mulattoes, Servants, and Slaves came from Assemblyman John F. Williams of the Sacramento mining district. Williams also proposed to ban future free black immigration, to require all current black residents to obtain licenses, and to fine whites who tried to import free or enslaved African Americans. The rest of his remarkable bill contemplated a slave code for masters and slaves already living in California. It validated the contracts that slaveholders made with their bondpeople and forced African Americans to abide by them. Enslaved people who were already in the state and "bound to servise [sic] by contract or indenture" would have to work out their terms faithfully or face fines and imprisonment. Slaveholders, on their part, had to refrain from cruel treatment and provide their bondpeople with adequate food, clothing, and shelter. They also had to release their slaves one year after the law went into effect and provide them with some sort of payment—in cash or goods—at the end of their terms. Beyond these limitations, masters would retain many of the customary rights accorded southern slaveholders. They could beat any slave who was "lazy, disorderly, [or] guilty of misbehavior"; they could compel slaves to work; they could capture runaways.[35] In short, Williams's bill both averted future black immigration and manumissions and obligated California to enforce master-slave contracts.

In the end, the legislature neither closed out future African American migrants nor validated contracts between masters and slaves. The more straightforward of the two exclusion bills did pass the assembly, mainly because of support from the mining districts, where fears of slaveholder monopoly and black competition ran high. Once it reached the senate, however, northern-born urbanities led by David C. Broderick defeated it. Free soil in outlook, these men likely opposed the manumission of slaves and competition from black workers but felt that excluding all African Americans was an inhumane (and possibly illegal) exercise of state power. Williams's proposal, which would exclude future black migrants but compel resident slaves to keep laboring for their masters, met a more ambiguous fate. A representative from San Francisco urged legislators to reject it outright. The state assembly did so, but by a margin of only one vote; nearly half the assemblymen wanted to continue considering it. Most of these supporters hailed from the mining districts and likely voted for the bill because they approved of its exclusionary provisions. But southern and slaveholding interests were also at play. Of the thirteen men who voted to reject the bill, seven came from the northern states, while only three were southern born. Conversely, at least seven of the twelve men who voted to keep considering the bill were southerners. One of these men, Madison Walthall from San Joaquin County, had great personal interest in enforcing slave contracts. Walthall's wife, Elizabeth, owned a family of slaves from Mississippi who were working out their freedom in California.[36] The vote suggests that the struggle over the state's early antiblack legislation was not merely between Californians who tolerated a free black population and those who did not. It was also a conflict between Californians who wanted to close out slavery and those who desired greater protection for masters already in the state.

The defeat of both assembly bills left the issue of slave contracts and manumission unresolved. No laws specifically prevented masters from bringing in slaves and manumitting them, but it also remained unclear whether masters could force slaves to abide by these arrangements. These questions stayed unsettled through the rest of the decade. As California's African American population increased—from 962 people in 1850 to 2,206 in 1852—the state legislature continued to debate black migration. The next two legislative sessions resulted in two more unsuccessful efforts to revive black exclusion bills.[37] These setbacks angered Governor Peter Burnett, who warned that legislative inaction had already eroded California's free-state status. "As was anticipated," he told the state legislature in 1851, "numbers of this race have been manumitted in the slave States by their owners, and brought to California, bound to service for a limited period as hirelings." In addition to increasing the state's dissolute and degraded black population, these arrangements established "practical slavery in our midst." Soon California would suffer the "distressing domestic controversies respecting the abolition of slavery" that plagued the rest of the nation.[38]

Consolidating Slaveholder Power: The Struggle over "Fugitive" Slaves

Peter Burnett's prediction that southern masters would flood California with manumitted black hirelings and embroil California in a bloody war of abolition never came to pass. Instead, the state's most ferocious battles over slavery centered around masters' rights to take their bondpeople out of California and back to the slave states. This struggle hinged on a central legal and political question: Did California's antislavery constitution free every slave who touched its soil, or were masters entitled to take their slave property back to the South and lifelong slavery? The debate over this issue immersed California in the bitter sectional politics that occupied the rest of the nation in the 1850s. Californians, far from being detached, distant, or unconcerned about slavery, battled over three of the most divisive political and legal issues of the era: the status of slavery in the federal territories, masters' rights to sojourn with their slaves in free states, and free states' obligations to capture fugitive slaves.

California's courts initially ruled against slaveholders by holding that bondpeople who touched California soil could not be held as slaves or returned to slavery in the South. These decisions prompted proslavery legislators to press for a new state law that guaranteed masters the right to remove slaves from the state. Despite stiff resistance from free-soilers, Chivalry Democrats managed to pass one such bill, the California fugitive slave law of 1852. The law gave masters who had brought slaves to California before its statehood one year to take them back to the South. It also criminalized enslaved people who ran away or refused to return to the slave states as "fugitives from labor" and guaranteed masters state aid in recovering them.[39] Upheld by the California Supreme Court and extended for two more years by the legislature, the law amounted to a three-year suspension of the antislavery constitution and eliminated much of the fluidity of early gold rush slavery.

Masters' entitlement to the slaves that they had brought with them to California involved a series of complicated and controversial questions about the legal status of slave property in federal territories and free states. The most divisive issue was whether the U.S. Constitution guaranteed slaveholders the right to carry slave property into the federal territories. From the Northwest Ordinance of 1787 to the Missouri Compromise legislation of 1820, Congress had long claimed the power to exclude slavery from federal lands. During the war with Mexico, free-soil advocates in the U.S. House of Representatives, including Democrat David Wilmot of Pennsylvania, proposed that Congress should exercise this power again by outlawing slavery in any territory seized in the conflict. The Wilmot Proviso never passed because it met intense opposition from proslavery ideologues who insisted that any interference with slavery in the federal territories was unconstitutional. Best expressed by John C. Calhoun in a series of 1847 anti-Wilmot resolutions, the proslavery doctrine held that the federal territories were the common property of all the states. The U.S. Constitution granted citizens, regardless of what state they came from, the right to carry their property into these lands. If free-state residents enjoyed full use of their property in the territories, the federal government could not deny the citizens of slave states the right to bring in their slaves. Before territories became states, any law restricting slavery in them—whether it came from Congress or from territorial governments—was unconstitutional and void. Only when a territory became a sovereign state and an equal partner in the Union could it outlaw the institution.[40]

The Compromise of 1850 temporarily resolved the impasse over slavery in the territories by admitting California as a free state and allowing the people of the New Mexico and Utah territories to settle the slavery question for themselves. Still, Californians had to resolve some thorny legal questions: Were slaveholders entitled to keep slaves that they had brought in while California was still a federal territory and before it became a free state? If so, did California become a free state as soon as voters ratified the antislavery constitution in November 1849, or not until Congress admitted California into the Union in September 1850? These issues raised, in turn, more questions about the scope of the state constitution and the rights of slaveholders in free states. The California constitution declared that slavery would not be tolerated in the state. It did not, however, contain an enforcement clause that explicitly liberated slaves who arrived before or after statehood. Without this enforcement clause in place, proslavery jurists in California might (and did) declare the antislavery provision a mere "declaration of a principle" that expressed an aversion to slavery but did not necessarily free any slaves.[41]

Even if the antislavery constitution had clearly freed every slave who set foot in California, legal precedents regarding sojourning masters might favor southerners who brought slaves to work the gold mines. Prior to the 1830s, many free states protected the property rights of masters who briefly transited through or visited free soil with their slaves. They did so based on comity, the legal principle that each state should enforce the laws of other states as a matter of mutual courtesy and national harmony. Masters who took up permanent residence in free states with their slaves, however, could be compelled to forfeit their bondpeople. As hostility toward slavery mounted in the antebellum North, free-state courts gradually rejected comity and liberated many slaves who arrived on free soil with their masters. But if California's courts interpreted goldseeking masters to be temporary sojourners (and they would), any bondperson brought in before or after statehood might remain in bondage.[42] California may have been a free state, but its power to restrict slaveholder property rights remained uncertain and contested across the 1850s.

Masters' rights to slave property in federal territories first emerged as a legal issue in California before the adoption of the antislavery constitution in November 1849. In this era, American magistrates usually followed Mexican antislavery law and ruled in favor of slaves' freedom. The earliest of these decisions came in 1846. Mary, an enslaved woman from Missouri, petitioned San José's new American justice of the peace, John Burton, asking for freedom. Burton found for Mary because Mexican law prohibited slavery.[43] A similar case gained national press in September 1849. B. W. Bean appeared before a Sacramento court to recover a $150 debt from an enslaved man named Charles. Bean tried to get his money by bringing suit against Charles's master. Magistrate J. L. Thomas dismissed the case against the slaveholder because "the Mexican law prohibited slavery in California . . . [and] there was no law to the contrary." Charles was now a free man and the only person responsible for the debt.[44] While these two early cases established that California slaveholders would lose their slaves, at least one other jurist disagreed. The U.S. Constitution was the only law of the land, he argued, and that document guaranteed slaveholders rights to bondpeople that they brought with them to federal territories. He jailed and flogged a fugitive black man and returned him to his master.[45]

The ratification of California's antislavery constitution and the Compromise of 1850 muddied rather than clarified the status of the state's slaves. On the one hand, California officially became a free state on September 9, 1850, after Congress finally approved its antislavery constitution. On the other hand, the Compromise of 1850 contained a new, harsher fugitive slave law. Like the 1793 law that preceded it, the 1850 measure permitted slaveholders and their agents to track down, arrest, and reclaim slaves who escaped across state lines into free states or territories. A concession to proslavery southerners, the new statute compelled free-state officials to cooperate with fugitive recapture and prescribed harsher criminal penalties for those who obstructed the recovery of slaves. It also contained a number of "gratuitously obnoxious provisions," including one that denied all due process rights to accused fugitives and another that allowed federal marshals to deputize bystanders and force them to chase down runaways.[46]

Slaveholders in California probably rejoiced at these greater federal protections for slavery. White southerners had pressed for tougher fugitive slave laws and greater free-state recognition of slaveholding property rights for decades. What was unclear, however, was whether the new law would be of any use to them. Nearly every slave in California traveled there under the control of his or her master; very few escaped from slave states and then journeyed thousands of miles in search of freedom on the Pacific Coast. California runaways came to the state with their masters' permission and crossed no state lines in seizing their freedom. Both of these circumstances might make the federal fugitive slave law useless.[47]

California masters soon tested the fugitive slave law and did indeed find it lacking. In late 1850, an enslaved man named Frank, who had arrived earlier in the year and before official statehood, escaped the mines and found refuge among free African Americans in San Francisco. The slaveholder, John Calloway, captured Frank in March 1851 and prepared to send him back to Missouri. Frank's free black allies convinced a judge to issue a writ of habeas corpus commanding Calloway to bring the man before the court. They also paid for his defense. Calloway's attorney argued that Frank owed labor in the state of Missouri but refused to return there. This made him a fugitive from labor under the federal law. Robert Morrison, the county judge who heard the case, disagreed. First, there was no solid evidence that Frank had been Calloway's slave in Missouri. Frank had confessed as much, but California's laws excluding black testimony made his statements inadmissible in court. Second, even if Frank was a slave, the federal fugitive slave law did not apply to him. Frank escaped after Calloway had already taken him into California (which was now a free state), and he crossed no state lines in his flight. Consequently, the enslaved man was not a fugitive from labor under federal law, but, by Calloway's own act, "ipso facto free, and at full liberty to go wherever he pleased."[48] Frank left the courtroom a free man.

The Frank case, widely reported in California and East Coast newspapers, stood as an early antislavery landmark. It suggested that slaveholders would have limited recourse to state or federal law and that they could expect little aid from California's courts. But this victory did not last long. The decision, in the words of historian Rudolph Lapp, "stunned the proslavery community" and stirred it to action.[49] The state's small population of slaveholders found allies in southern-born state legislators and jurists who, though they may have had no slaves in California themselves, were eager to defend slaveholding rights in the West. In the first two years of statehood, these lawmakers pressed for new legislation authorizing masters to return their bondpeople to the slave states and requiring California officials to cooperate with slave recapture. Their ultimate success severely constricted the antislavery constitution, rendered chattel bondage quasilegal, and eliminated much of the negotiation that characterized early gold rush slavery.

In April 1851, little more than a week after Judge Morrison let Frank go free, Chivalry Democrats in the state assembly devised a new statute to extend the federal fugitive slave law to bondpeople who ran away in California. Robert F. Saunders, an Alabama-born Democrat who now represented Butte County, proposed the Act Respecting Persons Escaping from the Service of Their Masters. Saunders's bill dealt with slaves exactly like Frank: those who arrived under the control of their masters before statehood and who subsequently ran away or refused to return to the slave states. Most of the bill simply restated the provisions of the 1850 federal fugitive slave law and declared California's commitment to enforcing it. It reaffirmed slaveholders' rights to pursue runaways who escaped into California from elsewhere, it charged state officers with aiding these masters, and it punished anyone who helped fugitives.[50] This was, in itself, a bold statement in favor of southern rights at a time when other free states actively resisted the federal fugitive slave law.[51]

The bill's remaining sections, those dealing with slaves brought into California by their masters, profoundly transformed the status of slavery in the state. Here legislators sought to uphold the proslavery principle that masters had the constitutional right to take their slaves into California while it was still a federal territory. The bill proposed that enslaved people "brought into this state before her admission into the Union" could be held by their masters and returned to the slave states. Those who ran away or resisted going back to the South would be treated as fugitives from labor and face the same penalties as slaves who ran across state lines. Their masters could enlist state officials to capture them and, once they had proven title, could ship them back to the South.[52]

These provisions gave slaveholders remarkable license. Most masters and slaves arrived during 1849 and 1850, the flush years of the rush. It followed, then, that nearly every enslaved person could be captured and taken out of the state. The law was also so vague that it accommodated slaveholders who wanted to remain with their bondpeople indefinitely. It placed no time limits on how long masters had to reclaim slaves. They might work their bondpeople in California for several years and then invoke the law to take them back to the South. It also said nothing about what would happen to captured fugitives. Slaveholders might apprehend runaways and then merely put them back to work instead of removing them from the state. Once the law went into force, only recently arrived slaves had the opportunity to get their freedom if they ran away in California; longtime slaveholding residents could keep working their bondpeople and take them back to the slave states at their leisure.[53]

Despite the law's significant challenges to free-state status, a large number of Whigs and Democrats in the assembly supported it. Some of these men were proslavery advocates and voted for it because they wanted to protect masters' property rights and expand slaveholders' claims in the territories. But even moderates on the slavery question could get behind the bill, at least after a few modifications. Allowing masters to reclaim slaves that they brought before statehood probably seemed like a reasonable legal compromise to many legislators. It placated those who demanded recognition of slaveholding rights in the federal territories and thus resolved that sticky constitutional question. It also preserved comity and spared the citizens of slaveholding states from being summarily dispossessed of their property when California became a free state. The bill's core supporters also reconciled moderates to the bill by adding a new clause that forced slaveholders to remove their slaves within sixty days or forfeit a $1,000 bond. After this concession, a bipartisan coalition passed the fugitive slave bill by a vote of eighteen to eight. In the end, though, the bill found no passionate advocates in the senate, where it arrived just a few days before the legislative session ended. The senate judiciary committee—which included at least one free-soil Democrat in Thomas Van Buren of San Joaquin County—considered the bill but apparently chose not to report back on it during the hurried days before the senate's adjournment. The bill died with the end of the legislative session.[54]

The future of California's slaves stayed unsettled until the legislature met again in 1852. This time around, a Whig, Henry Crabb, took up the charge. A Tennessee native reputed to be a "violent and aggressive pro-slavery man," Crabb later became famous for a botched 1857 filibustering campaign into northern Mexico that ended in his execution.[55] In the meantime, he led likeminded Whigs and Democrats in reviving the previous year's fugitive slave bill. Crabb proposed a measure nearly identical to the failed bill of the year before. His dedicated the state to enforcing the federal fugitive slave law, and, crucially, it allowed the arrest and removal of slaves who arrived with their masters before California statehood and who refused to return to the slave states. Like its predecessor, Crabb's bill also lacked specific deadlines concerning how much time masters had to take advantage of the law and how long they could keep slaves in the state after reclaiming them. Moderates and antislavery critics alike soon charged that the bill's vagueness allowed slaveholders to remain with their slaves as long as they pleased. Crabb and his followers assuaged these fears by appending a "sunset clause" to the bill that made it expire a year after its passage.[56] Slaveholders would have only this brief window of time to reclaim any runaways and take them east. The time limit seems to have brought moderate legislators, those interested in balancing state and slaveholder rights, on board with Crabb's plan. Assemblymen of all political stripes voted forty-two to eleven to pass the bill.[57]

The fate of the fugitive slave bill was far less certain in the senate. There, the state's most powerful free-soil Democrat, David C. Broderick, held sway. A master of parliamentary procedure, Broderick obstructed the bill with endless motions and amendments. He and his allies moved to postpone and table the measure at every turn. They also proposed unpopular amendments to extend greater legal rights to accused fugitives and to protect slaves who had contracted for their freedom. These maneuvers dragged out debate over the bill for nearly four days.[58] Broderick, however, met his match in James Estell, a Kentucky-born slaveholding Democrat who championed the bill. Estell's enthusiastic support probably had as much to do with personal interest as with promoting southern rights: he had more than a dozen of his slaves working on his Solano County farm. Estell rallied moderate and proslavery Democrats to the cause and defeated most of Broderick's amendments. Free-soil Democrats ended up with a lone concession. Slaveholders who recaptured their bondpeople could not hold them "in servitude" in California, but had to transport them out of the state. Even so, the wording of the provision was so imprecise that slaveholders might draw out this process for months or years. Senators nonetheless passed the bill by a vote of fourteen to nine, and after a signature from the governor, it went into force on April 15, 1852.[59]

Proslavery legislators' efforts to solidify slaveholding rights met with almost immediate challenge. Enslaved Californians, long accustomed to pressing the boundaries of slaveholder power, sought aid from antislavery free black and white allies to contest their deportation as fugitive slaves. These sympathetic advocates managed to bring a test case before the California Supreme Court just a month after the fugitive slave law's passage. During the spring and summer of 1852, the state courts ruled on the fate of Robert Perkins, Carter Perkins, and Sandy Jones. The men had arrived in California in 1849 with their master's son, Charles Perkins. Before Charles returned to Mississippi in 1851, he apparently set the men free as part of an informal emancipation bargain. The three went into business for themselves as teamsters, and by 1852 they owned $3,200 in property. In April of that year, just weeks after the fugitive slave law took effect, Charles Perkins decided to reclaim the men. Relying on the family networks that sustained slavery in California, Perkins wrote to a cousin who had stayed behind in the mines and instructed him to seize the former slaves. The cousin put together a makeshift posse, stormed the men's cabin in the middle of the night, and loaded the former slaves into their own wagon. He then took them before a Sacramento justice of the peace who approved their removal to Mississippi.[60]

Sacramento African Americans caught wind of the case and brought antislavery attorney Cornelius Cole to the men's aid. Cole took the matter to the Sacramento District Court, where he delivered a rousing ninety-two-page argument in defense of the men's freedom. "The relation of master and slave . . . was entirely annihilated" once California adopted its constitution, he argued, and fugitive recapture was solely the prerogative of the U.S. federal government. He exhorted the judge to strike down this grievous and uncon-stitutional fugitive law so that the American flag, which gracefully floated "over the rocky coast of the Pacific," would "continue to wave above only free-men forever."[61] Cole barely made it out of the courthouse alive. White south-erners, "many of whom were well armed for a possible conflict," packed the courtroom. One of these men, a former member of the state assembly, ap-proached Cole and threatened "personal violence on account of the case." Antislavery men rushed in to defend Cole, but the crowd got its way. The judge was thoroughly intimidated and remanded the former slaves to their former master's cousin.[62] Cole and his colleagues had no choice but to appeal to the state's highest court.

The black men would not find redress there, either. In one of the most deeply proslavery decisions ever rendered in a free state, the California Supreme Court ruled that the fugitive slave law did not violate California's constitution.[63] The two presiding justices, both southern-born Democrats, noted that Charles Perkins had arrived in California when it was still a federal territory. He could not, under the U.S. Constitution, be suddenly deprived of his slave property when California adopted an antislavery constitution. The justices then pronounced the antislavery provision of the California con-stitution a mere "declaration of a principle." It evinced an aversion to slav-ery, but it did not have an enforcement section that explicitly freed slaves. It contained no "provision . . . for emancipation" and was, therefore, "inert and inoperative." Until the state legislature passed statutes that liberated all slaves, California masters had a perfect right to reclaim their bondpeople and were "prevented by no law from the use of their services." Moreover, since most goldseeking slaveholders planned eventually to return to the slave states, they could reasonably be defined as temporary visitors whose prop-erty rights should be protected under the principles of comity. Following these two lines of reasoning, the justices asserted that any slave brought to California at any time remained in bondage. They returned the three men to their former owner.[64]

In his recent study of antebellum California politics, Leonard L. Richards interprets the California fugitive slave law as "largely symbolic," an abstract declaration of support for slaveholding rights.[65] A closer examination sug-gests, however, that the law, and the Perkins ruling that sustained it, had far-reaching legal consequences for California's 2,000 enslaved and free black residents. The law authorized the enslavement or reenslavement of a wide swath of African American society. Nearly all slaves were vulnerable to the law, because most had come with the pre-statehood torrent of goldseekers in 1849 and early 1850. Enslaved people who arrived after statehood, and even African Americans free from birth, could easily fall victim to fraud and kidnapping under the guise of the law. Statutes barring African American testimony against whites, compounded by the fugitive slave law's denial of due process to alleged runaways, made it difficult to dispute accusations of fugitivism. One anonymous antislavery writer explained African Americans' dilemma this way: "While this law is in operation," he observed, "every dark-skinned foreigner, more particularly if a child, negro, mulatto or Indian[,] may be made a slave by the connivance and rascality of three or four rogues." The perpetrators merely had to claim that their captive owed labor in another state. Unable to testify against whites in the state courts, accused fugitives could not defend themselves against such charges. In short, "A legislator hired to get up a bill for the especial benefit of kidnappers could scarcely devise a bill to give the intended victims less opportunity to be heard."[66]

The California fugitive slave law changed the dynamics of master-slave relationships in significant ways. When slaves ran away, refused to work, or resisted return to the South, slaveholders invoked the aid of legal authorities to capture and imprison them. Between 1852 and 1855, California and East Coast newspapers reported the stories of dozens of slaves dragged before state courts and remanded to their owners. When one enslaved woman married a free black man in late 1852, for instance, her master forced her before a San Francisco court. Once the slaveholder rendered "satisfactory proof of title" to her, the judge approved her deportation to Missouri. The same year, an Alabama man who worked in his master's Sacramento hotel escaped and found shelter in the free black community before suffering arrest and imprisonment. The man narrowly escaped deportation when a group of white residents purchased his freedom.[67]

If the fugitive slave law made the lives of runaways far more precarious, it practically rescinded the freedom of many slaves who had earned their emancipation by fulfilling contracts with their masters. The abolitionist *Liberator* reported the tragic story of Louisa, an enslaved woman who had labored in her mistress's San Francisco hotel for two years in exchange for her freedom. Armed men seized the woman and secured her return to slavery just before she completed her term. In Tuolumne County, Stephen Spencer Hill, a former slave who bought his freedom from his master and lived for more than a year as a free man, suddenly found himself arrested as a fugitive. Hill managed to escape from his former master, but he lost his prosperous farm in the process.[68] Slave contracts protected masters' rights to enslaved peoples' labor when slavery was illegal in California. They did little to sustain slaves' rights to freedom once the antislavery provision of the constitution had been overridden.

A Free State Reborn? Extending and Extinguishing the Fugitive Slave Law

African Americans and white free-soilers found some solace in the knowledge that the fugitive slave law was only a temporary measure. The sunset clause, appended to the law to win over moderates, stipulated that masters forfeited their right to reclaim their bondpeople after April 1853. What they did not anticipate was that growing sectional rivalries would keep the act from expiring quietly. For the next two years, Chivalry Democrats demanded the extension of the law to preserve southern rights. They argued that the law's original goal—preventing the dispossession of masters who arrived while California was a federal territory—could only be achieved by giving slaveholders more time to remove their bondpeople. In 1853 and 1854, they twice proposed, and twice succeeded in passing, one-year extensions to the fugitive slave law. Chivalry efforts to renew the bill coincided with the Kansas-Nebraska Act and bitter national struggles over slavery in the territories. These conflicts spilled over into California, where free-soilers and moderates alike protested southern efforts to press slavery into the West. This dissent found voice in renewed resistance to the California fugitive slave law. More legislators argued that accommodating slaveholders violated California's constitution and allowed slavery to exist in the state indefinitely. These arguments contributed to the sectional infighting that tore the state Democratic Party apart by 1854 and weakened its power statewide. Faced with the prospect of losing dominance in state politics, Chivalry Democrats ceased their demands for extension in the name of restoring party unity.

The first anniversary of the fugitive slave law in the spring of 1853 indicated little of the fight to come. Near the start of the legislative session, a Virginia-born Democrat in the assembly proposed extending the sunset clause for another year; and 85 percent of assemblymen—most Democrats, southerners, or both—approved it with no discussion. Supporters of the bill might have anticipated a harder fight in the senate, where free-soilers had nearly defeated them a year earlier. This time, however, David C. Broderick was not on hand to lead the opposition, and efforts to table and amend the bill made little progress. Senators approved extension by a margin of two to one. In the end, editors at the moderately free-soil *Alta California* voiced the only major criticism of renewal. The measure clearly conflicted with California's free-state status, they cried, and "the Legislature might have respected the Constitution so far as to let the law terminate with the present year."[69]

Protests against the fugitive slave law, muted in 1853, got louder the following year. The *Alta* editors' conviction that California had accommodated slaveholders long enough suddenly gained new converts when Chivalry Democrats proposed a second extension in the spring of 1854. This was likely because developments in national politics widened sectional rifts among California's Democrats. In January, Stephen A. Douglas of Illinois introduced the Kansas-Nebraska bill in the U.S. Senate. The bill, which would overturn the Missouri Compromise line and allow slavery by popular vote in the Kansas and Nebraska territories, generated nationwide furor over the possible westward and northward expansion of slavery. Chivalry Democrats brought the battle over the Kansas-Nebraska bill into the California legislature when they proposed a joint resolution approving it. Free-soil and moderate Democrats in the senate, including David C. Broderick, furiously condemned Kansas-Nebraska as a Slave Power conspiracy to foist southern institutions on the West. The legislature nonetheless approved the resolution and became the only free state, other than Stephen A. Douglas's home state of Illinois, to endorse the potential opening of Kansas and Nebraska to slavery.[70]

Both the Kansas-Nebraska bill and California's fugitive slave law dealt with the divisive question of slavery in the federal territories, and bitterness over Kansas-Nebraska crept into the 1854 debates over the California law's renewal. Chivalry Democrats continued to insist on state protection for the property rights of slaveholders who arrived while California was still a federal territory. This time around, though, a number of moderate and free-soil Democrats pushed back. They questioned whether California, a free state, should accommodate slaveholders any longer. Dissent was most striking in the assembly, where legislators had offered almost no resistance to the fugitive slave law in previous years. There, some Democrats complained that California had already given masters ample time to recover and remove runaways. Renewal would prolong slavery in the state indefinitely, allowing masters to "continue owning slaves in this State as long as they pleased, expecting to have the law extended from year to year," they argued.[71]

Chivalry Democrats shouted down all of these objections and pressed the bill through. Despite scattered protests from free-soil Democrats, the senate concurred, with a three-to-one vote in favor of extension.[72] The ease with which senators passed the renewal bill, however, masked explosive sectional rivalries. Immediately after the extension passed, a Chivalry Democrat, angered by a free-soil colleague's remarks that the law was unconstitutional, pulled out a sturdy cane and beat his rival in the middle of the senate floor.[73] Anticipating "Bleeding Sumner" (Preston Brooks's caning of free-soil senator Charles Sumner on the U.S. Senate floor in 1856), the confrontation exposed a growing divide between those who wanted to accommodate slaveholders at all costs and those who thought that a free state could no longer tolerate slavery.

These faults widened the following year. In the spring of 1855, the California fugitive slave law was set to expire unless the legislature chose to extend it again. By that time, the changing demographics of California slaveholding and the shifting terrain of state politics prevented extension. Declining gold rush prospects seem to have dampened slaveholder enthusiasm for California migration and prompted many to return home. Masters and slaves gradually disappeared from California newspaper accounts and court records by the mid-1850s.[74] At the same time that slaveholder presence decreased, Congress's passage of the Kansas-Nebraska Act in May 1854 fractured the state Democratic Party. Chivalry and free-soil Democrats broke off into separate conventions during the summer. The former pledged support for the Kansas-Nebraska Act, while the latter denounced the Chivalry for sectionalizing the party and breaking its unity. Come fall, the two factions ran on separate tickets with separate platforms. Meanwhile, the more radical antislavery dissenters from both the Whig and the Democratic parties called their own convention. They promised to defeat any future efforts to extend California's fugitive slave law and vowed to pass new laws restricting slaveholders' rights to return their bondpeople to the South.[75] Other dissident Whigs and Democrats united to found a California branch of the American or "Know-Nothing" Party. A secret nativist organization, the Know-Nothings opposed "foreign" influences and tried to mute sectional divisions by studiously avoiding the issue of slavery in the territories. The chaos and party fragmentation bred by Kansas-Nebraska shook up California's political order. The Chivalry routed the free-soil Democrats at the polls in the fall of 1854, but the split in the party allowed Whigs and Know-Nothings to capture legislative seats and important municipal offices.[76] For the first time in California's history, Democrats' hold over the state seemed to be slipping away.

When the legislature met in 1855, Democrats on both sides of the slavery question worried that sectional infighting might cost them statewide political dominance. They worked to mend fences and present a united front against new political adversaries. Chivalry Democrats probably feared that demanding the revival of the fugitive slave law would undermine this tentative reconciliation. The legislative session ended without a single effort to extend the law, and on April 15, 1855, it expired. The editors of the *Alta California* chalked up the death of the law to the "anti-Nebraska leaven" at work in state politics. In previous years, the Chivalry had cajoled northern Democrats into voting for the law as a litmus test of their commitment to southern rights. Any legislator who questioned the law's validity "was at once a marked man, to be hunted down by the epithet of Abolitionist." But in 1855, opposition to Kansas-Nebraska still ran so high that even the most "chivalrous of the chivalry" feared pressing the issue of fugitive slaves on their northern-born colleagues. "Passed each year to be used as a rod over the cringing backs of those who knew it was wrong, yet dared not vote against it," the fugitive slave law had finally met a quiet end.[77]

Or had it? Even though the fugitive slave law had expired and was unlikely to be resurrected, proslavery southerners held tight to the notion that California should acknowledge and protect slaveholders' interests in the West. As late as 1858, three years after the law had been swept from the statute books, California's proslavery jurists again defended masters' rights to bring their bondpeople into a free state. A Mississippi slaveholder named Charles Stovall took an enslaved man named Archy Lee to Sacramento in 1857. Stovall hired Lee out as a laborer and collected his wages until the young man finally ran away. The master had Lee arrested and unsuccessfully attempted to claim him as a fugitive slave before the Sacramento District Court. He then took the enslaved man before George Pen Johnston, the U.S. commissioner for California charged with overseeing the enforcement of federal statutes, including the 1850 fugitive slave law. Johnston ruled that he had no jurisdiction over the case because Lee had not escaped across state lines.[78]

Finally Stovall's attorney secured a hearing before the California Supreme Court. Two of the three judges, Justice Peter Burnett and Chief Justice David S. Terry, were "men of Southern birth and education, and were nurtured in the belief that slavery was a divine institution." Burnett had opposed the entrance of manumitted blacks into California during his governorship, but he was sympathetic to slaveholder rights. Terry, though a Know-Nothing, was an erstwhile Chivalry Democrat who vigorously supported the westward expansion of slavery. A year after the Lee case, he killed free-soiler David C. Broderick in a politically motivated duel.[79] Favored with this sympathetic audience, Stovall's attorney argued that the U.S. Supreme Court's recent decision in *Dred Scott v. Sandford* protected slavery not only in the federal territories but also in free states where the legislature had not explicitly banned the institution. What was more, Stovall was a short-term visitor who had traveled to California to recover his health. He should not, under the principles of comity, be deprived of his slave property. The justices rejected all of these arguments but still gave Lee back to his master. Stovall was a young and inexperienced man suffering from bad health and may simply have been ignorant of California's laws regarding slavery, they reasoned. It would be unjust to "rigidly enforce" the state's antislavery constitution against the hapless newcomer, even if he had no legal ground to stand on.[80]

If Burnett and Terry wanted to strike a blow for the proslavery cause, they were sorely disappointed. The changing political climate of the late 1850s made the court's decision the dying gasp of slaveholder rights in California. The justices' inept and distorted legal reasoning drew censure from across the political spectrum. Free-soil Democrats, and even some moderate pro-slavery Democrats, condemned it. Stockton's *San Joaquin Republican*, long af-filiated with the Chivalry Democrats, called the decision "a mockery and a trifling with Justice." Likewise, a proslavery southerner wrote home that "this way that ultra Southern men have of trying to force this [fugitive slave] law to cover cases for which it was never intended by its framers" only hurt the cause by stirring up abolitionist dissent.[81]

The loudest criticisms came from a new political party founded on the principle that the West should remain free soil. The Republican Party of Cali-fornia organized in 1856, two years after the establishment of the national Republican Party. California Republicans were largely political newcomers, augmented by a handful of old Whigs and free-soil Democrats. They were united by their opposition to the Kansas-Nebraska Act and slavery's west-ward expansion. Few in the party advocated full equality for black Americans. Most held deep prejudices against African Americans and claimed that they wanted to keep slavery out of the West to preserve the interests of white men. Even so, Republicans' unwillingness to tolerate slavery on free soil and their belief in equality before the law persuaded them to intervene on behalf of California's fugitive slaves.[82]

Although always small in number before the Civil War, Republicans made up for their size disadvantage by attracting some of the state's wealthiest and most important lawyers. Several of these men came to Archy Lee's aid. Edwin B. Crocker, brother to future railroad magnate Charles Crocker and the first chair of the state Republican Party, represented Lee before the Sacramento County Court.[83] Once the case went to the California Supreme Court, attorney Edward D. Baker, a former Illinois Whig, close friend of Abraham Lincoln, and California Republicans' greatest stump speaker, took on his defense. After the court ruled against his client, Baker, declaring that he "abhor[red] oppression and bondage," fought the decision by taking the case to the San

Francisco County Court, where a judge ignored the supreme court ruling and set Lee free. Baker cinched his victory when he convinced U.S. Commissioner Johnston—who heard the case again on a last-ditch second appeal from Stovall—that Lee did not qualify as a fugitive slave under the federal law because his master voluntarily brought him to free soil. Johnston dismissed the case and granted Lee final freedom.[84] Republican success in Lee's defense may have galvanized antislavery dissent in the legislature as well. Chivalry Democrats who were outraged by the defiance of the supreme court's decision proposed a new state fugitive slave law and yet another, particularly harsh, law banning black migration into California. Chivalry supporters in the assembly passed the anti–black migration bill by an overwhelming majority, but Republicans, joined by some free-soil Democrats, protested and obstructed the measures. Both died with the end of the legislative session.[85]

This temporary alignment between Republicans and free-soil Democrats coincided with the breakup of the state Democratic Party and gave a glimpse into the future of the state's antislavery politics. Between 1857 and 1860, the national debate over slavery's westward expansion made California's free-soil Democrats increasingly hostile toward the local Chivalry and the southern wing of the national Democratic Party. Free-soiler David C. Broderick, elected a U.S. senator in 1857, led his branch of the state Democratic Party in condemning the Lecompton Constitution—a proslavery document that would allow Kansas to join the Union as a slave state—and Democratic president James Buchanan for endorsing the measure. In 1858, Broderick's free-soilers (now called anti-Lecompton Democrats) joined with a handful of Republicans to run a slate of candidates against the Chivalry. They lost in most state races. Republicans declined to merge with free-soil Democrats in the 1859 election, and Broderick tried to rally support for his Democratic allies by embarking on a stump-speech campaign across California. He accused proslavery Democrats, Chivalry leader U.S. senator William M. Gwin, and James Buchanan of conspiring to "bring slave labor into the West to compete with free labor." Chivalry candidates prevailed again. Free-soil Democrats suffered their most devastating blow just after the 1859 election losses. David S. Terry, a Gwin ally and architect of the Archy Lee decision, exchanged insults with Broderick, challenged him to a duel, and killed him. On his deathbed, Broderick allegedly charged the Chivalry with engineering his murder because he "was opposed to a corrupt administration and the extension of slavery."[86] Many Democrats and Republicans agreed. Whatever the true motive behind the killing, Broderick's death helped unify California opponents of slavery. Anger over the Chivalry role in his demise, compounded by the fracture of the national Democratic Party during the election of 1860 and secession, aided Republicans in winning important state victories and paved the way for a full-fledged merger between Republicans and free-soil Democrats during the Civil War.

The 1860s would mark a new departure in California's politics of slavery. For nearly a decade, slaveholders attempted to carry southern slavery with them into California. They found, however, that enslaved people readily seized upon the peculiarities of California geography, law, and social relations to recast the conditions under which they labored. Uneasy with the new fluidity of master-slave relations on the Pacific Coast, slaveholders looked to the state legislature and courts for remedy. Sympathetic proslavery judges and legislators, eager to assert southern rights in the Far West, reworked free-state law to suppress slave resistance and cement rights to slave property. By 1852, these efforts resulted in a temporary suspension of the antislavery constitution that rigidified master-slave relationships and bolstered slaveholders' control over their bondpeople. Yet, as the resistance to the Archy Lee ruling and the outrage over David C. Broderick's death revealed, the effectiveness of proslavery influence in state politics started to erode at decade's end. As the nation moved toward civil war and emancipation, the state's rising antislavery leadership labored strenuously to resurrect the antislavery promise of California's constitution. By the 1860s, Republicans swept into power and, later joined by free-soil Democrats, broke the Chivalry's stranglehold on the state legislature and judiciary. Before then, though, California opponents of unfree labor waged a different kind of antislavery struggle, one against foreign-born "peons" and "coolies" who, they alleged, were slaves in fact if not in name.

CHAPTER THREE

Hired Serfs and Contract Slaves

Peonage, Coolieism, and the Struggle over "Foreign Miners"

When the California Assembly's powerful Committee on Mines and Mining Interests met in the spring of 1852, it proclaimed foreign immigration to be the greatest threat to the state's prosperity. Charged with recommending beneficial legislation for the mines, the committee urged state lawmakers to halt the "alarming inroad of hired serfs" who came from foreign nations to work the diggings. The committee highlighted the "importation by foreign capitalists of immense numbers of Asiatic serfs, and Mexican and South American peons" as a pernicious problem. Armies of servile foreign hirelings, commanded by Latin American and Chinese nabobs, crowded American-born whites out of the rich mineral lands that rightfully belonged to them as U.S. citizens. The committee found Asiatic serfdom, otherwise known as Chinese coolieism, particularly distressing. Men from China arrived "not as freemen" but were "brought as absolute slaves by their foreign masters and by foreign capitalists, and are held to labor under contracts." Free white men, working independently on modest claims, could never compete with wealthy Chinese masters and their contracted slaves. The committee recommended heavily taxing foreign-born miners for the privilege of working the mines and instructed California's congressional delegation to pursue a federal law banning Chinese and Latin American laborers from the gold country. Only by stemming the tide of foreign invaders could California "protect American labor on its own soil against the labor of imported and untaxed slaves."[1]

The Latino and Chinese miners who drew the condemnation of the assembly committee were transnational migrants who arrived in California under widely varying social and labor arrangements. The committee's report reveals, however, that both groups of workers occupied remarkably similar places in white imaginings of California's racial and labor order. Over the course of the gold rush, white Californians frequently recast Latinos and

Chinese into two new racialized labor categories of their own creation—the Spanish-speaking "peon" and the Chinese "coolie." Peons and coolies arrived in California under two analogous systems of bound labor that some whites dubbed "peonage" (sometimes "peonism") and "coolieism." They shared similar characteristics—degradation and dependency—and posed similar dangers—competition and dispossession—to California's free white laborers. Imagined workers rather than real groups of people, peons and coolies became crucial figures in California struggles over the meaning of slavery and freedom, race and nation, expansion and empire.

On one level, imagined peons and coolies became vehicles through which white Californians interrogated the troubling inequities of the emerging capitalist economy and the unfreedoms of wage labor. "Foreign capitalists," who drove their hired men like slaves and denied them the profits of their digging, came to represent the dangers that wage work posed to free laborers. In denunciations of serflike Mexicans and Chileans, who worked their masters' claims for next to nothing, and servile Chinese, who earned pitiful wages under overseas overlords, lay deep anxieties about the power of the wage market to reduce independent freemen to dependent and degraded slaves. But peons and coolies did more than merely illustrate the abuses of overreaching capital. Their very presence in the goldfields seemed to presage free white American laborers' own descent into wage slavery. Cheap and easily exploited, peon and coolie labor threatened to depress the high wages white labor commanded on the Pacific Coast to near-starvation levels. More troubling, perhaps, these foreign workers might hasten the death of rough economic democracy in the mines by pushing free white men out. With dozens of servile laborers at their command, foreign elites, and, later, American capitalists, could monopolize mineral land and drive independent white proprietors into poverty or the wage market. Occupying a liminal place between slavery and wage labor, peons and coolies both reflected what free white laborers might become and threatened to be the instruments of their undoing.[2]

In addition to being class-based critiques of the wage system, both antipeonism and anticoolieism quickly evolved into languages of race, gender, nation, and empire. The construction of Latino and Chinese laborers as unfree and degraded shored up racial boundaries around citizenship and helped to define both the nation and its citizenry as white. White Californians who called for the expulsion or exclusion of both groups contended that their innate servility, their willingness to be the virtual slaves of capital, placed them outside the category of freemen. They were unfit to participate in a republican government and, in fact, their very presence eroded American democracy. Imagined peons and coolies also menaced the nation by chipping away at American imperial claims to the West. Aiding foreign capitalists to carry off millions of dollars in California gold to distant lands, they deprived white Americans of the just rewards of their recent conquest of northern Mexico. More unsettling, the influx of degraded laborers from Latin America and China might loosen the grip of the United States on its recently conquered territories—lands that had been, just before the discovery of gold, the national domain of Mexicans, who now flocked northward. Expelling peons and coolies promised to preserve free labor from the ravages of capital, protect citizenship as the exclusive domain of white freemen, and preserve American empire on the Pacific.

Slaves and Hired Serfs: Inventing Peons

The Mokelumne River diggings boasted some of the richest gold deposits in the Southern Mines, and by the summer of 1849 they were among the most cosmopolitan places in California. Hundreds of Mexicans, Californios, Chileans, Hawaiians, and American Indians, all among the earliest goldseekers, worked alongside newer migrants from the eastern United States and Europe.[3] The crowded, polyglot character of the diggings soon upset the hundreds of newly arrived white Americans trying to make their way in the mines. In July, these men convened a mass meeting to protest the presence of "foreigners" in the district. They were stunned, they said, by the "sudden and unexpected appearance amongst us of influential men from the distant provinces of Mexico, Chili, Peru, [the] Sandwich Islands, &c., with large bands of hired men (who are nominally slaves)." Of these, Americans had most to fear from the "hordes of hired men who are weekly, nay, almost daily, flocking in upon them from the distant provinces of Mexico and South America." Serving their foreign masters, these degraded and dependent hirelings were little more than "slaves and hired serfs," probably "worse than Russian serfs." Well-versed in the tropes of free labor, the miners depicted this invasion of Spanish-speaking workers as a threat to the future of white workers in the new territory. The "honest laborer . . . relying upon his own independent and individual exertions for a livelihood, or the means of bettering his condition," simply could not compete against wealthy foreigners and their masses of laborers. For Spanish speakers to crowd out U.S. citizens was especially galling; the United States had just fought a bloody war to wrest California away from "Mexican misrule." The miners finally ordered all "foreign taskmasters and the men in their employ" to leave the diggings. They had two days to depart or face ejection by force of arms.[4]

The white Mokelumne miners' denunciation of Spanish-speaking "hired serfs" highlighted the unsettling, liminal place that Latin American workers came to occupy in the class imaginings of white goldseekers. In reality, Latino miners traveled to California in a dizzying array of labor relationships. Mexicans journeyed north as independent *gambusinos*, wage laborers, debt-bound servants, or hacienda *peones*. Chileans sought gold as entrepreneurs, as *inquilinos* and *peones*, or as waged contract laborers. The sheer diversity of these relationships was reflected in white miners' inability to name precisely the labor relationships that they were seeing. Mexicans and Chileans who labored for their countrymen were simultaneously "hired men," "serfs," and "slaves." The "influential men" and "foreign taskmasters" who made their way into the diggings appeared to both employ their hordes of workers and own them. The Mokelumne miners never acknowledged the seeming paradox that one could at once be both a hired man and a slave, but white Californians eventually adopted a word to describe Spanish-speaking people who were both employees and bondsmen: peons. In the heads of the whites who imagined them, peons were nominally free men who hired out their labor, but the conditions under which they worked resembled, at best, serfdom, and, at worst, chattel slavery. Peons neither earned nor demanded a fair cash wage for their labor, accepting instead a pittance or nonmonetary compensation. Servile and submissive, bound in archaic ties of social deference to foreign capitalists, peons endured (without protest) harsh working conditions fit only for slaves. In peons, white miners saw the nightmarish consequences of the wage market: capital, gaining the whip-hand over labor, could make freemen into slaves. In peons, too, they witnessed the capitalist monopoly of resources that heralded their own dispossession and degradation.

Peons were the product of not only class imaginings but racial and national imaginings as well. White American miners blamed the condition of peons as much on their racial deficiencies as on the abuses of capital. Poor Mexicans and Chileans willingly submitted to hard, unremunerated labor. This indicated that they possessed servile and dependent characters that made them more similar to black slaves than to white freemen. The "negroization" of Spanish-speaking workers established that peonage, like slavery, was inimical to free white labor and republican institutions and that peons were racially unfit to be autonomous and virtuous citizens.[5] If peons endangered American republicanism, the shadowy foreign capitalists who imported them appeared to throw American imperial interests into jeopardy. They commanded their servile laborers to siphon off California wealth that, by conquest, belonged to the American people, who had torn it away from "Mexican misrule." The invasion of Spanish-speaking capitalists, especially Mexicans, suggested the incompleteness and fragility of U.S. imperial claims to Mexico's former northern territories. Eliminating peonage thus became tied to the goal of defending and solidifying American continental empire.

Gold rush imaginings of peons had their roots in recent American imperial encounters with Latin America, including the Texas Revolution and the U.S.-Mexico War. During those conflicts, American proponents of empire rationalized American conquest by asserting that Mexico's free republican government was a sham. Instead, the bulk of Mexicans labored as peons and endured treatment more brutal and degrading than African American slavery. Before he and his bondpeople suffered expulsion from Rose's Bar in 1849, Thomas Jefferson Green wrote an account of his experiences in the Texas Revolution. Part proslavery rant, part anti-Mexican screed, Green's narrative advised Americans that "the boasted freedom of that country [Mexico] is a slavery in its horrid realities." Mexico's peons were technically free men, but "their freedom is only in name, for want and wretchedness, general ignorance and slavish humility, are seen there such as I have never, in a solitary instance, witnessed in the slave portion of the United States." When New Yorker W. S. Henry took part in the U.S. invasion of northern Mexico ten years later, he echoed his slaveholding countryman. Henry declared that the Mexican "'peone' system is fully equal to our slavery." In fact "the slave is a happy being compared with the peone."[6]

By the time of the gold rush, similar descriptions of peons seeped into the writings of overland migrants. Thomas B. Eastland, a Tennessean who traveled through El Paso with his own African American slave, Dow, could not resist comparing the condition of his bondsman favorably with Mexican "*peons* or slaves," who were "generation after generation held under bondage, upon obligations of debt which can never be canceled." Eastland found peonage most unsettling because it disrupted what, to him, were familiar and natural racial hierarchies. "In our country the *black man* is the servant of the *white man*," Eastland observed, but in Mexico "*free* and *independent* Mexicans, are the slave[s] of Mexicans and bound by fetters they cannot break." He alleged that even Dow, the enslaved man, scorned "dese Nigger Mexicans" as his own social and racial inferiors.[7]

The notion that Mexican laborers were peons, freemen "only in name" and nearly identical to black slaves in their legal and racial status, shaped early encounters between white American and Spanish-speaking miners. Finding many claims already occupied by earlier Latin American arrivals who mined with great success, white migrants demanded the withdrawal of "foreigners" from the gold country. Fusing strident declarations of American sovereignty with the anti-Mexican, antipeon rhetoric of the recent war, they accused any configuration of Spanish-speaking workers and employers of invading the mines and installing unfree peon labor there. Californios, Mexicans, and Chileans were not only trespassers on land that belonged exclusively to U.S. citizens, they alleged; these foreigners brought illegal slavery to the mines, which was inimical to both American free labor and U.S. territorial dominance in the West.

The conflation of peons with slaves and all Spanish speakers with peons proved devastating for large numbers of Latin American miners. Numerous and successful, Mexicans, Californios, and Chileans—many of whom had taught the earliest white arrivals how to work the mines—endured expulsion campaigns aimed at ejecting both "foreigners" and "peons" from the diggings. Some of this violence, like the ejection of Antonio Coronel, targeted Californios who, ironically, were now U.S. citizens under the 1848 Treaty of Guadalupe Hidalgo that ended the war with Mexico. White arrivals accused Californio miners who employed their Indian rancho laborers of transferring Mexican peonage to the mines. Ignoring the complexity and intricacy of rancho labor relations, they expelled both rancheros and Indians, "proprietors and peons," from numerous claims along the American River.[8]

Mexican and Chilean newcomers suffered similar ejections on the grounds that they imported noxious foreign slavery, peonage, into American territory preserved for free labor. In the summer of 1849, a group of Oregonians mining near the American River chased off a large party of miners from Mexico. They accused the Mexicans of being "a company of peons," enslaved debtors who worked to enrich their wealthy patrón. They alleged that the patrón, an American who had adopted Mexican citizenship, bailed his hirelings out of jail and bound them under contracts to work in California for two years at just under nineteen cents per day. Clearly "large contracts were being made, not only in Mexico, but in Chili and other South American states for prisoners or peons," argued one Oregonian. This labor system "would have excluded free American labor entirely" and replaced it "with a slavery like that of some of the South American countries, peonage, and even worse than the domestic slavery of the Southern States." The Oregonians resolved that the Mexicans, along with all foreigners, must leave the diggings. The Mexicans departed.[9]

When a large number of Chileans camped in Chili Gulch in the Calaveras diggings the following winter, a committee of nearby whites declared that only "*bona fide* citizens of the United States working for themselves" could remain in the area. They then passed a local mining code that, like the one that expelled Thomas Jefferson Green from Rose's Bar, prohibited masters from staking claims for their slaves. Since most of the Chilean miners were "peons" who "stood in relation to the headmen as dependents, in fact as slaves," white miners could justifiably eject them. Whites tried to drive off the Chileans, the Chileans resisted and killed some Americans, and a monthlong standoff ensued. The so-called Chilean War finally ended when white miners captured several Chileans. An informal tribunal executed two or three men, cut off the ears of two or three more, and horsewhipped the rest.[10]

Expulsion campaigns against Latin American miners pushed the issue of peonage into California state politics as early as the 1849 constitutional convention. There, the vague peons who populated miners' declarations became more explicitly linked to chattel slavery and were racialized as nonwhite or black. From the outset, delegates tied the presence of Spanish-speaking workers to the pressing question of whether California would permit slavery or African Americans (free and enslaved) within its borders. Delegates who opposed any black presence in the state pointed to the ills that degraded Chilean and Mexican laborers had already inflicted upon California. One delegate warned that the "fearful collisions" of whites and Latinos in the mines showed that American miners would never tolerate slavery or the importation of black workers. If either made headway in the mines, he warned, "you will see the same feeling, only to a much greater extent, that has already been manifested against the foreigners of Chili." Whites would again drive off any combination of masters and slaves.[11] Henry Tefft, a man who distinguished himself for his vicious condemnations of free African Americans, placed Mexican laborers in the same category as black slaves. He declared himself "opposed to the introduction into this country of negroes, peons of Mexico, or any class of that kind." Slaves and peons had the same degrading effect on white labor: they drove down wages and made manual labor dishonorable.[12] The equals or inferiors of African American slaves, peons posed nearly identical dangers to free white labor.

Convention delegates who voted to ban slavery in California failed to bar black migration or to combat the "peons of Mexico." Both issues fell instead to the first state legislature in early 1850. Alongside two bills aimed at restricting African American migration, new legislators took up two measures that addressed Latin American labor in the mines. These included a resolution to Congress regarding mineral rights on public lands and a state law to regulate mining by foreign nationals. The first dealt with the controversial question of how the federal government should treat miners who had staked their claims on public lands. Since most of the diggings were located on the public domain, anyone who extracted gold from them, even U.S. citizens, technically trespassed on federal lands. State legislators worried that any mass ejection of miners from the public domain would cripple California's economy. They hoped to convince Congress to adopt a liberal policy that would keep federal mineral lands open to individual exploitation with few restrictions or fees. A central question at stake was whether Congress should leave the mines open to all comers or whether it should reserve them for U.S. citizens alone.[13] The second measure, a proposed state law called An Act for the Better Regulation of the Mines and the Government of Foreign Miners (popularly known as the foreign miners' tax), asserted California's power to regulate foreign miners until Congress took action. Senator Thomas Jefferson Green, the man who had both railed against the peon slaves of Mexico and tried to install his own African American bondpeople in the diggings, was behind the law. Green proposed levying a sixteen-dollar monthly license fee on all foreign-born miners. Foreigners who refused to pay the fee would face eviction, jail time, and heavy fines. All revenue from the tax would go into the state treasury.[14]

Latino miners stood at the center of the debate over public lands policy and the foreign miners' tax. Whites who wanted to explain why the United States, a nation of immigrants, should suddenly ban the foreign-born from federal mineral lands latched onto the issue of peonage. They emphasized that the majority of foreigners in the mines were Latin American peons who, though technically free wage workers, were locked into labor relationships that differed little from slavery. Latin American capitalists subjected their peons to conditions intolerable to free white workers. Peons, submissive and subservient, bargained away their freedom and became the willing thralls of the capitalists who employed them. Peonage, in short, illustrated the perils of the wage bargain by turning workingmen into literal wage slaves. Allowing Latin American capitalists and their hired men to work California's mineral lands freely would, in the minds of their critics, be nearly equivalent to opening the state to chattel bondage.

Those who opposed Latin Americans in the mines contended that peons lacked a fundamental marker of freedom: a cash wage. Peons were hired men, but the wealthy capitalists who employed them rewarded them only with nonmonetary compensation such as food, goods, and clothing. The cash wage was hardly a hallmark of liberty in antebellum America, a place where most still associated wage labor with dependency and submission. Still, critics of peonage insisted that the absence of cash exchange in the capitalist-peon relationship indicated that Latin American laborers differed markedly from their white American counterparts. Complaining about the large numbers of foreign-born people working the mines, U.S. consul Thomas O. Larkin reported that "very many of our emigrants are Mexicans and South Americans—laborers (*peons,*) of the most abject class." The peons' employers, "men of ease and urbanity" from Chile, Mexico, and Peru, commanded their labor by giving them nothing more than a blanket, cigarettes, and steady access to a gaming table.[15] John Hovey, a white miner who helped expel Chileans during the Chilean War, pushed farther than Larkin and equated peons' lack of a cash wage with actual enslavement. Hovey asserted that most of the Chilean laborers were "*peons* or slaves" and that "these slaves obtain little else from their masters than their food and clothing." Assuming that these Chilean "slaves" had no cash to their names, Hovey and his fellow miners targeted their "masters" instead. They fined the men's employers one ounce of gold for every "slave" in their employ while letting the peons go free.[16]

For men like Larkin and Hovey, the sure proof of peons' descent into slavery was that despite being paid only in the bare necessities of life, they willingly toiled away for their masters. The peons whom Thomas Larkin described working for little more than a cigarette to smoke and a blanket to sleep in did so, according to his account, contentedly. Although naturally indolent, they were "mild and inoffensive" and "guided with ease" by their masters. The editor of the *Placer Times* asserted that Chileans were more successful as miners because "a life of servitude together with exposure to a hot climate" made them willing to bear conditions that most white men would not stand. A later correspondent to the *Times* concurred. He described Chilean gold diggers as "a half naked and servile class, who labored under the eye of masters." They endured hard labor, wading knee-deep in water and carrying baskets of earth on their heads, even in the height of the rainy season. Few white Americans would consent to working under such conditions.[17] George Tingley, part of an assembly committee charged with making recommendations to Congress on federal lands, repeated these kinds of complaints when he tried to explain why foreigners, especially Latinos, should be permanently excluded from California's mineral lands. Keeping the mines open to people of all nations would only "lure hither the foreign capitalist" together with his "degraded and debased hirelings." Worst among these were the "Mexican peon, Chilian slave, or Sandwich Island serf," who possessed "habits of life low and degraded; [and] an intellect but one degree above the beast of the field." They were capable of little more than hard toil in the mines. Importing these "hordes" of workers, the foreign capitalist would reduce American miners' earnings and quickly spirit away to foreign lands the "golden treasures" he had wrested from U.S. soil.[18]

Tingley's warning about the dangers of allowing servile labor in the mines struck on another central component of the antipeon critique: The enslavement of Latin American workers would ultimately dispossess and degrade white American miners who had thus far maintained a precarious hold on their own economic independence. Like southern slaveholders, foreign capitalists who employed peons promoted monopoly in the mines. With armies of workers at their command, they could occupy large tracts of land and seize an excessive amount of California's gold for themselves. Such monopoly violated economic democracy in the mines. The independent free white miner, working a small claim with his own labor, simply could not compete with "degraded and debased hirelings" who fanned out across the mines at the behest of their masters. They would be dispossessed or forced to accept little compensation for their labors, either as independent miners or as wage workers. Slaves to capital, peons might drive free white laborers into a similar form of bondage.

The linkage between Latin American peonage and monopoly stood at the heart of the argument to exclude foreign-born miners from federal mineral lands. One assembly committee urged Congress to avoid any land policy that favored large proprietors. The consolidation of mining lands into the hands of a few wealthy men always degraded free white labor. "Monopolists first render it unprofitable for the laborer to work for himself and on his own account," the committee warned, and then they recruited propertyless people, "cheap labor without character," to work for wages. Only by adopting a land policy that left independent proprietors "unawed and untrammeled by monopolists" could Congress ensure that a "moral, intelligent, and industrious class" developed the mines. Leaving the public domain open to Latin Americans precluded this economic democracy. Wealthy foreigners imported "'peons' or 'serfs'—a species of slaves" and thereby "accumulated wealth faster than the American citizen." California already denied southern masters the privilege of bringing in their bondpeople to compete with white miners. The committee wondered why the federal government forced California to "admit a South American with his slaves, where we will not admit one of our own citizens with his." Protecting California's free-state status, and the future of free labor itself, required congressional legislation expelling foreign monopolists and preserving small white claimholders' access to public mineral lands.[19]

The intertwined threats of peonage and monopoly also fueled the drive for the state foreign miners' tax. Thomas Jefferson Green, himself ejected from the mines for using slave labor just months before, promised that his proposed tax would diminish the power of "foreign employers" and "foreign proprietors" who worked their countrymen in the mines. Thus far, these men, with their swarms of laborers from "the Mexican and South American States, New South Wales, and the Southern Islands," extracted California gold "to the injury of the American people, who are rightful owners of this property." A tax on the foreign-born could reduce foreign monopoly or undercut its competitive advantages. Foreign capitalists, forced to pay hefty license fees for each man they employed, could ill afford to import dozens of servile workers. "Pass this bill," Green told his colleagues, "and the foreign proprietor of Chilian, Peon, Chinean, Canacker [kanaka] or convict gold digger, or the proprietor of gold diggers from any other nations, will pay some little tribute." This "little tribute" redirected the earnings of the wealthiest foreign monopolists into the state's coffers and expelled those who could not afford to pay the tax for their hirelings.[20]

Ever interested in developing a pliable labor force for the mines, Green also hoped that taxing foreign miners would open new opportunities for enterprising Americans. U.S. citizens could use the tax to bind foreign "operatives" by advancing them money to buy their licenses and then holding them to labor until they had paid off the loans. The foreign miners' tax, in short, extended to American entrepreneurs the "means of controlling this foreign labor upon equal terms with the foreign proprietor." To assuage any fear that his proposal contemplated a new form of peonage, one operated by American rather than foreign capitalists, Green concluded with a wistful appeal to free labor. Once the foreign operative completed his term of temporary bondage under his American employer, he could enter the ranks of independent proprietors and "go to work upon his own account."[21]

When Green complained that foreign proprietors and their hirelings denied Americans wealth due to them as the "rightful owners" of California, he highlighted a final concern about peonage: The practice might deprive the United States of the fruits of empire and even of empire itself. Employing an alien labor system antithetical to American free labor, Latin Americans took gold that was now, by conquest, the birthright of American citizens. Whites like Green argued that the U.S. seizure of the Mexican North meant very little if Mexicans and other Spanish-speaking people appropriated California's most precious resource to the exclusion of American citizens. The white Mokelumne miners who prided themselves on tearing California away from "Mexican misrule" complained that the unchecked migration of Latin American masters and their degraded serfs unraveled this new political order. Americans "who have conquered and own the soil" faced expulsion and dispossession at the hands of the people they had just subdued. A member of the California legislature likewise worried that the tremendous "outlay of money and life" in conquering California would be in vain if "swarms of foreigners" carried away Americans' "hard-earned and honorably purchased wealth."[22] Ramón Gil Navarro, the Chilean *patrón* who took his contract workers to the mines in 1849, summed up this postconquest hostility to Spanish-speaking miners. White Americans considered themselves the "rightful owners of mines bought from Mexico with Yankee blood" and would yield no part of them to foreign workers.[23] The struggle against Latin American peonage, then, was also a struggle to make the American conquest of California meaningful.

Antipeon arguments that cast Mexicans and South Americans as invaders eager to carry off the wealth of "American soil" also spoke to concerns about the fragility of American empire on the Pacific Coast. Having just assembled a transcontinental empire out of Mexico's former northern provinces, white Americans worried that the influx of Mexicans and other Spanish speakers might actually turn the tide on U.S. conquest. During 1849, rumors spread that thousands of northern-bound Mexicans were not just looking to take California gold but to take back California itself. One such report warned of Mexicans in "whole battalions, armed to the teeth," marching toward California. These legions, "gotten up by the great capitalists and friends of Santa Ana," were "one solid mass whose cry is 'California's recovery or death!'"[24] A military invasion led by Mexico's "great capitalists" never materialized, but anxious whites continued to associate the northward movement of moneyed Latin Americans and their bands of "peon" laborers with the unraveling of American empire. George Tingley, the assemblyman who complained about the intrusion of the "Mexican peon" and "Chilian slave," denounced the "suicidal policy" of open mining on the public lands because it allowed foreigners to overwhelm Americans on the Pacific Coast. Filled with the "subjects of Monarchies and Foreign Governments," California could easily fall to any alien power, including, presumably, the Republic of Mexico to the south.[25]

California's plea for congressional remedies to Latin American immigration catapulted peonage to the federal stage. In March 1850, California's assembly approved resolutions asking Congress to keep federal mineral lands free and accessible to all U.S. citizens but to prohibit all foreign-born people, even those who declared their intent to naturalize, from mining on them.[26] Accordingly, California's newly elected U.S. senators and representatives,

admitted to Congress just weeks before the end of the 1850 session, immediately pushed for a new law to regulate mining on federal lands. California
senator John C. Frémont, renowned free-soiler and explorer, recommended
a temporary plan for mineral land leasing in which all miners paid a monthly
one-dollar permit fee to work a thirty-by-thirty-foot claim. Frémont emphasized that both the fees and the claim sizes should remain small to "give an
opportunity to all people to get possession of some place to work upon." He
hoped to discourage monopoly by preventing "moneyed capital" from "driving out or overpowering the population who have no capital but their cour-
age and industry." Through this policy, the federal government could safeguard the rights of the small proprietor against the depredations of capitalist
speculators.[27]

Like California lawmakers before them, Frémont and his fellow California senator, slaveholder William M. Gwin, also insisted that excluding foreign miners helped stave off mineral monopolies. Frémont's Gold Bill, as his
leasing plan came to be known, allowed none but U.S. citizens to purchase
permits. When New York senator William Seward denounced this provision
for making invidious "distinctions among races and castes," Gwin countered
by calling up the specter of the Latin American peon. He warned his colleagues that any alteration to the bill would saddle the new state with "slavery
of the worst description—peonage." He predicted that "Mexicans with their
peons will come there and dig gold and go back to their own country with the
spoils." These comments alarmed at least one slave state senator, William
Dawson of Georgia, who connected a peon invasion to losing the spoils of the
recent war with Mexico. "Mexicans, from whom we took this property," could
easily cross into California and, "controlled by some intelligent leader, who
will direct the object of their labor," make off with Americans' hard-earned
treasure.[28]

These antipeon arguments seemed compelling. The Senate passed Frémont's Gold Bill with a compromise measure that closed out Latin Americans
and other nonwhites. Only European immigrants who declared their intent
to naturalize could mine on public lands alongside U.S. citizens; all others
would have to leave.[29] In the end, though, the bill never became federal law.
The House of Representatives did not have time to take it up before the session expired. Congress passed no comprehensive legislation governing mining on public mineral lands during the gold rush and declined to do so until
the 1860s and 1870s.[30] From a federal standpoint, the mines remained open
to citizens and noncitizens alike. The task of excluding foreign miners fell
back to California.

Congress's failure to regulate federal mining lands left the state law—Thomas Jefferson Green's foreign miners' tax—the prevailing remedy for Latin American immigration and peonage. Initially aimed at siphoning foreign capitalists' gold into the state treasury and making foreign labor available to American capitalists, the tax changed significantly during its journey through the legislature. The assembly, with the senate concurring, passed the bill and increased Green's onerous sixteen-dollar monthly tax to a prohibitively high twenty-dollar monthly tax. With this amendment, the tax became, more and more, a measure to remove Spanish-speaking people from the mines rather than one to exploit them for revenue or labor.[31]

Printed and distributed only in English and Spanish and enforced primarily against Spanish-speaking miners, the foreign miners' tax act amounted to expulsion. Faced with tax collectors demanding license fees that might amount to more than they earned in a month, Mexicans and Chileans fled the mines.[32] Others stood and fought the tax, just as they had resisted informal expulsions during the previous year. In May 1850, right after the tax became law, Mexicans, Chileans, and Peruvians living near the town of Sonora joined forces with French, German, and English miners to protest it. Determined to "guaranty security for us all, and restrain the rapacity of that horde who call themselves citizens of the United States," 4,000 foreign-born miners descended on Sonora to confront the new tax collector. After the sheriff drove them out of town, the disaffected miners camped in a nearby valley and allegedly vowed "not simply to resist the law, but to attack those who attempted to enforce it." The tax collector then assembled a makeshift posse of hundreds of Americans, many of them veterans of the recent war with Mexico. Donning their tattered uniforms and raising their old regimental colors, the volunteers prepared once again to conquer Mexican adversaries. They "marched out and drove this congregated mass of foreigners from camp to camp," persuading some to pay the license tax and forcing the remainder to leave.[33] In the wake of similar conflicts, several thousand Mexicans and Chileans abandoned the Southern Mines. Sonora, site of the most violent clashes, lost four-fifths of its total population. To top it off, state tax collectors raised only a fraction of the money that Green had projected.[34]

The exodus of Spanish speakers probably satisfied white miners who had long contended that expulsion was the only way to combat peon slavery and capitalist monopoly. The flight of Latin Americans was much less encouraging to American merchants whose commercial interests hinged on trade with foreign-born miners. In Stockton, the supply center for the Southern Mines, one such merchant complained that "business in many places, is at a complete standstill." He warned that hard times in the mining country threatened to spread to all of California's major cities as boomtown retailers closed up shop or curtailed their orders for supplies.[35] A group of anxious white merchants from the town of Sonora eventually pooled resources to test the legality of the tax before the California Supreme Court. They said that the state had no constitutional power to tax the use of federal mineral lands and that the tax's imposition on Mexicans violated the Treaty of Guadalupe Hidalgo's extension of equal citizenship rights to people of Mexican descent. The court adopted a distinctly states' rights stance and ruled against them. California, they declared, possessed the authority to tax federal lands and regulate the activities of foreigners within its own borders.[36]

The law stood, but not for long. To quell resistance and increase revenue, Governor Peter Burnett lowered the tax to twenty dollars for a four-month license. Finally, extensive lobbying by merchants in the Southern Mines convinced legislators to repeal the tax altogether in March 1851.[37] By then, the damage to commerce in the mines was irreversible. Some Mexicans and Chileans slowly made their way back to the diggings, but most left for their home countries. Others moved to California's cities, fled to isolated diggings, or founded their own camps distant from white Americans.[38] Surveying the devastating results of the tax, the Alta California proclaimed that the state only narrowly avoided ruination by a law that was "decidedly unconstitutional, unjust, impolitic, opposed to every principle of our free institutions, behind the age, illiberal and foolish."[39]

The Alta's declaration that the expulsion of Latinos from the mines, rather than their presence in the diggings, violated the nation's free institutions indicated changes under way in California. As Mexicans and Chileans left and took much of the lucrative gold rush trade with them, complaints about invading peon slaves subsided. Anti-Mexican violence persisted in the mines, but imagined Latin American peons would not emerge as a social, economic, or political problem again until large numbers of Mexican laborers arrived in California around the turn of the twentieth century.[40] Still, the questions that peonage raised about the relationship between capital and labor, between wage work and slavery, between citizens and aliens, and between empire and exclusion did not disappear with the repeal of the foreign miners' tax. Instead, white Californians transferred the class, racial, and national imaginings associated with peons to a new group of foreign-born laborers. Within just a year, imagined Chinese coolies took the place of peons and started to represent virtually the same threats and fears. The campaign for Chinese exclusion that emerged in California by 1852 had deep roots in the expulsion of Latinos that preceded it.

Asiatic Serfs and Contract Slaves: Inventing Coolieism

In April 1852, three years after the Mokelumne meeting to eject Latin American "slaves and hired serfs," whites in the Southern Mines gathered again to protest the arrival of a new, but strikingly familiar, labor system. In the largest mass meeting in Tuolumne County's early history, hundreds of people met in the town of Columbia to condemn "various measures now before the Legislature to establish land monopoly, peonage, and to degrade labor." Most distressing were two pending state bills permitting U.S. citizens to bind workers in foreign lands and bring them to California under long-term labor contracts. These measures, the crowd decided, would hasten the "introduction of the degraded coolies of China and the tattooed inhabitants of the South Sea Islands, as *peons*, to compete with the free laborers of this State." This new class of hirelings threatened to "bring down the price of labor and introduce a system of *Peonage*," one that "cannot fail of building up the capitalist and the extensive landholder at the expense of the honest, hard-working and industrious portions of the community." The revival of peonage was especially appalling because this time scheming American capitalists, rather than foreign proprietors, lay behind it. The state's legislators and moneyed men cooperated in a "conspiracy . . . to degrade and oppress labor, and establish among us extensive monopolies, [to] build up an aristocracy of money and a system of *Feudalism*." The meeting participants vowed "as Whigs and Democrats" to work within their respective parties to defeat the legislation and any politician who supported it.[41]

The Columbia miners' protest exposed the tangled relationship between racial categories and labor systems in California. In just a few sentences, the miners invoked labor designations usually associated with Latinos—*peons* and *peonage*—and then deftly re-racialized and redeployed them to condemn the arrival of Asian workers in the mines. In the process, they invented a new set of unfree, racialized laborers—Chinese coolies—who jeopardized the interests of free white workingmen in ways nearly identical to those of Spanish-speaking peons. Coolies, like peons before them, voluntarily bargained away the fruits of their labor, their freedom, and their autonomy to become the thralls of the wealthy capitalists who employed them. As the Columbia miners were quick to point out, coolies and peons alike threatened to degrade free laborers. Cheap and easily exploited, they depressed the wages of white workers and promoted "extensive monopolies" that shut out independent proprietors. Although the Columbia miners expressed little interest in the potential citizenship status of Chinese, their contemporaries proclaimed that coolies, like peons, exuded servility and dependence that made them akin to black slaves. Both groups, like the enslaved people they resembled, were unfit for participation in a free republic.

And yet the contests over imagined peons and imagined coolies diverged in fundamental ways. The miners who protested in Columbia during the spring of 1852 lived in a very different world from those who united along the Mokelumne River in the summer of 1849. The invasion of wealthy capitalists into the diggings, often only a vague menace in the early gold rush years, seemed much closer on the horizon in 1852. The slow decline of placer mining and the subsequent shift to large-scale, capital-intensive underground mining made corporate monopolies and widespread wage labor real possibilities in the mines. In this changing economic context, rapacious American capitalists often loomed much larger than shadowy "foreign proprietors" in the debates over coolie labor. The legal methods by which both American and foreign capitalists allegedly exploited coolies also shaped the debate over their labor in distinctive ways. Coolies could not escape their employers because they were bound under long-term wage contracts or contracts to pay debts. Whites who opposed coolieism, then, often confronted the unsettling possibility that the right of contract, one of the vaunted privileges of the free laborer, could be a badge of slavery rather than a hallmark of liberty. Working for wages under contracts for American capitalists, imagined coolies more closely reflected the futures that white laborers feared awaited themselves.

As the Columbia meeting's reference to Whigs and Democrats suggests, the debate over coolies also occurred in a much different political context. Political alliances and identities, vague and unformed in 1849 and 1850, coalesced into familiar party structures by 1852. Where Californians stood on coolie labor often correlated with whether they considered themselves Democrats or Whigs, free-soilers or Chivalry. These political identities were themselves linked to pressing questions of American expansion and empire in the Pacific. Where some politicians saw the exchange of people and labor with Asia as an opening to expand U.S. imperial interests into the Pacific, others warned that a poverty-stricken and overpopulated China would colonize its teeming millions of coolie laborers in California. Coolies represented both the opportunities and the perils of transpacific empire.

That white Californians would eventually settle on the term "coolie," rather than "peon," to describe Chinese contract laborers is not surprising.

Starting in the 1830s, coolies became central figures in emerging conversations about labor and race in the postemancipation Atlantic World. The word "coolie," which may be of Urdu-Hindustani, Tamil, or Chinese origin, initially meant "hireling" or "common laborer" and originally designated South Asian and East Asian workers who labored abroad in the eighteenth and nineteenth centuries. The term took on new meanings with the advent of abolition and emancipation in the Atlantic World. After the end of slavery in the British Caribbean, English authorities hoped that Asian laborers, especially Chinese, would supplement plantation workforces and ease the transition to a free-labor economy. In this context, "coolies" came to denote contracted or indentured Asian workers whom British officials systematically recruited to take up the occupations of former slaves. The abuses that Asian migrants suffered in their overseas journeys—including kidnapping, fraud, and cruelty at the hands of ship captains, labor agents, and employers—fueled a debate over the freeness of the "coolie trade" or "coolieism."[42]

As Moon-Ho Jung has convincingly argued, however, coolies never existed, in California or elsewhere in the world, as a real group of people or as a real legal category of workers. Instead, "coolies were a conglomeration of racial imaginings that emerged worldwide in the era of slave emancipation, a product of the imaginers rather than the imagined." Variously envisioned as free or enslaved, white or colored, potential citizens or perpetual aliens, coolies came "to embody the hopes, fears, and contradictions" surrounding slave emancipation and the rise of industrial wage labor. In the United States, some abolitionists identified coolies as a "conduit to freedom," a cheap and pliable labor force of free emigrants that could eventually supplant slaves in American agriculture. In contrast, southern proslavery ideologues depicted coolieism in the British West Indies as a brutal and degrading method of enslaving free workers, one that demonstrated the folly and hypocrisy of wage labor and abolitionism. The development of the "coolie" as an ambiguous, mutable class and racial construct was well under way before white Californians adopted the term in the 1850s.[43]

California's struggle to identify, define, and outlaw coolieism began in 1852, a year after the repeal of the 1850 foreign miners' tax. It emerged as a response to three trends: the arrival of an unprecedented number of Chinese migrants, the shift from small-scale placer mining to industrialized mining, and the legislature's consideration of new laws to ease the recruitment of foreign-born laborers. Before 1852, Chinese immigration drew little attention or alarm. State port authorities recorded only 3,494 Chinese arrivals between 1848 and 1851. Heartening news from returned gold rush migrants, as well as political upheaval caused by the start of the Taiping Rebellion in 1850–51, prompted a much larger migration the following year. In 1852, Chinese arrivals rose to an astounding 20,026 people, nearly six times that of all the previous years combined.[44] Most of these new arrivals made their way to the gold country, where they mined "worked-out" and abandoned claims. Applying hard labor and new techniques, Chinese extracted steady incomes from lands that American miners had supposedly exhausted.[45]

In the apt words of historian Susan Lee Johnson, these new Chinese arrivals "burst into a world of work already fraught with contention and inequity."[46] Chinese miners' success stood out against a backdrop of economic decline in the diggings. Early arrivals to the gold rush mined placers, alluvial deposits of gold in riverbanks and riverbeds that were close to the surface and could be extracted with picks, pans, and shovels. But accessible and abundant placer deposits soon gave out. In the Northern Mines, small-scale placer mining slowly gave way to industrialized underground (or lode) mining aimed at extracting gold from quartz veins deep beneath the earth's surface. Large subterranean mining operations, funded by wealthy investors and worked by wage laborers, gradually replaced independent prospectors digging on small above-ground claims. The Alta California summarized these changes as early as February 1851, lamenting that the placers would "never yield as they had yielded." The future of gold extraction lay in organized underground mining—"the man who lives upon his labor from day to day, must hereafter be employed by the man who has in his possession accumulated labor, or money, the representative of labor."[47] Industrialization was less dramatic in the Southern Mines where underground gold deposits were scarce and independent miners continued to eke out modest livings on declining placers. There a different kind of corporate threat, "water monopolies," which diverted water and sold it at high prices to prospectors who needed it to wash their gold, provoked class conflict.[48] All of these trends seemed to confirm long-standing anxieties, persistent since the antipeon movement, that free white miners would soon become the degraded dependents of capitalist masters.

Amid growing racial and class tensions came news from the legislature that appeared to link the arrival of Chinese laborers with the intrusion of moneyed capitalists into the diggings.[49] In early March 1852, members of California's Whig and Democratic parties supported new legislation that would make it easier for Americans to recruit, employ, and bind foreign-born laborers under long-term contracts. In the senate, George B. Tingley, a man who had railed against mining monopolies and peon labor in the assembly two years earlier, now proposed A Bill to Enforce Contracts to Perform Work and Labor.

A longtime Whig and a representative from the growing agricultural counties of Contra Costa and Santa Clara, Tingley may have changed his tune on foreign workers to satisfy wealthy landowning constituents who demanded inexpensive farm labor. Later critics, in fact, denounced Tingley's legislation as "one of those schemes which the whigs are now so busy concocting in this State to give capital an unfair advantage over labor."[50] Meanwhile, Assemblyman Archibald Peachy of San Francisco set forth a rival measure, A Bill to Enforce the Observance of Contracts. Born in Virginia, Peachy was a Chivalry Democrat. He had already responded to demands for cheap and pliant labor by sponsoring James Gadsden's 1852 petition to establish a slave colony in California. When the petition failed to bring results, Peachy may have looked abroad for alternatives.[51]

Both Tingley and Peachy hoped to alleviate the problem of contract breaking that had distressed employers of Chinese since the start of the gold rush. Their bills sought to make long-term labor contracts between U.S. citizens and foreigners valid and binding, mainly by requiring state officials to enforce them. Tingley's bill, the harsher of the two, allowed U.S. citizens living in California to enter into labor contracts with foreign-born workers. Such contracts, which could last up to ten years in duration, required workers to render specific performance. A legal instrument used to force compliance with contracts, specific performance subjected workers to criminal prosecution if they abandoned their employers. In the case of the Tingley bill, Chinese workers who broke contracts "without good and justifiable cause" would suffer jail time or criminal fines, in addition to wage forfeiture and other economic sanctions. Employers had only to pay workers a minimum wage of fifty dollars per year and refrain from inflicting "harsh and cruel treatment upon them." Peachy's alternative bill limited the contract period to five years instead of ten. Fulfilling contracts would nonetheless be strictly "obligatory" on the part of workers. Employers could withhold wages or use the courts to compel compliance. Recalcitrant workers were to be punished with jail time, paying damages to their employers, and forced labor on the public works. Peachy also put racial limits on his bill. In a nod to antipeon and antiblack agitations of previous years, Peachy's bill nullified contracts with "any free negro," restricted contracts to Chinese and Pacific Islanders alone, and prohibited contracts for mining labor.[52] Despite their differences, both bills had the same goal: creating a class of foreign-born contract laborers who would earn low wages, endure limited mobility for long periods, and suffer economic penalties, legal prosecution, and physical compulsion if they failed to perform their contractual duties.

Legislators gave both contract labor bills a warm reception at first. A senate committee dominated by Democrats almost unanimously recommended Tingley's bill for passage. Peachy's fellow Democrats in the assembly, including, inexplicably, several from the xenophobic Southern Mines, outvoted a coalition of Whigs and Democrats from the Northern Mines to pass his bill.[53] In a little more than a month, however, opposition to the measures swelled to a fever pitch in the diggings. Mass meetings like the one in Columbia denounced the legislation as part of a plot to introduce coolie labor, promote monopoly, and drive free labor from the placers. Makeshift vigilance committees assembled to expel Chinese. One such organization in Columbia denounced the legislative effort to "fasten, without the sanction of law, the system of peonage on our social organization." Members proclaimed that "no Asiatic or South Sea Islander shall be permitted to mine in this district either for himself or for others." Similar groups of anti-Chinese vigilantes in Nevada County and along the American River made good on these threats. They ejected hundreds of Chinese from lucrative claims, and local authorities refused to protect the refugees from physical violence or robbery.[54]

As the Columbia miners' declaration against both "Asiatics" and "South Sea Islanders" suggests, whites in the mining country often lumped native Hawaiians, particularly contract laborers, together with transpacific migrants from China. Denunciations of coolies and coolie bills frequently contained passing references to "Sandwich Island serfs," who posed nearly identical challenges to free white labor. Recall that the earliest anticoolie bill mass meeting in Columbia complained about the importation of both the "degraded coolies of China" and "the tattooed inhabitants of the South Sea Islands." One critic of the coolie bills vilified Americans who employed "Chinese or Kanaka carpenters, masons, or blacksmiths, brought here in swarms under contracts, to compete with our own mechanics."[55] Although far less numerous and visible in the diggings than Chinese, Hawaiians also suffered harassment and expulsion. White miners forcibly removed Hawaiians from claims in Mariposa County and along the Yuba River. By the fall of 1852, miners' conventions were calling for a $500 head tax on "all Kanakas, Islanders and Chinamen arriving in the State," and as late as 1854 mobs in Nevada County burned down a Hawaiian settlement in the hope of expelling its occupants.[56]

White miners hostile to both Chinese coolies and "Sandwich Island serfs" soon found new defenders among free-soil and moderate Democrats, many of them northern-born, who rallied against the "coolie" bills. In the senate, free-soil Democrats moved to kill both pieces of legislation. The powerful

David C. Broderick and his ally, Thomas B. Van Buren, struggled to defeat both measures through parliamentary maneuvering and even convinced a Chivalry-leaning colleague, Philip A. Roach, to issue a scathing pro-free-labor report against the Tingley bill. Governor John Bigler, a future free-soil Democrat and Broderick ally, followed up with an executive message that called for the prohibition of coolies and the restriction of Chinese immigration. Bigler's proposals won support from Democrats on the Assembly Committee on Mines and Mining Interests and a senate committee on "Asiatic immigration," all of whom joined the chorus against the Chinese and coolie labor.[57]

Free-soil Democrats' anticoolie campaign required depicting all Chinese labor relationships, even (or especially) contractual ones, as distinctly unfree. Free-soilers sought to establish that all or most Chinese were bonded coolies and that coolie labor closely resembled chattel slavery. This could be a difficult and perplexing task because most acknowledged that coolies voluntarily contracted their labor and received wages. Reading Chinese men out of the ranks of free laborers, then, necessitated casting both the wage bargain and contracts as markers of slavery rather than liberty.

Critics of coolie labor first accomplished this by focusing on the amount of compensation Chinese earned under their contracts. They acknowledged that Chinese freely entered into long-term contracts for wage work, but they argued that because they accepted such pitiful wages—far below what white men tolerated—they differed little from slaves. In his executive message denouncing coolie labor, Governor John Bigler complained that contracted Chinese worked "at merely nominal wages," making no more than three or four dollars per month.[58] The *Alta California*, a newspaper with a moderate free-soil bent, derided the paltry wages afforded Chinese workers under Tingley's plan. Employers had to pay contracted Chinese only fifty dollars per year, or $4.16 per month. This was a pathetic standard in California, where mining labor still netted, at minimum, six dollars per day. Chinese might accept this pittance, but it was certainly not enough to sustain life in the mines. Employers at least needed to provide contracted workers "a reasonable standard of remuneration."[59] The extremely low, almost negligible, wage bargains that coolies voluntarily entered into not only made them similar to slaves but also threatened to be the undoing of free white laborers who demanded reasonable, life-sustaining compensation for their labor. Capitalists who did not want to pay the high wages that free white labor commanded on the Pacific Coast would quickly switch from American to coolie workers once the state legalized Chinese contract labor.[60]

If incredibly low wages raised doubts about the freeness of coolie labor contracts, the methods capitalists used to enforce them seemed to confirm that they were mere instruments of slavery. Free-soil Democrats assured their listeners that coolies had to sign over their families to the control of their employers as a guarantee against contract breaking. Conjuring up images of vulnerable wives and children, their husbands and fathers powerless to protect them from death or bondage, they connected contract labor with the horrors of chattel bondage. The assembly's overwhelmingly Democratic Committee on Mines and Mining Interests reported that Chinese capitalists held their coolies "to labor under contracts, which our laws do not recognize, and whose penalties are revolting to our sympathies." The committee did not elaborate, but their Democratic colleagues outlined these repulsive practices in more detail. Governor Bigler asserted that Chinese employers enforced their contracts by wielding the power of life and death over coolies' families. Coolies depended on their employers to turn over a portion of their wages to their families in China. Employers could punish recalcitrant coolies by threatening their families with starvation.[61] Philip Roach concluded that the typical coolie contract bound over a worker's family as collateral to his employer. Vulnerable "mothers and children are held as hostages for their fulfillment," he reported, and the coolie thus had no choice but to keep laboring faithfully.[62] Coolie contracts were inherently unfree because they allowed employers absolute control over both the labor and the households of Chinese workers.[63]

Tingley and Peachy never contemplated transferring Chinese contract laborers' wives and children over to the control of American capitalists. Their critics worried, however, that their legislation still gave American capitalists too much power over contracted workers' lives. The length of Chinese workers' contracts generated great debate. Tingley's measure allowed employers to bind laborers for ten years; Peachy's bill permitted five-year contracts. The Alta California editors declared that any term above two or three years was "much too long." If labor and capital were to remain on equal footing, it would be unwise "to give the power to capitalists to control labor exclusively for so long a period." Wrangling in the senate knocked down Tingley's contracts from ten to five years, but some still questioned whether Chinese laborers should sign themselves over to American capitalists for such a long time. Even though he was sympathetic to the proslavery wing of the Democratic Party, Philip Roach agreed with free-soilers that workers who bargained away their freedom for years at a time resembled slaves. Tingley's bill to enforce coolie contracts was tantamount to "giving to capital, for the term of five years, the hand and heart of labor" and rendered the worker a "serf or bondsman" of his employer.[64]

Coolies, then, represented some of the dangers and contradictions of an emerging wage-labor economy in which capital owned the "hand and heart of labor." They voluntarily contracted with their employers, but contracts guaranteed them nothing but near-starvation wages, long-term dependence, and compulsion. Worst of all, coolies' bondage sentenced their own dependents, their wives and children, to starvation and servitude. But coolieism did more than illustrate the dangers of capital gaining an upper hand over labor. In turning Chinese men into slaves, making them available to capitalists for "nominal wages" and long terms, it also spelled the degradation and enslavement of freeborn white American men. Unable to compete with coolie labor or the capitalists who employed it, free white laborers became little better than coolies themselves.

Critics of Chinese contract labor juxtaposed the vision of California as a free-labor utopia with images of white men reduced to the slavelike conditions of their coolie competitors. Sometimes they blamed Chinese capitalists, like Spanish-speaking masters before them, for driving white laborers into poverty and servility. The senate committee on "Asiatic immigration" criticized wealthy Chinese who imported coolies and used them to take over claims that rightfully belonged to the "American freeman, whose father stood by Washington in the days of the revolution."[65] More often, Democrats warned that American capitalists would hire coolies to press their own countrymen into poverty and dependence. Philip Roach reminded fellow senators that labor had always been "perfectly free to find its rewards" in California. But American capitalists, crying that "labor is too high," would import "the surplus and inferior population of Asia" to undercut white labor. They plotted to make workingmen's "labor inferior, by law, to capital; and give to the latter a more than feudal right to dispose of their [laborers'] persons and happiness." Similarly, the Alta California editors declared that coolies heralded the end of white labor's rule on the Pacific Coast, a time when "capital was obliged to lift its hat and bow in obsequious respect to the sweating brow and brawny arms of the working man." They urged legislators to kill the coolie bills and prevent "capital from tyrannizing over and degrading labor."[66] The fate of white American labor rested entirely on the policy that the state adopted toward coolies.

Defeating coolieism preserved free labor by ensuring the independence of white American men who earned their bread with sweating brows and brawny arms. The death of the coolie trade, according to its critics, was also crucial to safeguarding the nation's republican institutions. Like peons before them, coolies embodied dependency and degradation, which made them unfit for citizenship in a free republic. Imported Chinese could not, in the words of one legislative committee, be accorded the same political status as European-born "freemen seeking liberty and the pursuit of happiness."[67] Coolies' willingness to accept unequal labor contracts proved their incapacity for political participation. Philip Roach welcomed the political enfranchisement of free European immigrants, but contracted Chinese "who would willingly doom themselves to bondage" were "not deserving of this privilege." Another committee bluntly asserted that "coolies, who are slaves of some master . . . do not understand our institutions." Representatives of "foreign serfdom," coolies stood "in direct opposition to all those principles of equality implanted in the mind of every true born American."[68] Banning coolies was essential to preserving a virtuous republic of free white men.

The dangers that coolieism posed to republicanism, might, in fact, undermine the territorial integrity of the American republic itself. Two years earlier, Spanish-speaking peons threatened to turn back the tide on the American conquest. This time around, their analogues, Chinese coolies, embodied the hazards to American empire that accompanied U.S. expansion into the Pacific. Prior to 1852, many white Californians, including the moderately free-soil editors of the *Alta California*, welcomed the arrival of Chinese migrants. Their presence promised lucrative new avenues of trade between the United States and the Chinese Empire. Even the senate committee that complained about "China serfs" emphasized the importance of the China trade, which was "destined to be the means of enriching us, and giving us a commanding supremacy on the broad Pacific."[69] Yet the expansion of an overseas trade empire also threatened to bring down American domestic empire. A poor and overpopulated China, home to over 400 million people, would inevitably look to California to colonize its subjects. Philip Roach warned that Asia's proximity to the Pacific Coast of the United States guaranteed that, left unchecked, Chinese laborers would soon "overrun our land." Half a million Chinese, most of them paupers and criminals exported by the Chinese government, would soon take over the state. "Myriads of tawny serfs are embarking for our shores . . . who will cover our land like the locusts of Egypt," a senate committee agreed. "They will meet our brothers and relatives in the rich mining regions" and claim it "to the exclusion of our own people."[70] California's response to coolies might determine the fate of the American empire on the Pacific.

Free-soil Democrats' campaign to eliminate coolies as threats to American labor, institutions, and empire met with little resistance. Only George

Tingley, the Whig senator behind one of the "coolie bills," defended Chinese contract labor to the bitter end. He did so, ironically, by adopting the xenophobic and antimonopoly arguments of his opponents. Tingley claimed that his bill eliminated the most dangerous form of coolieism: that in which "foreigners come under contract of foreigners, to rob our placers." Chinese contract laborers were already digging up California gold for their wealthier countrymen. The legislature needed to decide whether it would give Americans the exclusive right to recruit and control this labor, or whether it would continue to tolerate "foreign capitalists, who now unconditionally reap the benefits arising out of it." Allowing Americans to employ contract laborers, while invalidating contracts between foreign masters and serfs, actually promoted the interests of independent white miners by eliminating foreign competition for gold. Mixing antipeon and anticoolie arguments, he predicted that the death of his bill would ensure the continued flow of California gold into the "coffers of the rich mandarin or South American grandee," to the detriment of all white citizens.[71]

Tingley's impassioned plea to favor American capitalists over foreign capitalists won few converts when his opponents insisted that both endangered free white labor. Senator David C. Broderick and his followers orchestrated the defeat of both the Tingley and the Peachy bills by bringing them up for a vote at the same time. Right before the senate took them up, Democrat Paul Hubbs, a representative of miners in Tuolumne County, introduced An Act to Prevent "Coolie" Labor in the Mines, and to Prevent Involuntary Servitude. An antidote to the evils of both coolie bills, Hubbs's bill denounced the arrival of "hordes of Asiatic servants" bound under contracts to work in the mines. It singled out "capitalists of foreign countries" for disapprobation, but it also barred American citizens from engaging foreign laborers on contracts. Validating the Chinese expulsion campaigns already rife in the diggings, it allowed American citizens to seize any mining claim worked by foreign contract laborers. A few hours after Hubbs read his proposal, 90 percent of the state's senators voted to postpone consideration of the coolie bills indefinitely. Although Democrats would later take credit for protecting the state from coolie labor, the uproar in the mines guaranteed that every Whig except Tingley voted against it as well.[72] The legislature seemed poised not just to defeat Chinese contract labor bills but to outlaw both contract labor and Chinese labor altogether.

The successful campaign against the coolie bills did not, ultimately, translate into a ban on contract labor or Chinese immigrants. Paul Hubbs's bill never came up for a vote, and another last-minute senate measure to protect the mines from "excessive immigration from Asia" made little headway. Both acts proposed giving the state great power to restrict foreign immigration. Since federal courts were starting to interpret immigration law as the exclusive domain of Congress under the U.S. Constitution, legislators probably tried to steer clear of any measure that might be ruled unconstitutional. Anticoolie forces settled instead on the same solution that opponents of peonage had adopted two years earlier. By mid-April, both senators and assemblymen called for the revival of the foreign miners' tax that had expelled Spanish-speaking people from the mines in 1850 and 1851. To avoid the bloodshed and mass flight that followed the passage of the 1850 tax, assemblymen recommended a less onerous license fee of three dollars per month. All foreign-born miners would have to pay the tax, but legislators clearly intended it to fall most heavily on Chinese migrants. Moreover, once molded into its final form, the new foreign miners' tax also became a subtle anticoolie measure. Anyone who hired foreign-born workers, including U.S. citizens, had to pay their employees' taxes and could face jail time or fines if they did not comply.[73] Employers who brought "hordes" of Chinese to the mines would pay dearly for the privilege of exploiting their labor.

Supporters of the new foreign miners' tax who hoped that it would press alleged Chinese coolies out of the diggings were probably disappointed. Despite claims that Chinese laborers earned but three or four dollars per month, hardly enough to afford the three-dollar monthly license fee, most Chinese stayed in the mines and paid the tax. Chinese immigration did decline in 1853, probably because Chinese merchants wrote home to publicize the new tax and inhospitable conditions in the gold country. Nonetheless, Chinese arrivals rebounded by 1854, and the Chinese presence in the mines became a major boon to the state.[74] Until overturned in 1871 during Reconstruction, the foreign miners' tax injected $58 million into the state and county economies. During these eighteen years, California derived between one-quarter and one-half of its annual revenue from the tax. Tuolumne County, site of some of the greatest anti-Chinese agitation, got more of its revenue from the foreign miners' tax than any other source. By 1855, the California senate warned that restricting Chinese immigration might bankrupt the state.[75]

This may explain why, with each new wave of anti-Chinese protest in the mining counties, the legislature opted merely to tax Chinese more heavily rather than to ban them altogether. In 1855, the legislature raised the license fee to six dollars per month (with an automatic increase of two dollars per month each succeeding year) and placed a fifty-dollar head tax on all incoming Chinese migrants. Chinese residents and their white representatives ensured that this taxation rarely amounted to expulsion or prohibition. They successfully lobbied to have the foreign miners' tax reduced back down to four dollars per month in 1856, and they launched two test cases before the state courts that established the unconstitutionality of head taxes.[76] Chinese thus persisted in the gold country across the 1850s, and by the Civil War many had moved firmly into agriculture, railroad work, and industrial production as well. By then, a revived anticoolie movement, one that explicitly linked the project of Chinese exclusion to the national abolition of slavery, again gripped the state.

In the aftermath of the coolie bill debate, California Chinese wrote letters of protest to Governor John Bigler, author of the most virulent anti-Chinese reports of the 1852 legislative session. Determined to prove that Chinese immigration posed no dangers to American labor or institutions, two San Francisco merchants, Hab Wa and Tong Achick, refuted Bigler's accusations that most Chinese came to California as coolies. Their letters, probably composed with aid from their white lawyers and spokesmen, argued that Chinese workingmen resembled the free white laborers vaunted by the anticoolie movement far more than they did slaves. None of the Chinese in California were "'coolies,' if by that word you mean bound men or contract slaves," they asserted. Instead, the average Chinese man came to California "because of his desire for independence." He paid his way to the state by taking out loans given to him "by the charity of his countrymen, which they bestow on him safely, because he is industrious and honestly repays them." Once in the mines, Chinese men behaved precisely like their free white American counterparts. They worked with "patience, industry, temperance and economy" and saved their money so they could return home and "buy rice fields, build houses and devote themselves to the society of their own households." Far from sacrificing their wives and children to their creditors, they felt "the deepest anxiety to provide for their descendents" and strived to "live orderly, work hard, and take care of themselves, that they may have the means of providing for their homes and living amidst their families."[77] Chinese migrants were not dependent, degraded slaves, but men who embodied the virtues of industry, upward mobility, independence, and mastery over household dependents that lay at the very heart of free-labor ideology. In the merchants' summation, "The Chinamen in this country are not 'serfs' or slaves of any description, but are working for themselves."[78]

The Chinese merchants' efforts to recast the coolie debate, to divorce Chinese workers from slavery and move them firmly into the ranks of free workers, bore little fruit. Despite assurances that Chinese men were independent proprietors who labored industriously to support their families in comfort, anti-Chinese Californians would continue to link Chinese with coolieism and coolieism with vicious and degrading forms of bondage. Just days after the merchants sent their first letter to the governor, the *Alta California*'s editors commended the people of California for defeating the coolie bills. They had staved off the horrors of the coolie trade and narrowly avoided having "the evil and burden of slavery strapped to the shoulders of our already afflicted state."[79] This was not the first time that white Californians congratulated themselves on warding off slavery. Just two years before, many of those who attacked coolieism took pride in expelling another breed of slaves, Latin American peons. Free men who bargained away their liberty and the rewards and dignity of their labor to their hirers, peons and coolies came to stand as powerful illustrations of the degradation of labor under the wage system. The consenting slaves of their employers, they hastened capitalists' monopoly of land and resources that would eventually pull independent white laborers down to their own servile condition. Peonage and coolieism, dual evils, loosened the nation's grip on its Pacific Coast empire and threatened to erode the foundations of free-labor republicanism by turning white American freemen into slaves themselves.

CHAPTER FOUR

Enslaved Wards and Captive Apprentices

Controlling and Contesting Children's Labor in 1850s California

In 1856, Benjamin Davis Wilson and his wife, Margaret Hereford Wilson, faced a household crisis. The Wilsons were among the wealthiest landholders in Los Angeles, but they were never able to find reliable domestic laborers. The "only privation" the family suffered in California, Benjamin wrote, was the want of a "good house servant." Margaret, the daughter of St. Louis slaveholders, felt the absence of domestic help as an acute hardship. She returned to Missouri in 1856 with plans to bring back "a house servant or two" for her California estate. The Wilsons first considered buying enslaved African American women and transporting them west. But slaves were expensive, and, since California was a free state, Margaret predicted that any bondwoman "would leave me as soon as I got home." Benjamin suggested hiring a white woman, "as they (the black) would perhaps give you a great deal of trouble and the white or free one you can discharge when she gets impertinent." Still, Margaret worried that most white women would refuse to work for reasonable wages in California and would abandon the family for more lucrative employment.[1]

When all of these schemes to obtain the labor of adult women proved unworkable, the Wilsons pursued a different strategy. In 1857, Benjamin asked a business associate in far northern California to "secure" several Indian children from local villages and send them to Los Angeles. Under California's 1850 Act for the Government and Protection of Indians, he could petition a justice of the peace to become the children's guardian and retain their "care, custody, control and earnings" until adulthood.[2] These plans fell through, but the Wilsons found another way to procure youthful domestic laborers. When Margaret returned from St. Louis, she brought her mother, sister, and two enslaved girls, Emily and Maria, from her mother's household. Benjamin soon helped his mother-in-law, Esther Hereford, petition the Los Angeles

County Probate Court to become the girls' legal guardian. The court, which periodically awarded masters custody of enslaved black children under the state's guardianship laws, granted the request. Hereford could hold Emily and Maria until they turned twenty-one. Judicial alchemy transformed Missouri slaves into California wards.[3]

The Wilsons' quest to secure household workers and the diverse legal strategies at their disposal to hold young servants highlighted the importance of bound labor to domestic life in 1850s California. During the gold rush, California's struggle over unfree labor usually centered on the business of mining. Denunciations of slaves, peons, and coolies that filled the state's newspapers and legislative journals emphasized the economic, social, and political threats that these workers posed to the free white men who worked the state's gold mines. These free-soil discourses privileged mining work—associated with men—over domestic work—associated with women and children. In doing so, they obscured the unfree labor that took place in California households and how the home became a major site of struggle over California's free-labor destiny.

While legislators and newspaper editors complained that degraded, servile workers would glut the mines with cheap labor, California suffered a chronic shortage of domestic labor. The arrival of thousands of unattached men generated enormous market demands for skills such as cooking, cleaning, and laundering. Sometimes these demands reinscribed older assumptions about gender and race as women of all backgrounds and men of color were relegated to (and often profited from) selling domestic services to white miners. Sometimes they unsettled and remade the racial and gender contours of domestic work as white men kept house or worked for wages as cooks and servants. Even as the flush times waned and white women arrived in greater numbers, white emigrant families bemoaned the lack of "good house servants," which stymied their efforts to reproduce middle-class domesticity on the Pacific Coast.[4]

Many families, like the Wilsons, searched for ways to bind long-term domestic servants. White southerners used or hired out their bondpeople in household service, Californios relied on Indian rancho laborers and debt-bound Sonorans to perform domestic chores, and American entrepreneurs contracted Chinese and Hawaiian men as cooks and servants. Across the 1850s, though, children made up the majority of bound servants in Californio and emigrant homes. The first California legislature responded to demands for abundant and inexpensive domestic labor with statutes that encouraged householders to claim American Indian and African American children as long-term wards. The 1850 Act for the Government and Protection of Indians perpetuated older Spanish-Mexican practices of "adopting" captive children by granting white residents guardianship rights over Indian minors. The same legislature rejected a scheme to bring enslaved black children into the state as apprentices, only to approve an expansive general guardianship law that gave white householders leeway to hold African American youths, as well as Indian children, as wards. Indian and black children worked as bound house servants under these laws into the 1860s.[5]

Unlike chattel slavery, "coolieism," or "peonism," the unfree labor of American Indian and African American wards generated little protest or comment. Once absorbed into new households, children's bondage became legally and culturally invisible. When the law transformed young people from captives or slaves into wards, it recast relations of labor exploitation as family relations. Wardship turned black and Indian children into the domestic dependents of white and Californio householders, who now had legitimate parental and paternal rights to their labor. Male heads of household were entitled to the labor and earnings of their nonwhite wards, just as they controlled the work and earnings of other dependent family members, their wives, minor sons, and minor daughters. As a household relationship, wardship both concealed and justified the forced expropriation of Indian and African American children's labor. Most important, once the law remade children into dependent family members, white guardians demanded, and often received, the right to command them with little interference from the state. Regardless of where they stood on the slavery question, state officials generally supported white men's authority over their dependent family members. Throughout the 1850s, legal authorities steadfastly upheld the claims of white and Californio householders to the Indian and black children they claimed as wards. They almost always approved petitions for guardianship, and they supported men's claims to their wards against the rights of the children's parents and intrusions by third parties. Like other familial relationships such as marriage or parenthood, wardship vested adult white men with mastery over household dependents and shielded the coercive, unequal relationships inside homes from external scrutiny or interference.[6]

The exploitation of Indian and black children's labor went uncontested only so long as it remained in the legal realm of wardship. Legislators who had few qualms about white householders controlling the labor of Native or African American wards rebelled against proposals to expand and formalize children's servitude. Starting in 1853, rancheros, farmers, and some state legislators pressed for a system of Indian apprenticeship designed to force impoverished Native parents to bind out their children as laborers. Later in the decade, proslavery whites in southern California looked for ways to apprentice black children in the slave states and bring them west. These two interests merged in an 1859 effort to rewrite the state's new general apprenticeship law—a measure aimed exclusively at poor white children—to permit the binding of Indian, black, and Chinese children as well. Free-soil interests defeated each of these proposals. They argued that the apprenticeship of nonwhite minors threatened to introduce slavery into the state and bring yet another group of servile workers into competition with free white labor. By 1860, however, the dire state of California's Indian affairs trumped these concerns. In the name of "civilizing" the state's Native peoples and quelling warfare, Democratic legislators created an apprenticeship system that encompassed nearly all Indian children and adults. This regime of forced labor persisted until California, like the rest of the nation, embarked on the age of emancipation.[7]

Guardians, Wards, Apprentices, and the Gold Rush Politics of Domestic Labor

In September 1849, delegates to California's constitutional convention turned their attention to the problem of domestic labor. Throughout the convention, mining district representatives pushed for a constitutional amendment banning African American migration to the state. This prohibition, they insisted, would protect free white mining labor from competition with degraded black labor. Opponents of antiblack laws, on the other hand, defended African American migration as a solution to the state's chronic shortage of domestic workers. William Shannon, the man who proposed the antislavery amendment to the constitution, observed that African Americans provided crucial household labor for East Coast whites and were "absolutely essential to the comfort and convenience of domestic life." A law banning them amounted to "depriving the people of California of the services of a class of men who are required by the people of every State in the Union."[8] Shannon and other opponents of exclusion dismissed the idea that unrestricted black migration might encourage slaveholders to sneak their enslaved house servants into California under contracts and indentures. The constitution's antislavery provision freed these men and women as soon as they touched California soil. But their confidence wavered when they considered the enslaved children who might arrive with their masters' families. Kimball Dimmick, a New Yorker and an ally of Shannon, fretted that California might have to recognize apprenticeship arrangements in which "colored boys in the [southern] States are indentured to the age of twenty-one and brought here before the expiration of the indenture." These children would be "required to serve" until they became adults. Only then would they "undoubtedly become free."[9] In this, Dimmick anticipated an emerging legal reality in the new state. Californians who wanted to secure long-term household servants without violating the antislavery constitution would look to bind the labor of children.

Many of California's early legislators proved sympathetic to the project of transferring nonwhite children into emigrant and Californio households. At the same time that they denounced slavery, peonage, and coolieism as threats to white miners, state lawmakers proposed new legislation aimed at creating a class of unfree domestic laborers. In 1849–50, the year of the antislavery constitution and the first foreign miners' tax, state legislators considered three different bills that made Indian and black children vulnerable to forced wardship. The most successful bill, the Act for the Government and Protection of Indians, allowed white residents to claim Indian children as their wards and obtain their "care, custody, control and earnings" until adulthood.[10] Meanwhile, lawmakers mulled over a second statute that empowered slaveholders to import African American minors as apprentices and hold them until they turned twenty-one. The apprenticeship of black minors was too bound up with the enslavement of African American adults to win broad support. Still, the legislature inadvertently helped masters by passing an expansive general guardianship law. This statute authorized the probate courts to assign new guardians for orphaned children or the offspring of incompetent and unsuitable parents. It made it easier for whites to tear enslaved black children—as well as Indian minors—away from their families and absorb them into their own households as wards. The same legislature that tried to preserve the goldfields as a haven for free white labor made the home a refuge for Californians who wanted to exploit unfree Indian and black domestic labor.[11]

California's chaotic Indian affairs made regulating Native American labor a priority for the first state legislature. The sudden arrival of thousands of miners brought California Native communities into conflict with non-Indian invaders and exposed them to devastating rounds of war, disease, starvation, and dispossession. Although Indian affairs fell under the constitutional purview of the federal government, the U.S. Office of Indian Affairs (OIA) intervened little in California during the early years of the gold rush. It took until 1851 for federal agents to start making treaties with California Native people. These agreements extinguished Indian title to the gold country, promised Indians food, clothing, and protection, and set aside reservation lands for their exclusive use. Even then, the U.S. Senate left the fate of the state's Indian population in limbo by refusing to ratify these unpopular and expensive treaties. California's state legislators filled the vacuum in federal power by assuming control over domestic Indian policy. They raised militias to suppress "hostile" Indians and launched haphazard, ad hoc negotiations to keep the peace.[12]

In the spring of 1850, legislators also considered two sweeping bills, one from the senate and one from the assembly, designed to regulate every aspect of Indian life in California. Both bills proposed placing Native people under the authority of white magistrates and created mechanisms to punish Indians who committed offenses against white residents. Formulated by white and Californio rancheros, the laws also sought to establish a stable, accessible Indian workforce by institutionalizing labor practices that had long sustained the Mexican rancho system. These included sections that authorized the binding out of Indians convicted of vagrancy or other crimes and provisions that made it easier for whites to track down and punish Indian workers who absconded without paying their debts.[13] Once in control of its own Indian affairs, California opted to extend and bolster unfree labor practices that closely approximated the debt servitude that white miners condemned in their campaigns against peons and coolies.

The labor of Indian children played a central role in this new legislation. With both bills, lawmakers looked to replicate the old ranchero practice of "adopting" Native children—usually orphans, captives, and "godchildren" recruited from local Indian communities—and holding them as domestic servants. The senate Indian bill, the work of Butte County ranchero John Bidwell, allowed whites to apply for the guardianship of Native children whom they wished "to keep and raise." Petitioners could go before a special justice of the peace for Indians, a white official elected by white and Indian men of voting age, and bring the child's parents or relatives. Once the family consented to the arrangement, the justice granted the petitioner a certificate giving him or her the child's "care, custody, control and earnings" until adulthood. Guardians needed to provide Indian wards with adequate food and clothing. Those who "inhumanely and barbarously treated" children risked hefty fines and might have to give the children back to their parents or have their wards assigned to new guardians. When children became adults and wardship expired, guardians had to provide their former charges with a small amount of "useful property" and two suits of clothing.[14]

Legislators never recorded responses to Bidwell's Indian bill, but its legislative history suggests that many favored a more coercive and extensive law.

The senate gave Bidwell a hearing, only to scrap his proposal in favor of a harsher assembly bill, the Act for the Government and Protection of Indians, concocted by another American-born ranchero, Elam Brown of Contra Costa County. In contrast to Bidwell's plan for special justices of the peace for Indians, Brown put regular justices of the peace, elected by whites alone, in charge of nearly all aspects of Indian affairs. One of their tasks was to hear petitions for the guardianship of Indian children. Brown, like Bidwell, allowed whites to apply for the custody of Indian children in their possession. But his version made it much easier for whites to obtain Native wards and granted children fewer benefits and protections. Petitioners did have to establish that they used "no compulsory means" to acquire a child. To do this, though, they needed only to bring the child's "parents or friends" before the court to assent to the arrangement. This looser wording allowed virtually anyone, including kidnappers who had obtained children through "compulsory means," to stand as "friends." Bidwell's protections for Indian wards also found little place in Brown's version. Guardians who mistreated children risked trivial fines. Judges were to appoint new guardians for abused wards rather than returning them to their families. Children received no compensation at the end of their wardship.[15] When Brown's bill finally came up for review by the senate, the judiciary committee—which included prominent rancheros such as Mariano Guadalupe Vallejo and John Bidwell himself—recommended its passage. The senate then approved it with no discussion or debate.[16] The Act for the Government and Protection of Indians became law in April 1850 and determined California Indian policy for decades to come.

Rancheros' successful campaign for Indian wardship may have given hope to slaveholding interests. During the deliberations over Indian labor, a new bill allowing the apprenticeship of enslaved African American children also made its way before the legislature. The Act Relative to Free Negroes, Mulattoes, Servants, and Slaves, the bill that Assemblyman John F. Williams proposed to legalize slaveholders' contracts with their bondpeople, also let masters bring apprenticed black children into the state. The bill stipulated that African American adults—men over twenty-one and women over eighteen— could be held under contract for only one year and had to receive some kind of compensation when their terms expired. No such restrictions applied to black youths under the age of majority, meaning that masters could hold them for longer terms and did not have to compensate them. Williams's bill also stated explicitly that black children apprenticed in other states and then transported to California would be exempt from the one-year contract limitation placed on adults. Slaveholders who wanted to bring enslaved children into the state and keep them had only to claim that they had apprenticed the young people in the slave states before going west. Once in California, these children would remain under their masters' control until adulthood.[17]

Ultimately, this bid to allow enslaved black apprentices into California met with far less success than efforts to convert Indian children into wards. Recall that Williams's bill met with outright rejection right after he introduced it.[18] This defeat probably had little to do with legislators' aversion to apprenticeship and more to do with their opposition to adult enslaved men working in the mines under contracts. Unlike the Act for the Government and Protection of Indians, which obscured minors' status as bound laborers by absorbing them into white families as wards, black apprenticeship was too intimately tied to slavery to find many supporters during the first year of statehood.

Legislators who frowned upon the blatant apprenticeship of enslaved African American children nonetheless approved general guardianship legislation that (unwittingly) meshed with slaveholder interests. Like similar laws in other states, the new guardianship statute charged probate courts with assigning custodians to minors.[19] Whenever "necessary and convenient," probate court judges were to appoint nonparental guardians for two classes of children: those who had no living or identifiable biological parents and those whose parents were not "competent to transact their own business" or were "otherwise unsuitable." Under these provisions, people who wanted to obtain guardianship over a particular child could approach the local probate court, declare that the child was orphaned or being raised by incompetent or unsuitable parents, and request custody. Once appointed, new guardians filed a bond that they agreed to forfeit to the state if they failed to care for the child. They then retained custody of their ward until the child turned twenty-one, married, or was emancipated by the court.[20]

In the long run, the paternalistic features of the new guardianship law that removed children from incompetent or unsuitable parents—usually those deemed impoverished or immoral—proved a vital resource for both slaveholders and those who wanted to bind Indian children. These petitioners could report that children were orphans or that their parents were unfit to care for them and ask for guardianship. Probate judges usually took these claims at face value and handed over both Indian and black children to new guardians. Incorporated into white households through the same general guardianship laws governing white children, Indian and black youths became nearly invisible as unfree workers.

In the first few months of 1850, California legislators constructed a legal framework for channeling American Indian and African American children into white households as bound domestic workers. The Act for the Government and Protection of Indians, reinforced by state guardianship laws, created a formal system of wardship that continued older Mexican practices of integrating youthful Indian laborers into non-Indian homes. Legislators who hoped to build a formal system of black apprenticeship did not enjoy similar success, largely because it was impossible to disassociate the binding of African American children from chattel slavery. The passage of these general guardianship laws nonetheless gave slaveholders important new legal tools for strengthening their hold over enslaved children. Remaking Indian and black minors into wards, domestic dependents who owed their labor to the white heads of household who cared for them, this tangle of 1850 guardianship statutes obscured the coerced nature of children's labor. Together they built an important labor force of young unfree domestic workers at the same moment that California pressed for admission into the Union as a free state.

The Liberties of a White-Man: Guardians, Indian Wards, and California Law

In 1853, a white Sacramento County farmer named Jesse Snyder was murdered in his home. The killer, George Hendry, was Snyder's former business partner and boarded with the Snyder family. During his stay in the Snyder home, Hendry had acquired an Indian boy named Dick, identified as "a thick set, intelligent Indian lad, about 10 years of age, belonging to the Payute tribe." He kept the child as his servant and might have claimed him as a ward under the Act for the Government and Protection of Indians or through the probate courts. After a time, Jesse Snyder decided that he wanted the child for himself. He began bullying Hendry in an effort to "seduce his Indian boy" away from him. Snyder's insults and threats often focused on Hendry's manhood (or lack thereof). One witness remembered that Snyder constantly teased Hendry by asking him whether or not he had "any 'Penis.'" One spring day, Snyder made his last "taunting remark." He urged Dick to disobey Hendry's commands and ridiculed Hendry's attempts to keep the boy's affection. A heated exchange escalated into a fistfight. Hendry drew a knife and stabbed Snyder to death in front of the man's horrified family. At his trial, Hendry brought in witnesses who testified that Snyder's incessant threats and interference with the Indian child drove Hendry to kill. A Sacramento jury eventually found Hendry guilty of manslaughter rather than murder and "recommended the prisoner to the mercy of the Court." The district court judge complied and sentenced Hendry to only six months in prison for the crime. Hendry served the term but still refused to give up the child. He abducted Dick from the child's new white guardian and fled for parts unknown.[21]

The murder of Jesse Snyder illustrated how strongly control over Indian wards came to be linked to manhood and mastery in 1850s California. For white men like George Hendry, Indian children were a valuable source of domestic labor. More than that, the ability to command the labor of Indian children became an important signifier of free adult manhood. California's Indian policy and guardianship laws changed Native children into wards, the domestic dependents of the white patriarchs who made claim to them. These patriarchs, in turn, expected to command the bodies, labor, and obedience of Indian children living in their households—as they did their own wives and children—with no interference from other citizens or the state. They demanded full legal control over the Indian children in their possession, often in defiance of Indian parents' rights. They appealed to state authorities to defend their mastery against the competing claims of other men. And, like George Hendry, they sometimes countered interference with their wards, whether from other householders or government agents, with swift and furious violence.

Jesse Snyder's invasion of George Hendry's domestic relations—which, tellingly, involved sexual taunts that emphasized Hendry's emasculation and impotence—did more than drive Hendry into a murderous rage. It may also have won Hendry the sympathy of the Sacramento jury and judge who granted him leniency. Extant court cases suggest that California legal officials, themselves male heads of household, defended the prerogatives of men who claimed Indian wards. Justices of the peace and probate judges rarely questioned non-Indian men's petitions for custody of Indian minors, often granting them with little investigation into the children's history or regard for Indian families. They also defended guardians' rights to Indian children against the competing claims of other non-Indian men. On occasion, they inflicted only minor punishments when guardians like Hendry resorted to extralegal violence to retain their wards. Legal officials facilitated the incorporation of Native children into non-Indian households and then staunchly defended guardians from interference in their domestic relations.

White and Californio men who wanted to gain possession of Indian children pressed legal officials to grant them guardianship, regardless of whether they complied with state laws or obtained consent from Indian families. Local justices of the peace supported these claims, often ignoring or loosely interpreting section 3 of the Act for the Government and Protection of Indians, which required "parents or friends" to appear in court and assent to the wardship. In Santa Barbara County, for instance, justices enforced these requirements inconsistently and took few pains to make sure that white petitioners obtained the approval of Indian parents. On November 26, 1853, Santa Barbara justice of the peace R. W. Lee bound out three Indian adolescents to two different white petitioners. Henry Carnes, who hoped to gain custody of ten-year-old Miguel, appeared before the court with the child's father, Joaquín, who gave his consent. Lee approved the arrangement. The same day, Thomas Hope requested to bind out two boys, Gabriel and Juan de Dios. He appeared alone, never explained how he obtained the children, and provided no evidence that parents or friends agreed to the wardship. Lee granted the request anyway.[22] Far to the north, Sonoma County justice of the peace Peter Campbell was far more assiduous in granting the requests of a Californio petitioner than he was in establishing the consent of an Indian mother. Sometime around 1852, Campbell recorded that Timotea, "an Indian little girl about ten years of age," had "been bound in [his] books to live with M. G. Vallejo till she arrives at maturity." The petitioner, General Mariano Guadalupe Vallejo, was one of the state's wealthiest Californio rancheros. Vallejo agreed to "cloathe and support her [Timotea] during her minority." She would stay in his home where, presumably, she would work as a domestic servant until she turned fifteen. Campbell had Timotea affix her mark to the record, but the child's parents did not appear before him. He included only a vague note that the child's mother, whom he never mentioned by name, had given "her assent" to the arrangement at some point in the past.[23]

Petitioners who wanted to lay claim to Indian children also used alternative legal channels to get around the restrictions in the Act for the Government and Protection of Indians. They appeared before the probate courts and argued that they should be appointed guardians for the children of dead, absent, or unfit parents. Probate judges sympathized with these requests and often granted guardianship without probing into Indian children's histories or investigating claims against Indian parents. In 1852, Rafael González petitioned the Santa Clara Probate Court to be appointed guardian of Refugia, "an infant Indian girl," who he alleged was an orphan. Without even looking into the claim, the judge gave González "immediate custody" of the child. He did so despite evidence that another family was already caring for Refugia. When William Gibson appeared before the Los Angeles Probate Court, he made a similar claim to Chapo, an eight-year-old Native boy who he said was an orphan. Gibson provided no details about the child's origin, but Judge William G. Dryden instantly granted the request.[24]

This Maidu boy, photographed in Marysville, Calif., in the 1850s, was likely the ward of a white family and charged with caring for his guardians' children. The photograph resembles portraits of enslaved nursemaids posing with their masters' children that were commonly produced in the slave South during the same period. Robert H. Vance, *Untitled [Maidu Boy]*, ca. 1850, ambrotype, 12.07 x 9.37 x 1.59 cm, San Francisco Museum of Modern Art, purchased through a gift of Lucinda Watson, the Evelyn and Walter Hass Jr. Fund, an anonymous gift, H. Marcia Smolens, Tony and I'lee Hooker, and the Accessions Committee Fund. Reproduced by permission of the San Francisco Museum of Modern Art, San Francisco, Calif.

As a probate judge, Dryden also took at face value claims of Indian parents' incompetence and readily approved guardianship petitions that invoked the unfitness of Native mothers. In 1858, Dryden heard a petition from John Reed, a white resident who applied for guardianship of Santiago Barton, a child of mixed white and Indian heritage. Reed claimed that the child's mother, an Indian woman, "live[d] in adulterous intercourse with different classes of persons." Her "habits and mode of life" made her "incompetent to maintain, educate and care for, her son." Dryden agreed and granted Reed custody. Two years later, Dryden appointed a new guardian for Joseph Benton, a child of mixed Indian and African American descent whose "besotted" Indian mother allegedly abandoned him.[25]

Ignoring parental consent, neglecting to investigate children's family history, or accepting arguments about unfit Indian parents, justices of the peace and probate judges established that non-Indian men's mastery over Indian minors in their households superseded Indian parents' rights to their children. Once Native children were absorbed into non-Indian households, these same officials defended guardians' rights to their wards against the incursions of other non-Indian men. Most of the surviving court cases involving Indian wards came about when guardians complained that other men enticed, kidnapped, or meddled with the children in their care. Dedicated to protecting non-Indian male householders' rights to the bodies and labor of their dependents, justices of the peace pursued, prosecuted, and punished men who interfered with other men's Indian wards or looked the other way when guardians took the law into their own hands.

In Sonoma County, guardians relied on Justice Peter Campbell to ward off other men, both Californios and white newcomers, who tried to take possession of valuable Native children. In 1851, Felix Gallardo complained to Campbell that another man of Mexican descent, Juan Mendos, broke into his house and "forcibly stole" a six-year-old Indian girl named Francisca. Gallardo described the child as "the property" of his wife and demanded her return. Campbell recorded the incident and pursued the case, but was seemingly unable to track down Mendos or recover the girl.[26] He had more success prosecuting a white man who enticed an Indian child away from his Californio neighbor. Not long after Campbell had bound out Timotea to Mariano Guadalupe Vallejo, the ranchero testified that the girl had fled. Nicholas Carigen, a Tennessee-born farmer who lived nearby, illegally harbored the child. Campbell instructed his deputies to apprehend Timotea and remove her from Carigen's home. Carigen later had to answer to the court for concealing the girl from her legally appointed guardian.[27]

Cave Johnson Couts, a ranchero who also frequently served as a justice of the peace in San Diego County, often found himself embroiled in conflicts over Native wards. In 1858, Couts appeared before a fellow justice of the peace, William Farrell, to complain about the escape of an Indian boy named Francisco. Couts's Californio wife, Ysidora Bandini Couts, became the child's godmother during the Mexican era. "According to the custom of the country at that time," she held him as her ward and brought him into Couts's household when they married. The young man had been working on the family's rancho, well cared for and provided with "suitable food and clothing," until suddenly "inticed away by others." Couts requested that the boy be formally bound to him as a ward until he came of age. Farrell approved the petition for guardianship and ordered Francisco's arrest and return to Couts's custody.[28]

As a justice of the peace, Couts also intervened in similar disputes among his neighbors. In 1860, José Arguello alleged that two young Native girls, one from his household and one belonging to a neighbor, had been kidnapped or enticed away by Jesús Dominguez and his female companion. The couple took the girls to Los Angeles, where they may have planned to sell them. Couts ordered the sheriff to pursue the couple and secure the girls' return to San Diego. Just a few months later, Couts seemingly decided not to intervene in a near-fatal altercation over an Indian ward. Patrick O'Neil rushed to Couts's home to protest that a Californio neighbor, José Yberra, had assaulted him on his own property. The dispute arose when Yberra confronted O'Neil about "whipping an Indian boy, that he [Yberra] claimed as a servant of his." Yberra then grabbed a gun and chased O'Neil around with the intention of shooting or striking him. O'Neil probably expected swift punishment against the man who threatened his life in his own home. Couts, however, may have sympathized with Yberra's efforts to shield his ward from interference. He took no further action on the case.[29]

Californians who controlled Indian wards came to expect that legal officials would support their claims to mastery over Native children living in their homes, whether against Indian parents or other householders eager to obtain Indian labor. These expectations became so entrenched across the 1850s that some men fiercely resisted any state effort to intervene in relations between guardians and wards. Men jealously guarded their wards from state interference, confronting legal officials with violence and bold assertions of racial and gender privilege.

During his stint as justice of the peace in Sonoma, Peter Campbell learned that challenging claims to Indian children could be a deadly affair. In July 1851, Campbell refused to give up two Indian children to a pair of brothers named Berryessa. The Berryessas belonged to a large Californio ranching family scattered throughout Sonoma, Napa, Solano, Santa Clara, and Contra Costa counties. Throughout the 1850s, various Berryessa men carried on the old Mexican practice of invading the countryside, gathering up Indians of all ages, and forcing them to work on their ranchos. One kidnapper, Ramón Berryessa from the Contra Costa branch of the family, had even lost his life in 1850 when two of his Indian victims escaped and stabbed him to death. Federal Indian agents eventually worked with state officials to convict several Berryessa men for kidnapping.[30] In fact, Campbell himself wrote to the U.S. commissioner of Indian affairs complaining that a party of local men—a group that probably included the Berryessas—had abducted nearly a hundred Native people and forced them to work on their mining claims. Shortly thereafter, Campbell somehow obtained two of the Indian youths claimed by the Sonoma Berryessa brothers. One of the brothers, Francis, got drunk, confronted Campbell, and demanded that he relinquish the children. Campbell refused, and Francis stabbed him. Campbell survived the attack, and a mob assembled to hang his assailant. Then other Sonoma residents, sympathetic to Berryessa's cause, broke him out of jail and helped him escape to Napa County. Campbell later resumed his office, probably a bit more wary about interfering with local practices of procuring Indian children.[31]

Much like Francis Berryessa, Cave Johnson Couts—though he often served as a justice of the peace himself—resisted state interference with the Indian wards in his home. A white southerner, Couts framed any attempt on the part of state and federal authorities to regulate his relationships with Indian servants as an affront to his household mastery and racial privilege. As late as 1865, for instance, John Quincy Adams Stanley, the newly appointed special agent of Indian affairs for San Diego County and an avid Republican, investigated a complaint that Couts was holding an Indian boy named Reyes against the wishes of the child's parents. Stanley wrote Couts a stern letter ordering him to "at once liberate the boy Reyes and permit him to return to his father."[32] Couts sent back a scathing response, asserting that his gender and race entitled him to control over his household dependents, which trumped any claim that legal officials or Indian parents might have to the child. "As a *white-man*, [I] do not feel at liberty to comply with your orders," Couts told him. He brazenly dared Stanley to try and force him to "*liberate*" all his servants. "I have some dozen or more," he bragged, "and nearly all of them Indians and Negroes." There was no state law that could compel him, as a white man and master of his home, to give them up. "No servant of mine," he repeated, "can be taken from me on the order of any 'Especial Indian Agent.'"[33] Although federal officials may have secured Reyes's return to his family, Couts tried to prevent future state intervention in his domestic affairs. When he petitioned for guardianship of another Indian ward, he drafted a special provision, supposedly at the request of the child's mother, that "no Indian agent, Indian Captain or Alcalde" should "interfere" with the boy during his time in the Couts household.[34]

Cave Johnson Couts's refusal to yield up Reyes on the grounds that he was a "*white-man*" encapsulated the racialized and gendered meanings that adhered to Indian wardship in 1850s California. Non-Indian men who possessed Indian wards felt entitled, as free white men, to mastery over their household dependents. They expected (and demanded) that local legal authorities defend their rights to the Indian children living in their households. For their part, judges generally sympathized with and validated these claims to mastery, upholding them over Indian parental rights and intrusions by other would-be guardians. This tacit understanding occasionally broke down when officials like John Quincy Adams Stanley (an antislavery Republican) refused to acknowledge the liberties and privileges of white men. For the most part, though, judges regarded Indian wards as domestic dependents whose custody and labor rightfully belonged to white and Californio patriarchs.

From Masters to Guardians: Making Slaves into Wards

During the same years that Cave Johnson Couts worked to secure his rights to the Indian children in his San Diego household, Simon Hammersmith, a resident of San Francisco, made similar claims to an African American child. Sometime in the middle of the 1850s, Hammersmith moved to California with his family and an enslaved or indentured black woman named Mary Williams. After her arrival, Mary gave birth to Charles, a "mulatto child," who may have been the son of Hammersmith or a white lover. Mary eventually fled the Hammersmiths' home to live with a white man named James Frizzelle. When she tried to take her son with her, Hammersmith refused to part with him. Hammersmith petitioned the San Francisco Probate Court for guardianship of Charles by alleging that Mary "was not a suitable person to have charge of the child." The court agreed with Hammersmith's assessment and granted him custody of Charles until he became an adult. The case made it into the newspapers in November 1857 when Mary, desperate to reclaim her son, enlisted Frizzelle's help to kidnap him. When one of Hammersmith's young daughters took Charles out for a walk, the couple seized the child and ran. The police eventually caught up with the pair and charged Frizzelle with assault and abduction. Charles returned to the Hammersmiths' care.[35]

Throughout the 1850s, slaveholders like Hammersmith searched for ways to exploit the labor of enslaved children without running afoul of the state's prohibition on slavery and involuntary servitude. They faced a number of challenges. The defeat of John F. Williams's bill in 1850 meant that slaveholders had no formal mechanism for apprenticing African American children. Moreover, the legal obfuscation of binding enslaved people under contracts, common during the gold rush, only worked for adult slaves and not for children. As minors, they could not enter into the kinds of contractual arrangements that masters used to extract labor from African American men and women. For these reasons, slaveholders sought aid from the probate courts and the general guardianship laws that petitioners for Indian children often used. Like Hammersmith, they requested to become the legal guardians of the black children living in their households.

Once enslaved children became wards, slaveholders legally controlled and profited from their labor. With the power of the law behind them, they used children as leverage in their relationships with recalcitrant enslaved parents like Mary Williams. Slaveholders also expected unmitigated control over their youthful domestic dependents. They asserted their entitlement to black children over the rights and interests of enslaved parents, usually by denying their kinship ties to enslaved families or accusing slave mothers of being unsuitable caretakers. The probate courts supported these claims, and, with only one major exception, they ruled in favor of masters' guardianship. On rare occasions when whites like Frizzelle intervened to release black children, the courts upheld the rights of masters to black wards. California masters-turned-guardians could expect dominion over enslaved children not far removed from that which they enjoyed in the slave states.

Slaveholders had a number of reasons to press for and defend their control over enslaved children. The brisk market for domestic labor inaugurated by the gold rush made the labor of enslaved youths nearly as important to masters as that of adult slaves. Some slaveholders, including Reuben Knox and Esther Hereford, deliberately took enslaved children west. They employed them as domestic servants in their own homes or profited from hiring them out. In fact, census records reveal that around 26 percent of all African American slaves in California were under the age of twenty-one in 1850; this proportion increased to just under 34 percent by 1852.[36] Employing enslaved minors as servants also came with fewer risks. They had less mobility than adult slaves, making it more difficult for them to resist, run away, or seek other employment. Holding onto enslaved children also helped slaveholders compel obedience from enslaved parents. While Simon Hammersmith's petition for custody of Charles failed to lure Mary Williams back into his household, other slaveholders used their power over enslaved children to gain influence over adult slaves. The profitability and pliability of enslaved children's labor, then, gave slaveholders many incentives to press for custody.

Slaveholders' efforts to obtain guardianship of enslaved children are best documented in Los Angeles, the same town where Benjamin Davis Wilson successfully converted his mother-in-law's Missouri slaves into wards. Los Angeles lay at the end of the Gila Trail, a major southern overland route to California. Slaveholding southerners from the Deep South and Texas, some of them with bondpeople in tow, came through the city on a regular basis. Most, like the Texas emigrant Thomas Thorn—the man who nearly lost several runaway slaves in the village in 1850—merely passed through on their way to the mining country. Others stayed and became merchants, farmers, and ranchers.[37] Some of these new residents kept their slaves with them. By 1852, the town had around forty-five black and mulatto residents, many of them enslaved or newly free. This number included at least twenty-five enslaved people who arrived in nearby San Bernardino (then part of Los Angeles County) in 1851. These African Americans belonged to southern-born members of the Church of Jesus Christ of Latter-day Saints and came with their masters from Mormon Utah to establish an agricultural colony.[38]

By the middle of the 1850s, the influx of white southerners, including a small but persistent population of slaveholders, made Los Angeles one of the strongest centers of proslavery sentiment on the Pacific Coast. Los Angeles representatives led yearly legislative campaigns to divide off southern California into a separate state. They demanded independence in the name of greater local self-governance and lower property taxes. Most contemporaries charged them with secretly plotting to turn southern California into the nation's next slave state. These suspicions seemed confirmed when a large number of white Angelinos left California to fight for the Confederacy in 1861.[39] It is not surprising, then, that masters, slaves, and enslaved children appeared before the Los Angeles courts on several occasions during the 1850s. Los Angeles judges heard at least six separate cases, involving the guardianship of seventeen different enslaved children, between 1852 and 1858.

Guardianship cases usually began when slaveholders petitioned the probate courts for custody of the enslaved children living in their homes. Some of these slaveholders, much like their counterparts who requested Indian wards, represented children as orphans without family ties. Slaveholders who separated children from their parents in the slave states and took them to California could easily claim that they had no nearby kin to take charge of them. Esther Hereford, the slaveholding mother-in-law of Benjamin Davis Wilson, used this ruse to become the guardian of Emily and Maria, the two enslaved girls whom she brought from Missouri. In April 1857, almost immediately after arriving in Los Angeles, Hereford appeared before the probate court asking to be appointed the children's guardian, as they had "no relations or next of kin in the state." She could state this in all truthfulness because she had just torn the girls away from their families in Missouri. Judge William Dryden, the same man who had so readily granted the requests for Indian wards, took Hereford at her word and made her guardian.[40] Despite his anxieties about African American apprenticeship when he served in the 1849 constitutional convention, Judge Kimball Dimmick, Dryden's predecessor, granted a similar slaveholder request in 1855. A man named McCatrick testified that he had a "certain negro boy named 'Tom'" in his "care and custody." He failed to say how he obtained the child but stated confidently that Tom had no relatives living in the state. In this case, McCatrick used the law to transfer the child and his services to someone else. He asked that John Shore, another white man, be named Tom's guardian. Shore was a Virginian, and the 1860 census reveals that he had at least one black man living in his household as a "servant." The petition for guardianship may have been a cover for the sale or transfer of Tom to another master. Dimmick immediately approved the guardianship.[41]

Hereford and McCatrick capitalized on the probate court's power to appoint guardians for "orphaned" slave children. Other Los Angeles slaveholders exploited a different provision of the guardianship law: the section allowing probate judges to appoint guardians for children whose parents were financially incompetent or unsuitable caretakers. Slaveholders resorted to this appeal to gain custody of the children of the adult slaves that they brought to the state. In Los Angeles, every one of these petitions asserted that enslaved mothers were unfit to care for their children. Some masters sought guardianship over the children of enslaved women currently living in their homes. Others tried to gain custody of children whose mothers had already escaped in California or had been manumitted. In these cases, masters probably hoped to not only secure the labor of enslaved children but also discourage slave mothers from running away and punish, harass, or control women who no longer lived in their households. Invoking racialized constructions of womanhood and motherhood rooted in proslavery ideology, they alleged that enslaved women lacked the virtues of chastity, temperance, and industriousness necessary to provide for their children's future comfort and moral well-being. In every instance, probate judges accepted these claims and converted children into the wards of their masters.[42]

Two guardianship cases, those of eighteen-month-old Rose and three-year-old Cassady, reveal the ease with which slaveholders could wrest enslaved children away from their mothers. In 1856, John and Charlotte Rowland, longtime residents of southern California, petitioned the Los Angeles Probate Court for guardianship of Rose. The child's mother, a black woman named Amanda, lived in the Rowland household. Mother and daughter were most likely slaves that Charlotte Rowland had brought from her home state of Kentucky a few years earlier. Amanda may have had a falling out with her master's family, because both John and Charlotte separately importuned the judge to give them custody of the child. They alleged that Amanda was unfit to keep Rose because she was "not married—nor has any means of supporting the child and herself." Charlotte even argued that Amanda was a helpless vagrant who should be put in the Rowlands' custody along with her daughter. The judge granted the Rowlands custody of Rose for the next sixteen years. Amanda avoided a similar fate—California law allowed the wardship of adults only in cases of insanity—but she may have had to stay with her master's family to avoid separation from her daughter.[43] Two years later, a white Arkansas-born woman named Civility Dorsey made a similar claim to Cassady. The girl's mother, known only as Sally, was probably a slave that Dorsey or her husband, Hilliard, had brought to California. Sally apparently agreed to let Hilliard Dorsey have custody of Cassady in 1858 but may have tried to get the child back when he died shortly afterward. Instead, the widow made claim to the child, arguing that Sally, a "single woman" who had "no permanent residence," was "incapable of educating the said child." This portrait of Sally as an unwed mother, a pauper, and a vagrant achieved the result that Dorsey desired. Judge Dryden turned Cassady over to the Dorsey family.[44]

The guardianship proceedings for Rose and Cassady, founded on depictions of enslaved mothers as unfit parents, went uncontested by everyone but the women themselves. Only one case, In the Matter of the Guardianship of Lucy, a Mulatto Child, involved competing white claims to enslaved children. The fate of Lucy suggests that judges may have been strongly disposed to support masters' claims to enslaved minors against those of other white petitioners. When the case began in 1850, Lucy was six years old. She came to Los Angeles with her masters, John and Laura Evertsen, and her enslaved grandmother, Julia (sometimes known as Judah or Judy). After suffering a terrible public beating at the hands of her master—so bad that police arrested Evertsen for assault—Julia escaped and took Lucy with her. Evertsen went straight to the probate court. He claimed that Julia was a "dissolute" character and asked to be appointed Lucy's permanent guardian.[45]

Other white Angelinos intervened. John Nichols, a New Yorker by birth, protested that Evertsen should not get Lucy because he "claim[ed] property in the said child as his slave" and had abused her grandmother. These arguments may not have been wholly altruistic. Nichols petitioned the judge to give him, not Julia, guardianship of the girl. The case dragged out for several months until another claimant, Benjamin Davis Wilson, came forward. Wilson, of course, later engineered his mother-in-law's 1857 bid for guardianship of the enslaved girls Emily and Maria. In 1850, though, he was a recent widower who had taken on Lucy's grandmother, Julia, as his housekeeper. He accused Evertsen of beating the child and plotting to return her to the slave states. He, too, requested Lucy's guardianship, perhaps seeking to reunite grandmother and grandchild or perhaps hoping to bind both to his own household. Evertsen countered that Lucy should never be allowed near Julia, who was "a woman of loose, lewd and immoral habits" and unsuitable "to be brought into contact with or to acquire influence over a female of tender years." Wilson was also unfit to care for a young girl because he did not have a wife. Invoking paternalist proslavery tropes, he made a fatherly claim to Lucy. She "was born and has ever lived in his family and has been treated kindly and paternally," he testified. The probate judge ultimately sided with the master and gave Evertsen guardianship. In 1860, eight years later, a census taker recorded the teenaged Lucy still living as a "servant" in the Evertsens' Los Angeles home.[46]

Los Angeles probate judges often sympathized with slaveholders' desires to bind enslaved children and upheld their claims over those of African American mothers and competing white petitioners. Still, there were limits on how far the courts were willing to take slaveholder rights. At least one major Los Angeles slave case suggests that judges, even southern-born slaveholding ones, might balk at granting guardianship when masters tried to take black children back to the slave states. In January 1856, two enslaved women, Biddy Mason and Hannah, appeared before the Los Angeles County District Court on a writ of habeas corpus. They were accompanied by their twelve children and grandchildren, who ranged from seventeen years to two weeks of age. All were slaves of Mississippi-born Mormon migrant Robert Mays Smith. Most had come with Smith's family to California from the Utah Territory in 1851. The youngest had been born in California. The women and children spent five years working on the Smith ranch in the San Bernardino Mormon colony before Smith decided to relocate his family and slaves to Texas. Someone, perhaps a member of the town's small free black community, warned authorities that Smith planned to take the fourteen bondpeople with him to the slave South. Another anonymous person petitioned for a writ of habeas corpus forcing Smith to bring the enslaved people before Judge Benjamin Hayes of the District Court.[47]

When he appeared before Hayes, Robert Mays Smith framed his claims to the women and children in paternalist language. Like John Evertsen before him, he argued that ties of affection and dependence, not coercion, bound the African American people into his family. Biddy Mason and Hannah left Mississippi with "their own consent," and he "supported them" and their children while they worked on his California ranch. His relationship to them was strictly that of a kindly father. He was "subjecting them to no greater control than his own children, and not holding them as slaves." They all wanted to go with him to Texas "voluntarily, as a portion of his family." Since all the enslaved people except Biddy Mason and Hannah were minors under the age of twenty-one and had lived in his household since birth, Smith felt entitled to guardianship or some kind of "patriarchal rule" over them.[48]

Judge Hayes, though a southerner and former slaveholder, rejected Smith's claims. As a non-Mormon, Hayes probably had little sympathy for the rights of his fellow southerner. As a judge determined to uphold free-state law, he was adamant that Smith had no property rights in Biddy Mason or Hannah. The women had arrived well after California statehood, and the state fugitive slave law had expired the year before. He also denied that Smith had "supported" the women and children as his family members. In light of "the urgent wants of this country for domestic servants," the master had surely profited from their labor. Nonetheless, Hayes, who had been a lawyer in the case of Lucy and Julia four years earlier, admitted that Smith might benefit from guardianship precedents already set by slaveholders and those who obtained Indian wards. He noted that, "in default of a good law of apprenticeship, the law of guardianship has been liberally construed in this section of the State." Smith, therefore, might have petitioned the probate courts to "retain the care" of the children "and, perhaps, receive unmolested the fruits of their labor, as others are doing with the Indians, and, occasionally with persons of color." In short, Smith possessed the "ordinary qualifications" stipulated in the general guardianship statute and "under other circumstances than the present, might be guardian of those under 21 years of age." But this case was extraordinary. Smith planned to take the children out of California and into Texas, a slave state. Texas law prohibited the in-migration of free African Americans, and thus Smith could only legally take them there as slaves. Smith's move would doom all the children, including those born on California soil, to lifelong bondage. Fearing that the children's "liberty will be greatly jeopardized, and there is good reason to apprehend and believe that they may be sold into slavery or involuntary servitude," Hayes found against the master. He proclaimed

Biddy Mason, Hannah, and all the children "free forever." Smith left for Texas empty-handed.[49]

When Benjamin Hayes denied Robert Mays Smith guardianship and "patriarchal rule" over the children of Biddy Mason and Hannah, his decision marked a departure from most judicial rulings in Los Angeles. As Hayes himself admitted, slaveholders often used the state's guardianship laws to hold black children and "receive unmolested the fruits of their labor." In all but this case—in which guardianship would lead directly to enslavement in the South and in which the defendant's Mormon faith won him little sympathy—the Los Angeles courts supported slaveholders' entitlement to slave children. Designating enslaved children "orphans" with no family ties or the offspring of unfit mothers, the probate court favored the rights of white southern householders over those of enslaved parents. On rare occasions, it also upheld slaveholders' claims against other whites who intervened to return children to their parents or who hoped to seize their labor for themselves. Converting enslaved minors into wards and defending slaveholders' rights to their custody, legal officials obscured children's enslavement and allowed masters to continue exploiting their labor in a free state.

The Struggle over Indian and African American Apprenticeship

Throughout the 1850s, state legislators and local legal officials both tolerated and promoted the wardship of American Indian and African American children. New laws covered over the unfree status of these children by binding them as domestic dependents into white households, and the courts upheld white men's claims to their bodies and labor. The servitude of Native and black youths remained relatively unnoticed and uncontested so long as they were bound in familial ties of wardship and guardianship. When eager employers of Indian and black labor, together with Indian policy reformers, pressed for new statutes that might force hundreds of youths into formal, state-regulated systems of apprenticeship, they ran up against familiar free-soil opposition. In 1853 and 1854, free-soilers defeated two efforts to establish formal systems of Indian apprenticeship by arguing that they placed Native laborers in competition with free white workers. The state legislature also rejected at least three general apprenticeship bills that permitted the voluntary and involuntary binding out of children of any racial background. Not until 1858, when economic depression and urban poverty wracked the state, did California finally pass a comprehensive apprenticeship act aimed at forcibly removing children from impoverished parents and compelling them to labor.

Even then, free-soil legislators took great pains to craft a "whites-only" apprenticeship law that prohibited the systematic binding out of Indian, black, and Chinese youths. Advocates of Indian and black apprenticeship pressed for the elimination of these racial restrictions in 1859 but met fierce opposition from free-soilers, who accused them of conspiring to introduce slavery into the state. The following year, however, an upsurge of Indian warfare in California's far northwestern counties and the dire need for new Indian policy buried these free-soil objections. In the spring of 1860, less than a year before the start of the Civil War, California passed a far-reaching Indian apprenticeship law that made thousands of Native children and adults vulnerable to long-term servitude.

The campaign for a formal system of Indian apprenticeship began as early as 1853. That year, legislators from southern California tried to pass a revised Act for the Government and Protection of Indians in order to make it easier for whites to obtain Indian children and to bind them as laborers. The original act only allowed whites to apply for guardianship of minors whose "parents or friends" had consented to the arrangement, but this new one would force scores of Native men and women to give up their children. Impoverished Indian parents, "not having the means for the suitable maintenance" of their sons and daughters, had to go before the local justice of the peace. He would then bind out each child for the rest of his or her minority to any "householder or freeholder" in order "to learn any art, trade, mistery [mystery, or secret craft knowledge], or occupation, or to perform ordinary and respectable labor." The law also instructed justices of the peace to seek out poor Native parents who refused to comply with the law and to "immediately bind out" their children. Since most California Indian families suffered some degree of poverty, justices might accuse almost any Native parent of not providing a "suitable maintenance" and take their sons and daughters. At the same time that the law denied Indian mothers and fathers rights to their children, it also explicitly established the paternal rights of white patriarchs over their new apprentices. Each person who obtained Indian apprentices would "have the moral and religious training of the same, as the head of a family over his children."[50]

This earliest effort to institute a formal system of forced apprenticeship for Indian children withered in the face of free-soil opposition. The *Alta California*, sympathetic to the free-soil cause, denounced the new Indian bill. The argument against apprenticeship stemmed partly from humanitarianism. Compulsive binding out would "reduce the Indians to a state of slavery," the editor argued, and make them "the servants and dependents of their exterminators." Other free-soilers agreed and called the new act "a glaring, bare-faced and outrageous attempt to engraft the barbarous peon laws of Mexico on our free institutions." They dubbed the measure "McFarland's peon bill," after J. P. McFarland, the Los Angeles assemblyman who first proposed it. Given the recent antipathy against Mexican peons, these arguments resonated with Californians who were anxious to protect free white American labor from competition with "cheap" nonwhite labor. In fact, the *Alta* editor framed the new law as just another attempt to "effect a reduction in the wages of labor and to lower and degrade it by bringing into competition with free white labor that of inferior races." Capitalists had attempted "at various times to introduce negro, Asiatic, Kanaka and every other kind of labor that could be had at a cheaper rate than can that of American citizens." He predicted that an act so amenable to slavery and so threatening to white workers would "be indignantly voted down."[51] Indeed, although the assembly's Committee on Indian Affairs recommended passing the new Indian bill, assemblymen never took it up for a vote.[52] Persistent southern Californian assemblymen introduced an almost identical bill the following year. This time, the Committee on Indian Affairs, now headed up by a Democrat from the mining counties, rejected the bill in favor of keeping the provisions of the 1850 Act for the Government and Protection of Indians. On the committee's recommendation, the assembly again voted to postpone apprenticeship indefinitely.[53]

Despite back-to-back defeats, calls for Indian apprenticeship grew louder as the decade went on. California's age-old problem of labor scarcity generated much of this demand. The expanding population of permanent white residents and the growth of commercial agriculture and ranching after the gold rush created needs for field hands and domestic servants that might be met by apprenticing Native youths.[54] The dismal state of Indian-white relations in California also spurred interest in an apprenticeship system. While Native peoples had suffered violence and displacement at the hands of invading Americans since 1846, the mid-1850s push of white squatters into northwestern California provoked a particularly bloody and protracted conflict. The rural northwest, especially Mendocino, Tehama, Trinity, Humboldt, and Shasta counties, saw dozens of violent confrontations between whites and local Native peoples. Most started when ranchers and farmers sought retribution against alleged Indian murderers and cattle thieves and organized paramilitary "Indian hunting" campaigns to punish the wrongdoers. Militias, some made up of vigilantes and some authorized by the state, killed thousands of Indian people in battles and massacres, usually on the flimsiest of pretexts. Native resistance and retaliation met, in turn, with more violent retribution from whites. This warfare against northwestern California Native peoples, genocidal in scale and scope, did not subside until after the Civil War.[55]

Many white Californians who surveyed the northwestern violence prescribed forced apprenticeship for Native children. Removing Indian children and binding them out to whites might "civilize" Native people and quell warfare. J. Ross Browne, a longtime California resident who reviewed the state's Indian policy and recommended federal reforms, insisted on a regime of compulsory schooling and apprenticeship for Indian children. California's Indian affairs hinged "wholly upon the policy pursued towards the rising generation of Indians." Not yet fixed in the habits of their ancestors, Native boys and girls could benefit from a rigorous course of forced labor. Browne advocated the "total separation of the children from their parents," a goal that federal agents might achieve "gradually, or by purchase, or by force, if necessary." Children would then live on a "school farm," where boys would learn skilled trades and girls would be trained in rudimentary housework. After this initial reeducation, federal agents should bind all children out to "respectable white settlers" for three- or four-year terms. Browne, who may have been thinking back to the defeat of Indian apprenticeship bills a few years earlier, worried that his plan would be misconstrued as "a new species of slavery." He emphasized, however, that apprenticeship was the only alternative to Indian extermination. "Let the minors be apprenticed and the adults put to work on ground set aside for them," he wrote to his superiors, "and some good may be accomplished."[56] At least one California military official agreed with Browne's sentiments but wanted the state government to operate its own system of compulsive labor. William Kibbe, California's quartermaster and adjutant general who coordinated militia campaigns against northwestern California Indians, contended that a comprehensive state apprenticeship system could transform Native people into useful and productive laborers. After a long term of apprenticeship, the savage and degraded California Indian could "emerge from his temporary and conditional bondage, a civilized, christianized, educated being," Kibbe asserted. He could then enter into honest employment "as a mechanic, laborer, or master of some industrial pursuit" and join the ranks of free laborers.[57]

While Browne and Kibbe advanced plans for compulsive Indian apprenticeship, events in southern California seemingly rekindled interest in African American apprenticeship. For years, white southerners in Los Angeles relied on the state's general guardianship laws to control the enslaved children that they brought to the state. As the 1856 case of Biddy Mason and Hannah demonstrated, however, slaveholders' guardianship rights to enslaved children were not absolute. The courts shied away from allowing slaveholders to shuffle enslaved children back and forth between free and slave states at will. Meanwhile, southern California politicians' yearly bids for independent statehood—proposals that many feared (or hoped) would open up the region to slavery in the future—floundered in the state legislature. In light of these developments, apprenticing enslaved youths may have appeared a promising option for southern California whites who wanted to continue bringing African Americans into the state and profiting from their labor.[58]

The interests of those who wanted Indian apprenticeship and those who hoped to secure black apprentices began to merge in 1858, the year that California passed its first general apprenticeship law. Before this time, California had no law that provided for the binding of white youths as apprentices. Voluntary apprenticeship—the practice of parents binding children out to master craftsmen—was a dying institution in many free states by the 1850s. The rise of industrial wage labor, coupled with the tendency of the courts to favor contractual labor relations over patriarchal ones, spelled its decline in all but specialized trades. On the other hand, involuntary apprenticeship—in which state officials forcibly bound out the children of poor parents deemed morally unfit or incapable of supporting them—continued to thrive throughout the United States.[59] Neither initially found a foothold in gold rush California, where legislators, eager to promote their state as a haven for free white labor, hesitated to subject white youths to an archaic form of servitude. A proposal for a general apprenticeship law failed in 1852 when one Whig senator made a "powerful speech against the apprentice system." The legislature also refused to pass similar bills in 1855 and 1857.[60]

Lawmakers overcame this aversion to apprenticeship during the economic crisis of the late 1850s. California suffered from the depression that followed the Panic of 1857. Poverty and unemployment grew rapidly, especially in San Francisco. The most worrisome symptom of economic decline was the large number of poor, homeless, and idle white boys who turned to scavenging, begging, or theft. The predicament of urban youths was so grim that California's governor, J. Neely Johnson, devoted a portion of his annual executive address to them. Johnson lamented "the number of wayward boys who now infest the community . . . with no employment or the means of education." Legislators could only "improve and elevate [the boys'] present and future condition in society" and save California from their immorality and idleness by adopting "salutary legislation" for general apprenticeship.[61]

The state legislature followed Johnson's suggestions and passed a statute allowing children of both sexes to be bound as apprentices, clerks, or servants "in any profession, trade, or employment." The measure permitted both voluntary apprenticeship of children to learn craft skills and the involuntary binding out of poor children to manual and domestic labor. It required county legal officials to apprentice any child whose parents were, or were likely to become, public charges. Once apprenticed, these children endured a variety of coercions. Any child "held to service" could be arrested and "return[ed] to the care and custody of the person lawfully entitled to such service or labor." Unrepentant runaways faced a one-month jail term. Apprentices did enjoy some benefits and protections. Masters had to instruct them in reading, writing, and arithmetic or send them to a public school. Those who beat apprentices "without just cause or provocation" would lose their services.[62] A piece of class legislation, the general apprenticeship law aimed at tutoring working-class youths in habits of industry by separating them from impoverished parents and forcing them to work.

California legislators finally acquiesced to a general apprenticeship law because they hoped it would impose social control over the state's growing population of urban poor whites. But old anxieties about apprenticeship's consequences for free white labor seeped into the act. Senator Samuel Bell, one of the state's earliest free-soil Republican leaders, drafted the bill and carefully crafted its racial language to exclude all but whites from its provisions. Reaching back to the free-soil arguments that had defeated Indian apprenticeship in 1853 and 1854, the bill prohibited the apprenticing of Native youths. It also shut out African Americans and Chinese. One provision allowed minors from other states, territories, or nations to bind themselves as apprentices to California residents who paid their passage to the state. To take advantage of this section, however, the prospective emigrant had to prove that he was "a white person capable of becoming a citizen of this state." This clause prevented both the apprenticeship of Chinese immigrants to work off their passage money and the binding of African American minors whose masters might bring them to the state under the ruse of apprenticeship. In this way, legislators extended the "salutary" discipline of apprenticeship to white youths without bringing American Indian, Chinese, or African American apprentices into competition with white labor.[63]

Californians who favored Indian and black apprenticeship were likely disappointed with the racial exclusions built into the state's new apprenticeship law. In less than a year, a small coalition of proslavery southerners and politicians from counties with large Indian populations tried to amend it to their advantage. In March 1859, Senator Cameron Thom, representing Los Angeles, San Bernardino, and San Diego counties, proposed to strike out or revise all of the general apprenticeship law's racial restrictions. One of his amendments sought to eliminate the section that prohibited the apprenticeship of American Indian children so that they, like white children, could be seized from poor parents and forcibly bound out. Here, Thom likely sought to appease his southern California ranchero constituents, who depended heavily on Indian labor and who had pressed for the earlier failed Indian apprenticeship bills of 1853 and 1854.[64]

Crucially, Thom's bill also reopened the possibility of unfree African American labor in California. Thom was a Virginian from a wealthy slaveholding family, and, just a month before trying to revise the apprenticeship law, he stirred up sectional controversy by advocating independent statehood for southern California. Free-soilers condemned this campaign, like those before it, as a plot to open up southern California to slavery. Thom's proposed amendments to the apprenticeship bill seemed to confirm these suspicions. He advocated striking out the section barring Californians from apprenticing nonwhite minors and paying their passage to the state. Declaring that "any person may bind him or herself to service" in exchange for passage to California, Thom's amendments implicitly authorized whites to apprentice African Americans (as well as Chinese) and transport them into the state. Finally, Thom added in new racial exclusions that relieved masters of having to educate nonwhite apprentices. Only apprenticed white children would have the right to home tutoring or public schooling.[65] Masters could enjoy all the benefits of apprenticing nonwhite minors without shouldering the expense of educating them.

Thom's bill made some progress at first. The senate referred it to its judiciary committee, a group that included Thom, at least two other southern-born Democrats, and two senators from northwestern counties wracked by Indian violence. With one telling exception—a Democrat from the mining counties, where opposition to bound or imported labor always ran high—this seven-man committee recommended the bill. Then the issue of black apprenticeship sank the entire proposal. The editor of the *Sacramento Daily Union*, sympathetic to the northern-born branch of the state Democratic Party, warned his readers that Thom's seemingly innocuous changes to the bill's wording "savor[ed] very strongly of the 'peculiar institution.'" Most were aimed at transplanting slavery in California. "The dropping of the word 'white'" from the section governing apprentices brought into the state from elsewhere was clearly designed so that "negroes under the age of 21 years, the property of Southern gentlemen emigrating to this State, may be admitted and held in bondage until they have reached a majority." Thom's efforts to exclude all but white children from the law's educational benefits supported this idea. It was hardly believable that Thom wanted "to prevent our citizens from educating, if they thought proper, the Indians, Chinese and Mulatto children whom they may have taken to service." Rather, he wanted to shield southern masters who viewed educating black children as a threat to the slave system. "Mr. Thom's amendments to the Apprentice Act have but one end in view," the Union concluded, "and that is to smooth the way for the introduction by Southern men of their household servants under age, and to remove the disabilities for their continuance in servitude until of age." Here was a "foretaste" of the kinds of policies southern Californians would pass if they managed to break off as a new state.[66]

These anxieties about a proslavery conspiracy probably spelled Thom's defeat. By mid-April, the Union reported that the senate had tabled the amendments to the apprenticeship bill for good.[67] The 1859 campaign to split off southern California as a new state also failed, as did a subsequent state division movement in 1860. A disappointed Thom eventually left Los Angeles to fight a new battle for slaveholder rights. In 1862, he went back to Virginia and enlisted in the Confederate army.[68]

The failure of Cameron Thom's revised apprenticeship bill revealed the limits of tolerance for children's unfree labor. Across the 1850s, white householders profited from the labor of Indian and black wards with little challenge or opposition. Justices of the peace and probate judges upheld white householders' claims to the children living in their families, readily granting them guardianship and discounting the interests of Indian and African American parents. Once these youths became wards, the coercive nature of their labor disappeared from view. Legally redefined as domestic dependents—rather than as captives or slaves—white guardians could control their labor with little interference. California legal officials, invested in fortifying white men's authority over their household dependents, defended guardian-ward relations from challenge or invasion. The exploitation of Indian and black youths drew opposition, however, when rancheros and southern masters pressed for formal systems of apprenticeship that might expand their access to minors and their labor. Free-soil Californians, suspicious of slavery and any other labor system that put "inferior races" into competition with free white workers, defeated every proposal to apprentice nonwhite children that came up in the legislature before 1859. American Indian and African American children could continue to labor in white households, but only so long as they bore the legal status of "wards" rather than "apprentices."

By 1860, however, arguments against slavery and "cheap" apprentice labor no longer held against the deteriorating state of California Indian affairs. In the face of the constant warfare that plagued the northwestern counties, Cameron Thom's efforts to expand the general apprenticeship law inspired a renewed movement for Indian apprenticeship. More than a year after Thom's bill expired in the senate, the *Sacramento Daily Union* revisited the measure. Thom's proposal, aimed at "nothing less than an introduction of colored 'apprentices' into the State," started a dangerous precedent. It awakened legislators to the possibilities of using apprenticeship laws to make "servants of the inferior races in this country." Now it would be American Indians, rather than African Americans, who suffered most from this "apprenticeship dodge."[69]

This was because Democrats in the 1860 state legislature created a full-blown system of apprenticeship that encompassed thousands of Indian children and adults. Eager to suppress Indian resistance, dispossess Indians of their land, and convert Native people into laborers, northwestern Democrats pressured their colleagues to amend the 1850 Act for the Government and Protection of Indians. Binding out Indians to white families for long terms was the only way to pacify and civilize them and bring permanent peace to northwestern California, they argued. As J. B. Lamar, a Georgia-born Democrat from Mendocino County put it, the state of California had to "adopt a general system of peonage or apprenticeship" if it wanted to quell northwestern violence. Such a system would not only civilize Indians and provide them with "permanent and comfortable homes," but white settlers would get "profitable and convenient servants." Democrat Lewis Burson of Humboldt County took up the charge. He proposed to repeal the old wardship sections of the original 1850 Act for the Government and Protection of Indians and replace them with a harsher apprenticeship provision. Burson allowed whites to apprentice any Indian children in their possession so long as they could prove that they had obtained them from their parents or the "person or persons having the care or charge" of them. They could also apprentice Indian adults and children taken as prisoners of war or alleged vagrants with "no settled habitation or means of livelihood." All adult Indians were to serve ten-year apprenticeships. Children, depending on gender and age at the time of apprenticeship, would serve up to anywhere from age twenty-one to age thirty. The heavily Democratic state legislature passed the measure—after a few revisions to make Burson's original bill harsher—with no dissent or discussion.[70]

The *Union* editor denounced the new apprenticeship amendments as a violation of California's free constitution. "If this does not fill the measure of the constitutional term, 'involuntary servitude,'" he wrote, "we shall be thankful if some one will inform us what is lacking."[71] The *Union*'s criticism gained force as the nation embarked on a war over slavery and the state came into the hands of new Republican leadership. Free soil and antislavery in outlook, Republicans condemned Democrats' Indian apprenticeship system as a barbarous and outmoded form of slavery. This anger mounted as apprenticeship statutes encouraged and expanded captive raiding against Native communities in northwestern California. But Republicans firmly believed that Indian people would have to be tutored in the graces of civilization and work discipline before they could be properly integrated into the wage-labor market. Torn between the desire to convert Native people into "civilized" free laborers and their aversion to slavery, Republicans struggled to end the apprentice system while enacting new reforms that forced Indians to work.

CHAPTER FIVE

For Purposes of Labor and of Lust

California's Traffics in Women

In 1863, a reporter for the *San Francisco Bulletin*, a strong Unionist newspaper, took his readers to Jackson Street in the Chinese district. He asked them to picture the Chinese prostitutes who lived in the brothels along the crowded thoroughfare. These women spent their waking hours tapping at their windows to attract customers. They had little choice in the matter. Kidnapped in China and sold to brothel keepers as slaves, they kept up their incessant rapping to generate profits for the men who owned them. The brothel inmates rarely questioned their fate. It was "the condition of women born in the oldest empire of the world," China, to be bought and sold in such a manner. Then the reporter wondered what these women might be thinking as they watched the throngs of people who passed by their windows. What did Chinese prostitutes think of "our ladies"—that is, white American women—"as they passed in all the glory of Christian costume?" They undoubtedly watched white female passersby with great curiosity, because there was "something in American women which they could not understand." They could not fathom why "all these mothers and wives and daughters were not fulfilling the destiny of their sex and drumming the funeral march of their own souls on window-panes for the benefit of their masters." White wives and daughters moved freely through the city, their bodies and sexuality seemingly exempt from being bought and sold in the market. But Chinese women, bound by a cultural tradition that countenanced degrading commerce in female bodies, were "imported in droves like cattle . . . [and] penned up in moral shambles."[1]

The *Bulletin* reporter's speculations about the inner lives of Jackson Street prostitutes and his contrast between enslaved Chinese women and free white women reflected a long-standing struggle over commerce in women's bodies and sexual servitude. Starting with the gold rush, many enslaved and indentured women worked in California. Women from the eastern United States,

China, Australia, Mexico, Chile, Europe, and the Pacific Islands entered California's burgeoning world of commercialized sex, many through kidnapping, indenture, and enslavement.[2] Others, especially African American and Native American women, served as bound domestic servants. Bound women of diverse backgrounds were also incorporated into California households in complex, intimate ways—as long-term sexual partners and concubines and, sometimes, even as wives. The enslaved Jackson Street prostitute, tapping at her window at the behest of her master, was only the most visible symbol of the commerce in bound women's bodies, labor, and sexuality that became commonplace in California by the beginning of the Civil War.

California's traffics in women engendered a complex discursive struggle over the meaning and content of female freedom, the commercialization of sex, and the nature of male desire. As they faced lucrative traffics in women, white Californians critical of these practices—mostly middle-class male Republicans and free-soil Democrats—confronted difficult questions about women's marketability. In what contexts could women's labor power, sexuality, and bodies be bought, bartered, and sold, and in what contexts could they not? These questions were troubling not just for white Californians. The emergence of a national market economy and the corresponding rise in female waged work and the urban sex trade brought concerns about women's salability to the forefront of politics in many U.S. cities during the nineteenth century.[3] The sale and sexual exploitation of African American women in the antebellum slave trade also made commerce in women's bodies a focal point of abolitionist literature and, later, the Republican Party's critique of the slave system.[4] How, whether, and when women should enter the market as objects of commerce became questions of national political significance in the face of slave emancipation, rising industrial wage work, and the growth of the commercialized vice economy.

In California, where not only female labor power and sexuality but even diverse female people were for sale, free-soil whites identified commerce in women's bodies as a form of slavery incompatible with free-state status. They attempted to mark boundaries between legitimate and illegitimate economic exchanges in women by drawing upon emerging middle-class discourses about marriage, gender, and family. Like the *Bulletin* reporter, these critics of woman trafficking evoked idealized white, middle-class gender relations to highlight the horrors of buying and selling women. They envisioned the bonds of home and family as women's greatest protection from the market. Husbands and fathers commanded the labor of their wives and daughters, but they also shielded them from the ravages of the capitalist marketplace and the overt commodification of their bodies, labor, and sexuality. Ignoring the economic exchange and dependency that structured middle-class American marriage, white critics depicted other types of commerce in women as antithetical to the normative gender and family relations of free society. Instead of protecting women from the worst abuses of the market, men who bought and sold women as prostitutes, domestic workers, concubines, and wives reduced them to commodities. They subverted proper, natural relationships between women and men by turning intimate sexual and household relations into mere economic transactions. Woman trafficking reflected, in short, a nightmarish merger of the domestic sphere and the market that transformed family relationships—sex, household labor, and even marriage and childbearing—into matters of bargain and sale.

These assumptions about gender, marriage, family, and the market structured discursive, legal, and political struggles over the two most prominent California traffics in women. These were the trade in captive indigenous women on the white-Indian frontier and the international commerce in bound Chinese prostitutes. These two traffics differed from each other in significant ways. The trade in Indian women was an older and primarily rural phenomenon that involved the incorporation of female captives into non-Indian households as apprentices, domestic servants, long-term sexual partners, or wives. The traffic in Chinese prostitutes, in contrast, was largely an urban affair. It emerged in the middle of the 1850s in conjunction with the transpacific expansion of global capitalism and the migration of thousands of Chinese to California. Both trades, however, involved very visible economic exchanges in women whom whites constructed as nonwhite. Together, they not only raised vexing questions about the marketability of women; they also became vehicles through which white middle-class Californians expressed new racialized understandings of gender, household, and family relations.

Critiques of the traffics in Indian and Chinese women rested on depictions of homes and domestic life invaded by the imperatives of the market. Accounts of the captivity of Native women described horrific scenes in which unscrupulous poor white frontiersmen—known colloquially as squaw men—kidnapped, bought, and sold Indian men's wives and daughters and forced them into domestic and sexual servitude. Squaw men, often called "white Indians" because they flouted prevailing norms about interracial intimacy, severed sacred bonds of home and family and denied Indian husbands and fathers their rights to their female kin. Narratives about the traffic in Chinese prostitutes described similar scenes but cast Chinese husbands and fathers as perpetrators rather than as victims. Whites attributed the enslavement of bound Chinese prostitutes to the women's own male kinfolk. They contended that Chinese men possessed excessive patriarchal control over female family members and regularly sold their own wives and daughters into sexual servitude. Chinese women were often willing accomplices to their own downfall because they lacked proper feminine virtues of modesty and chastity. Representations of both trades, then, attached deeply racialized meanings to the buying and selling of women's bodies. Indian men and women were victims of the lust and greed of racially degraded white frontiersmen. Chinese women labored as enslaved prostitutes due to defective Chinese conceptions of manhood and womanhood. Blind to the economic exchange that underlay their own gender relations, white critics depicted both traffics as dangerous aberrations from the natural gender and domestic order, perpetrated by men who were either nonwhite or ambiguously white.

Representations of female trafficking, as well as the racialized and gendered meanings attached to them, had real consequences for bound women and the men in their lives. The ways that whites depicted the sale of Native and Chinese women's bodies shaped state legislation—including antikidnapping, antimiscegenation, and antiprostitution laws—that politicians designed to stamp out these practices. Discourses about woman trafficking also influenced what happened to Indian and Chinese women when they appeared before the California courts. White judges, acting on their own assumptions about proper domestic and gender relations, granted some women's bids for freedom and denied or ignored others. But whites did not exercise complete discursive control over female trafficking. Native and Chinese women and men approached the courts with their own narratives about marriage and family relations and their own attitudes about the relationship between economic and gender relations. By the dawn of the 1860s, the California courts had become sites of discursive contest where white, Native, and Chinese Californians struggled over the meaning of buying and selling women.

Trafficking Native Women in California

In 1939, ninety-year-old Lucy Young sat down with an anthropologist to dictate reminiscences of her childhood in northwestern California. Young, whose birth name was T'tcetsa, was born sometime near the start of the gold rush. She belonged to the Lassik people, who made their homes in present-day Humboldt and Mendocino counties. A child when warfare between whites and Indian peoples broke out in northwestern California in the 1850s,

T'tcetsa narrated her youth as a story punctuated by cycles of violence, captivity, sale, and sexual exploitation. At the height of the northwestern wars in the early 1860s, U.S. troops massacred most of the men in her band, including her father and older brother. Soldiers captured the twelve-year-old T'tcetsa, her mother, and her younger sister and marched them to Fort Seward. There T'tcetsa first entered the local captive trade. A white hog farmer came to the fort in search of a servant to help his wife, an Indian woman, care for a newborn child. He settled upon T'tcetsa and wrested her away from her mother. T'tcetsa kept house for the couple and endured terrible beatings until she finally managed to run away. She reunited with her mother and sister at Fort Seward, but the hog farmer returned and recaptured her. This time, he traded her to another white man, who probably intended to sell her as a servant in the coastal settlements. T'tcetsa fled her captors again and walked fifty miles back to Fort Seward. During the remainder of her stay at the fort, several young girls from her band, including her younger sister, were kidnapped by whites. T'tcetsa only evaded capture a third time when her mother spirited her away to the distant home of a cousin.[5]

As she matured into young womanhood, T'tcetsa found herself the victim of a different kind of trafficking. When she was around thirteen, a white man named Abraham Rogers took her from her family to live with him. He renamed her Lucy, and when she grew older, he married her. The couple apparently lived together happily for a time and had four children. At some point, the marriage ended and T'tcetsa found herself a captive yet again. According to her own account, she lived for five years in virtual slavery in the household of a white man. He shackled her so that she could not escape and beat her so mercilessly that she miscarried several children (likely the products of forced sexual encounters). Her captor finally released her when a white woman, whom he deemed a more desirable partner, agreed to marry him. After two decades in and out of the California captive trade, T'tcetsa, a free woman, married a Native man from a related band and started her own farm.[6]

T'tcetsa's narrative reveals how the exchange of captive Native women and girls became a vital part of the social fabric in northwestern California during the decade following the gold rush. Through individual acts of kidnapping and violence and informal networks of trade, northwestern whites trafficked Native women and girls as domestic servants, as long-term captive sexual partners, and even as wives. Whether bound legally through California's wardship and apprenticeship laws or held illegally through kidnapping and forced captivity, Native women and girls experienced dual exploitation. As

Lucy Young (Lassik), born T'tcetsa, survived repeated captivities before marrying a man from a related band and settling on the Round Valley Reservation. As an elder, she became the primary ethnographic informant on Lassik culture. Lucy Young, July 1, 1922, Zenia, Calif., A/1j/P1 no. 1, C. Hart Merriam Collection of Native American Photographs, BANC PIC 1978.008, Bancroft Library, University of California, Berkeley. Courtesy of the Bancroft Library.

bound domestic servants, they endured the expropriation of their labor. As women, many also suffered sexual servitude as their captors subjected them to forced concubinage and marriage. Many even bore their captors' children. T'tcetsa's story also makes clear that the exploitation of female captives was strongly tied to the U.S. conquest of California's northwest. The whites who seized Native women and girls as servants and sexual partners were often the same people who coveted Indian land and clamored for state and federal aid in subduing "hostile" Indian neighbors. The kidnapping and sale of female captives usually followed in the wake of military campaigns aimed at suppressing, dispossessing, and removing the region's Indian peoples. Thus, the politics of female trafficking were almost always linked to the politics of empire in California.

The trade in captive Native women that flourished in California's northwest during the 1850s and early 1860s had deep historical roots in indigenous and Spanish-Mexican communities. Since the eighteenth century, Native Californians and Spanish-Mexican newcomers had developed far-flung systems of captive raiding and trading. This trade was never as robust in California as it was in other parts of the Spanish empire such as New Mexico and Texas. In those provinces, the exchange of captive women and children cemented male honor and prestige, forged diplomatic relations among diverse peoples, sustained household economies, and increased the population of both European and indigenous communities.[7] Nonetheless, Native captives, especially women, played important roles in colonial California. Starting in the 1790s, Spanish soldiers raided Native communities in the California interior to secure captive laborers and converts—many of them women and children—for the missions. After Mexican independence and secularization, Mexican rancheros also relied on captive raiding to supply their ranchos with workers. Some, like the German-born Swiss ranchero John Sutter, specifically targeted indigenous women and children. During the same period, California also became enmeshed in complicated networks of captive trading that spanned the Great Basin. Mexican, American, and Ute traders exchanged horses for enslaved Paiute women and children, and many of these captives ended up in California households.[8]

During the gold rush, Californios and indigenous peoples adapted these older practices of female captive raiding and trading to the new American social order. Gold rush demands for labor, particularly the need for domestic workers, prompted some Californios to venture into the interior to seize Indian women and girls. In 1855, a federal Indian agent in Mendocino reported that a group of "Spaniards"—probably ethnic Mexicans from coastal ranchos—terrorized local Indian communities in a search for female captives. The party abducted "twenty or twenty-five young women" from a neighboring village and killed one female prisoner before leaving the area. Some of these captive women may have been bound for Californio ranches, but others may have been destined for domestic servitude in the mines or cities. At least one ethnic Mexican, Marcus Vaca, appears to have developed a small-scale business supplying female captives to white households in Sacramento. In 1854, a Sacramento grand jury indicted Vaca for kidnapping three

Indian girls, all under the age of fourteen, and transporting them into the city. He sold them as domestic servants to white housewives for one hundred dollars each.[9]

The profitability of female captive raiding attracted white entrepreneurs as well. Just weeks after his abortive attempt to chase down the band of "Spanish" kidnappers, the frustrated Mendocino agent reported another mass abduction. A pair of white men from Clear Lake, accompanied by a force of fifty or sixty well-armed Indian auxiliaries, kidnapped thirteen people from a nearby village. The captives, which included both children and adults, were "all females." The agent succeeded in tracking down the kidnappers and returning the women and girls to their families, but he was unable to bring charges against the white men. In some regions, white men replaced Californio raiders as the primary suppliers of female Indian captives. Pierce Asbill, among the first Americans in northwestern California, profited from selling captive women to ethnic Mexican men on the northernmost ranchos. Wailacki women from the mountainous interior were among the most valued captives in Mexican communities, Asbill remembered, because they "made good wives" and "domesticated very quickly." During the winter of 1855–56, Asbill and his partners captured around thirty-five Wailacki, mostly teenaged girls. They shackled them together and marched them to a rancho near Red Bluff. There, Mexicans paid the whites three fine horses for every "good, young squaw."[10] Over the course of the 1850s, then, female captives not only became important laborers in emigrant and Californio communities, but the procurement, transportation, and sale of these women also turned into a profitable business for Californio and white entrepreneurs and their indigenous allies.

Once torn from their communities, captive Native women and girls suffered diverse fates. Some girls and young women were legally incorporated into non-Indian households through the state's guardianship and Indian apprenticeship laws. San Diego ranchero Cave Johnson Couts "adopted" a young girl named Sasaria in 1855. The girl, allegedly an orphan, belonged to an ethnic Mexican couple who transferred custody over to Couts in exchange for fifty dollars. Sasaria was to stay with Couts's wife, Ysidora Bandini Couts, "to serve her as a servant until she arrives at the age of 18 or 21 years (as the law may be)." Once the state legislature created a formal system of Indian apprenticeship in 1860, dozens of whites appeared before the Humboldt and Colusa county courts to bind captive girls as apprentices to perform domestic and household labor. Most claimed that they had captured the girls during recent military campaigns, that they had purchased them from their destitute parents, or that they had obtained the consent of the girls' parents at some date in the past. The courts granted all of these requests.[11]

The formal, legal incorporation of Native girls into non-Indian households constituted only a part of the female captive trade. Many girls and women came into white and Californio homes through informal, extralegal, and violent networks of exchange that crisscrossed the state. In northwestern California, local militiamen and vigilantes who waged war against Indian peoples simply appropriated female captives for their own use. When a white posse from Trinity County killed an entire village of 150 Wintu people in 1852—an event known ever after as the Bridge Gulch Massacre—the men spared only a handful of young women and girls. They carried them back to the town of Weaverville and gave them to white families who kept them as servants. One white woman eventually sold her young female charge to a passing teamster for forty-five dollars.[12]

Traffics in female captives remained vibrant in Trinity County across the 1850s. After a party of Trinity whites attacked a Native village and killed three people, one man "brought home a young squaw, he said for a cook." In another part of the county, a Kentuckian "lawfully purchased" an eight- or nine-year-old girl "for his seraglio" to serve as his wife or mistress. When the child ran away with the help of her uncle, the southerner pursued "the juvenile squaw" and killed four members of her band in the chase. Commerce in Native women and girls became so common that it may have generated a semi-institutionalized slave market in some parts of the county. One resident claimed that a Hyampom newspaper reported the current prices for "squaws" in the same manner that southern papers advertised rates for purchasing slaves. Prices for four classes of Indian women—"good, middling, inferior [and] refuse"—appeared in the paper's columns, and anyone who wanted to purchase a "good to middling" woman would have to give her captor five oxen, seven deerskins, and five blankets.[13]

Incorporated into new households, captive women and girls filled crucial roles as domestic servants. In the far northwestern counties, where nearly one in every four white families may have held Indian children as servants, the labor of captive girls sustained household economies. Helen Carpenter, a Mendocino white woman who enjoyed the services of at least nineteen indigenous apprentices, including seven adult women and one small girl, viewed young female apprentices as crucial helpmates to rural California housewives. These youngsters, she noted, were in great demand as servants, because even the smallest and most awkward girl could soon be taught to wash dishes and "rock the baby." In nearby Humboldt County, ten-year-old

Kate, allegedly "purchased of her parents . . . by their voluntary consent," performed "household and domestic duties" for the family of her new master, William B. Hagans.[14]

While white families made up part of the market for captive women and girls, most of the demand probably came from unmarried white men. Early in the Civil War, the Mendocino Herald, a Democratic paper that was critical of the Lincoln administration but often sympathetic to the plight of bound Indian laborers, exposed a "crime of the darkest dye." According to the editor, around fifty single white men in the county were "living in concubinage with squaws from 10 to 14 years old," presumably captives taken in the recent Indian wars.[15] The staunchly Republican Marysville Appeal alleged that a thriving traffic in these young girls plagued northern California. White frontiersmen, "unmarried, but at housekeeping," readily paid one hundred dollars for a "likely young girl." In this case, "likely"—a word southern slave traders used to describe especially promising slaves—designated female captives who had both the skills to be competent household laborers and the personal attractions to be desirable sexual partners. These captives sold for more than twice the price of young boys. Thus, the editor lamented, Indian women and girls suffered two forms of exploitation. They were bought and sold for "purposes of labor and of lust."[16]

As the Marysville editor was quick to point out, men who controlled female captives' bodies could appropriate both their labor and their sexuality. In many instances, whites captured, bought, and sold women and girls to serve as domestic laborers and as coerced sexual partners. Some captives suffered shorter-term sexual abuse involving temporary confinement and repeated rape. Bands of white raiders reportedly seized Native women from their villages and held them in their homes for weeks or months at a time before releasing them. Others, like T'tcetsa, endured long-term forced cohabitation and concubinage. In Trinity County, where mixed white and Indian households were commonplace by 1860, a large number of Indian women entered domestic partnerships with white men by force. Some cohabitation involved the "consent of both parties," a local man reported, but it was common for white men who could not "obtain a squaw by fair means" to "drag off" a woman and "knock down her friends if they interfere." Many women fled to the mountains to escape capture, and their families were "driven from their homes in the dead of Winter by crowds of drunken men."[17] Some of these pursuers claimed captive women as their wives, forcing them to live with them permanently or to bear their children. William Macon lived in Tehama County with a Native woman whom he "had compelled to become his wife for the time being." Described as "a person of very dissolute habits, and low associations," Macon murdered several Indian people who took an interest in the woman's plight. A woman living in Butte County left the home of a white man named Downs after bearing him a child. She returned to her people and married a Native man, but Downs declared that he would "have her back if he [had] to kill the whole tribe." The woman and her husband fled their village several times, and sympathetic white miners finally locked up the couple in their cabin to prevent Downs from "forcibly carrying [her] off."[18]

By 1860, the trafficking of Native women and girls for "labor and lust" became so commonplace in war-torn northwestern California that the *Sacramento Daily Union*, a paper with ties to the northern branch of the Democratic Party, declared that a new form of slavery gripped the state. Ignoring the traffic's roots in indigenous and Spanish-Mexican practices of captive raiding, the paper blamed it on northwestern California white men who dominated the trade by the middle of the 1850s. The state's wardship and apprenticeship laws subjected all Indian people to compulsory labor unbefitting a free state, the editor argued. "But the most disgusting phase of this species of slavery," he declared, "is the concubinage of creatures calling themselves white men with squaws throughout various portions of the State."[19] Neither entirely human nor entirely white, these kidnappers—white unmarried frontiersmen—subjected female captives to such vile and disgraceful servitude that their acts were "unfit to commit to paper." While the *Union* was reluctant to explore the issue further, California's Republican and free-soil Democratic press avidly denounced frontier whites who kidnapped and enslaved Native women. They accused kidnappers, people merely "calling themselves white men," of degrading California's free-state status, violating sacred bonds of home and family, and transgressing the boundaries between whiteness and Indianness.

Squaw Men and Helpless Husbands:
Representing the Trade in Captive Women

The warfare that gripped northwestern California brought the plight of captive Native women and girls to the attention of free-soilers in the late 1850s. Like abolitionists who focused on the dual labor and sexual exploitation of African American women to illustrate the horrors of southern slavery, these free-soil critics often used captive Native women to discredit California's coercive Indian labor systems.[20] The captive woman, torn from her home and stripped of both her labor and her chastity, became a potent symbol of the enslavement and abuse that the state's Indian people suffered. Although the enslaved Native woman was, herself, an object of pity and concern, many depictions of the captive trade focused on the violation of Indian men's rights. Kidnappers did more than subject Native women to repugnant forms of sexual slavery. They also denied Indian men the right to control and defend their female kin—rights that naturally belonged to them as male heads of household. In other words, critics of women's captivity (at least rhetorically) extended to Indian men a particular set of manhood rights that were both central to republican ideology and usually reserved for white men alone.[21] At the same time, they depicted the perpetrators of the captive trade as morally and racially degraded whites—"squaw men." Ruthlessly breaking up Indian homes, severing Indian men's authority over female kin, and selling women as sexual partners, wives, and concubines, squaw men transformed sacred family relationships into vulgar commercial transactions. These men represented the unholy convergence of market forces with unbridled male lust, which threatened the sanctity of marriage, family life, and manhood rights.

Free-soilers' depiction of the female captive trade, together with its emphasis on the rights of Indian men to the persons of their wives and daughters, departed significantly from older ways of writing about Indian gender relations. Since the gold rush, white depictions of Indian life in California cast Native women as the slaves of their lazy and tyrannical male kin. Following in a long tradition of Euro-American writing about indigenous divisions of labor, white Californians, according to Albert Hurtado, "described native women as slaves because they appeared to work harder than men."[22] This stereotype of the "squaw-drudge" was almost ubiquitous in the 1850s. One California Indian agent advised his superiors, for instance, that indigenous wives were "great slaves to their Lords and Masters" and bore all the responsibility for gathering and processing food. White writers also cited indigenous marriage practices to illustrate Native women's slavelike status. Polygamy, harsh punishments for adultery, and the payment of bride prices among California Native people all rendered women the slaves of their male kinfolk. One writer asserted that a California Indian man was allowed to have as many wives as he pleased. "This is natural; for as the wife is but a slave, the greater number possessed, the richer the possessor," he explained.[23] These stereotypes were so pervasive that the Trinity Journal speculated that kidnapping and enslavement might be an improvement on Indian women's usual lot in life. Forced to live with new white masters, captive women would come to "despise" Indian men, "the squalid, lazy creatures who used to make them slaves."[24] Lumping the remarkably complex gender relationships of dozens of California bands together, many writers concluded that Native gender and marriage practices were indistinguishable from chattel slavery.

As the trade in female captives widened in the late 1850s, however, free-soil critics cast the seizure of Indian women as an illegal and immoral intrusion of the market into intimate family relations. Portrayals of the female captive trade evoked nightmarish images of violated Indian homes. White men who kidnapped, sold, and enslaved Native women sundered the most sacred of domestic ties—those that bound husband and wife—depriving Indian men of their female dependents and Indian women of their chastity. They linked the violent uprisings among Indians to the natural, even laudable, efforts of Native men to redeem their female kin and defend the honor of their families. A correspondent to the Republican *Marysville Appeal* complained, for instance, that kidnappers, "unscrupulous whites," took every opportunity to "invade by force, cajolery or deceit the marital privileges of the Diggers." The violation of these marital rights would "demoralize and dissatisfy the Indians more than anything else," he warned. Bret Harte, a strong proponent of Indian rights who was affiliated with several prominent Republicans, defended Indian men's rights to protect their kinswomen from capture and abuse. "Just let us imagine that a Digger has the same nice principles that a member of Congress has . . . that they [Indian men] have the right to defend the chastity of a wife or daughter," he wrote. It was only natural that Indian men would "demand 'an eye for an eye, tooth for tooth' or even life for life" when their families came under attack. If whites wanted an end to Indian violence, they needed to demonstrate that "civilization carries with it something stronger than simple lust and might."[25] The Democratic *Sacramento Daily Union*, only moderately free soil in its views, also decried the captive trade's dissolution of Indian men's family ties. Since the first whites had arrived in California, the Indian man found that "his inalienable rights have been ruthlessly infringed." These included his most sacred rights to family ties. His "children are taken from him, his wife plucked from his bosom, his daughters prostituted in his very presence," the editor lamented. It was unreasonable to expect Indian men to submit to this "monstrous wrong" in silence.[26]

Desecrated Indian marriages and homes, torn asunder by "simple lust and might," also influenced emerging critiques of the new federal Indian reservation system. While Congress failed to ratify the treaties that the Office of Indian Affairs made with California Native peoples in 1851–52, it did appropriate money for the establishment of reservations on government lands. In northwestern California, these included the Nome Lackee Reservation in Tehama County, the Mendocino Reservation and Nome Cult Farm in

Mendocino County, and the Klamath River and Smith River Reservations in present-day Del Norte County. Federal agents hoped to remove Native people from their homelands—by military force, if necessary—and relocate them to the reserves. Once resettled, Native people would work under the supervision of federal employees and learn the rudiments of "civilization," including farming and housekeeping. Agents would protect Indians from intruding white squatters and also make sure that Native people stayed on the reservation. The reserves, however, generally failed to meet these expectations. Most suffered from poor funding, corruption, and inefficiency. Critics of the reservation system charged federal agents with everything from neglecting and starving Indians to defrauding the government of money, land, food, and equipment. Many of the reservations also encompassed lands coveted by whites, and federal Indian agents faced constant challenges from invading squatters. Finally, federal agents' inability to contain Native peoples—who fled from starvation, disease, and harassment—prompted northwestern California whites to call for the abolition of the reserves. These problems became so severe by the 1860s that the federal government abandoned most of the pre–Civil War northwestern California reservations.[27]

In the meantime, reform-minded Republicans and free-soilers reviled the reservations for promoting the captivity and exploitation of Native women. Instead of protecting the Native people in their charge, federal reservation employees kidnapped and trafficked in Indian wives and daughters. They rendered Indian men powerless to protect the women in their households. The *San Francisco Bulletin* ran an account by a northwestern California correspondent, who accused reservation employees of being "daily and nightly engaged in kidnapping the younger portion of the [Indian] females, for the vilest of purposes." In a nightmarish reversal of the idealized white, middle-class home, he explained that "the wives and daughters of the defenceless Diggers are prostituted before the very eyes of their husbands and fathers." Instead of teaching Indian people the values and graces of civilization, reservation agents were nothing more than "civilized monsters." The *Sacramento Daily Union* editor who argued that Indian men's rights to their wives and daughters had been "ruthlessly infringed" derided the reservations for promoting these abuses. He argued that "the severest penalties should be imposed for any, even the slightest improper advances toward the women" living on the reservations. "When this security is not afforded," he asked, "what inducement is there held out for the Indian to resort thither with his family?"[28]

Depictions of broken Indian homes and powerless Native men were so potent that even white squatters, people who sympathized little with Indians, invoked them to discredit the reservation system. Rural whites insisted that Indians learned little about civilization on the reservations. Instead, federal employees condoned the captivity and sexual exploitation of Indian women that degraded Indian marriages and home life. Disgruntled whites near Nome Lackee, eager to get their hands on Indian lands, petitioned the secretary of the interior to reduce the size of the reservation and remove its agent. They bolstered their claims by citing the plight of Native women and their male kin. "Instead of endeavoring to elevate and improve the character and condition of the Indians," the petitioners reported, reservation employees were "dragging them down to a level with themselves by compelling the squaws, even in the presence of their Indian husbands, to submit to their lecherous and beastly desires." These sexual improprieties were so outrageous that local whites had taken to calling Nome Lackee "the Government Whore House."[29] One farmer made a similar protest against the Mendocino Reservation. At the reserve, "if a young man Indian, has a pretty squaw, the Bowie knife and revolver takes her *from him*; and they keep so many hired white men up there, that the common saying [nickname] for that place is the U.S. Brothel."[30] In "Government Whore Houses" and "U.S. Brothels," federal agents denied Indian women their freedom and their chastity and Indian men their most sacred rights to female kin.

Free-soil critics of the traffic in Native women developed a distinctly gendered narrative about female captivity and sexual exploitation that emphasized the violation of Indian homes and the denial of Indian men's rights to their families. When these same critics turned their attention to the white men who perpetrated these crimes, their arguments took on other racial and class meanings. They adopted a name for white men involved in the captive trade: "squaw men." The term, which did not come into common use across the United States until the post–Civil War era, appeared in northwestern California newspapers by the middle of the 1850s. "Squaw man" initially designated any white man who lived with or married an Indian woman, especially a man who made his home with his wife's people. Northwestern Indian agents and white farmers often blamed these men for stirring up trouble by selling alcohol and firearms to Indians and interfering with their removal to the reservations. With the escalation of violence and female captivity in northwestern California, the term took on additional connotations. White men who lived with Native women consensually were still squaw men, but the term often became an epithet for those whites who bought and sold Indian women or compelled them to live in their homes as wives and concubines.[31]

In popular renderings, squaw men were race traitors and social outsiders. Ostensibly they were white, but their habits continually brought their whiteness into question. They were outlaws who, by abducting Native women, provoked Indian retaliation against innocent and "respectable" white settlers. They also violated white racial and gender norms by forging sexual and domestic relationships with Indian women. So promiscuously did they cross the boundary between whiteness and Indianness that they became, in the words of their critics, "white Indians," "white-skinned diggers," "men calling themselves white," and men "claiming to be white." As one Indian agent summed it up, squaw men were a "class of individuals who, forgetting their origin, cut themselves loose from their fellows, and bow at the shrine of Digger prostitution."[32] Assumptions about class also permeated the squaw man stereotype. Squaw men allegedly came from the dregs of frontier communities. Poor, transient, and illiterate, they operated on the margins of civilized society. They were, in the strong words of one editor, "the lowest, meanest, most contemptible, worthless and abandoned trash that ever disgraced the earth."[33]

These portrayals of squaw men placed the traffic in Native women outside "respectable" white society. Middle-class whites, including married men and women with children, avidly bought, sold, and held Native women and girls. The captive trade nevertheless became associated with poor, unmarried, transient, and dissolute frontiersmen. Motivated by little more than lust and gain and unwilling to abide by the sexual and racial mores of their white neighbors, they could make few claims to respectability or whiteness. Thus, the traffic in Native women and the violation of Indian homes it entailed could be neatly divorced from middle-class families' demands for domestic labor. It is not surprising, then, that California's first efforts to curb the trade in Native women and girls focused on suppressing squaw men and the interracial intimacy—forced or consensual—that gave them their name.

The Politics of Captivity

When warfare ripped across the counties of northwestern California in 1858, the editor of the *Red Bluff Beacon*, Tehama County's largest newspaper, blamed the flare-ups on the ubiquitous "squaw men" who abducted and lived with Native women. The only way to suppress such men was to outlaw race mixing of any kind. Compelled to associate only with "persons of their own color and race," squaw men would cease to threaten the lives and livelihoods of respectable white settlers.[34] The *Beacon* editor was just one of many white Californians who called for the elimination of squaw men and the criminalization of interracial intimacy. Mounting violence spurred north-western California vigilante organizations and state legislators to confront the female captive trade. Some sought to punish kidnappers with extrale-gal violence and tougher legislation. They also struck at the most visible outcomes of the captive trade: interracial sex, cohabitation, marriage, and mixed-blood children. Local and state laws against Indian-white intimacy proposed to draw new racial boundaries around the institutions of marriage, home, and family and penalize those who transgressed them. Restricting who could marry, cohabit, or have sex with whom, these laws not only sought to suppress squaw men; they also looked to establish racial homogeneity as a vital component of a legitimate family.

The first efforts to curb squaw men and interracial intimacy began in Cali-fornia's northwestern counties, the heart of the female captive trade. Con-vinced that squaw men brought "assassination and death upon decent citi-zens," groups of northwestern whites worked to criminalize and expel them.[35] Mass meetings of settlers resolved that squaw men would have to abandon their domestic association with Native women or face ejection from the com-munity. After an upsurge of violence in Humboldt County in 1858, whites in the Mattole Valley gathered and declared that they "discountenance[d], and [would] not permit any white men to go into the Indian rancherias to inter-fere with squaws or children, or in any way molest them." They ordered all squaw men to vacate the valley or be driven out. Local newspapers reported, with satisfaction, that the squaw men complied with the settlers' demands.[36] A similar group in Tehama County blamed most Indian conflict on a certain class of white men, "those filthy and abandoned beasts in human shape who have squaws, with whom they live in concubinage." They warned these men that they would have to give up the Indian women living in their households, leave the vicinity for good, or risk being treated "as nothing better than In-dians themselves." One month later, they organized a vigilante militia called the Antelope Rangers to remove local Indians to the reservations. Declar-ing that white men "who are keeping squaws in concubinage are no better than savages themselves," the Rangers made a special effort to remove Indian women from reputed squaw men's homes.[37]

As vigilantes prowled northwestern California, legislators from the region devised formal statutes to prevent the abduction of Indian women and to restrain interracial intimacy. In the spring of 1858, Senator Ephraim Garter, a Democrat who represented Tehama, Shasta, and Colusa counties, proposed new amendments to the Act for the Government and Protection of Indi-ans that took aim at squaw men. The first strengthened the antikidnapping provisions of the law by imposing fines and jail time on white men convicted of "taking away any squaw from her tribe." More than that, Garter hoped to prohibit any kind of sexual, familial, or domestic relations—coercive or not—between Indians and whites. Laws against miscegenation were nothing new in California. The first state legislature had banned marriage between whites and African Americans in 1850. Still, the state's Spanish-Mexican past and its long history of social, cultural, and sexual mixing among Indians and Europeans had exempted white-Indian marriages from these prohibitions. Garter wanted to change all that. Any white man who married or was found "habitually living with an Indian female . . . or sustaining illicit relations with such" could be convicted of a misdemeanor. Jail time and steep fines would follow. Garter won the support of fellow Democratic senators on the Committee for Public Morals, but the senate ultimately tabled his proposal.[38] Four years later, northwestern California senators introduced a petition from whites in Mendocino County who complained about "white men cohabiting with squaws" and asked the legislature to ban the practice. Senators rejected the petition because any law against white-Indian intimacy would be unenforceable. They explained that "as long as 'flesh is weak' and 'temptation strong,' the evil cannot be remedied."[39] Despite their failure, both proposals represented legislative efforts to stamp out interracial intimacy and to police the racial boundaries of the household.[40]

The failure of Garter's bill and the Mendocino petition may have reflected growing unease with state intervention in white men's households. However much some northwestern California whites and free-soilers disapproved of the female captive trade and squaw men, at least some worried that efforts to break up Indian-white households undermined white men's control over their intimate domestic relations. In an article entitled "Legislature Interfering with 'Domestic Institutions,'" the editor of the *Humboldt Times* sympathized with the intent of Garter's bill but feared that it went "too far in its sumptuary restrictions in matrimonial alliances." Domestic relations between Indians and whites were undesirable, but the state legislature should not have such expansive power to "control any man's 'love matters.'" To the east, in Shasta County, one editor complained about the vigilante militias that invaded white men's homes and sent Indian women off to the reservations. "Household ties . . . have been ruthlessly severed on several occasions," he cried.[41] It is unclear how many northwestern California whites shared these sentiments, but it is possible that anxieties about state intrusion into white men's domestic affairs may have tempered efforts to suppress squaw men or the captivity of Native women.

Ambivalence or hostility toward state interference in Indian-white house-holds may also have made it much more difficult for Native women and their families to contest their captivity. Marginalized people whose enslavement was often informal and extralegal, individual captive women rarely appear in the historical record. A few extant sources suggest, though, that the political and discursive wrangling over the captive trade and squaw men did little to change the status of individual women. Despite growing criticism that the female captive trade ripped apart Native households and violated the rights of Indian husbands and notwithstanding mounting criticism of squaw men and miscegenation, legal officials often balked at depriving white men of the captive women in their households. Sharing northwestern California settlers' anxieties about state interference in domestic affairs, state judges and fed-eral Indian officials were reluctant to overrule white men's claims to Native women. Even in cases where white men blatantly ripped apart Native families by seizing married women, legal authorities ruled that the prerogatives of white captors superseded those of Indian husbands. They upheld white men's mastery over their domestic relations, even in the most blatant cases of kid-napping, and often at the expense of Indians' family ties.

The legal travails of two Mendocino County Indian residents, Mary and George Barham, illustrate how ideas about white men's mastery shaped the fates of captive women. In October 1861, George Barham, an acculturated Indian man who worked as a servant in a white household, petitioned the county court judge to issue a writ of habeas corpus for his fifteen-year-old wife, Mary. Barham, represented by a sympathetic white attorney, com-plained that C. S. Williams of Ukiah had kidnapped Mary and was holding her against her will. The petition alleged that the young woman's captivity was illegal, not just because she was held without her consent, but also be-cause it violated George Barham's marital rights. As her husband, George was "entitled to the custody of said Mary as his wife." To validate these claims, the attorney produced the Barhams' marriage certificate and white witnesses who testified that Williams seized Mary "out of the care, custody and under the control of her husband" shortly after their wedding. The judge issued the writ, but Barham got little satisfaction. Williams avoided the charges by claiming that Mary had fled his home and that he could not find her to bring before the court.[42]

Mary did manage to escape and rejoin her husband. Just six months later, Williams made his own petition for a writ of habeas corpus in which he de-manded custody of the young woman. In it, he swore that he was entitled to Mary because he had recently apprenticed her under the amended Act for the Government and Protection of Indians. Williams complained that George Barham's employer, John Barham, retained the young woman as a servant and refused to render her up. He thus deprived Williams of Mary's "care, custody, control and earnings" due to him as her new master. When he delivered Mary Barham to the court, John Barham countered Williams's petition by emphasizing that the Native woman's presence in his household was natural and legitimate. She was the wife of his servant, George Barham, and, as such, remained with him in the Barham home voluntarily. Moreover, any apprenticeship was "fraudulent, illegal and void" because her husband never consented to it. The rights due George Barham as Mary's husband invalidated any claims Williams might make to her as an apprentice. The judge, however, ultimately ruled against Indian family rights. George and Mary Barham had no marital privileges that the courts were bound to respect. C. S. Williams was to have custody of Mary and enjoy her services for ten more years, until she turned twenty-five.[43] Once formally apprenticed, captive women owed their labor first to their white captors and only secondarily, if at all, to their Native husbands.

Around the same time that the Barhams entered the Mendocino County court, federal officers on the Mendocino Reservation wrestled with similar questions about the competing rights of husbands and captors. In 1860, a U.S. Army officer arrested and jailed a white man named Simpson for "removing an Indian woman, the wife of an Indian from the Reservation[,] against the wishes of her husband and herself." Simpson protested his incarceration by claiming that the woman and her husband had, until recently, been servants in his household. Moreover, he alleged that the husband abused the woman and had threatened to kill her if she did not run away with him to the reservation. Drawing upon timeworn stereotypes about Indian men's mistreatment of their wives, Simpson stated that "he had acted from the finest motive of humanity" by rescuing the woman. Simpson then argued that his rights to the woman overshadowed those of her husband. Like C. S. Williams, Mary Barham's captor, he claimed that he had recently bound his captive under the Act for the Government and Protection of Indians. The arresting officer remained unsympathetic to Simpson, but the federal agent in charge of the reservation intervened on the kidnapper's behalf. He contended that state Indian apprenticeship laws mandated the separation of husband and wife to satisfy Simpson's claims to the woman's labor. He let Simpson keep the woman in his custody.[44] Like the judge in the Barham case, the agent declined to interfere in the domestic affairs of white men and determined that the claims of captors superseded those of husbands.

The fates of women like Mary Barham and the anonymous reservation captive revealed an important contradiction. Critics of the captive trade argued that white men's buying and selling of Native women's bodies usurped the gender and household relationships that underpinned free society. This commerce in women represented a dangerous intrusion of male lust and the market into the sacred institutions of family and marriage. Yet, these same kinds of arguments about the sanctity of the home ultimately gave captive women and their male kinfolk little recourse before the law. State legal officials, unwilling or unable to interfere with the intimate domestic affairs of white men, rarely intervened to remove women from the households of their captors. Condemning the trade in captive women as a dangerous subversion of Indian family relations was one thing; providing legal protections for Indian households that safeguarded Native women from the domestic claims of white men was quite another. This dissonance between discourse and legal reality repeated itself throughout the 1850s as Californians struggled to make sense of a newer, transpacific traffic that brought thousands of Chinese women to California's shores.

Trafficking Chinese Women in California

In 1861, the *Trinity Journal*, a northwestern California newspaper that carried dozens of stories about the dangers of squaw men, turned its attention to a different social evil. Since the early 1850s, gold deposits had lured thousands of miners to the Trinity-Shasta area. Among these new migrants were hundreds of Chinese men and a lesser number of Chinese women. Like many other California newsmen before him, the Trinity editor fretted about the dangers of this new population, and he repeated familiar anti-Chinese arguments. Chinese men depressed white men's wages by working cheaply; they carried the state's mineral resources off to China; they were coolie slaves owned by Chinese merchants. He concluded, however, that Chinese gender relations posed the greatest problem for the state. "Most Chinese women in California are slaves," he assured his readers, "as abject and servile as the blackest, kinky-headed negro in Louisiana." Chinese women's enslavement was predicated on sex rather than on race. It was their fate, as women, to be "bought and sold among male Chinamen as any other property."[45] Combating California's "Chinese Problem" required eliminating the sale of women that underpinned Chinese gender relations.

The *Journal* editor's focus on the enslavement of Chinese women illuminates the shifting ground of anti-Chinese sentiment in California across the

1850s. Ever since the gold rush, calls for Chinese exclusion focused on the alleged unfree status of male Chinese "coolies." The arrival of greater numbers of Chinese women, many of whom worked in the commercialized sex trade, brought the status of Chinese prostitutes to the forefront of the anti-Chinese critique. Taking aim at Chinatown brothels, opponents of Chinese immigration insisted that the way Chinese migrants organized their sexual and gender relations posed as much of a threat to the state's social and moral order as the coolie trade. Much like the protests against Indian women's captivity, criticisms of Chinese prostitution focused on women's sexual servitude and the way it subverted idealized white visions of middle-class home and family life. Anti-Chinese critics argued that rather than being wives and mothers, almost all Chinese women in the state were enslaved prostitutes whose bodies, labor, and sexual virtue were freely bartered among their countrymen. At times, whites blamed this trade on male Chinese procurers and brothel keepers, brutal slaveholders who profited from buying and selling both the persons and the sexual services of Chinese women. At other times, however, they attributed the traffic in bound prostitutes to Chinese gender, family, and household relations. They argued that all Chinese men were tyrannical patriarchs who claimed outrageous property rights in their female kin and freely bought and sold their wives and daughters into prostitution. Instead of shielding women from the market, Chinese men regarded them as commodities and treated intimate relations of home and family as mere economic transactions. Chinese women were never wholly innocent victims in these narratives. They lacked natural feminine virtues of modesty and chastity, and these weaknesses often contributed to their downfall. Ultimately, traffics in Chinese women came to represent a troubling intrusion of the market into (supposedly) nonmarketable domestic relations that grew out of defective Chinese manhood and womanhood.[46]

The assertion that many Chinese women arrived in California as bound prostitutes had some basis in social reality. During the early 1850s, a small number of Chinese women like Ah Toy achieved financial independence and upward mobility by selling sexual services and companionship to a multiracial clientele. Some of these women even employed or purchased other women to work for them. Opportunities for these independent prostitutes diminished, however, by around 1854. Control over prostitution and its profits passed out of the hands of female entrepreneurs and into those of Chinese men, as tongs, secret societies and brotherhoods, consolidated their control over commercialized vice establishments. Chinese women who worked in tong-operated brothels had very little control over their earnings and labor.

Most had arrived in California as part of a complex transpacific traffic. Procurers purchased young women from their poverty-stricken families in southern China or kidnapped and decoyed them in port cities. They then transported them to California and sold or transferred them to Chinese already resident in the state.[47] Sale was indeed the lot of many young Chinese women who arrived in California's ports.

While anti-Chinese critics were quick to cast nearly all imported Chinese women as chattel slaves bound for brothels, the reality was far more complex and ambiguous. Many young peasant women and girls sold by poverty-stricken families did end up in the world of sexual commerce in China or in Chinese communities abroad. Still, not all became bound prostitutes. Some might be purchased by wealthy men as secondary wives and concubines. Chinese law recognized these relationships, and the children that came from them, as legitimate. In fact, one missionary acquainted with Chinese women in California speculated that instead of being bound for brothels as slaves, most became secondary wives who lived with migrant men "in a respectable way according to Chinese domestic customs." Finally, a significant number of bound female immigrants did not end up in the sex trade at all. Many younger women and girls arrived as mui tsai, "indentured domestic servants," who performed household chores and cared for young children in Chinese American homes.[48] The claim that most Chinese women were enslaved prostitutes resulted from whites' failure to recognize a range of household relationships—from polygamy to concubinage to domestic servitude—in which economic exchange in women might take place.

Even the assertion that bound Chinese prostitutes were chattel slaves whose condition resembled that of southern African Americans simplified a messy, ambiguous set of labor relationships. Tongs and brothel keepers did buy and sell women, but this commerce was often tangled in shadowy webs of debt and contractual relations. Many Chinese prostitutes worked under a system of debt bondage in which they labored to pay brothel keepers and tongs for their passage to California and money advanced them for their living expenses. In theory, a woman could escape the system by paying back her creditors in full. In reality, most got trapped in an endless cycle of debt, and their employers sold them to other men to recoup the money. Sometimes women who did not arrive in California as prostitutes wound up in the trade if their families accumulated debts. California newspapers reported many cases of tongs seizing and selling women into brothels when their husbands defaulted on loans.[49]

Over the years, this system of debt bondage seems to have developed into formal, contractual indentured servitude. Brothel keepers eventually required women to sign contracts or "bills of sale" in which they ostensibly agreed to work as prostitutes until they had repaid their debts. In an 1873 contract, the earliest known to exist, a woman named Ah Ho "distinctly agree[d] to give her body" to a man named Yee-Kwan "for service as a prostitute for four years." All of her earnings would go to pay back money advanced for her transportation and living expenses. The promise of future freedom was probably illusory. Yee-Kwan could extend Ah Ho's term of labor for every day of work that she missed due to illness, which probably included time lost to menstruation and pregnancy. He might also increase her debt by charging her steep fees for room and board.[50] In this way, temporary debt bondage could extend indefinitely. Ah Ho and women like her were neither freely contracting individuals nor absolute chattels. Like "peons" and "coolies" before them, they occupied a confusing, indeterminate status between free and unfree that unwitting whites simply labeled "slavery."

"Harlot-Serfs": Representing Traffics in Chinese Women

The complex labor, economic, gender, and family relationships that brought some Chinese women to California defied easy categorization as slavery. And yet, whites who dissected the traffic in Chinese prostitutes either ignored or failed to appreciate this complexity. Instead, they marked prostitutes as victims of degenerate and unnatural Chinese gender and sexual relations. All Chinese men claimed extensive property rights in female bodies. All (or most) Chinese women were commodities bought and sold in the market. Like anticoolieism, the critique of prostitution cast anti-Chinese arguments as antislavery arguments. Chinese were dangerous and undesirable immigrants not just because Chinese men worked as abject coolies, but because these same Chinese men regarded all women, even their own family members, as slaves.

Throughout the 1850s, anti-Chinese depictions of Chinese prostitution abounded in the imagery of the slave market. They dehumanized and animalized Chinese women, representing them as so many pieces of property, so many head of cattle, traded back and forth among Chinese men. A writer for the Alta California explained in 1857 that "the Chinese enslave their women and hold them more in the light of cattle than human beings." An interior paper agreed and alleged that the animal-like status accorded Chinese women made their lives almost worthless. Once Chinese men had forced their female "slaves to the commission of the vilest crimes, and when sickness and disease come upon these unfortunate creatures . . . they are taken out like beasts and unmercifully put to death."[51] For the editor of the *Sacramento Daily Union*, the Chinese treatment of women rivaled the coolie system in brutality and moral turpitude. "In the control and management of Chinese women, a system of slavery is known to exist, worse, in our estimation than Southern slavery," he declared. Southern masters had to provide for their bondpeople's upkeep, but "the owners of those miserable human beings called Chinese women" readily disposed of their chattels' lives without any restraint. He concluded that Chinese prostitution was such a "stigma upon American civilization" that it justified the complete expulsion of Chinese from California.[52]

The brutal slave trade in Chinese women was all the more disturbing because it was neither limited to prostitutes nor unique to California. Critics of prostitution insisted that the condition of Chinese women in California brothels reflected the servile and degraded status of all women in the Chinese Empire. Ignoring the economic exchange in women's bodies that structured their own marriage practices, they alleged that Chinese husbands regarded marriage as an economic transaction, a property relation rather than a family relation. They avidly bought and sold their wives and profited from their shame. Chinese family and domestic relations were a sham. Marriage and prostitution were interchangeable and nearly indistinguishable from one another. Male Chinese migrants were utterly unassimilable, critics of Chinese immigration concluded, because their womenfolk were always marketable.

Anti-Chinese analyses of woman trafficking drew frequent comparisons between Chinese wives and Chinese prostitutes. They charged that the two groups of women occupied similar positions in Chinese society and that, in fact, many prostitutes were former wives sold into sexual slavery. The *San Francisco Bulletin* referred to enslaved Chinese prostitutes and their employers as being married "according to the Chinese fashion," suggesting that there was little difference between wives and prostitutes. That same year, a *Bulletin* reporter explained that the status of married Chinese women differed little from that of the miserable slaves who worked in Chinatown brothels. "As is tolerably well known, the relations between Chinamen and their women in this country is generally a mere matter of bargain and sale," he noted.[53] Other observers argued that marriage between Chinese immigrant men and women was little more than a method for conveying Chinese women into sexual servitude. In an 1858 article called "A Traffic in Chinawomen," the *Alta California* alleged that many Chinese men went through "the formality of a marriage with some Chinese female." These marriages were "valueless for all moral purposes, in the eyes of the parties to the hymeneal bond," and were merely preludes to sale and slavery. Once the woman was safely in the "possession

Mug shot of Ah Jim, "kidnapper," 1875. Sacramento authorities arrested dozens of men who were accused of kidnapping and enslaving Chinese prostitutes. "Ah Jim," photographed and described here in a police mug shot book, was indicted for abducting a Chinese woman and forcibly conveying her to another county (presumably to sell her to a brothel). Center for Sacramento History, Sacramento Police Department Collection, 1995/13/0079. Reproduced by permission of the Center for Sacramento History, Sacramento, Calif.

of her so-called husband," he transported her to an interior mining town "where he sells her for a sum varying according to the diminutiveness of her feet, and other personal attractions." This dual system of marriage and slavery was so widespread in California, the *Alta* charged, that state lawmakers should prohibit justices of the peace from marrying any Chinese couple.[54]

In many of these anti-Chinese narratives, the "sold wife" became a powerful symbol of normative gender relations turned upside down. Descriptions of Chinese "domestic life" charted the perils of Chinese women in a marriage market that was little different from a slave market and who faced the horror of sale at any time. In 1860, the *California Police Gazette*, known for its sensation-alized crime stories, recounted the harrowing story of "a Chinaman named Pow How." When Pow How caught his wife gambling, he immediately sold her to another man for $400. The woman, the *Gazette* reported, found that death was her only escape from sale. She committed suicide by overdosing on opium. A decade later, the narrative of the sold wife had changed little. In 1869, the *Gazette* reprinted "Sale of a Wife." This much more lighthearted story recounted the trials of "Miss Ti-Ting, a beautiful, accomplished and dove-like daughter from the Flowery Kingdom." Ti-Ting arrived in Califor-nia a bought woman; a Grass Valley Chinese merchant had purchased her as a wife. Her new husband soon grew jealous of her friendship with another Chinese man, but as "he had bought and paid for her . . . how to get his money back was the only thought that kept him awake o'nights." The story concluded with the husband recouping his investment by selling Ti-Ting off to another merchant.[55] Whether real or fictionalized, Ti-Ting embodied the commodified Chinese wife—purchased by her husband, she could be sold at any time.

As much as anti-Chinese critics denounced Chinese men for selling wives like prostitutes and prostitutes like cattle, many suggested that female traf-ficking could not be blamed on Chinese manhood alone. Defective Chinese womanhood also spurred the trade. Historian George Anthony Peffer argues that, by the 1870s, California whites who sympathized with young victims of "white slavery" usually depicted Chinese prostitutes as semi-willing accom-plices in their own enslavement. They tempered their outrage at Chinese fe-male slavery by asserting that most of its victims were immoral women easily tricked or lured into bondage by promises of easy fortune. These attitudes also pervaded anti-Chinese writing in the 1850s and early 1860s. Whites portrayed bound prostitutes as both victims of a cruel system of slavery and debauched women whose lack of virtue brought them to their fate. The *Alta California* editor that expressed sympathy for enslaved Chinese prostitutes through-out the 1850s also denounced them as "a class of beastly creatures . . . more disgusting than brutes and more repulsive than vermin." These "abandoned creatures" sat in the windows of their "vile dens" beckoning to passersby and exposing white children to displays "too revolting to be told in the columns of a public newspaper." The women "should be exterminated at once from the country," he concluded. The *Trinity Journal* editor who cried that women were "bought and sold among male Chinamen as any other property" also cast these female victims as grotesque purveyors of disease and immorality. They were "miserable, wretched harlot-serfs—putrid, festering, moral sores in every community where they exist."[56] As the use of the term "harlot-serf" suggests, anti-Chinese writers could not decide whether trafficked Chinese women were pitiable victims of forced sexual servitude or whether their innate immorality made them willing slaves.

In the 1850s and 1860s, anti-Chinese writers represented the international traffic in Chinese women as a peculiar outgrowth of the way that Chinese migrants ordered gender, marriage, family, and sexual relations. The intensely patriarchal nature of Chinese society reduced most Chinese women, even wives, to objects of "bargain and sale." Some concluded, too, that trafficked Chinese women might bear some of the blame for their own condition. Chinese women's defective womanhood, their lack of a proper sense of decency or morality, made it easy for procurers and brothel keepers to bind them in the first place. The Chinese "harlot-serf," a woman who was both a victim of Chinese men's greed and lust and a slave to her own vile passions, remained a staple of California anti-Chinese literature for decades to come.

Bound Chinese Women and the Courts: The Case of In Re Quin Ti

Representations of female trafficking extended outside the realm of discourse. They shaped both the administration and enforcement of the law and the lives of bound Chinese women. Doubly oppressed by gender inequalities in the Chinese community and the racism and sexism of dominant white society, Chinese prostitutes had limited power to contest their conditions.[57] Still, these women regularly appeared before the courts in the 1850s and 1860s and tried to use the legal system to their advantage. Some women, particularly those who had escaped from brothels, appealed to the courts for protection when their former employers tried to kidnap them or have them arrested on false charges. Others relied on Chinese men—husbands, husbands-to-be, and lovers—to petition judges for writs of habeas corpus that would release them from brothels.[58] In all of these cases, bound women and the men in their lives found their futures shaped and constrained by white assumptions about Chinese gender and family life. Images of tyrannical slaveholding Chinese men could work to the advantage of Chinese women when they sought to escape their employers. On the other hand, stereotypes about degenerate Chinese womanhood could hamper women's claims to protection and freedom.

But whites never had complete narrative control over legal proceedings. Chinese women and men presented their own stories, which appealed to or challenged Anglo discourses about Chinese gender relations. Chinese women and their attorneys played to stereotypes about Chinese female slavery to convince judges to intervene against their employers. Chinese men, from brothel keepers to community leaders to husbands and lovers, also tried to shape court proceedings by setting forth their own interpretations of Chinese gender, family, and marriage practices. California's courtrooms became key sites of discursive struggle, among both whites and Chinese, over the buying and selling of women.

These conflicts emerged most clearly in *In Re Quin Ti*, a kidnapping case that came before the Sacramento District Court during the fall of 1859. It revolved around a Chinese woman named Ma Ho—who was either a fugitive from forced prostitution or a delinquent wife—and her relationship to a man named Chu Quong—who was either a scheming, slaveholding brothel keeper or an abandoned husband. Both sought custody of Ma Ho's daughter, six-year-old Quin Ti. Throughout the proceedings, Anglo and Chinese participants struggled to exercise narrative control over the case and to uncover the "true" identities of Ma Ho and Chu Quong. They offered up competing, often contradictory representations of Chinese gender relationships and the trafficking of women in Chinese American communities.

The case began in Sacramento's small Chinese quarter in November 1859. There, Ma Ho supported herself and Quin Ti by working as a prostitute. Unlike many Chinese women in the world of sexual commerce, Ma Ho appears to have been an independent operator who kept her earnings for herself. This was hard-won independence. Between 1857 and 1859, she endured at least three different kidnapping attempts. Brothel keepers had her arrested on "frivolous" and "trumped-up" charges so they could capture and sell her. She thwarted her abductors every time, usually by appealing for help from Sacramento police and judges.[59] On the morning of November 3, 1859, Ma Ho faced a new threat. While she slept, a party of Chinese men led by Chu Quong seized Quin Ti and spirited her out of the city. Ma Ho reported the abduction to the Sacramento police. They tracked down and arrested the kidnappers.[60] The *Sacramento Daily Union* announced that the recovery of Quin Ti saved Ma Ho from almost certain slavery, as "the object of the kidnappers [was] to secure possession of the mother, supposing that she would follow in pursuit of her child." But events soon took an unexpected turn. The imprisoned Chu Quong secured white attorneys and petitioned for a writ of habeas corpus for Quin Ti. He claimed that he was Ma Ho's husband and Quin Ti's biological father. He also demanded custody of the child. Ma Ho protested that Chu Quong had once held her as a slave in a brothel and that he was not Quin Ti's father.[61]

What began as a seemingly cut-and-dry case of thwarted kidnapping soon turned into a more complicated matter as different white and Chinese participants constructed competing narratives of Ma Ho and Chu Quong's relationship. At stake were central questions: Was Chu Quong married to Ma Ho or did he own her? Were the couple husband and wife or master and slave? And what was the difference between these positions in Chinese communities? Throughout the case, most whites held fast to the notion that Chinese men regarded women as property and sold them as slaves. In its reports on the case, the *Sacramento Daily Union* observed that a "system of genuine slavery exists among the Chinese, so far as their women in this country are concerned." Women were "bought and sold as regularly as negroes are in Texas," and most of them were "forced to live the life of prostitutes for the pecuniary benefit of their Chinese masters."[62] Since Chinese women were often or always marketable, some whites reasoned that it might be impossible to determine whether Ma Ho was Chu Quong's wife or his slave. Ma Ho's lawyer, for instance, asked witnesses if Chu Quong had purchased Ma Ho before marrying her and, more tellingly, inquired whether Chinese husbands frequently put their wives into houses of prostitution. The judge, John McKune, chalked up the confusion over Chu Quong and Ma Ho's status to the peculiar habits of the Chinese. The difficulty of distinguishing wives from enslaved prostitutes, he remarked, "could not occur except for the introduction of a large population of Mongolians among our Anglo Saxon race."[63] For white observers, relations between Chinese men and women were predicated on sale and enslavement, making marriage and sexual servitude nearly indistinguishable from one another.

White legal officials and newspaper reporters exerted narrative dominance over the hearing, but Chinese participants, both litigants and observers, attempted to seize discursive control over the proceedings. They challenged (and sometimes appealed to) white assumptions about defective Chinese gender relationships by presenting their own narratives about Chinese family, marriage, and domestic life. For his part, Chu Quong, the alleged kidnapper, invoked discourses about marital duty and female virtue that highlighted stereotypes of Chinese women's immorality. He stated that Ma Ho had married him in China, lived with him in California for three years, and given birth to his daughter. But she "violated her marriage vows" by running away with the child and voluntarily taking up the life of a prostitute. In the formulaic legal phrasing of Chu Quong's lawyer, Ma Ho was morally degenerate and "unfit to superintend the raising, education, and morals of said child." Chu Quong, in contrast, was a devoted patriarch whose only crime had been rescuing his daughter from an immoral and unfaithful wife.[64]

For her part, Ma Ho, with the help of her lawyer, disputed these claims. She testified that Chu Quong was her former owner, not her husband. Her narrative of events echoed that of white observers by emphasizing the repeated sale of her body. She had arrived as an imported prostitute in 1852, and Chu Quong had purchased her for $600. He took her to a mining town and forced her to work as a prostitute until she finally escaped from him. In the emphatic words of her attorney, the couple had never lived as husband and wife, and "the only relation that ever existed between them was that of master and slave." Moreover, Chu Quong had no legitimate claims to Quin Ti. The little girl was Ma Ho's child by a white man. Countering Chu Quong's accusation that she was an unfit wife and mother, Ma Ho's lawyer invoked a language of maternal rights. "She, as the mother of said child, is her natural guardian and entitled to [her] custody, care and control," he argued.[65] Chinese litigants and their lawyers presented their own narratives—of faithful husbands betrayed by immoral Chinese women and innocent mothers forced into sexual slavery—that both undermined and appealed to prevailing white assumptions about Chinese gender, family, and sexual relationships.

Nonetheless, white assessments of Chu Quong and Ma Ho's relationship, not Chinese ones, prevailed. When it came time to make his ruling, Judge McKune decided that the identities of Chu Quong and Ma Ho were still inscrutable. One thing was clear. Regardless of whether Chu Quong and Ma Ho were husband and wife or master and slave, neither was fit to keep Quin Ti. Chu Quong was a kidnapper and probably a brothel keeper. Ma Ho (even if she had been a slave) was an immoral woman and a prostitute. The child's moral welfare was best served by putting her in the care of a local white family. McKune resolved the dilemma at the heart of the case by placing Quin Ti beyond the reach of both Ma Ho and Chu Quong.[66]

But even then, McKune did not have the last word. After the habeas corpus hearing, a Sacramento jury found Chu Quong and one of his accomplices, Ah Chon, guilty of kidnapping. Each faced a year in prison at San Quentin. After appealing to the California Supreme Court and losing his case, Chu Quong served his full term.[67] At that point, several prominent members of the Chinese community met and wrote a petition to Governor John Downey asking him to pardon the accomplice, Ah Chon. The petitioners (all men) declared that Chu Quong and Ma Ho were legally married and that Quin Ti was Chu Quong's legitimate daughter. Ma Ho was an immoral woman who had "violated her marriage vows, and become a prostitute" while her husband toiled away in the mines to support the family. Chu Quong wanted to secure the child so that he could send her back to his family in China "to be raised, and make [her] feet small, according to the custom of China."[68] This narrative, which cast Ma Ho as an immoral Chinese woman and Chu Quong as a dutiful patriarch, struck a chord with Governor Downey. He pardoned Ah Chon, declaring that the man had been "simply . . . assisting [the] Father to take his legitimate child away from a house of prostitution." His actions demonstrated more "merit than criminality" and he should go free.[69] Unlike McKune, Downey concluded that the relationship between Chu Quong and Ma Ho was self-evidently and unambiguously that of a faithful husband betrayed by an immoral wife.

The trials of Ma Ho, Chu Quong, and Quin Ti exposed the discursive struggles that raged over Chinese women's status in the courts. The whites to whom Ma Ho appealed for aid assumed that slavery was simply Chinese women's lot in life. Most Chinese women, even wives and daughters, were marketable. There were no meaningful distinctions among marriage, prostitution, and slavery in Chinese communities. Most also blamed Chinese women's condition on their defective moral characters. For both Judge McKune and Governor Downey, Ma Ho's alleged immorality was as important to explaining her descent into prostitution as her history of sale and enslavement. These representations were unstable and subject to contestation. Chinese like Chu Quong, Ma Ho, and the men who defended Ah Chon set forth alternative narratives of the relationships between husbands and wives that challenged or took advantage of white assumptions about Chinese women's absolute marketability. White men may have held the power in the courts, but they rarely retained total narrative power over legal proceedings involving trafficked Chinese women.

The discursive and legal contests over the fate of bound Chinese women represented a larger struggle over the meanings of female freedom in nineteenth-century California. Like the journalists and attorneys who decried Ma Ho's enslavement, white Californians who were critical of woman trafficking held a particular set of assumptions about proper relations between men and women. Drawing on idealized visions of the middle-class household, they considered marriage and home as institutions that lay outside of the realm of the market. Within them, men shielded women's labor and bodies from being made objects of commerce. The buying and selling of female bodies disrupted these expectations. For white observers, the trade in captive Native women, as well as the international traffic in Chinese prostitutes, represented disturbing intrusions of the market into domestic life that made intimate sexual, gender, and household relations into commercial transactions. They blamed these horrifying traffics on deficient and degraded gender relations perpetrated by men who were either nonwhite—like the tyrannical Chinese brothel keepers—or ambiguously white—like the northwestern California squaw men. All the while, white opponents of these traffics remained blind to the irony that they held up white middle-class gender relations, founded on women's economic and physical subordination to men, as safeguards of women's liberty. These contradictions extended into the Civil War and Reconstruction eras as California's new Republican leadership confronted woman trafficking in the wake of national slave emancipation.

CHAPTER SIX

Emancipating California

California's Unfree Labor Systems in the Crucible of the Civil War

Six months after the Confederate surrender at Appomattox, Peter Anderson, African American editor of San Francisco's *Pacific Appeal*, rejoiced that the Union victory in the Civil War had transformed California. A "free-born state" that was "in her infancy . . . nurtured and taught slave State proclivities," California was being reconstructed just as surely as the former Confederacy. Anderson had good reason to be optimistic. Chivalry Democrats, who had long supported involuntary servitude, slaveholder property rights, and the westward expansion of slavery, had fled to fight for the Confederacy or faded into the background of political life. Up-and-coming Republican leaders joined northern-born, free-soil Democrats who had been alienated by southern Chivalry Democrats' incessant demands for slaveholding rights in the West and the killing of David C. Broderick. Together they formed a new Union Party dedicated to preserving the Union, crushing secession, and supporting Abraham Lincoln's administration. During the height of its power, from 1862 to 1865, the Union Party endorsed the Emancipation Proclamation and denounced slavery as "an institution condemned by God and abhorrent to humanity." Four months after the Emancipation Proclamation took effect, the new party voted to repeal California's prohibitions on black testimony, which had once subjected African American residents to abuse and reenslavement. By the end of the war, the state, in Anderson's words, resembled "a regenerated Southern man who has declared in favor of unrestricted freedom." He hoped state legislators would complete California's emancipation by giving African American men the vote. After all, it would not do for California to play the "hypocrite" by endorsing black suffrage in the South "without the least disposition of granting the right herself."[1]

While Peter Anderson framed the death of slavery as a victory for California's African Americans, the Civil War and emancipation also brought far-reaching changes for the state's diverse peoples and labor systems. As East Coast Republicans dismantled African American slavery, California's Republicans and free-soil Democrats, fused together in the Union Party, identified, denounced, and eradicated a variety of state labor systems that seemed incompatible with the national march toward emancipation. Systems of slavery, apprenticeship, contract labor, and sexual trafficking that had persisted since the gold rush all came under scrutiny. In the aftermath of the war, some forms of bound labor began a long decline; others dissolved altogether or took on new forms. California embarked on its own journey through emancipation and reconstruction alongside the North and the South.[2]

Emancipation and Reconstruction, uneven and incomplete processes across the United States, were especially complex in California. The state's tangled web of bound labor systems, its racial and ethnic diversity, and the tenuousness of the Republican-Democratic fusion in the Union Party ensured that emancipation had radically divergent consequences for different groups of Californians. Radical Republicans in the Union Party successfully mobilized free-labor, pro-Union, and antislavery arguments to repeal the anti–black testimony laws that had once propped up the proslavery regime and African American bondage. Still, when these same men pressed for testimony rights for American Indians and Chinese, they ran up against former Democrats in the Union Party who argued that the measures would collapse all racial hierarchies and degrade whites. Republicans' own ambivalent attitudes about American Indians' capacity for civilization and citizenship also limited emancipation for Native peoples. Republicans abolished Indian apprenticeship in 1863 and worked to suppress trafficking in Indian women. Yet they supported laws that punished Indian "vagrants" and convicts with compulsory labor and subjected Native reservation dwellers to a harsh regime of labor discipline.

Emancipation had especially contradictory outcomes for Chinese men and women. The fragile Union Party coalition split on the issue of Chinese immigration. Radical Republicans argued that Chinese workers should be granted the same rights and privileges as workingmen of other races, while more conservative Republicans and Democrats insisted that they were coolie slaves whose presence endangered a nation newly dedicated to free labor. Republicans who condemned the kidnapping and captivity of American Indian women also took a far more ambivalent stance regarding sexual trafficking in Chinese women. Union Party efforts to break up Chinese prostitution cast Chinese women either as abused slaves of their tyrannical countrymen or as immoral women whose degraded condition resulted from their own depravity. The first depiction affirmed Chinese men's unfitness for immigration and citizenship. The second justified the exclusion and expulsion of Chinese women in the name of preserving public moral welfare. In California, then, emancipation did not solely, or even centrally, involve questions of African American freedom, nor did it follow a straightforward trajectory from bondage to liberty for the state's diverse peoples.

"Relics of Barbarism and Slavery": Dismantling California's Proslavery Regime

In August 1860, just a few months before secession, a free black man petitioned a Napa County court to release his teenaged son from slavery. Aaron Rice alleged that his former master, William Rice, held his son Nathaniel in bondage. Like dozens of westward-bound slaveholders before him, William Rice had made an informal arrangement with his bondpeople. He promised Aaron Rice and his entire family freedom in exchange for a period of labor in California. The elder Rice had either managed to escape from his master or had completed his end of the bargain; now he wanted William Rice to grant the freedom that had been promised to his son. The Napa County court judge issued a writ of habeas corpus and ordered William Rice's arrest. At Rice's hearing, however, the judge concluded that the master had used "no coercion" to keep the family laboring for him in California. To all appearances, father and son had voluntarily traveled to California and entered into contracts to work for William Rice there. There was simply "no evidence" that Rice had worked the African Americans as slaves in violation of the state constitution. In reality, there was probably considerable evidence of the men's enslavement, it was just not admissible in California's courts. The state's refusal to allow African American testimony against whites—a prohibition that had long worked against the interests of slaves—prevented Aaron and Nathaniel Rice from taking the witness stand. The judge dismissed the suit. William Rice continued to hold Nathaniel until his "contract" expired and brought charges against Aaron Rice for perjury. The outcome of the case is unknown, but Aaron Rice may well have suffered fines and imprisonment for trying to secure his child's freedom.[3]

Incidents like the Rice case were rare in California by the 1860s. Fugitive slave trials declined rapidly after the departure of southern slaveholders in the mid-1850s, the liberation of Archy Lee, and the exodus of many Chivalry Democrats to the Confederacy in 1861. Nathaniel Rice was one of only four enslaved African Americans who tried to claim freedom in the California courts between 1861 and 1864.[4] Nonetheless, few black California activists were ready to celebrate the death of slavery and Chivalry rule. The anti–black testimony laws that kept Nathaniel Rice in servitude and left thousands of black Californians with little security for their persons or property were throwbacks to the state's earlier proslavery past. African American leaders maintained that California would remain a virtual slave state as long as these measures stayed on the books.

These arguments gained more force when Republicans and free-soil Democrats merged in 1862 to form the Union Party. Republicans in the Union Party, dedicated to equality before the law, contended that the prohibition of black testimony was a lingering vestige of slavery foisted upon the free state by proslavery Democrats who now rebelled against the federal government. They urged fellow legislators to emancipate California from treacherous laws that supported slavery, created invidious racial distinctions, and poisoned the state with the taint of secessionism. Divisions within the Union Party ensured, however, that attacks on race-based legal inequalities extended only so far. The moderate and conservative end of the new party, mainly made up of Democrats, balked at lifting all racial restrictions on testimony, especially those imposed on Chinese. They also stood firm against Republican efforts to expand suffrage to black men. The Union Party ultimately installed a limited version of Reconstruction that erased the remnants of the state's proslavery past without drastically remaking its racial order.

Prior to the Civil War, African Americans gained some support for testimony rights from the new branch of the state Republican Party. Many Republican legislators endorsed black petitions for testimony rights in the late 1850s, and Republican newspapers condemned the exclusion of African American evidence against whites. The ascendance of Republicans in national politics, the election of Republican Leland Stanford as California's governor, and strong Republican gains in the state legislature in the 1861 elections encouraged black rights activists.[5] They quickly mobilized pro-Union, antisecession, and antislavery arguments to appeal to the new Republican leadership. If California was to become a free state in earnest and break out of the grip of treacherous slaveholding southern Democrats, they proclaimed, it needed to remove the testimony laws that reduced black residents to a degraded and slavish condition. The premier issue of the *Pacific Appeal* denounced testimony restrictions as unworthy of a true free state. The laws were "relics of barbarism and slavery," editors Peter Anderson and Philip A. Bell wrote, and proslavery legislators used them to "degrade our manhood and inflict irreparable injury on our rights and liberties." A group of black

Californians sent yet another petition to the legislature asking for repeal in the name of ending slavery. In the United States, only people "held as slaves" suffered exclusion from the witness box, they observed. The ban on African American testimony had been entirely "incident to slavery," an artifact of the state's proslavery past. Human bondage was on its deathbed, and restrictions on black testimony should terminate along with it.[6]

These petitions won the support of those Republicans who genuinely embraced equality before the law and hoped to seize on the issue to discredit supporters of slavery and secession. Assemblyman Caleb Fay, a Republican who helped free a fugitive slave in 1852, proposed abolishing the ban on black testimony in both criminal and civil cases. Fay and his followers echoed African American petitioners' arguments. California needed to throw off proslavery, prosouthern rule and take its place among the nation's other free and loyal states. Repealing the ban on black testimony was the first step. Fay called the testimony law "a disgrace to the State" and one of California's "youthful follies" committed under the yoke of early proslavery dominance. Now the "spirit which would oppress the negro would be behind the spirit of the age," he remarked. Fay's fellow Republican from San Francisco, Samuel C. Bigelow, directly connected repeal and defeating slavery and secession. California remained a virtual slave state—out of step with the rest of the Union and held in the grip of treasonous slaveholder policies—as long as its black residents could not testify against whites. Repeal alone could "remove the last mark and badge, and burning brand of shame fixed upon this State by that class of men whose sympathies [are] with the men now in arms against the Government of the United States." Extending the metaphor of a branded slave, Bigelow urged fellow legislators to "remove this burning brand, this last remaining mark of ownership placed upon the State by [the] chivalry, nullification, pro-slavery, blow-the-top-of-your-head-off, secession crowd."[7]

Republicans faced opposition from Democrats, who, with the exception of a handful of northern-born free-soil men, condemned repeal on the grounds that admitting black testimony eroded white supremacy. As one Democratic assemblyman put it, "The negro race was universally recognized as an inferior race, and any attempt to elevate them would only result in degrading the white race to their level."[8] Resistance to black testimony reflected a broader set of racial anxieties. Most Democrats, and even some Republicans, feared that lifting prohibitions against African Americans might open the door to all nonwhite testimony. The 1850–51 statutes that barred black testimony against whites extended the same exclusions to people with more than one-half Indian ancestry in cases tried under the regular criminal and civil law. Through a series of tortured ethnological arguments, the California Supreme Court ruled in 1854 that the prohibition on Indian testimony also applied to Chinese because the two groups were nonwhite and descended from the same racial stock.[9] All of these exclusions might crumble away if the state admitted some nonwhites to the witness box.

In light of these arguments, most California Republicans, including Caleb Fay himself, insisted that only African Americans, not Chinese, should benefit from repeal. Some worried, in fact, that Chinese testimony would lead to an influx of slavish and degraded labor into the state. As William H. Sears, a strong Republican supporter of black testimony put it, black Californians were fellow Americans and Christians who deserved equality before the law. Chinese were dishonest "heathens" controlled by the Chinese Six Companies. They would testify to anything the Six Companies wanted and would use their access to the witness box to overturn the foreign miners' tax and other laws that kept their immigration in check. Throngs of Chinese would come to California, preventing "white men and women from gaining an honest livelihood" and driving "white girls" out of respectable employment altogether.[10] Far more was at stake than whether Chinese should enjoy equality before the law. Democrats and Republicans alike worried that any extension of legal rights to Chinese would encourage a coolie invasion, which would undermine the legal and economic supremacy of white Americans.

A few of the most radical Republicans countered that the only way to "break the coils of the proslavery, chivalric sentiment which has been thrown around the free state of California" was to lift all racial restrictions on testimony.[11] These arguments won little ground, as even the suggestion of extending testimony rights to Chinese torpedoed Republicans' efforts on behalf of American Americans. Republicans who managed to rally support for the measure in the assembly watched in dismay as the senate, where Republicans and Democrats were more evenly matched, indefinitely postponed the vote on both of Fay's criminal and civil testimony bills.[12]

The African American editors of the *Pacific Appeal* condemned the failure of the repeal bills as "unjust, illiberal, and oppressive." They held out hope that the fall elections would bring a clean sweep of the legislature and fill it with loyal Republicans eager to cut down any legislation associated with the old proslavery regime. "Another year," they projected, "and the people of California will be convinced that it is no longer to their interest to yield obedience to the demands of the Slave Oligarchy."[13] This prediction came true sooner than the editors anticipated. Over the spring and summer of 1862, Republicans gained considerable strength by cultivating ties with prominent northern-born, free-soil Democrats who shared their views. The two groups eventually fused into the Union Party, a new political party that emphasized the preservation of the Union, support for the war effort, and cooperation with the Lincoln administration. In the fall, the party ran candidates against the Union Democratic Party—moderate Democrats who supported the Union but who were critical of Lincoln and emancipation—and so-called Breckinridge or Lecompton Democrats—the remnants of the Chivalry who denounced Lincoln and advocated compromise with the Confederacy. Unionists, as party members styled themselves, won enormous majorities. They took 94 of 120 seats in the senate and assembly. The *Pacific Appeal* rejoiced that the Chivalry Democrats, the men who authored the "Mississippi-and-South-Carolina sections to the Civil and Criminal Practice [testimony] Act of this free state," had been ousted once and for all.[14]

Fusion did favor the African American cause. In 1863, the Unionist coalition revived the attack on the anti–black testimony laws, calling them backward, disloyal, proslavery enactments at odds with both liberty and Union. The "colored disability was placed upon the statute book at a time when the refuse ruffianism of South Carolina and Mississippi held high carnival in these halls," one new Unionist proclaimed; it harked back to the days when the "chivalry of the slave pen cracked their whips over the heads of recreant Northmen." He urged Unionists, "men who loved freedom," to "vote to destroy the last relic of slavery in California." Another Unionist, a former Democrat, cheered the law because it would "destroy the last remnant of copperhead Democracy, which had ruled the State so long." Repealing anti–black testimony laws was the new Union Party's first and best chance to roll back more than a decade of proslavery rule.[15]

Outnumbered almost ten-to-one in the senate and almost seven-to-one in the assembly, remaining Democrats could not outvote Unionists. Instead, they hammered away at the fault lines in the fragile Union Party alliance by again invoking the specter of Chinese testimony. Knowing that only some Radical Republicans and almost no Democrats in the Union Party supported Chinese entrance to the witness box, they insisted that permitting black testimony would force the state to accept Chinese testimony as well. If the Union Party opened the courts to African Americans, it could hardly deny similar rights to 60,000 California Chinese, who were far more "industrious, enterprising and wealthy" than their black counterparts. Unionists were either hypocrites who unwarrantedly elevated degraded African Americans above more qualified Chinese or they were enemies of white supremacy who secretly sought to admit all nonwhites to testimony rights. The latter course would ruin California, because, as one Democrat claimed, it would be "the first step toward the elevation of the inferior races upon the Pacific coast to terms of equality with the white race."[16]

Democrats' protests that knocking down one racial barrier might collapse all racial distinctions failed to sway the Union Party on the issue of African American testimony rights. Both houses voted to strike out antiblack language from the state's Criminal and Civil Practice Acts. But Democratic assertions that testimony reform threatened to destabilize all racial hierarchies may have widened rifts in the Unionist ranks. Most Unionists ignored calls for race-neutral testimony laws from the Radical Republican end of the party. Unionists' revised testimony law retained language banning Indian evidence against whites in regular criminal and civil cases. It also formalized, for the first time, the prohibition on Chinese testimony that the California Supreme Court established in its 1854 ruling. No "Mongolian, or Chinese" would be "permitted to give evidence in favor or against any white person."[17] Unionists who rallied to destroy the anti–black testimony law as "a relic of slavery" moved quickly to shore up racial barriers against other groups of people who stood to benefit from the collapse of the proslavery regime.

African Americans in California hailed repeal in 1863 as the overthrow of Chivalry politicians who had "persist[ed] in keeping us down on the level of slaves." Now able to testify against whites in court, black Californians enjoyed rights to defend their liberty and their property denied them since the gold rush. Other events in 1863 suggested, however, that the destruction of California's proslavery political regime was far from complete. Lincoln's Emancipation Proclamation, issued on September 22, 1862, and effective on January 1, 1863, weakened the Republican-Democratic alliance of the Union Party and invigorated Democrats who were sympathetic to slaveholding rights. In January 1863, California's Unionist-dominated legislature became the first in the nation to pass resolutions endorsing the Emancipation Proclamation. The gesture both heartened and surprised Republicans, who marveled that a state "so long chivalry-ridden" was the first to come out in favor of black freedom.[18] But this symbolic unity masked growing fractures in the Union coalition. Unionists in the assembly only reluctantly voted for the Emancipation Proclamation resolutions. They refused to approve it until their colleagues scrapped a strong statement endorsing slave liberation in favor of a lukewarm declaration that emancipation was merely a wartime necessity. Even this was too much for some Democrats in the Union Party. Alienated by the repeal of the anti–black testimony laws and emancipation, they rejoined their former party in the spring of 1863. Reunited with anti-Lincoln Democrats, they adopted a party platform that "denounce[d] and unqualifiedly condemn[ed] the emancipation proclamation" as an unnecessary measure that encouraged slave rebellion in the South.[19]

Democratic resistance to emancipation dogged Unionists in the legislature for another two years. As late as December 1865, a small group of Democrats tried to obstruct California's ratification of the Thirteenth Amendment. Black freedom would automatically lead to black suffrage and black domination, they said. The state should not ratify the measure without sending a remonstrance to Congress denying the power of the "Federal Government to interfere with, the right of suffrage or the elective franchise in any of the States." The states should be able to exclude black voters as they saw fit. The Thirteenth Amendment still passed easily, but the vocal protests against black freedom and political participation indicated that Chivalry was not yet dead in California.[20]

The question of black suffrage ultimately helped break the Union Party coalition. In the two and a half years after the end of the Civil War, many Democrats bolted the alliance and joined the reinvigorated Democratic Party. Linking black voting rights to black domination, white degradation, and the eventual enfranchisement of servile Chinese "coolies," Democrats made up for wartime losses. They swept California elections in 1867 and won back a majority of the state's political offices by pledging "no negro or Chinese suffrage."[21] Once in office, they refused to ratify the Fourteenth and Fifteenth amendments and fought African Americans' efforts to secure public schooling for their children. Peter Anderson's 1865 declaration that California had been reconstructed, finally transformed from a quasi–slave state to a state dedicated to "unrestricted freedom," appeared premature.

"An Unholy Traffic in Human Blood and Souls": Emancipating California Indians

In April 1863, as Unionists in Sacramento congratulated themselves on reforming state testimony laws and eliminating "the last relic of slavery in California," the Mendocino County coroner held an inquest into the death of a ten-year-old Indian servant. The girl, known as Rosa, had been "apprenticed to Mrs. Basset" of Ukiah. When the coroner arrived, he found the dead girl "nearly naked, lying in a box out of doors." At first it appeared that Rosa had died of exposure. Witnesses remembered that the child had been sick and had become so "troublesome in its illness" that the Basset family had shut her out of the house in the middle of a raging snowstorm. But massive bruises on the child's abdomen suggested that there was more to the story. One of the Bassets probably beat the sick child before forcing her out into the cold. Local officials never filed charges in the case.[22]

Rosa's captivity and her early, violent death gave the lie to enthusiastic declarations that slavery was dead in California. Like thousands of indigenous people, Rosa had been bound into a white household under the 1860 apprenticeship amendments to the Act for the Government and Protection of Indians. The new amendments allowed whites to bind Indian children in their possession, as well as adult Native war captives and "vagrants," for ten or more years at a time. The northwestern California Democrats who pressed for apprenticeship claimed that the institution was a humane and enlightened alternative to Indian extermination. A period of temporary bondage might domesticate and civilize Indians, provide whites with workers, and bring peace to northwestern California. In reality, apprenticeship laws encouraged the illegal captivity and enslavement of Native people and fed back into the cycles of warfare that already wracked the region.[23]

The violence that accompanied the captive trade eventually prompted many northwestern California whites to demand the abolition of apprenticeship. More important, horrific stories of the murder, kidnapping, and enslavement of Indians drew criticism from the state's rising Republican leadership. These men painted Indian apprenticeship as a Democratic plot to fasten a new form of slavery on the state. California needed to liberate its Indian slaves, just as the Union emancipated black slaves in the South. For all their emphasis on freeing captive Indians, California Republicans believed that most Native people needed to undergo compulsory labor before they could be properly civilized and incorporated into the market as free laborers. The same men who worked to eliminate the most egregious forms of kidnapping and enslavement did not repeal laws that punished Indian vagrants and convicts with forced labor. They also insisted that Indians on federal reservations should learn civilized habits through stints of supervised, compulsive agricultural toil. Indians would be free from outright enslavement, but not free to choose whether, or even how, they would work.

Republican assaults on apprenticeship grew in response to the violence, suffering, and chaos that followed the 1860 amendments to the Act for the Government and Protection of Indians. Originally aimed at quelling warfare in northwestern California by channeling Native people into a formal, orderly, and regulated system of supervised labor, the apprenticeship amendments exacerbated the illicit slave trade that long provoked turmoil in the region. The provision that allowed Indian war captives to be bound as apprentices encouraged the organization of white kidnapping parties that scoured the countryside in search of prisoners to sell.[24] Several thousand Indians probably suffered apprenticeship during the three years that the new amendments were in operation. The practice was so widespread, in fact, that Indian apprentices made up nearly 40 percent of the population of some northwestern California townships.[25]

Although hundreds of Indian adults entered white households as apprentices, children like Rosa became the special targets of the new law. The apprenticeship amendment loosened the antikidnapping provisions of the original 1850 Act for the Government and Protection of Indians by no longer requiring whites to establish the consent of children's "parents or friends" before a judge. Petitioners now needed only to apply to the county court, state that they had obtained Indian children from their parents or the "person or persons having the care or charge" of them, and then ask for a certificate of apprenticeship.[26] The laxity of the clause made it easy for white farmers and ranchers to purchase children from kidnappers and apprentice them for most of their youths. Some groups of northwestern California whites, dubbed "baby hunters" in the California press, waged small-scale war on northwestern Indian peoples to supply this market for young Indian laborers. These mobile, armed companies scoured the mountains in search of isolated villages. They would then "stealthily creep into the Indian camp at night while its inmates were asleep," attack, and snatch up as many children as they could in the ensuing chaos. Some assailants murdered Indian parents who refused to give up their children. Despite these well-publicized horrors, some kidnapping parties developed into semiformal paramilitary groups that capitalized on state-sponsored violence against Indians. "Regular organized companies," complete with elected officers, followed close on the heels of state militias and federal troops sent out to attack Indian villages. Once soldiers had killed or captured adult Indian men and women, these companies seized any children who had been separated from their parents, orphaned, or abandoned in the confusion of battle. Highly organized, efficient auxiliaries to sanctioned military campaigns against Indians, kidnapping parties made little effort to conceal their activities.[27]

Kidnapping and apprenticeship triggered cycles of resistance and retribution that fueled horrific violence in northwestern California. In the summer of 1861, two teenaged Yuki boys living in Mendocino County allegedly attempted to poison their master, former Indian agent Thomas Henley. They slipped strychnine into his family's food. The Henleys detected the problem, but not before the servants fled. Henley caught up with one of the young men and hanged him. A year later, in April 1863, a fifteen-year-old Yuki apprentice allegedly murdered his master by decapitating him with an axe. He escaped and rejoined his people. A federal reservation agent then took two hostages from the young man's band and threatened to execute them if the accused murderer did not turn himself in. Local whites finally tracked down the former apprentice and gave him to military authorities. They hanged him without process of any kind.[28]

These incidents prompted some local whites to demand the end of the apprenticeship system. Groups of whites in Humboldt County called a mass meeting condemning Indian warfare and declaring it the duty of "all good citizens to discourage, by all lawful means, the further apprenticing of Indians of any age or either sex." They formed vigilante militias that seized apprentices from white homes and removed them to the reservations. One Humboldt County resident reported that by early 1862 "all the tame and apprenticed Indians in the county have been sent to the reservation." The removal had "been an act of the people and brot about by Lynch law." The few Native people who remained in white households were "shot down at their work," as "no quarters is shown to an Indian."[29]

Growing opposition to apprenticeship in northwestern California coincided with a mounting Republican campaign against the institution. New Republican lawmakers denied that apprenticeship civilized American Indians. They condemned binding out Indians as a cruel, archaic form of slavery. They accused proslavery and southern-sympathizing Democrats of installing a labor regime that bore striking similarities to black bondage in the American South. Apprenticeship reduced Native people to dependency and servitude, conditions at odds with the state's constitution and the national turn toward emancipation, they argued. Once in power, Republicans sought to eliminate the state's apprenticeship laws and replace them with a policy of Indian removal and resettlement. They advocated prosecuting kidnappers, liberating apprentices from their masters, and removing all Indians to reservations, where they would labor for their own subsistence under the watchful gaze of federal agents. Enemies of arbitrary and unjust Indian apprenticeship, Republicans ultimately condoned dispossession and compulsory reservation labor as the means to turn Native people into self-sufficient free workers.

The Republican crusade against the Indian apprenticeship law began in earnest in 1861. As secession discredited Democrats nationwide, California Republicans blamed the state's long and troubled history of Indian affairs on the proslavery sentiment of their Democratic rivals. Southern-sympathizing proslavery Democrats invented apprenticeship, Republicans argued, so that they could remake California in the image of the Old South. Since the earliest days of statehood, the editor of the Unionist *San Francisco Bulletin* fumed, Democrats had promoted an "abominable system of Indian apprenticeship, which has been used as a means of introducing actual slavery into our free State." A Republican editor in Columbia railed against Democratic officeholders who opposed Chinese labor but who insisted on promoting Indian apprenticeship. "There is such a hubbub about Coolie labor, such an antipathy against 'slavery,'" he observed, "[that] it seems somewhat strange that our State and Federal officers, should aid in introducing it into this State." He continued: "There never was such a thing as a slave if these poor Indians are not slaves to the parties to whom they are 'apprenticed.'" These criticisms became all the louder when Vincent Geiger, a prominent Virginia-born Democrat and former agent at Nome Lackee Reservation, apprenticed seventy-two reservation Indians and took them across state lines to mine in Nevada Territory. The incident, the Republican *Marysville Appeal* cried, "smack[ed] of cottondom."[30] These laments abated when Abraham Lincoln appointed George M. Hanson, a fellow Illinois Republican and avowed opponent of slavery, to the post of superintendent of Indian affairs for northern California. Republicans and Unionists predicted that Hanson's appointment would bring "humane and Christian men, philanthropists of enlarged ideas, and having the good of both the white and Indian races at heart," into the Office of Indian Affairs. They would replace Democratic "salary-seekers, graduated into positions upon Indian Reservations from corner groceries and the precincts of ward elections and political conventions." Many hoped that Hanson would launch an investigation into apprenticeship that would stimulate federal pressure for repeal.[31]

Hanson did not disappoint. He proved to be a relentless critic of the apprenticeship system and made its repeal central to Indian policy reform. He rejected the argument that apprenticeship was a natural step toward Indian civilization. Instead, it was both a moral and a legal wrong. It encouraged "crimes against humanity" by facilitating the kidnapping of Indian people and their sale into "virtual slavery." The apprenticeship law also violated California's constitutional ban on slavery and federal power over Indian affairs established by the U.S. Constitution. Hanson recommended that Congress should "provide a remedy" to California's system of Indian slavery. In the meantime, he pledged that he would work with the state courts and the legislature to stamp out this "unholy traffic in human blood and souls" that caused all the "so-called Indian Wars" that plagued the state.[32]

Hanson first targeted those who kidnapped and sold Indian children. He appointed private citizens as special Indian agents who reported on the movements of kidnappers through the countryside. He also enlisted the help of local law enforcement and prosecutors to bring charges against kidnappers and to confiscate their captives. In October 1861, Hanson worked with officials in Marysville to apprehend three white men who had kidnapped nine Indian children in Humboldt County and carried them south to sell. The men, who claimed they were doing "an act of charity" in finding good homes for Indian orphans, later admitted to killing the children's parents. They eventually got their freedom by paying a $500 bond and skipping bail.[33] A few months later, officials in Mendocino County, acting at Hanson's behest, arrested George Woodman just as he was about to cross over into Napa County with sixteen Yuki and Pomo children. A jury convicted Woodman of kidnapping, and the judge confiscated the captives. Woodman then appealed to the Mendocino County district and county courts to bind the children out as his apprentices.[34] To protest his innocence, Woodman also wrote open letters attacking George Hanson and those who arrested him. He asserted that the children were orphans and that servitude in white homes would do more to civilize them than Republicans' misguided antislavery principles. "There is a school of philanthropists who consider that unlicensed and boundless freedom is the highest boon that mankind can enjoy," Woodman wrote. But it was a much greater act of humanity to place Indian children in white households where they would be freed from the "degradation of savage life" and "the absolute and immediate danger of starvation."[35] The district court nonetheless found against Woodman and put the children in the custody of the county's district attorney.

In each of these cases, Republicans excoriated the kidnappers for perpetuating a noxious slave trade in California. The *Marysville Appeal*, the same newspaper that likened apprenticeship to the practices of "cottondom," called the Humboldt abductors "vile kidnappers in human flesh." Killing Indian parents, taking their children, and "packing them about the country, like so many sheep or swine, to sell at retail or wholesale" was "enough to chill the heart of a man." George Hanson, who responded to George Woodman's protests through newspaper editorials of his own, scoffed at the idea that humanitarianism and benevolent paternalism motivated kidnappers. Instead, he located these transactions firmly in the realm of the slave market. He ridiculed the "professed philanthropy" of men like Woodman who went "hunting Indian children in the mountains ostensibly in order to 'find good homes for them.'" Their true motive was only "to sell them, and profit by the proceeds."[36]

In the end, neither the legal outcomes of the cases nor stern Republican denunciations of Indian slavery resulted in the liberty of kidnapped children.

All met fates little different from those that kidnappers had planned for them. Once he successfully seized the nine children in Marysville, Hanson made no effort to return them to their people or to take them to the reservations. He placed each with local white families.[37] In Ukiah, the plight of Woodman's captives sparked so much interest that one hundred white residents, "desirous to get possession" of the children, applied to apprentice them. The district attorney—who probably had Hanson's blessing—apparently determined that the children could never be properly civilized if returned to "their parents and native wilds." They were "better off among the whites" and should be furnished with "guardians and comfortable homes." He gave the children over to eager white applicants. Helen Carpenter later remembered that Woodman's captives endured difficult labor, brutal treatment, and neglect at the hands of their new masters. In fact, one of these children was Rosa, the apprentice whom the county coroner found beaten to death in the April snow just a year later.[38]

The fate of Rosa and the two dozen children that Hanson "liberated" revealed the contradictions in California's policy toward Native peoples. Hanson and other Republicans denounced the kidnapping and forced labor of Native children as a horrifying, dangerous, and illegal brand of slavery. Yet they held tight to the notion that civilizing Indian people might come only at the cost of subjecting them to some sort of temporary servitude. Indians should be freed from the most egregious forms of slavery, but, like African American freedpeople in the South, they would not enjoy freedom from work or labor discipline altogether. Republican efforts to emancipate Indians in California during the Civil War were always tempered by the desire to transform Native people into civilized and productive laborers.

The Republican determination that Indians would be free to work for themselves, but not free from work, emerged in their proposals to end the apprenticeship system. True to his promises, George Hanson sent messages to the state legislature calling for the repeal of the state's apprenticeship laws. He found allies in Assemblymen Charles Maclay and Caleb Fay, two staunch Republican supporters of African American testimony rights. In the spring of 1862, just as the legislature debated whether to allow black evidence against whites, the two men presented Hanson's messages and proposed two new bills. One would repeal the apprenticeship system set up by the 1860 amendments to the Act for the Government and Protection of Indians. The other abolished the sections of the original 1850 law that called for the whipping and binding out of Indian convicts. Maclay and Fay let one key part of the state's coercive Indian labor policy stand. Local legal officials would still be able to arrest Indian "vagrants" who had no visible employment and bind them out to white employers on four-month terms. This section of the law, which resembled the vagrancy laws aimed at freedpeople in the postemancipation South, compelled Native people to enter the market economy as workers and cut them off from other subsistence activities. In spite of (or because of) the decision to retain this vestige of bound labor, assembly Republicans voted for both bills.[39]

Even with their restricted vision of Indian freedom, the repeal bills faced a hard road in the senate, where Democrats still held substantial power. Mendocino County Democrat William Holden, a strong advocate of apprenticeship, argued that the system "embodied one of the most important measures for [Indians'] improvement and civilization." Native people fared so much better in white homes that keeping the law was "a matter of humanity and kindness to the Indians." The law merely needed to be "perfected" rather than erased altogether. He wrote a watered-down substitute bill that allowed any Indian child to be apprenticed so long as the California superintendent of Indian affairs approved each transaction. Republicans rejected the substitute. It did nothing to curb the abuses of apprenticeship and would, in fact, make the system worse by rendering all Native children (not just orphans, war captives, and vagrants) subject to binding out. The bill died, and apprenticeship lived on for another year.[40]

Fortunes changed in 1863 after Republicans swept into power and joined forces with free-soil Democrats to form the Union Party. Four months after the Emancipation Proclamation went into effect, Unionists repealed the 1860 apprenticeship amendments to the Act for the Government and Protection of Indians without any dissent, discussion, or debate.[41] Historians have often interpreted the vote in favor of repeal as an effort to bring California in line with national slave emancipation. In the words of Robert Heizer and Alan Almquist, ending Indian apprenticeship constituted "a local version of the Emancipation Proclamation."[42] While Republican antislavery sentiment and attentiveness to African American freedom certainly influenced repeal, the measure may actually have passed because it did not bring full emancipation for California's Indian workers. The new Unionist coalition paired Republicans with free-soil Democrats who were more conservative on racial issues and whose former party took a more aggressive stance on subduing Indians. As a result, Fay and Maclay's already limited 1862 repeal bills—which abolished Indian apprenticeship and convict labor without getting rid of bound labor for Indian "vagrants"—became weaker. The bill that passed in 1863 repealed the 1860 apprenticeship amendments but did not touch many of the other compulsory labor provisions of the original 1850 Act for the Government and Protection of Indians. Indian vagrants could still be bound out to work four-month terms. Native convicts still faced whipping for certain crimes and could be forced to work for whites who paid their bail.[43] Moreover, the language of the repeal bill may have placated those Democrats who had a strong vested interest in apprenticed Indian labor. It only prevented future apprenticeships and made no provisions to emancipate Native people bound out prior to repeal. Union Party Republicans' own desires to incorporate Indians into the labor market, combined with Union Party Democrats' racial conservatism, produced an imperfect and incomplete Indian Emancipation Proclamation.

State records illustrate the limits of Indian emancipation. Thousands of Indians remained in white households and suffered sale, exploitation, and violence after 1863. In both 1864 and 1865, California's superintendent of public instruction counted nearly 6,000 Indian children under the age of seventeen still living in non-Indian households.[44] Legal records reveal that some of these children endured chattel slavery. In 1864, for instance, Mendocino resident John Gardner approached a justice of the peace and accused another white man, John McGill, of "grand larceny by kidnapping." The "property" that McGill stole was an Indian child named Dick, valued at $250. The justice, who never questioned Gardner's proposition that Dick was property and that his kidnapping constituted grand larceny, facilitated the child's return to his master. Native adults also endured abuse and compulsion after repeal. During the summer of 1865, Mendocino County rancher Robert Hildreth went on trial for murdering Ben, an Indian man he claimed as an apprentice. When Ben left to work for another white man, Hildreth captured him, bound him, and tethered him to a horse. The animal escaped from Hildreth's control and dragged Ben to death. Hildreth claimed that the incident was an accident, but witnesses testified that he had spurred the horse on. The court dismissed the charges and set Hildreth free. The story broke at the same time as the ratification of the Thirteenth Amendment and outraged journalists across California. Even the *Police Gazette*, a working-class paper unsympathetic to Native people, concluded that "slavery exists in California in precisely the same condition that it did until lately in the Southern States." Republicans eliminated apprenticeship, but the freedom they extended to indigenous people was fragile and tenuous.[45]

Nowhere were Republican visions of Indian freedom more contradictory than on the federal reservations. Although the federal government abandoned most of the original antebellum Indian reserves in war-torn northwestern California, Republicans kept high hopes that reservations would solve the state's "Indian problem." Men like Superintendent George Hanson who protested forced Indian labor in private white households held out removal and resettlement of Indians as the most humane and efficient way to civilize them. In theory, this involved persuading Indians to give up mobile subsistence strategies in favor of sedentary agriculture on reservation farms. In practice, it meant removing Indians by force to the reservations and compelling them to perform agricultural labor under the supervision of federal agents. In 1863, the same year that the Union Party abolished Indian apprenticeship, Republican officials instituted just such a system of compulsory labor on the Nome Lackee Reservation. Elijah Steele, a Republican who replaced George Hanson as superintendent of Indian affairs for northern California, ordered his agents to compel all "able bodied Indians" living on the reservation to work on the farm. Hunger enforced labor discipline. Only those who were "actually employed" received federal rations. A similar policy prevailed at nearby Round Valley Reservation, where one visitor remarked that Indians were kept "under tolerable discipline, and work pretty well under overseers."[46]

By the late 1860s, Republicans in the Office of Indian Affairs hoped to make compulsory labor standard practice on the California reservations. One suggested that to "promote subordination and civilization" Native people should work under close supervision and never be allowed to leave the reservations without passports. Following the maxim that "the hoe and the broadaxe will sooner civilize and Christianize than the spelling book and the Bible," he advocated compelling California Native children to work until they had been "humanized by systematic labor." These policies prevailed at Round Valley, one of the few northwestern reservations to survive beyond the 1860s. There, one critic observed in 1874, "compulsion is used to keep the Indians and to drive them to work." Indian workers received "no payment [for] labor and no opportunity to accumulate individual property." All of this seemed especially disconcerting in a nation that now professed to extend liberty and due process to all.[47]

Republicans in California adopted a fractured and contradictory stance toward Indian labor. Professing opposition to slavery, they battled the idea that compulsory labor in white homes would civilize or educate Indian people. They attacked forced apprenticeship as a barbarous and dehumanizing form of bondage that conflicted with free-state status and the nation's inexorable march toward liberty. And yet Republicans remained amenable to some forms of compulsory labor. Indians might be exempt from laboring for white masters as apprentices, but they could not choose to live outside the market altogether. Able-bodied people who had not attached themselves to a white employer could be convicted of vagrancy and bound out, as could those found guilty of crimes. Those living on Republican-run federal reservations faced a stark choice between hard manual labor and starvation. For some indigenous people, freedom was even more elusive. With no statute on the books directing masters to release bound laborers, many Indians who were apprenticed before the repeal bill stayed in white households as servants.

Discrepancies between Republicans' professed antislavery sentiment and the reality of their Indian policy gave Democrats fodder for discrediting the Union Party. In 1864, John Bidwell of Butte County ran for Congress on the Unionist ticket. Bidwell was a longtime ranchero who relied heavily on Indian labor, and he had drafted the milder, unsuccessful version of the 1850 Act for the Government and Protection of Indians. A former Democrat, he had abandoned his home party to join the Union coalition before finally becoming a Republican. The Democratic press soon branded Bidwell and his Unionist constituents as hypocrites. One scathing 1864 editorial alleged that the "abolitionist" Bidwell operated a "(digger) slave pen" where he accorded his Indian workers more "vile treatment" than enslaved African Americans. "As you are such a stickler for freedom of the slaves," the paper asked, "why not set the example and comply with the request of your neighbors by giving freedom to your (Indian) slaves?" After Bidwell won the congressional seat, he loudly condemned both slavery and black disfranchisement as "purely arbitrary and despotic . . . wholly inconsistent with the fundamental principles of democratic republican government." The Democratic *Colusa Sun* took him to task for the inconsistencies in Republican policy at home. "If Gen. Bidwell is of the opinion that every line of distinction is arbitrary and is so contrary to republican government," the editor wondered, "why don't he admit Chinese and negroes and Diggers to his parlor, to his table and to his bed?" As Democrats were so enthusiastic to point out, the Republican dedication to black rights in the South did not necessarily translate to a policy of full emancipation or racial equality in California.[48]

"Masters and Unfree Servants": The Coolie
Question during the Civil War

The *Colusa Sun's* indictment of John Bidwell suggested that Republican support for African American emancipation and civil rights would mean "social equality" among all of California's peoples, the intimate mixing of whites with "Chinese and negroes and Diggers." The comment revealed not only how quickly questions about economic and political liberty morphed into anxious tirades about social and sexual intermixing, but also how tightly the issue of black freedom was tied to the question of Indian and Chinese rights. The destabilization of one type of race-based inequality could knock down and undermine others. By the time that the *Sun* editor wrote his rebuke in 1866, Republican efforts to end African American slavery and civil inequality had already raised new questions about the status of other California groups. Debates about racial restrictions on testimony rights as well as the repeal of Indian apprenticeship followed hard on Republican campaigns to improve the status of black Americans. Most controversial of all was what expanding civil rights legislation would mean for California's thousands of Chinese residents. For, the *Sun* declared, if Republicans could punish white southerners for failing to grant African Americans liberty and equality, they could easily declare "a war upon the people of California who do not recognize their equals in the Chinese who infest our State."[49]

In reality, Republicans' approach to the "Chinese Question" was far more complex than the *Sun* editor imagined. Political divisions and ideological conflicts within the party made it difficult for Republicans to reach consensus on what emancipation and Reconstruction should mean for Chinese residents. Specifically, Republicans' adherence to antislavery principles conflicted with their dedication to equality before the law. Party members could not agree on whether Chinese workers were coolie slaves who needed to be excluded from the state or voluntary immigrants and free laborers entitled to the same legal protections as their white counterparts. Moderate and conservative Republicans, as well as former Democrats who joined them in the Union coalition, tended to adopt the former view: Chinese were unfree workers whose presence endangered free white labor and threatened to undo the accomplishments of emancipation. California Republicans who identified most with the Radical branch of the national party disagreed. In their eyes, Chinese were not coolies or slaves but merely free laborers who worked hard and cheaply. They deserved the same immigration opportunities and protection for their lives and property as other groups enjoyed. Still other Unionists took a more complicated stance. Chinese were coolies, but they lay somewhere between slave and free; while technically voluntary immigrants, they worked for such low wages under such poor conditions that they may as well have been slaves. The key divisions in the party revolved, in short, around whether Chinese were coolies and whether coolies were slaves. The answers to these questions determined whether the party should work toward Chinese exclusion or toward securing civil equality for Chinese immigrants.[50]

Republicans' struggle to identify and define "coolies"—to determine whether Chinese migrants were free laborers or slaves, voluntary immigrants or imported servile workers—was not new. Since the 1852 debates over the Tingley and Peachy "coolie bills" and the second foreign miners' tax, California's legislators had confronted similar questions. These debates subsided in the late 1850s, only to reemerge with greater force amid 1860s economic transformations that changed the role of Chinese workers in the California labor market. Most Chinese men continued to work in the mining industry—in 1860, 70 percent labored as miners. But the gradual decline of mining, the construction of the transcontinental railroad line, and the rapid growth of California's agricultural and manufacturing sectors spurred Chinese movement into farm and nonmining industrial labor. Chinese populations in the state's largest cities increased as migrants moved to urban areas to take up jobs in construction, manufacturing, and domestic and personal service work. The greater concentration and visibility of Chinese in urban areas made them targets of white industrial workers, who, like white miners a decade earlier, charged them with being "cheap labor" and competitors for jobs. Eventually, anticoolie leagues—white, urban, working-class organizations—emerged to combat the coolie menace by closing Chinese out of the labor market and agitating for immigration restriction.[51] Republican efforts to make sense of coolies and to determine the future of Chinese laborers emerged from these new social and economic conditions.

At the same time that California Republicans responded to changes in their home state, they also participated in a national struggle over coolies. Historian Moon-Ho Jung documents how investigating and outlawing coolieism became a major Republican project at the national level during the Civil War. In February 1862, Republicans in Congress passed an anticoolie act that prohibited U.S. citizens from participating in the so-called coolie trade. The phrasing and construction of the law revealed the ambiguous status of coolies in Republican ideology. As Jung argues, the anticoolie law was both the last U.S. anti–slave trade law and the first major statute restricting foreign immigration. It barred Americans from shipping any Chinese subjects "known as 'coolies'" and "held to service and labor" to any world port. Republicans unabashedly framed this part of the law as an anti–slave trade provision. They hoped it would quash a traffic in coolies that, they believed, rivaled the African slave trade in its brutality. And yet the same law also stipulated that Chinese who were free and voluntary immigrants could take passage to the United States. The message behind the law, according to Jung, was that "the United States deplored the importation of human beings," but it "embraced immigration." Crucially, though, the law never specified which Chinese workers counted as "coolies" and what differentiated them from free and voluntary immigrants. Thus, imagined coolies occupied a liminal legal and cultural status between imported slaves and free entrants.[52] California Republicans' heated debate over whether Chinese were free laborers or coolie slaves paralleled a national struggle to determine the racial, class, and citizenship status of Asian laborers in the age of emancipation.

California Republicans' first major confrontation with the coolie question came in 1862 when rival Democrats proposed the Act to Protect Free White Labor against Competition with Chinese Coolie Labor, and to Discourage the Immigration of Chinese into the State of California. Nicknamed the Chinese Police Tax, the act would levy a $2.50 monthly tax on all Chinese engaged in occupations other than mining or merchandising. Chinese miners were already paying a hefty license fee, and the bill would subject virtually all Chinese residents to a similar system of taxes. It also made employers liable for paying their workers' taxes, placing a heavy burden on Chinese who employed their own countrypeople and dissuading whites from hiring immigrants from China. The bill's proponents argued that it would discourage future Chinese immigration, prompt Chinese nationals to leave the state, and provide a lucrative source of income in counties where Chinese hung on.[53]

In its very title, the police tax bill constructed a sharp dichotomy between "white labor," marked free, and "Chinese labor," marked "coolie." It proclaimed that these types of labor were in direct opposition to each other and that white labor needed protection from competition with coolies.[54] The attempt to exclude Chinese from the category of free laborers provoked a wide range of responses from Republicans in the legislature. Republicans with radical leanings attacked the police tax as an intolerant and unenlightened law that unjustly singled out Chinese workers for persecution. In their view, Chinese labor and free white labor were nearly identical. Coolies might be slaves, but Chinese in California were not coolies; they were merely hard-working and inexpensive free laborers whose presence benefited California industry. One Republican-led committee investigating Chinese labor maintained "that there is no system of slavery or coolieism amongst the Chinese of this State." Instead, thousands of free Chinese laborers, voluntary immigrants, helped develop the state's manufacturing and agricultural enterprises through their "cheap labor" and contributed nearly $14 million to the state economy as taxpayers and consumers. The committee opposed taxation to further "oppress and degrade" Chinese migrants and urged fellow politicians to "legislate as becomes a great liberal, magnanimous people." Like-minded Republicans in the assembly concurred. Enlightened legislators had the duty to "protect the weak, to lift up the oppressed; to open the doors of freedom to those who were in chains," ideals wholly at odds with racially discriminatory taxation.[55]

Republicans who opposed the police tax contended that no one who opposed slavery and revered freedom and justice—by which they meant their fellow Republicans—could possibly vote for it. Nonetheless, nearly half of the Republicans in the assembly joined Democrats in passing the bill. Many explained their stance by invoking the antislavery principles that drove the party in this period. Chinese laborers were coolies, they said, and coolieism was identical to (or at least bore many similarities to) slavery. Some insisted that Chinese across the state ran virtual slave markets where "a man could buy a Chinaman at any time for from $400 to $800." Others alleged that Chinese "head men" hired out "coolies" to the highest bidder in the same way that southern masters hired out black bondpeople. The only difference was that hired slaves received better treatment than their coolie counterparts.[56]

Still other Republicans highlighted the instability of "coolie" as a labor category by arguing that Chinese were virtual rather than actual slaves. They admitted that coolies were not chattel slaves because they did labor voluntarily and receive pay. The problem was that Chinese willingness to work for starvation wages made them nearly the equivalent of slaves. One Republican who charged that "slavery existed among the Chinese" conceded, in the next breath, that coolies were wageworkers whose low standard of pay would "drive out white labor." He announced that "although he was a Republican," he would support the tax. A legislative committee dominated by Republicans who wanted the tax warned that "whilst the influence of slavery is losing territory in our Eastern sister States," unrestrained coolie immigration was making California a society of "masters and unfree servants." Even they conceded, though, that the Chinese were at least "nominally free." It was just that their wages were so pitiful that their "labor rank[ed] no higher in the public respect than slave labor." They asked Congress to restrict the immigration of wage-working Chinese slaves so that an "irradicable system of involuntary servitude" would not rise on the Pacific Coast just as black slavery died on the Atlantic Coast.[57]

Radical Republicans failed to persuade their colleagues that the police tax was an odious, discriminatory measure out of step with the spirit of the times. There was enough Republican support for the police tax that both the assembly and the senate passed it by large margins. Leland Stanford, the state's first Republican governor and a critic of Chinese immigration, signed it into law. When May came, tax collectors began making their rounds to gather the monthly $2.50 tax. But just as they had fought the foreign miners' tax and the head taxes of the 1850s, Chinese merchants swiftly mounted a legal challenge to the new law. In June, a San Francisco merchant named Lin Sing filed suit against a tax collector named Washburn when the latter forced him to pay the tax for one of his Chinese employees. Prominent Republicans took up the case to test the constitutionality of the police tax.[58]

Lin Sing's suit eventually made its way to the California Supreme Court, in July 1862. John Dwinelle, a Republican and counsel for Lin Sing, contended that the police tax was a dead letter. Like California's previous anti-Chinese laws that the court had overturned in the late 1850s, this one also interfered with federal power to regulate commerce with foreign nations. He also called into question the allegations of Chinese coolieism embedded in the police tax. Whenever white workers felt threatened by industrious Chinese migrants, they cried that free white labor was under siege by the "yellow skin of the 'Chinese coolie.'" California Chinese were not coolies but free laborers entitled to enter the country under the recent federal anticoolie act. The odious police tax allowed these free and legal migrants to be stripped of their property, hunted down, and imprisoned until they paid their taxes.[59] Attorney General Frank Pixley, a Republican who later became a lead figure in the anti-Chinese movement, countered that the sovereign state of California could use its police powers to regulate noxious groups of people. The Chinese fit this description because they threatened the moral welfare and economic interests of white Californians and could never become naturalized citizens.[60] The court, made up of a mix of Democrats and Republicans, found for Lin Sing. Justices ruled that the police tax, an act of "special and extreme hostility to the Chinese," discouraged their immigration and, by extension, interfered with foreign commerce. The law also conflicted with the federal anticoolie act of 1862 that "expressly authorize[ed] voluntary immigration" from China. The court came down closer to the Radical Republican side of the coolie question, finding Chinese to be free immigrants whose entrance and residence could only be proscribed by federal law. The police tax was unconstitutional, and no Chinese could be forced to pay it.[61]

The decision in *Lin Sing v. Washburn* and the nullification of the police tax proved a signal legal victory for Chinese across the state. It did not, however, heal the split in the Republican ranks over the coolie question. Some Republicans held tight to their conviction that Chinese men were slaves (or near slaves) who should be excluded because they endangered free labor. Others insisted that Chinese workingmen were free laborers who deserved equality before the law. The ambiguous and unstable meaning of coolie labor remained at the heart of these debates. Imagined at once as slave and free, desirable immigrants and dangerous imports, "coolies" exposed the tensions among different factions of Republicans and the contradictions between Republican antislavery ideology and dedication to equality before the law. These rifts widened in 1863 after Republicans joined free-soil Democrats in the Union Party coalition. California Democrats had a long history of anti-Chinese agitation and pressed their new Republican colleagues for laws restricting Chinese immigration and legal rights. The Union coalition later fell apart when former Democrats bolted to rejoin their old party on a platform pledging the end of Chinese immigration and coolie labor. Appropriating the antislavery idiom of their erstwhile Republican colleagues, Democrats used the coolie question to sweep back into power at the end of the decade.

"Bought and Sold as Any Other Property": Republicans Confront California's Traffics in Women

In March 1862, at the height of the debates over the Chinese Police Tax, Republican assemblyman William Sears rose to defend the measure against his colleagues who thought that it was inhumane and unjust. While most proponents of the tax fixated on the dangers posed by male Chinese "coolie" laborers, Sears turned his attention to Chinese women. One of the virtues of the police tax, he proclaimed, was that it would reduce the growing number of Chinese women in the state. Sears "denied that any of the Chinawomen were respectable"; in fact, most of these women, even those purported to be wives, were enslaved by Chinese men. He related an incident in which a Chinese man "pawned his wife to another Chinaman" and "never redeemed the pledge." The police tax would both expel a vicious and noxious class of women from the state and eliminate a perverse system of woman trafficking rooted in Chinese gender relations.[62]

Sears's concerns about the enslavement of Chinese prostitutes illuminated a final dilemma that California Republicans faced during the Civil War era: how to eradicate the state's distinctive traffics in women. Slave emancipation in the U.S. South brought questions about the marketability of women's bodies to a prominent place in national political discourse. In the eastern United States, these discussions often focused on African American freedwomen's self-ownership, including rights to control their own bodies, reproduction, and wages. White women also embarked on their own campaign against "woman slavery" by pressing for suffrage and married women's rights to own property and to keep their wages. Finally, the proliferation of prostitution in the urban East focused renewed attention on sexual commerce. Reformers debated whether women who exchanged sex for cash were freely contracting individuals who exemplified the triumph (and dangers) of free-labor capitalism or victims of archaic sexual slavery.[63]

In California, the most profound struggles over the meaning of female freedom centered on the traffics in Chinese and Native American women, which first emerged during the gold rush. Committed to antislavery, California's Republicans grew uneasy about these traffics and envisioned a strong role for the state government in suppressing the buying and selling of Indian and Chinese women. Republicans conceptualized these two traffics in very different ways, leading to divergent and uneven consequences for bound women. They attributed traffics in Indian women to degraded whites, secessionist "squaw men" who violated the rights of Indian husbands by stealing and enslaving their wives. Republicans tried—with only partial success—to suppress squaw men, to restore Indian women to the authority of their husbands, and to reconstitute Indian families according to their own visions of middle-class domesticity. Alternatively, Republicans explained traffics in bound Chinese prostitutes as the result of perverse and deficient Chinese gender relations. Republicans expressed concern and pity for Chinese women who, they believed, were victims of sexual slavery perpetrated by their countrymen. Still, many asserted that Chinese women's moral deficiencies caused their descent into prostitution and bondage. Republicans' efforts to abolish the traffic in Chinese women alternated between antislavery laws intended to punish Chinese men as "slaveholders" and measures that treated trafficked women as nuisances to be expelled rather than as slaves to be liberated. Eager to eliminate commerce in women's bodies and to define proper market relations between men and women, Republicans protested assaults on Indian men's rights to their female kin while denouncing Chinese gender relationships that seemed to promote woman slavery.

Republicans' efforts to end the captive trade in Native women went hand in hand with the movement to repeal the 1860 apprenticeship amendments to the Act for the Government and Protection of Indians. Party members' critique of apprenticeship often focused on the plight of Native women and girls, who increasingly suffered kidnapping, sexual abuse, and long-term servitude in white homes under the guise of the new apprenticeship laws. Echoing prewar critiques of the captive trade, Republicans focused on the break-up of Indian homes and the violation of Indian men's rights to their female family members. George Hanson, the Republican superintendent of Indian affairs for northern California who prosecuted baby hunters and who warned the legislature about the evils of apprenticeship, took special interest in these matters. Writing from Round Valley, Hanson lamented that the reservation was under attack from "a class of unprincipled white men, whose business alone it is to mix with the Indians, and at every opportunity make merchandise of their children and wives of their squaws." These men would "constantly excite the Indians to jealousy by taking their squaws from them."[64] Indian men who brought their families to the reservation seeking safe haven suffered similar abuses at the hands of federal employees. Hanson reported directly to President Lincoln that one agent enticed an Indian woman from her husband to use "for his own purposes." Unmarried white male employees retained "from one to three squaws to use when they pleased to do so." Such abuses were so rampant on the reservation that Hanson complained he was "opposed by the entire squaw fraternity" in his efforts at reform.[65]

Like their predecessors, Hanson and other Republicans complained bitterly of these "squaw men," debased whites who, they alleged, kidnapped Native women and lived with them on terms of sexual intimacy. In the context of the war, though, Republicans often wedded squaw men's criminal, racial, and sexual transgressions to a new kind of treachery: secessionism. A large number of southern whites—particularly Missourians—lived in northwestern California and in areas adjacent to the reservations. Secession sentiment ran high among these southern-born settlers, and rumors of pro-Confederate plots to seize federal forts and Indian reservations set Republican officials on edge. In their efforts to subdue "squaw men" and Indian kidnappers, Republicans cast the perpetrators as rebels whose outrages against Native people and treason against their own race were also assaults on the Union and the power of the federal government. George Hanson insisted that one notorious abductor of Indian women and children on the Round Valley Reservation was a "malicious, copperhead kidnapper." Another staunch Union man declaimed against the "squaw men" whom he met in his travels. Almost all of them were "rank Secessionists" and "'poor white trash' from the frontier slave states, Missouri, Arkansas, and Texas." The correlation between interracial intimacy and treason was so high that he had never met any squaw man who was also a Union man. Squaw men were both race traitors—men who abandoned their whiteness by kidnapping and cohabiting with Indian women—and treasonous outlaws whose crimes tore at the fabric of federal authority and union.[66]

The Republican campaign against squaw men involved two components. First, Republican officials sought to reform the reservations to make them bastions of middle-class respectability, safe from the depredations of degraded squaw men. Second, they worked to reconstitute Indian families by prosecuting kidnappers. George Hanson pursued the first goal by clearing out the "squaw fraternity" of single young white men who were most guilty of abusing Indian women. These he replaced with white "married men of good deportment" who brought their white wives to live with them on the reservations. The presence of respectable white families could make the reservations "self-protecting against the kidnappers, squaw-men, and all intruders."[67] Moreover, Hanson hoped that married middle-class white women would provide an important unpaid service on the reservation. They might counteract the "baneful influences" of squaw men by instructing Native women in morality and domesticity. "The example and precepts of good white women, cannot but have a telling effect and happy influence among the female indians," Hanson reported, and he boasted that a handful of white reservation wives were already busying themselves "instructing the young Indian women in the advantages of domestic economy and civilization."[68] Under the supervision of settled white families and virtuous married white women, Indian women would no longer be victimized by unstable, predatory communities of single white men. Re-creating respectable white home life on the reservations could dampen the female captive trade, eliminate noxious interracial relationships, and put Indian families on the path to civilization.

Hanson and his employees also took a more aggressive stance against kidnappers of Indian women. The repeal of the 1860 apprenticeship amendments to the Act for the Government and Protection of Indians made it harder for kidnappers to claim Native women as apprentices. Hanson used this new circumstance to advantage. He commanded Indian agents at the Round Valley Reservation to take legal action against any whites who kidnapped, harbored, or detained any reservation Indians, "particularly the squaws."[69] U.S. Army officers stationed at the reservation were to aid in the capture, arrest, and trial of any offenders. Just such an incident came to light in July 1863, a few months after the repeal of Indian apprenticeship. Henry Abbot, the man whom Hanson described as the "malicious, copperhead kidnapper," took a young Indian woman off of the reservation and refused to give her up. While earlier kidnappers had been able to secure Indian women by binding them as apprentices, Abbot could make no such claims. The reservation agent and an army captain arrested Abbot, held him for several days, and pledged that they would only release him when he gave up the woman.[70]

The legal campaign against squaw men proved only partially effective as courts and juries often found in favor of kidnappers. Abbot refused to disclose the whereabouts of the woman and won the sympathy of local citizens. He sued the reservation agent and the army captain for false imprisonment, claiming that they had no authority to arrest him. In the words of Hanson and his employees, Abbot used "Secesh attorneys" and played on the sympathies of a "rebel court" to get a decision in his favor. The jury found for the kidnapper, and the court commanded federal officials to pay him $3,000 in restitution.[71] At least two other cases involving captive Native women, one in Shasta County in 1867 and another in Mendocino County in 1871, ended in a similar fashion. In both cases, local juries and authorities refused to part victims from their abductors or to prosecute kidnappers.[72] Republicans may have eliminated the legal basis for women's captivity, but local courts continued to support white men's mastery over female Indian captives. The emancipation of captive Native women, like Indian emancipation more generally, remained unfinished.

The Republican campaign against squaw men paralleled a much more prominent legislative movement to break up Chinese prostitution and traffics in Chinese women. Republicans who worried that Indian men enjoyed no rights to their womenfolk were even more concerned that Chinese men wielded excessive, tyrannical mastery over their countrywomen. If the state needed to shield the family rights of Indian men from degraded white interlopers, it also needed to protect Chinese women from their own countrymen. Republicans painted Chinese prostitutes as hapless victims of sexual servitude perpetuated by Chinese men who viewed women as little more than commodities. Invoking the language of antislavery, they argued that the state needed to eliminate the buying and selling of women that lay at the heart of Chinese gender relations.

Some Republicans, especially those with radical leanings, expressed genuine concern for Chinese women bound into the sex trade. They approached the traffic in Chinese women as an illegal and immoral form of slavery and pressed for antislavery legislation aimed at liberating Chinese women from brothels. As early as 1860, assembly Republicans pressed for a new state law to criminalize the buying and selling of Chinese women. Entitled An Act to Prohibit the Sale of Chinese Persons of Either Sex, the new law would not only stamp out the alleged coolie trade in Chinese men. It also made it a crime to buy and sell a Chinese woman and imposed up to five years of jail time and a $1,000 fine on convicted offenders. The bill got lost in the shuffle at the end of the session, but the principles behind it elicited great interest in the

Republican press. The Republican-leaning editor of the *Trinity Journal* supported this kind of legislation to stop Chinese women from being "bought and sold among the male Chinamen as any other property." The state needed to make it a felony "to own or buy or sell a Chinese woman." A few years later, a staunch Unionist paper advocated harsh measures to eradicate California's own "peculiar institution" of Chinese prostitution perpetuated by Chinese men. Republicans racialized female trafficking as a distinctly Chinese problem and implied that the state needed to intervene to protect Chinese women from their rapacious countrymen, who treated them as slaves.[73]

Once Republicans merged with free-soil Democrats and formed the Union Party in late 1862, Radicals' pleas to liberate Chinese women were often drowned out by new voices. Democrats in the new Union coalition, steeped in their party's long tradition of anti-Chinese activism, favored legislation to suppress and punish Chinese prostitutes. Proponents of this approach wanted to clean up urban sexual commerce and singled out Chinese prostitutes on the grounds that they were more depraved and pestilent than other groups of women who sold sex for cash. In response to public outrage over the visibility of Chinese brothels in San Francisco, Senator Horace Hawes, a Democrat now in the Union Party, proposed an Act for the Suppression of Chinese Houses of Ill Fame in 1866. In its initial form, the bill punished all men who patronized Chinese brothels "for the purpose of fornication or lewdness." They could be fined or jailed. Later, though, the senate replaced it with a harsher measure that mainly targeted Chinese women. The new law declared all buildings "kept, managed, inhabited or used by Chinese women for the purposes of common prostitution" to be public nuisances. Men who visited these brothels faced no legal prosecution, and landlords who knowingly leased property to brothel inmates only had to forfeit the rents they collected. Most of the burden fell on the female occupants. Residing in a suspected brothel served as prima facie evidence that a woman was a prostitute and made her vulnerable to arrest, eviction, fines, and imprisonment.[74]

The Act for the Suppression of Chinese Houses of Ill Fame elicited complicated responses. Some Union Party members, mostly Radical Republicans, opposed the bill and condemned it for the same reason that earlier Republican legislators opposed the police tax: it was a racially intolerant bill that meted out punishment to helpless and oppressed people. They argued that it promoted "unjust discrimination against a particular class of unfortunates, who were entitled to more consideration than others less ignorant and helpless." Singling out "one race" for punishment would be unfair and illegal. They favored striking out racial language so that the bill would apply equally to all women in the sex trade. On the other side of the Union Party, Democrats and more conservative Republicans voted for the measure. They argued that the law was necessary because Chinese prostitutes behaved in ways that were "peculiarly deleterious to the public morals." They managed to push the bill through both houses. San Francisco officials began arresting, jailing, and trying dozens of alleged Chinese prostitutes.[75]

Chinese women in the sex trade, marginalized in both their own communities and the larger white society, had little power to contest the laws that treated them as nuisances and threats to public morality. But fleeting glimpses of Chinese prostitutes' responses to the Act for the Suppression of Chinese Houses of Ill Fame suggest that women used their limited means to resist the law or to shape it to their own advantage. Some white newspapermen asserted that Chinese prostitutes purposely sought arrest under the law to escape servitude. Imprisonment meant at least temporary escape from brothels and "comparative freedom" when measured against the "serfdom" they suffered at the hands of their employers. More fortunate women looked to the courts for redress. Several imprisoned Chinese women enlisted the aid of Frank Pixley, the former Republican attorney general from the Lin Sing case. Although later a vocal opponent of Chinese immigration, Pixley pleaded with the judge to grant his clients "fair play." He thought that the law was inequitable (and possibly unconstitutional) because it targeted Chinese while "American, German, French and Spanish prostitutes who flaunt their full-blossomed vice" walked the streets unmolested. Pixley managed to secure a full jury trial—rather than summary judgment—for each woman he represented.[76]

As repression became more brutal and arrests more numerous, prostitutes' options shrank. Police repression forced many Chinese women out of the city. Newspapers noted, with glee, that hundreds of Chinese prostitutes and brothel keepers fled to Oregon and interior mining towns. The law drove other women underground. The San Francisco press reported that some Chinese prostitutes and the brothel keepers who controlled their labor reached an informal compromise with city police. Arrests would stop so long as the women confined their activities to specific neighborhoods and kept out of sight. The Act for the Suppression of Chinese Houses of Ill Fame had come to function as a kind of informal exclusion measure. It eliminated the most visible trafficked Chinese women by expelling them from the state's largest cities and driving them to the margins of civil society.[77] The law stayed in force for nearly two years, until the state courts finally ruled that its provisions singling out Chinese women for punishment violated the federal Civil Rights Act of 1866.[78]

The ascendance of the Republican Party and the process of national emancipation and Reconstruction changed the landscape of race and labor in nineteenth-century California. The dense tangle of bound and semibound labor systems that had sustained sectors of the state economy for more than a decade began to unravel as Republicans attacked slavery, apprenticeship, contract labor, and sexual trafficking as outmoded forms of servitude inimical to the project of emancipation. African American slavery, and the anti–black testimony laws that sustained it, perished. The apprenticeship of American Indian peoples was discredited and abolished. Coercive labor systems involving Chinese men and women (both real and imagined) came under greater scrutiny. Republican vows to remove the last vestiges of bondage, the last "burning brand" of slavery from California, appeared to have come to fruition. California would be reconstructed, reborn as a free state, just as surely as the states of the former Confederacy.

Or would it? The Republican rise to power revealed that the complexity of California's race and labor systems precluded any kind of straightforward transition from bondage to freedom. Republicans, hopelessly split by ideological differences, mobilized the language of freedom in multiple ways, resulting in contradictory outcomes for the state's diverse peoples. In the name of defeating slavery, Republicans simultaneously authorized the "liberation" of Indian apprentices and the exclusion and legal subordination of Chinese "coolies." They mandated the repeal of discriminatory testimony laws as remnants of slavery but condoned systems of forced labor to bring Indian "vagrants" into the free market. They called for the emancipation of bound Chinese women in the sex trade but also clamored for their expulsion from free society. If California emerged from the Civil War era reconstructed, its transformation was as incomplete and imperfect as that of the rest of the Union.

CHAPTER SEVEN

Reconstructing California,
Reconstructing the Nation

When the steamship *Japan* docked in San Francisco in August 1874, it brought 589 Chinese passengers to California's shores. Among the new migrants were twenty-year-old Ah Fook and her nineteen-year-old sister, Ah Fung. The women had suffered intense poverty in their home country. They took passage aboard a ship in Hong Kong and sailed to San Francisco, where they hoped to join Ah Fook's husband and to find work in the needle trades. Upon arriving in the port city after a long sea voyage, the women embarked on another difficult journey through the California legal system. California's state-appointed commissioner of immigration boarded the ship and examined the Chinese passengers. He pronounced the sisters and twenty other female Chinese migrants to be "lewd, debauched and abandoned women." An 1870 California law, the Act to Prevent the Kidnapping and Importation of Mongolian, Chinese, and Japanese Females, for Criminal or Demoralizing Purposes, restricted the landing of women from Asia. Only women of "correct habits and good character" who "desire[d] voluntarily to come into this State" would be allowed to immigrate. Women who did not meet these qualifications—according to the commissioner of immigration—could not land, and the shipping company would have to take them back to China at its own expense. Ah Fook, Ah Fung, and their twenty countrywomen waited aboard the *Japan* in preparation for their deportation.[1]

The case of the twenty-two Chinese women, as the legal proceedings against the *Japan*'s passengers came to be known, would change the face of U.S. immigration law and racial policy during the Reconstruction era. After the Civil War, both Democrats and Republicans in California struggled to reconcile the exclusion of Chinese immigrants with new federal civil rights legislation that guaranteed all persons the equal protection of the laws. They did so by invoking the legacy of emancipation and the Thirteenth Amendment.

Drawing upon a decade and a half of free-soil and antislavery arguments against Chinese coolies and enslaved prostitutes, California's legislators carefully crafted racially discriminatory immigration measures that evaded civil rights legislation by masquerading as antislavery laws. The 1870 statute under which the twenty-two Chinese women were detained purported to restrict the immigration of Asian women because they were potential enslaved prostitutes, not because they were nonwhite. An almost identical California law, passed on the same day, targeted Chinese men in a similar fashion. The Act to Prevent the Immigration of Chinese Criminals and to Prevent the Establishment of Coolie Slavery required transpacific carriers to prove that their passengers were not coolies but people of good character who "desire[d] voluntarily to come into this State."[2] Together, the 1870 laws avoided explicitly excluding Chinese on the basis of race or national origin alone, a proposition that would violate the Fourteenth Amendment and the Civil Rights Act of 1870. Instead, they claimed to break up the transpacific slave trade and to guarantee that only free laborers and voluntary emigrants came to the nation's shores.

Although the federal courts later struck down these laws, California's 1870 bills eventually became the models for the first federal anti-Chinese exclusion act, the Page Law of 1875. Horace Page, the California Republican who championed it, framed it to exclude enslaved Asian prostitutes and coolies—consonant with the Thirteenth Amendment—rather than to prohibit all Chinese as a racial group—a policy at odds with Republican civil rights legislation. Restricting Chinese immigration by targeting specific undesirable groups of "unfree" Chinese rather than the Chinese as a whole, the Page Law set the stage for the Chinese Exclusion Act of 1882. That act purported not to deny entry to all Chinese, only to Chinese laborers who were cast as imported, servile workers who threatened American free white labor. California's struggle over Chinese "slavery," a contest that stretched back to the early 1850s, thus transformed national postwar racial policy. What happened in California helps to explain how Reconstruction, the era of civil rights and equal protection, simultaneously became the era of Chinese exclusion.[3]

The Democratic Reconstruction of California

California's postwar campaign against Chinese "slaves" began almost immediately after Appomattox. The rift between Republicans and Democrats in the state's Union Party widened once the war ended. During the fall of 1865, many Democrats in the Union coalition were disillusioned by Radical Republicans' stand on black and Chinese civil rights. They bolted and rejoined old Democratic stalwarts "upon the principle of opposition to negro suffrage."[4] The rupture became nearly complete when the question of Chinese immigration and civil rights reemerged during the state elections of 1867. A postwar economic downturn, increased Chinese migration via the new Pacific Mail steamship route from Hong Kong, and the movement of Chinese workers into manufacturing jobs contributed to a growing tide of anti-Chinese agitation among urban, working-class whites. Anticoolie leagues made up mainly of Irish immigrants, trade unionists, and Democratic supporters cropped up in California's cities. The most prominent, the Pacific Coast Anti-Coolie Association, pledged to protect free white labor from coolie competition, to press for the legal restriction of Chinese immigration, and to expel Chinese immigrants from the state.[5]

The stance of the Union Party's 1867 nominee for governor only helped fuel the Democrats' fire. A moderate Republican much criticized for his political opportunism and corruption, George C. Gorham tried to walk a middle ground on the Chinese question that would mollify diverse constituencies—Radicals, moderates, and a dwindling number of old Democrats—within the disintegrating Union coalition. Gorham embraced the Thirteenth Amendment and declared himself "opposed to human slavery, and to all its substitutes and aliases; coolieism, peonage, contract systems in which one side makes the bargain for both." While this stance made him sympathetic to fears of coolie labor, he proclaimed that it did not make him the foe of Chinese workers. Repeating arguments California's Radical Republicans had made during the Civil War, he emphasized that the solution to the "coolie" problem was to liberate and uplift Chinese migrants rather than to exclude or persecute them. "Because I am opposed to the Coolie system, I am not the enemy of its victims," he explained. Even if Chinese in California were slaves or coolies (a claim he disputed), they still belonged to the brotherhood of man, and "no man of whatever race has any better right to labor, and receive his hire therefor, than has any other man." He ended by likening the exclusion of Chinese to the perpetuation of southern chattel slavery. "I am as emphatically opposed to all attempts to deny the Chinese the right to labor for pay," he concluded, "as I am to the restoration of African slavery whereby black men were compelled to labor without pay." Gorham's simultaneous embrace of anticoolieism and antiracism did little to heal rifts in the Union Party that had been growing since the Chinese Police Tax and the Act for the Suppression of Chinese Houses of Ill Fame during the Civil War. Gorham also opened himself up to assaults from Democrats who, in a play on his initials, jokingly dubbed him "G. Coolie G." and denounced Republicans for welcoming unfettered coolie immigration. Erstwhile Democrats in the Union coalition continued to desert in droves to the revived Democratic Party.[6]

As the fall elections approached, the reunited and revitalized Democrats capitalized on the racial and labor ferment in the state to attack the Union Party on the issues of Radical Reconstruction, black suffrage, and Chinese immigration. They hammered especially hard on the latter issue. Few Democrats were overtly enthusiastic about emancipation. Nonetheless, they realized that they could use the putative status of Chinese men as coolie slaves and Chinese women as enslaved prostitutes to discredit the (now predominantly Republican) Union Party. They appropriated the Republican wartime idiom of free labor and abolition and turned it back on Union candidates. Declaring themselves the enemies of slavery, Democrats insisted that excluding the Chinese was the only way to protect the accomplishments of emancipation and safeguard the nation from human bondage. Chinese were bound laborers, slaves, whose presence violated the Thirteenth Amendment's prohibition on slavery and involuntary servitude and federal laws and treaties prohibiting the coolie trade. Chinese men also turned back the clock on emancipation by enslaving, trafficking in, and prostituting their own womenfolk. Finally, Democrats harked back to the antimonopoly arguments of the gold rush era and contended that capitalists and corporations would import Chinese bondsmen, control their votes, and reduce free white men to economic and political slavery. Unlike Republicans, who sympathized with both the Chinese and big business, Democrats promised to eradicate the Chinese slave trade and protect free white labor on its own soil against coolie slaves and capitalist masters. The party of African American slavery before the war, the California Democratic Party tried to remake itself into the party of coolie abolition in the postwar era.

Democrats' deliberate effort to align the cause of Chinese exclusion with abolition and emancipation began even before the 1867 election. Early in the year, one anonymous Democrat contended that the party's success depended on casting itself as the new champion of antislavery. Chinese were analogues to the African American slaves of yesteryear: "The Chinese are now sold and passed from master to master, just as slaves were in the South not long ago," he claimed. In destroying Chinese slavery, the Democrats had the full weight of the law and popular will on their side. "The law denounces this conduct; here we have the law with us. The community abhors slavery; here we have public opinion in our favor," he reminded his readers. Democrats could triumph by claiming to strike a blow against Chinese bondage.[7]

Henry Huntley Haight, the Democratic candidate for governor in 1867, successfully merged anti-Chinese and antislavery rhetoric into a critique of the Union Party and capitalist monopoly. Haight skillfully erased Democrats' long association with slavery, recast his party as California's savior from Chinese servitude and capitalist domination, and set up Republicans as the true proponents of human bondage. Haight had once been a Republican himself. Now he condemned Republicans' liberal racial policies, especially their toleration of Chinese immigration, for refastening unfree labor on the nation. Keeping the national gates open to China ensured that "all the serfs and scum of pagan countries" would come to the United States and claim equal citizenship. Peons and slaves who had "lived for centuries in abject obedience to one of the most despotic governments which ever existed," Chinese men degraded free American institutions. If Republicans succeeded in removing racial restrictions on federal suffrage or naturalization laws, Haight declared, "gangs of Chinese would be imported for their voting as well as working qualities." Corporate interests would use their control over Chinese slaves' votes to manipulate state politics and virtually enslave free white men. White Californians needed to ask themselves whether they would submit to political rule by "a servile, effeminate and inferior race of Mongolians."[8] The Democratic Party presented the only alternative to Chinese slavery and, eventually, white slavery.

Democrats' anti-Reconstruction and anticoolie appeal met with resounding success. Haight beat George Gorham soundly. Democrats gained a massive majority in the assembly, came a few seats shy of taking the state senate, and won two congressional seats. California was one of the first states that Democrats "redeemed" after the war. The Union Party dissolved as its Republican members started calling themselves Republicans once again. They strove for the rest of the century to achieve the dominance that they had enjoyed during the early 1860s.[9] In the meantime, Republicans battled ascendant Democrats who followed up on their victory with a vigorous repudiation of national Reconstruction policy. During the 1867–68 session, Haight and the Democrats simply chose to sit on the Fourteenth Amendment and not ratify or reject it. California went on record as the only free state that did not ratify the Fourteenth Amendment in the 1860s.[10]

The real rebellion against Reconstruction came in 1869–70 with the debates over the Fifteenth Amendment. In the struggle to defeat the amendment, Democrats continued to represent themselves as the party of freedom and antislavery. Republicans, they said, would use the votes of degraded African Americans and imported Chinese to consolidate corporate power, control elections, and make slaves of white freemen. Despite Republican protests that Chinese could not become naturalized citizens and would remain disfranchised, Democrats insisted that the Fifteenth Amendment contemplated extending suffrage to Chinese men as well as African American men. In the former Confederacy, the amendment threatened the "subjection of the white population . . . to the rule of a mass of ignorant negroes." In California, it portended both the revival of slavery and the political domination of a new class of masters and slaves. The Fifteenth Amendment, according to the Democratic Party platform, "degrade[d] the right of suffrage" and "ruin[ed] the laboring white man, by bringing untold hordes of Pagan slaves (in all but name) into direct competition with his efforts to earn a livelihood." It also promoted corporate domination. Universal manhood suffrage built up "an aristocratic class of oligarchs in our midst, created and maintained by Chinese votes," Democrats proclaimed. In Henry Haight's formulation, enfranchising Chinese who were "virtually owned and controlled here by a few companies" would be tantamount to giving the state over to the political "control of capitalists and corporations."[11]

Democrats took special exception to the wording of the Fifteenth Amendment. The amendment's declaration that states could not discriminate against voters based on "previous condition of servitude" could put the entire California government into the hands of Asian slaves and their capitalist masters. Democrat Eugene Casserly, California's newest U.S. senator, fumed: "No matter what may have been the depth of the degradation to which slavery of any kind may have reduced a hundred thousand, or any number of people from Asia, either Chinese or Hindoo, who may be imported here, no matter what their unfitness for the franchise, it shall not be in the power of California to prohibit in any degree to those degraded beings the right of suffrage in her borders. This amendment takes them all in." Enfranchising the enthralled Chinese laborer posed, in Casserly's estimation, an enormous threat to American democratic government. The Asian slave was "ready to work when and where he is bid, and for whatever wages he is bid to work, and, above all things . . . ready to vote as he is bid." If Republicans allowed Chinese laborers to enter the state in defiance of the Thirteenth Amendment, free white men would rapidly lose political ground to the wealthy capitalists who controlled Chinese labor and votes.[12]

Chinese gender relations also played a central role in Democratic protests. Enfranchising Chinese men, they argued, would overturn the proper roles and relationships of men and women in a free society. On the one hand, coolie slaves lacked the manly virtues necessary to become virtuous republican

"The Reconstruction Policy of Congress, as Illustrated in California." This Democratic campaign cartoon from 1867 illustrated the party's racial arguments against the Unionist coalition. Here Union Party gubernatorial candidate, George C. Gorham (depicted at the bottom of the tower), threatens to collapse all racial barriers to citizenship by supporting Reconstruction legislation for black suffrage and civil rights. Heathen Chinese, savage Indians, and even monkeys could clamber up the shoulders of white Unionists and African Americans to demand the vote. Library of Congress, Prints and Photographs Division, LC-USZC4-5758.

citizens. They were "effete," "effeminate," and "servile," abjectly obedient and dependent, easily controlled by their employers. On the other hand, Chinese men were also cruel slaveholders who bought, sold, and enslaved the women of their own communities. Henry Haight alleged that, among the Chinese, "women are degraded almost to a level with the brutes." In nearly the same breath that he condemned the "servile competition" posed by male Chinese laborers, he railed against the Chinese practice of "importing Chinese females by the hundred, for the vilest purposes." The 1869 Democratic State Convention denounced Chinese men for arriving under a "system of servitude" at the same time that it accused them of perpetuating a perverse form of sexual slavery. Chinese men in California had "no families, having thus far imported women solely for purposes of prostitution." They attributed women's condition to degenerate and inequitable Chinese gender systems: Chinese men believed that "women have no souls." Even though the Fifteenth Amendment would not enfranchise female Chinese migrants (or any other group of women), Democrats asserted that Chinese women's enslavement would nonetheless corrupt American politics. "In nearly every case," U.S.-born men of Chinese descent eligible to vote under the Fifteenth Amendment would be "the polluted and spurious offspring of Chinese brothels."[13] Chinese gender relations, based on immorality and abject slavery, corroded the nation's foundation of liberty.

Democrats appropriated and bent the Republican idiom of antislavery to good effect. Their tirades against the Fifteenth Amendment, filled with depictions of slavish Chinese laborers, overreaching capitalist masters, tyrannical woman traffickers, and brutalized Chinese women, resonated with white voters. Democrats routed Republicans in the 1869 state elections. They won control of the senate and increased their majority in the assembly by fifteen seats.[14] This overwhelmingly Democratic legislature then rejected the Fifteenth Amendment on January 28, 1870. California stood as one of only two former free states (the other was Oregon) never to ratify the measure during the Reconstruction era. Less than a week after California's repudiation, the Fifteenth Amendment gained the approval of enough states to become part of the U.S. Constitution.[15]

Radical Reconstruction extended its grasp into California, with or without the consent of the state's legislators. The Reconstruction Amendments, combined with a wave of civil rights statutes passed by Radical Republicans in Congress, obstructed Democrats' quest to rid California of Chinese immigrants. Policies originally aimed at aiding southern freedpeople threatened to undermine California's existing (and any future) anti-Chinese statutes. The federal Civil Rights Act of 1866, a law that extended basic legal rights to all people born in the United States, regardless of race, would likely overturn California's testimony laws barring U.S.-born people of Chinese descent from the witness box. The Fourteenth Amendment posed a more direct challenge to anti-Chinese laws. It decreed that states could not deprive any person within the jurisdiction of the United States (citizen or noncitizen) of life, liberty, or property without due process of law, nor could they deny any person the "equal protection of the laws." Measures that singled out the Chinese for special exclusions or penalties might be overturned as unconstitutional. This likelihood increased when a Republican Congress passed the Civil Rights Act of 1870, also known as the Enforcement Act of 1870 or the Ku Klux Klan Act. In addition to bolstering black voting rights in the South, this act explicitly extended equal protection to noncitizen aliens. It also prohibited states from singling out some immigrant groups for special charges or taxes; all immigrants had to be taxed equally.[16]

Any direct effort to restrict Chinese immigration also interfered with the federal government's power to make treaties and regulate foreign commerce, outlined in the U.S. Constitution. California's legislators had to take special care not to violate the Burlingame Treaty of 1868, the nation's most recent treaty with China. The project of Anson Burlingame, a Radical Republican with a strong belief in civil equality for all, the treaty extended generous and liberal terms to China. Recognizing "the inherent and inalienable right of man to change his home and allegiance," it allowed unrestricted voluntary emigration from China and gave Chinese in the United States all the privileges and immunities extended to the subjects of other favored nations. But the Burlingame Treaty did contain one significant loophole that anti-Chinese forces could (and would) exploit. Reflecting the Republican aversion to slavery, it condemned "any other than an entirely voluntary emigration" and prohibited importation of Chinese "without their free and voluntary consent." The treaty charged both nations with passing laws to ensure that all immigration was consensual and voluntary.[17]

Faced with a slate of federal laws and treaties that appeared to preclude anti-Chinese legislation, California Democrats resorted to creative lawmaking. They crafted two 1870 Chinese exclusion laws that purported to uphold the Thirteenth Amendment and the antislavery provisions of the Burlingame Treaty by restricting Chinese entry. Claiming that they merely sought to prohibit Asian slaves and quell the coolie trade, not to exclude the Chinese based on their race, Democrats proclaimed that immigration restriction was fully consonant with the letter and spirit of federal Reconstruction law. Federal courts later overturned Democrats' exclusion measures for violating the Fourteenth Amendment, but the laws found new life when the state's Republicans successfully pressed to get them incorporated into the federal immigration code. Federal Reconstruction law remade anti-Chinese politics in California, but California's struggle over Chinese "slavery" would, in turn, shape the trajectory of national Reconstruction policies regarding labor and race.

In March 1870, less than a month after the passage of the Fifteenth Amendment, California Democrats passed a pair of linked bills that they claimed were crucial to upholding the national abolition of slavery. The first, the Act to Prevent the Kidnapping and Importation of Mongolian, Chinese, and Japanese Females, for Criminal or Demoralizing Purposes, was the law that California authorities would use to detain the sisters Ah Fook and Ah Fung four years later. Like much of the anti-Chinese prostitution legislation that came before it, this 1870 act criminalized and hypersexualized Asian women. Its preamble declared the arrival of Asian prostitutes to be a threat to "public decency" that caused "scandal and injury" to the state. Each woman hoping to disembark in California had to demonstrate to a state-appointed commissioner of immigration that she was a "person of correct habits and good character" before she could land. She would then be interrogated to determine whether or not she was a prostitute.[18]

The provisions of the 1870 law were clearly discriminatory and probably violated the Fourteenth Amendment by subjecting Asian women to legal penalties that immigrant women of other nationalities did not face. Democrats were able to garner support for the law, even among Republicans, by framing it as a measure to suppress a broader slave trade between Asia and California, rather than as a law that prohibited the immigration of all Chinese women. The preamble to the bill alleged that one of its main purposes was to prevent the importation of enslaved women. Most female Chinese in the sex trade were "kidnapped in China, and deported [to California] at a tender age, without their consent and against their will." Moreover, the law, in addition to requiring proof that women were not prostitutes, also demanded evidence that they "desire[d] voluntarily to come into this State." Not all Chinese women would be denied entry; only women who failed to prove that they were not kidnapped and imported prostitutes would be prohibited from landing. Finally, the measure did not single out Chinese women. Women from China, Japan, and "any of the islands adjacent to the Empire of China" would face examination and potential exclusion.[19]

Democrats neatly tied the exclusion of Chinese men to that of Chinese women by linking the antiprostitution bill to a second (nearly identical) bill barring "coolie" immigration. The Act to Prevent the Importation of Chinese Criminals and to Prevent the Establishment of Coolie Slavery made Chinese men vulnerable to the same kinds of examinations and restrictions that Asian women faced. The bill started with familiar anti-Chinese rhetoric. The preamble blasted the arrival of "criminals and malefactors . . . constantly imported from Chinese seaports" and charged them with exhausting the state criminal justice system. Again, though, Democrats emphasized that it was Chinese migrants' status as "imported" men that was the basis for their exclusion. By the importation of Chinese criminals, "a species of slavery is established and maintained which is degrading to the laborer," it stated. The reintroduction of slavery was "at war with the spirit of the age" and had to be eliminated. Like female passengers from Asia, every "Chinaman and Mongolian," whether born in China, Japan, or the islands adjacent to China, would have to provide the commissioner of immigration with satisfactory evidence that he was a voluntary immigrant of good character. Failure to do so would mean detention and deportation.[20]

Democrats' efforts to restrict Chinese immigration on antislavery grounds met with protest from some Republicans. Charles Tweed, a Radical Republican in the state senate, condemned the bill restricting female immigration as a species of "class legislation." It unjustly singled out Asian immigrant women for deportation as prostitutes while exempting women of other nationalities from any legal penalties. It also unfairly criminalized female Chinese immigrants because it operated on the faulty "supposition that all women coming from [the Chinese] empire are prostitutes, and that there are no virtuous women among them." He proposed that no racial or national discrimination should be made. The law should apply to all female immigrants from all nations or be discarded completely. Tweed cried that the idea that "slavery exists among these people in this country" was simply false. Democrats only added antislavery language to the laws to create a "pretense for a necessity for their enactment." If passed in their current form, both bills would be "disgraceful to the State, and in direct opposition to the spirit of the age."[21] The Unionist editor of San Francisco's Alta California agreed. The legislature's failure to place immigration restrictions on "Jezebels of Caucasian blood" indicated that the 1870 law was motivated more by "hatred of the Chinese" than any real concern about unfree prostitution. "Who is interested in this shameful discrimination," he wondered, "and why not have a law that shall searchingly apply to all alike?"[22]

Democrats countered charges of "shameful discrimination" by contending that the laws were primarily antislavery measures. They restricted Chinese slavery and did not bar all Chinese wholly on the basis of race. One Democrat insisted that the anticoolie bill "was not to prevent Chinese immigration." It only sought "to prevent the influx of Chinese criminals, or of Chinese brought to this country against their will."[23] Another proclaimed that the laws were necessary, not just because the Chinese were immoral, but because "they are simply in a state of bondage worse than any which ever prevailed in the Southern States."[24] These explanations were convincing enough that Democrats turned some Republicans over to their side. When the bills came before the assembly, the restriction of Chinese female immigration "was passed without debate." The anticoolie bill raised more Republican dissent. Still, newspapers reported that although all of the "no" votes against it came from Republicans, "several Republicans voted with the ayes."[25] The law went into force in March 1870, and the state's new commissioner of immigration began screening and detaining Chinese women in July. Dozens of women suffered examination, detention, or deportation in the first four years of the law's operation.[26]

California Republicans Reconstruct the Nation: The Antislavery Campaign for Chinese Exclusion

The mild approval that some Republicans gave the Democrats' 1870 antiprostitution and anticoolie bills was a subtle sign of the party's changing response to the Chinese question. Whereas California Republicans during the Civil War had split between discountenancing arbitrary racial discrimination and the necessity of excluding Chinese "slaves," the 1870s saw the party increasingly united behind restriction. The national postwar resurgence of the Democratic Party—especially pronounced in California—left once-dominant Republicans vying for votes with their former rivals. California Republicans, who had declared arbitrary immigration restrictions against the Chinese "contrary to the spirit of the age" in their 1869 convention, changed their tune. By 1871, the state's Republicans advocated federal legislation against the Chinese "as shall discourage their further immigration to our shores."[27] The transformation of the California Republican Party portended changes in the national party. Confronting the economic depression of the early 1870s, rising worker protest, and cutthroat competition with Democrats, Republicans nationwide began to abandon the racial politics of the Civil War era. As the party turned away from civil rights and equal protection, it became more willing to embrace the anti-Chinese cause to attract votes.[28] California Republicans were at the forefront of this retreat from Reconstruction. They realized that they could more easily sway East Coast Republicans to Chinese restriction if they could square exclusion with the party's standing record on slavery and race. Success would come by following the model of California Democrats. California Republicans began casting exclusion as an antislavery expedient—one that preserved the Republican legacy of abolition—rather than as a racially discriminatory measure at odds with the party's ostensible advocacy of equal protection.

Horace Page, California Republicans' most influential anti-Chinese advocate in Congress, was quick to grasp the utility of antislavery in turning his party toward exclusion. Page won election to the U.S. House of Representatives in 1872 by portraying himself as a staunch advocate of immigration restriction. He introduced seven anti-Chinese bills and resolutions into Congress during his first two-year term.[29] Page argued that prohibiting Chinese entry was not a matter of racial exclusion but an issue of slavery's suppression. In a speech about one of his 1874 bills to prohibit Chinese "coolie labor," Page began by denying that racism lay behind the legislation. He claimed that he had no "prejudice against any people on account of race or color" and that he was "willing at all times and under all circumstances to accord to every people, of whatever nationality or color, the equal protection of the laws." The Chinese were an exception. They introduced immorality, paganism, disease, and poverty into California. Most damning, they undermined the nation's new birth of freedom. Chinese immigrants arrived under conditions "in comparison to which African slavery was a paradise." They came to California "as slaves to the companies which pay their passage." More distressing, slavery defined nearly every aspect of family life among the Chinese. "Woman, when not used as a slave, is something worse," Page confided. "The relations between parent and child are like those of master and slave" because the Chinese father "sells his son into servitude and his daughter for prostitution."[30] Chinese should not be excluded merely because they were Chinese but because they practiced types of slavery inimical to the postemancipation nation.

Page ultimately failed to get his coolie bill beyond committee, but the exercise taught him a valuable lesson for the future. As he outlined in an 1875 campaign speech, he had learned that only a law designed to restrict Chinese as unfree laborers had any chance of succeeding in the prevailing legal and political climate. "You cannot prevent voluntary immigration, but you can prevent involuntary immigration," he explained to his anti-Chinese constituents. "So long as the Eastern members of Congress believe that the people of California are prejudiced against this class of people simply on account of their race," Page observed, "just so long it will be impossible to do anything more about it."[31] Overcoming the Republican distaste for racially discriminatory legislation necessitated appealing to the party's regard for free labor.

The arrest of Ah Fook, Ah Fung, and their fellow passengers aboard the *Japan* in August 1874 came just two months after Page's calculated denunciation of Chinese slavery, and it helped him build his case for immigration restriction. California had already detained and deported dozens of Chinese women under the state's 1870 antiprostitution law. This time was different. Ah Fook angrily declared that "she had brought her sister here with a good intention" and managed to secure legal counsel with the help of Chinese in San Francisco and the steamship company who transported her to California. Her lawyers petitioned for a writ of habeas corpus alleging that immigration officers were illegally holding the twenty-two women. The 1870 California law under which the women were being deported was unconstitutional. It usurped federal power to regulate international commerce, violated the Burlingame Treaty, and conflicted with the Civil Rights Act of 1870. The case made its way through the California District Court and the California Supreme Court. Both ruled that the exclusion of Asian prostitutes was a legitimate and constitutional exercise of state police power.[32]

When the case went before the U.S. Circuit Court of California on appeal, however, the women received a much more sympathetic hearing. At the head of the court, temporarily presiding over its affairs, was U.S. Supreme Court Justice Stephen J. Field. A longtime California resident, Field advocated an expansive interpretation of the equal protection clause of the Fourteenth Amendment. In his dissenting opinion in the famous *Slaughter-House Cases* just one year earlier, Field rejected the idea that the amendment applied only narrowly to newly freed African Americans. Rather, he argued, it protected every "citizen of the United States against hostile and discriminating legislation against him in favor of others."[33] U.S. naturalization rules prohibited Chinese from becoming citizens, but the language of the equal protection clause specifically granted all *persons* immunity from discriminatory laws. Some immigrant women could not, therefore, be subjected to deportation as prostitutes if other immigrant women did not suffer similar penalties. In Field's mind, this was not merely a point of law but a matter of basic justice. Even though Field had no sympathy for the Chinese, he had little respect for laws that singled out "low and despised Chinese women" for persecution while allowing "the bedizened and painted harlot of other countries to parade our streets . . . without molestation, and without censure." Declaring the 1870 antiprostitution law unconstitutional, he released the women. At least one woman agreed to remain in custody so that Field's decision could be tested before the U.S. Supreme Court. In 1876, the case of the twenty-two Chinese women—under the title *Chy Lung v. Freeman*—became the first involving Chinese immigrants to come before the nation's highest court.[34] There the justices upheld Field's ruling. It seemed, at least for a time, that Reconstruction policy trumped any California attempt to exclude Chinese migrants.

The overturn of the 1870 antiprostitution law in the federal courts drew angry reactions from around the state. The *San Francisco Bulletin*, an erstwhile Unionist paper once sympathetic (or at least neutral) to Chinese immigration, issued a cutting review of Field's decision. The editor predicted that brothel keepers would soon whisk away the twenty-two "chattels" to Chinatown brothels, while legal officials stood helplessly by. "Had it been foreseen how broad a construction . . . has actually been put upon the Constitutional amendments designed for the protection of the enfranchised blacks," he later complained, "there would not have been anything like the same unanimity of sentiment over their adoption."[35] Reconstruction amendments aimed at reforming the South had rendered California helpless against Chinese immorality and slavery.

Horace Page used the outrage over the decision to press for exclusion at the federal level. Two months after Field released the women, Page started collecting affidavits from the state's leading white "experts" on Chinese immigration. His efforts focused on the "slave traffic" in Chinese women. He presented the documentation, including an "original bill of sale" for a Chinese prostitute, to the House Committee on Foreign Relations in December 1874. Page urged the House committee to pursue renegotiation of the Burlingame Treaty. China had not lived up to its treaty obligations because it had failed to enforce the section prohibiting involuntary immigration. The arrival of coolies "under servile labor contracts" and "the importation of Chinese women as slaves for prostitution" resulted. The United States needed a revised treaty to "operate as a wall between free and servile labor." The committee reported positively on Page's proposal.[36] It also looked as if Page would get the support of the highest-ranking Republican official in the country, President Ulysses S. Grant. In a December address to Congress, Grant sympathized with the antislavery impulses behind exclusion. "The great proportion of the Chinese immigrants who come to our shores do not come voluntarily . . . but come under contracts with headmen, who own them almost absolutely," Grant reported. He lamented that Chinese women imported into California for "shameful purposes" suffered from an even "worse form" of servitude than their male coolie counterparts. He conceded that some sort of restriction on Chinese immigration was necessary to halt "this evil practice."[37]

Page capitalized on Republican antislavery declarations against the Chinese to propose a supplement to the federal immigration code in early 1875. The Page Law, as the supplement came to be called, purported to enforce existing treaty stipulations by ensuring that all immigration from China and other Asian countries was "free and voluntary." Modeled closely on California's 1870 antiprostitution act, it prohibited the importation of Asian prostitutes and women who "entered into a contract or agreement for a term of service within the United States, for lewd and immoral purposes." In this way, as Kerry Abrams has observed, the Page Law treated suspected prostitutes as "female coolies" who could be excluded because they were imported under contracts and did not arrive voluntarily.[38] The law charged U.S. consuls in Asian nations with examining all prospective female immigrants, turning away women who appeared to be prostitutes or involuntary migrants, and issuing certificates to those who passed the test. American immigration officials in U.S. ports would examine the certificates and re-interrogate women upon arrival. A woman could be turned away and deported at any point in the process. Any ship captain who brought an unsuitable woman to the United States had to pay a $500 bond guaranteeing her future return to China or forfeit his vessel to pay for the cost of the woman's deportation. The Page Law also put harsher restrictions on coolies. It subjected those who imported Asian laborers "without their free and voluntary consent, for the purpose of holding them to a term of service" to stiffer financial penalties and jail time.[39]

Page's challenge was to convince a Republican-dominated Congress to pass an immigration restriction measure that targeted the Chinese and subjected them to legal penalties that other racial groups did not face. He did so by claiming that the supplement was necessary because China did not abide by the Burlingame Treaty and sent thousands of slaves to California's shores. In keeping with the law's stringent prohibitions against Asian women, Page made female slavery the centerpiece of his case. Affidavit after affidavit, collected in California and read into the *Congressional Record*, verified that Chinese men mercilessly bought and sold Chinese women for vile purposes. One missionary's testimony averred that "it is a very common practice among them to buy and sell young girls for purposes of prostitution." As they grew into adulthood, these women were "transferred from owner to owner like so many cattle . . . and retained in this slavery by menace and even force." A law enforcement officer wrote that "most of the Chinese women who are brought to San Francisco come here for the purposes of prostitution, and they are brought here as the slaves or property of individuals, firms, and companies, and sold here to other Chinese as chattels." Page followed these pronouncements by reading a bill of sale for a Chinese prostitute. He concluded with a plea for protection against Chinese slavery. If China did not enforce the Burlingame Treaty, it was up to Congress to end this notorious slave trade. American legislators had to "teach these traffickers in human beings that in this land of ours, where virtue is respected and honest toil appreciated, we will no longer submit to their infamous practices."[40]

Page's piles of evidence on Chinese slavery, combined with his pleas to stifle ruthless human "traffickers" by excluding involuntary immigrants, seems to have appealed to Republicans. The Page Law passed the Republican Congress "with virtually no opposition." Page gloated that even though Democrats had long claimed the mantle of the anti-Chinese cause, "it was left to a Republican Congress to secure some proper legislation on this subject."[41] In less than a decade, the national Republican Party would take credit for passing the first major federal law restricting Chinese immigration. When Democrats stalled and balked on the Chinese question, Page's law "*passed a Republican House and Senate,*" a Republican campaign text boasted nine years later.[42]

The underlying intent of the Page Law—Chinese exclusion—became clearer in its operation and enforcement. Instead of creating a mechanism for separating free Chinese women from unfree Chinese women, it shut down nearly all female immigration from China. The total number of Chinese female immigrants entering the United States per year plummeted. Whereas an average of 626 Chinese women came every year between 1869 and 1874, a total of only 265 Chinese women were admitted between the passage of the Page Law in 1875 and 1881.[43] This was not because most Chinese immigrant women were imported prostitutes who failed their examinations. While the law may have weeded out kidnapped women and potential prostitutes, it often ended up excluding Chinese women from all backgrounds. George Anthony Peffer has argued that U.S. immigration officials "demonstrated a consistent unwillingness, or inability, to recognize [Chinese] women who were not prostitutes." This attitude subjected all prospective Chinese female immigrants to lengthy interrogations and intrusive visual examinations that forced them to prove, beyond a shadow of a doubt, that they were "respectable" and migrated legally. The immigration process often shut out women like Ah Fook and Ah Fung who identified themselves as the wives, daughters, and relatives of Chinese men in the United States but who did not pass immigration officials' stringent tests. The lengthy, humiliating, and expensive process of gaining entrance to the United States, combined with the threat of deportation at any point, also probably discouraged Chinese women from attempting to immigrate at all. The call to defeat Chinese female slavery proved a convenient pretext for outright, and nearly total, exclusion of Chinese women.[44]

And so it was that the party that had recently discountenanced arbitrary and invidious distinctions based on race passed the most racially restrictive immigration measure in U.S. history up to that point. Republicans could explain away this contradiction, and even brag about it, because California members had inextricably linked the cause of Chinese exclusion to the party's time-honored stance as the party of free labor and antislavery. After 1875, the Republican Party turned ever farther from Reconstruction civil rights legislation. Republicans began to endorse blatantly racist arguments against Chinese immigrants. They complained that Chinese were inherently immoral, that they were pagans and idolaters, that they were filthy and diseased, that they were alien and completely unassimilable. But the accusation that the Chinese were unfree (or at least ambiguously free) and that their exclusion sustained (rather than violated) Republicans' ideals of freedom and equality continued to be central to the party's anti-Chinese campaign. By 1884, in fact, the Republican Party platform asserted that closing out Chinese immigrants was wholly consistent with the party's history. "The Republican party having its birth in a hatred of slave labor, and in a desire that all men may be free and equal, is unalterably opposed to placing our workingmen in competition with any form of servile labor, whether at home or abroad," it declared. This sentiment grew not from race prejudice, Republicans reasoned, but from intolerance for unfree labor. The party "denounce[d] the importation of contract labor, whether from Europe or Asia, as an offence against the spirit of American institutions," though, tellingly, it only called for immigration restrictions on Chinese contract laborers.[45]

If the Page Law amounted to the wholesale exclusion of Chinese women, the near-total exclusion of all Chinese was not far behind. The rise of the Workingmen's Party of California (WPC) in 1877 made restriction a priority for both Democrats and Republicans. An independent labor party that advocated the eight-hour day, checks on corporate power, and the expulsion of Chinese from the labor market, the WPC blasted the two major parties for being soft on the "coolie" question. When WPC candidates managed to win one-third of all the seats to California's second constitutional convention in 1878–79, they made the elimination of Chinese coolie labor a keystone of state policy and a requirement for workingmen's support. The new state constitution that WPC delegates helped to draft retained the old 1849 prohibition on slavery and involuntary servitude but now specifically added Chinese contract labor to the list of working relations that the state would no longer tolerate. California's 1879 constitution declared that "Asiatic coolieism, is a form of human slavery, and is forever prohibited in this State." It voided all "contracts for coolie labor," prohibited corporations from hiring any Chinese, and charged the state's future legislators with passing laws to cut off Chinese immigration.[46] In the eyes of California state law, Chinese workers and slaves were now officially one and the same.

In the wake of the WPC revolt, California's congressional delegation pushed East Coast colleagues harder to modify the Burlingame Treaty's promise of unrestricted Chinese immigration. California Republican congressman Horace Davis begged "men of all parties who hate the memory of slavery [to] relieve our young State from the blight of contract labor."[47] Democrats in Congress responded in 1879 with the Fifteen Passenger Bill, a law that prohibited American ships from bringing more than fifteen Chinese passengers to the United States at one time. Republican president Rutherford B. Hayes vetoed the law, not because of its invidious racial distinctions, but because it violated the Burlingame Treaty. Hayes was optimistic, however, that the unfree laboring status of the Chinese gave the United States a way out of this predicament. Article 5 of the Burlingame Treaty banned the immigration of coolies and was supposed to grant the United States "protection against servile importation in the guise of immigration." The Chinese government's failure to enforce article 5, its unwillingness or inability to suppress the importation of coolie slaves to the United States, provided Americans with grounds for demanding a revised treaty.[48] Hayes's successor, James A. Garfield, agreed. In his acceptance letter for the Republican nomination, Garfield boasted that the United States had long opened its doors to all immigrants. But Chinese immigration was substantially different. "It is too much like an importation to be welcomed without restriction; too much like an invasion to be looked upon without solicitude," he wrote. Taking the new Republican line, he objected that the ease with which Chinese slaves masqueraded as free immigrants necessitated treaty renegotiation and, ultimately, restriction. "We cannot consent to allow any form of servile labor to be introduced among us under the guise of immigration," Garfield warned.[49]

Garfield's claim that the United States needed to bar Chinese immigration to prevent imported and servile Chinese from sneaking into the country under "the guise of immigration" provided a powerful rationale for the revision of the Burlingame Treaty. In 1880, a special diplomatic delegation traveled to China to modify existing treaty provisions regarding immigration. By November, diplomats had negotiated a revised treaty that permitted the

VOL. VII.–No. 175.   JULY 14, 1880.   Price, 10 Cents.

"What fools these Mortals be!"
MIDSUMMER-NIGHTS DREAM

Puck

PUBLISHED BY
KEPPLER & SCHWARZMANN.   NEW YORK   OFFICE No. 21 – 23 WARREN ST.
TRADE MARK REGISTERED 1876.
"ENTERED AT THE POST OFFICE AT NEW YORK, AND ADMITTED FOR TRANSMISSION THROUGH THE MAILS AT SECOND CLASS RATES"

"Where Both Platforms Agree—No Vote—No Use to Either Party." This cartoon shows the convergence of the national Democratic and Republican party platforms on restricting Chinese immigration by the early 1880s. Republican James Garfield and Democrat Winfield Scott Hancock nail their parties' anti-Chinese platforms together to box in the Chinese on both sides. Puck, July 14, 1880, Library of Congress, Prints and Photographs Division, LC-DIG-ds-00868.

United States to restrict or suspend the entrance of Chinese laborers when it felt that these immigrants threatened the nation's "interests" or "good order." Chinese merchants, Chinese traveling for education or pleasure, and Chinese laborers already living in the United States enjoyed exemption from these restrictions. In singling out Chinese *laborers* for potential exclusion and allowing other Chinese to immigrate freely, the new provision seemed to validate California Republicans' evolving exclusion argument. Restricting Chinese immigration was a matter of keeping out an undesirable group of servile and unfree workers; no one aimed to exclude all Chinese purely on racial grounds.[50]

The revision of the Burlingame Treaty laid the groundwork for a broad exclusion law two years later. In 1882, John F. Miller, a Republican senator from California, proposed the original bill that eventually became the Chinese Exclusion Act. Miller's bill purported merely to enforce the revised Burlingame Treaty by suspending the entrance of Chinese laborers for the next twenty years. Miller cast his measure not as an all-purpose Chinese exclusion bill but as an antislavery and anticoolie bill. If Congress failed to pass the measure, its inaction would guarantee "the introduction of Chinese coolies into the United States in the future." Miller went on to paint a grim portrait of the nation under the grip of this Chinese slavery: "An adverse vote now is to commission under the broad seal of the United States, all the speculators in human labor, all the importers of human muscle, all the traffickers in human flesh, to ply their infamous trade without impediment under the protection of the American flag, and empty the teeming, seething slave pens of China upon the soil of California!"[51] Defeating coolieism, a type of bondage identical to or worse than African slavery, required the exclusion of all Chinese laborers, regardless of character, background, or skill.

Miller's fellow Californian, Representative Horace Page, rallied Republicans in the House to the cause. Adopting arguments nearly identical to those he had used to ram the Page Law through in 1875, Page contended that restricting Chinese immigration grew from opposition to unfree labor rather than blind, irrational race prejudice. Exclusion did not conflict with the Republican Party's age-old principles; in fact, Page proclaimed that he was "proud as a Republican" to endorse it. "I belong to . . . that party which has always extended its hands to the downtrodden and oppressed of all lands," Page declared, affirming Republicans' long-standing dedication to civil equality. This belief was not at odds with exclusion because Chinese were contract slaves, not freemen seeking to better their condition. Page welcomed the latter, but he "would not extend [his] hand to a cooly slave brought here under a contract to be placed side by side with the white laboring-men of this country." His fellow Republicans could not, with any consistency, permit Chinese immigration to continue. Time and again, Republicans had eradicated all vestiges of human bondage. After working for the "suppression of African slavery," they had, just hours earlier, voted to eradicate Mormon polygamy, "a twin relic of the barbarism of slavery." Now the party had to complete its work and eliminate that other holdover of slavery, "the Chinese cooly contract system as found on the Pacific Coast." Other House Republicans joined Page's chorus and dismissed objections to Chinese exclusion as old-fashioned, maudlin, "sentimental philanthropy" on behalf of the colored races.[52]

California Republicans' plea that their colleagues would cast aside Republican promises of equal protection and civil equality in favor of banning coolie slavery won little ground at first. The exclusion bill provoked weeks of debate in the Senate and House. An emerging opposition coalition of East Coast Republicans, mostly aging Radicals, dismissed the clamor against the Chinese as the kind of outmoded, illiberal race prejudice that the party had long struggled to overturn. "The Republican party is founded on sentiment," Representative Ezra Taylor of Ohio exclaimed, and a "party born out of the anti-slavery sentiment, born out of the principle of liberty, cannot disregard sentiment." He personally deplored Chinese immigration but would not "sacrifice" his party's noble sentiments to vote for a bill that promoted race hatred and inequality. Senator George Frisbie Hoar, a long-time Massachusetts Radical and the bill's most vocal opponent, accused exclusionists of pandering to "the old race prejudice" that had enslaved African Americans and caused the Civil War. The Republican Party was above this kind of race-baiting, one Radical argued, and it should leave such shameful tactics to Democrats.[53]

Radicals also rejected exclusionists' antislavery appeals as disingenuous. If exclusionists sincerely wanted to ban only enslaved coolies and prostitutes, not construct racial barriers to all Chinese, then they would have framed the law more narrowly. By prohibiting the entrance of all laborers from China, exclusionists clearly wanted to bar free, voluntary Chinese immigrants who did not come under contracts. Only race distinguished these free and honest toilers from European immigrants. Senator Hoar admitted that coolies were noxious and that "no person whose labor is not his own property" should be allowed to enter the United States. But the exclusion bill made no such distinction. It targeted "not importation, but immigration . . . not importation, but the free coming" of Chinese. In short, it was "not the slave, or the apprentice, or the prostitute, or the leper, or the thief, but the laborer at whom this legislation strikes its blow."[54] The embargo on all Chinese laborers regardless of character or status, the lengthy twenty-year ban on these workers, and the numerous bureaucratic hardships imposed on exempt classes of Chinese who tried to prove their legal right to enter had but one end in mind. In the words of one Republican, the bill was designed "to throw such obstacles in the way as will, without regard to the [renegotiated Burlingame] treaty, greatly limit, if it does not prevent, all Chinese from coming to this country."[55]

Republican (and Democratic) proponents of exclusion countered this opposition by insisting that there was no such thing as a free Chinese laborer. "A cooly is a laborer and a laborer is a cooly . . . all of them are slaves," one testified.[56] Anything short of a total ban on all Chinese laborers would permit the revival of slavery in the United States. Others denied that the bill amounted to a racial prohibition on all Chinese. Laborers from China might be barred from entering, but the "coming of other classes for other purposes is unrestricted," one exclusionist pointed out. More than that, these exempt classes enjoyed greater rights than most immigrants because they had the full privileges and protections given to all citizens of most favored nations.[57] Republicans who supported the bill also sought to demonstrate its reasonableness and mildness by conceding a reduction of the exclusion period from twenty years down to ten years.[58] With a shorter time of operation, they argued, the exclusion bill would become a moderate measure for the temporary and experimental suspension of coolie importation, not a draconian policy that sought the total, eternal exclusion of all Chinese. Legislators of all stripes could vote for it without violating American principles of liberty and equality.

In its final form—after much wrangling, a presidential veto, and a hasty revision—the Act to Execute Certain Treaty Stipulations Relating to Chinese prohibited the landing of "both skilled and unskilled laborers and Chinese employed in mining." To quiet those who worried that a twenty-year suspension was too harsh and violated the spirit of the 1880 revised treaty, the bill's proponents agreed to the ten-year exclusion period instead. After these modifications, nearly half of all Republicans in Congress joined with Democrats to pass the bill. Republican president Chester A. Arthur signed it into law in May 1882.[59]

Like the Page Law before it, the Act to Execute Certain Treaty Stipulations Relating to Chinese ostensibly aimed only to restrict an undesirable class of ambiguously free laborers. The true intent of the law soon became evident in its semiofficial nickname—the Chinese Exclusion Act. It shut out vast numbers of Chinese. Most prospective Chinese immigrants labored in some capacity and could be denied entrance. Chinese women married to laborers could not enter the United States, further compounding the difficulties posed by the Page Law. The immediate effect on Chinese immigration was stunning. A rush of 39,579 Chinese arrivals came in 1882 to beat the exclusion deadline; by 1887, immigration officials permitted a mere ten Chinese to land.[60]

Immigration rebounded from this low as Chinese used the courts to challenge the exclusion law, gained entry by claiming merchant status, or established family connections to resident Chinese to evade the ban.[61] Congress nonetheless continually tightened up loopholes in the Exclusion Act to prohibit nearly all Chinese entry. Amendments in 1884 barred Chinese laborers embarking from non-Chinese ports from coming into the country. They also placed strict limits on who counted as "merchants" and made it difficult for exempt classes of Chinese to verify their status as legal entrants. The Scott Act of 1888 eliminated the old section that allowed Chinese laborers already legally resident in the United States to come and go freely. Any laborers who went back to China, even those who left family and property in the United States, could not return. Finally, the 1892 Geary Act exposed the fallacy of giving exclusion a moderate and limited trial. It lengthened the 1882 Exclusion Act another ten years. A subsequent treaty pushed exclusion forward another two years to 1904. When that year arrived, China refused to renew its treaty and Congress voted to extend the exclusion law indefinitely. It stayed in force until World War II.[62] Framed in part to keep out Chinese "slaves," the Chinese Exclusion Act severely restricted free and voluntary Chinese immigration for more than sixty years.

California politicians' careful re-racialization of slavery to encompass Chinese immigrants thus helped give rise to the United States' most virulent, enduring, and racially discriminatory immigration laws. Just as surely as national Reconstruction policy reached west to remake California's racial order, California's peculiar amalgamation of anti-Chinese and antislavery arguments stretched east to shape the contours of national racial policy in the 1870s and beyond. By emphasizing that the destruction of coolie slavery, rather than racial prejudice, lay beneath efforts to curb Chinese immigration, California Republicans legitimated racial discrimination within federal law. This strategy helps explain how the Republican Party, ostensibly dedicated to equality before the law, could become a major force for Chinese restriction. It also illuminates how the Reconstruction era, which saw the nation's farthest-reaching civil rights legislation, simultaneously became the era of Chinese exclusion. California's decades-long struggle over unfree labor, a conflict often overlooked or relegated to sideshow status in national history, played a critical role in remaking the racial landscape of postemancipation America. Unraveling Reconstruction in all its messiness, ambiguity, and complexity requires us to attend to postwar clashes over slavery and freedom on the nation's Pacific as well as Atlantic shore.

Conclusion

Beyond North and South

By most measures, Basil Campbell lived out the free-labor promise of the nineteenth-century American West. An African American man born in Missouri, Campbell arrived in California in 1854 with nothing to his name. In the next twenty-five years, as the nation went to war and reconstructed itself, Campbell raised himself from obscure poverty to secure independence to sizable wealth. From humble origins as an agricultural worker in Yolo County, California, Campbell began buying livestock and amassed a small fortune of $10,000 by the time that South Carolina seceded from the Union. He spent the early 1860s purchasing Yolo County real estate, and by the decade's end he owned a patchwork of 2,000 acres of prime ranchland near the small settlements of Cottonwood and Fairview, California. The postwar era found Campbell constructing a respectable middle-class life. He built a substantial farmhouse, married a black woman, adopted her children, and even began renting out some of his acreage to white tenants. Just after Reconstruction ended, Campbell's fortune had increased tenfold and he ranked as one of the wealthiest African Americans in the state. He voted in state and federal elections and served on county juries. He died a rich man in 1906 and left more than $80,000 to his heirs.[1]

But beneath Basil Campbell's classic rags-to-riches westering tale lies an unsettling story of a western journey taken by force and a term of bondage on the Pacific Coast. In 1910, two elderly African American men from Missouri sued Basil Campbell's widow in the Yolo County courts seeking a share of his estate. G. Wyatt Wheeler and John W. Wheeler claimed that they were Campbell's sons, born to him and a previous wife, Mary Stephens, under slavery in Missouri. Basil Campbell was born a slave and did not go to California in 1854 as a free man. A slaveholding Missourian named J. D. Stephens purchased him for $1,200 and took him to a farm 1,500 miles away in Yolo County.

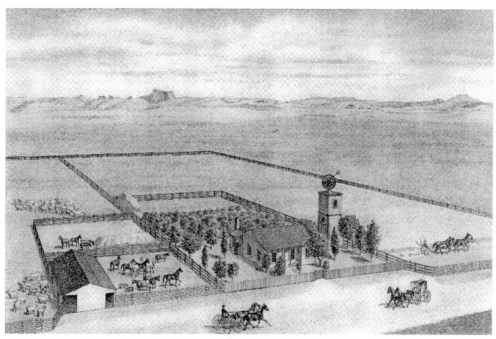

A seeming embodiment of the western free labor promise, Basil Campbell acquired this substantial ranch and became one of the wealthiest African Americans in California. "Residence and ranch, Basil Campbell, near Fairview, Yolo County," in Frank T. Gilbert, *The Illustrated Atlas and History of Yolo County, California* (San Francisco: DePue, 1879), plate 21.

Campbell's forced migration dissolved his Missouri family. Neither Mary nor her children ever saw him again. Moreover, Campbell's arrival on free soil did not mean immediate freedom. Like many California-bound masters before him, Stephens required Campbell to work out a term of labor before getting his freedom. He demanded that Campbell serve a full ten years. Campbell received, in turn, $100 a year from his annual earnings and the opportunity to end the arrangement early if he accumulated enough money to pay off his purchase price. Campbell invested his yearly stipend in livestock to raise the funds for his free papers. Finally, in 1861, he managed to buy his way out of bondage by paying Stephens $700 in lieu of his final three years of labor. Thus, despite California's constitution banning slavery and involuntary servitude, Campbell spent his first seven years in the Golden State laboring as an indentured slave.[2]

Campbell did build a new, prosperous life in freedom, but the legacy of his involuntary westward migration would haunt his family for another half

The California Supreme Court's 1910 repudiation of Basil Campbell's slave family exposed the coercive nature of western labor for many nineteenth-century Californians and the persistent legacy of the state's unfree past. *San Francisco Call*, May 8, 1910.

a century. In 1910, three California courts, including the California Supreme Court, ruled that the family that Basil Campbell had created in slavery had no legal standing. A marriage between slaves, "which neither party has the capacity to create and which either party could terminate at will, or which could be terminated by their master, is not a marriage relation, and it is mockery to speak of it as such," an appellate judge concluded. The Wheelers could claim no legitimate kinship ties to Basil Campbell and were not entitled to any part of his estate. Neither man could inherit the fruits of a father's labor reaped under California slavery or California freedom.[3]

Basil Campbell's biography is at once the most familiar and the most unrecognizable of western stories. In Campbell's rise to self-sufficient respectability, we see the standard hallmarks of the mythic western narrative: a poor man moves west and through his hard work and enterprise turns the region's abundant resources into a more prosperous life. In this version of the westering story, the region stands as a landscape of freedom. Untouched by the blight of slavery, the West presented hardworking, entrepreneurial free laborers with unlimited opportunities for geographic mobility, economic improvement, and landownership. The West's promise of freedom was so strong that even impoverished African Americans could overcome racial intolerance and previous servitude to become self-owning, independent citizens. Other parts of Basil Campbell's story puzzle and confuse. His journey west, involving a forced migration over long distances and resulting in the permanent break-up of a family, appears to have more in common with the antebellum interstate slave trade than the overland westward migration. Campbell's life in California, a life constrained by forced labor, white property rights in non-white bodies, and people of color's loss of legal rights to kin relations, seems more properly to belong to the American South than to the American West. In Campbell, a mythic vision of the West as a free-labor refuge, remote from the national crisis over slavery, sits uneasily with an alternative, almost antithetical, unfree West that reproduced the coercions and inequalities that prevailed on the East Coast.

That we see two conflicting, irreconcilable stories in Campbell's life speaks to the profound disjuncture between the history of the American West and the history of American slavery. In a mythic West purged of slavery and unfreedom, where relations of free labor are simply assumed to be triumphant, Basil Campbell and thousands of other Californians entangled in coercive labor relations have no place. They seem mere aberrations, insignificant and innocuous abnormalities in an otherwise free land. But the view changes once we weave together the experiences of California slaves, indentured servants, captives, apprenticed wards, contract laborers, and trafficked women into a broader story about western unfreedom. It suddenly becomes clear that the West was not an exceptional or isolated place during the Civil War era but that it endured battles over human freedom and human difference that paralleled those of the North and the South. If the West is the quintessential American region, that is because its history reflects both the nation's ferocious conflict over slavery as well as its promises of untrammeled individual liberty.

Just as California's struggles over unfreedom force us to rethink old tales of westering freedom, they also press us to create a new national narrative of slavery, emancipation, and Reconstruction that more fully takes into account the Far West. Breaking black-white and slave-free binaries at every turn, California's incredibly complex labor relations give us new insights into the contradictions of the emerging wage-labor economy, the demise of slavery and the rise of "free labor," and the remaking of American race in the nineteenth century. Adding the Far West to the story does more than give greater depth and complexity to our rendering of the period. The power of California antislavery and racial discourse in shaping national Reconstruction politics, particularly immigration policy, reminds us that the Far West was actually critical in the making of the postemancipation racial order of the United States. We cannot fully understand the trajectory of Reconstruction or the failures and contradictions of American race relations in this period without first looking to the struggle over slavery on the Pacific Coast. Reimagined as integral rather than peripheral to the story of American slavery and American freedom, the Far West becomes a new starting place for rethinking this most turbulent era in U.S. history.

Shifting our gaze toward the Pacific Coast is all the more important because in the 135 years since the end of Reconstruction the rest of the nation has come to look more and more like California. In its human diversity, in its proliferation of transnational labor systems, in its intense conflicts over how to draw the color line around national borders, nineteenth-century California foreshadowed (even anticipated) the demographic transformation of the United States and enduring national contests over race, work, and citizenship. Home to the nation's largest immigrant population, its most racially diverse population, and its largest prison population, modern California continues to be at the forefront of American struggles over freedom and belonging. Now, perhaps more than ever, we can better understand where the nation has been, and where it is going, by looking beyond black and white, beyond free and slave, beyond North and South, and lighting out for the West.

Appendix

Masters and Slaves in 1850s California

Scope and Methods

The following tables summarize data on probable California masters and slaves that I have compiled from the 1850 federal manuscript census and a special 1852 state census. Determining the slave or free status of African Americans living in 1850s California was a difficult and necessarily imprecise process. The 1850 federal census recorded 962 African Americans in California, and the 1852 state census reported 2,206 black and mulatto residents. But census takers generally failed to note (except in rare instances) whether these African Americans were free or enslaved. I therefore had to rely mainly on context to ferret out master-slave relationships.

I used a two-step process to identify probable masters and slaves. First, I cataloged every black or mulatto person reported in each census. This task was made easier by the recent digitization of the full manuscript census by Ancestry.com, a private genealogical data company that grants online access to paid subscribers. Ancestry.com allows for the searching of census records by race and color, and this powerful tool allowed me to compile a list of every person designated "black," "negro," "colored," or "mulatto" by census takers.

In the second step, I examined the manuscript census entries for every black and mulatto person that I found in step 1 to make an educated guess about his or her slave or free status. I analyzed surname patterns, household makeup, occupations, age, birthplace, and last place of residence. I determined that African Americans were likely to be slaves if they met at least two of the following criteria:

1. They lived in a mixed black-white household in which all or most household members were born or last resided in slave states.
2. They were born in or last resided in a slave state.
3. They were listed without a surname or shared the same surname as a white person living in the same household.
4. Their occupation was listed as "slave" or "servant" and they lived in a mixed black-white household.
5. They were African American children living in an all-white household.
6. I was able to determine the enslaved status of the individual by comparing his or her name against other records such as court cases, indenture contracts, or newspaper articles.

I have recorded the findings of this two-step process in the four tables that follow. Table 1 documents the birthplace of probable slaves, broken out by sex and age, as well as the birthplace of the master or head of household that I was able to associate with each enslaved person. Table 2 documents the number of probable slaves present in each of the California counties that reported data for the 1850 federal census. It is broken out by sex and age. It also includes the number of probable slaveholding households in each county as well as the average number of slaves per slaveholding household. Note that the number of masters documented in Table 1 is not identical to the number of slaveholding households in Table 2 because multiple masters often lived in each slaveholding household (such as when two slaveholding relatives lived together). Table 3 summarizes data on the birthplace and last place of residence of both probable masters and slaves drawn from the 1852 census. Last place of residence, a category not included in the 1850 federal census, allows a more nuanced looked at the migration patterns of slaveholders and the enslaved. We can see, for instance, that most slaves and masters from North Carolina went directly from that state to California. On the other hand, many more masters and slaves last resided in Missouri than were actually born there, indicating that slaveholders had moved to Missouri with their bondpeople before later embarking for California. Some slaveholders may also have claimed Missouri as their last place of residence because they left from there on the overland trail to California. Finally, Table 4 replicates the format of Table 2 and presents data from the 1852 state census.

Sources and Accuracy

The incomplete nature of both the 1850 and 1852 censuses may have resulted in a substantial undercount of masters and slaves in my study. The extreme mobility of population in gold rush California and the far-flung dispersion of miners across vast and isolated areas led to underreporting across the state. It is likely that census takers in both 1850 and 1852 missed hundreds (even thousands) of people, including possible masters and slaves. Missing and lost census data also make a complete picture of master-slave relationships impossible. The 1850 federal census reports for Contra Costa, Santa Clara, and San Francisco counties were destroyed in a fire or lost in the mail on their way to Washington, D.C. Therefore, the 1850 tables here do not document possible masters and slaves in San Francisco, California's largest city. The 1852 state census poses even greater challenges. The manuscript census sheets from Colusa, Sutter, and Marin counties are missing, and the Butte County entries are largely illegible. Also, since only whites were eligible for citizenship in California, some counties simply omitted Indians, Chinese, and African Americans from their 1852 counts. In all, this census snapshot probably represents only a partial picture of African American slavery in California during the gold rush.[1]

TABLE 1. Origins of Probable California Masters and Slaves, 1850

Birthplace	Total Slaves	Male Slaves	Female Slaves	Slaves under Age 21	Master or Head of Household
Alabama	8	6	2	3	6
Arkansas	16	12	4	5	6
California	2	1	1	2	0
England	0	0	0	0	1
French colonies	1	1	0	0	0
Georgia	4	2	2	1	4
Illinois	0	0	0	0	1
Kentucky	27	21	6	5	11
Louisiana	3	3	0	0	3
Maryland	4	3	1	2	4
Mississippi	3	2	1	1	1
Missouri	27	22	5	8	14
New Hampshire	0	0	0	0	1
New York	0	0	0	0	3
None listed	3	3	0	0	0
North Carolina	18	15	3	2	4
Pennsylvania	0	0	0	0	2
South Carolina	4	4	0	0	5
Tennessee	27	24	3	7	18
Texas	13	7	6	9	1
Virginia	43	35	8	8	19
TOTAL	203	161	42	53	104

Source: U.S. Bureau of the Census, Seventh Federal Population Census, 1850, Record Group 29, Microfilm Publication M432, National Archives and Records Administration, Washington, D.C.

TABLE 2. Probable California Masters and Slaves, by Age and Sex, 1850

California County	Total Slaves	Male Slaves	Female Slaves	Male Slaves under Age 21	Female Slaves under Age 21
Butte	7	6	1	0	1
Calaveras	20	20	0	2	0
El Dorado	37	33	4	8	3
Los Angeles	6	0	6	0	4
Marin	1	1	0	1	0
Mariposa	43	28	15	4	9
Monterey	1	1	0	0	0
Sacramento	16	9	7	2	6
San Diego	2	1	1	0	1
San Joaquin	2	1	1	0	1
Solano	15	14	1	2	0
Sutter	4	4	0	1	0
Trinity	4	4	0	1	0
Tuolumne	11	10	1	0	1
Yolo	3	3	0	0	0
Yuba	31	26	5	3	3
TOTAL	203	161	42	24	29

Source: U.S. Bureau of the Census, Seventh Federal Population Census, 1850, Record Group 29, Microfilm Publication M432, National Archives and Records Administration, Washington, D.C.

Male Slaves Aged 21–45	Female Slaves Aged 21–45	Male Slaves over Age 45	Female Slaves over Age 45	Total Slaveholding Households	Average Slaves per Household
6	0	0	0	4	1.75
16	0	2	0	13	1.54
20	1	5	0	22	1.62
0	2	0	0	4	1.5
0	0	0	0	1	1
22	6	2	0	11	3.91
1	0	0	0	1	1
6	0	1	1	12	1.33
1	0	0	0	2	1
1	0	0	0	2	1
12	1	0	0	1	15
3	0	0	0	2	2
3	0	0	0	2	2
10	0	0	0	6	1.83
3	0	0	0	2	1.5
23	2	0	0	19	1.63
127	12	10	1		

TABLE 3. Birthplace/Last Residence of Probable California Masters and Slaves, 1852

	NUMBER OF SLAVES BORN IN			NUMBER OF SLAVES LAST RESIDING IN		
Location	Male	Female	Unknown Gender	Male	Female	Unknown Gender
Alabama	1	0	0	4	0	0
Arkansas	3	0	0	5	1	0
California	1	0	0	1	0	0
Florida	0	1	0	0	0	0
Georgia	5	1	0	2	0	0
Germany	0	0	0	0	0	0
Illinois	0	0	0	0	0	0
Indiana	1	0	0	0	0	0
Iowa	0	2	0	0	0	0
Ireland	0	0	0	0	0	0
Kentucky	6	1	0	0	1	0
Louisiana	0	3	0	3	6	0
Maryland	1	0	0	0	0	0
Mississippi	9	10	0	4	0	0
Missouri	15	7	0	27	8	0
New Hampshire	0	0	0	0	0	0
New Jersey	0	0	0	0	0	0
New York	0	0	0	0	0	0
North Carolina	51	1	0	45	0	0
Ohio	0	0	0	0	0	0
South Carolina	4	2	0	2	1	0
Tennessee	16	5	0	14	4	0
Texas	1	7	0	5	10	0
Unknown	6	1	1	4	1	1
Utah Territory	2	0	0	13	12	0
Virginia	10	4	0	3	1	0

Source: State of California, California State Census, 1852.

Slaves under Age 21 Born in	Slaves under Age 21 Last Residing in	Birthplace of Master or Head of Household	Last Residence of Master or Head of Household
0	0	2	2
0	1	0	3
1	1	0	0
1	0	0	0
0	0	4	2
0	0	1	0
0	0	0	1
0	0	0	0
2	0	0	0
0	0	1	0
3	1	12	1
1	1	1	4
0	0	0	0
12	0	1	0
10	13	6	27
0	0	0	0
0	0	1	0
0	0	2	0
7	6	12	10
0	0	1	0
1	1	2	2
8	6	10	6
7	10	0	4
3	2	7	7
2	16	0	0
2	2	9	3

TABLE 4. Probable California Masters and Slaves, by Age and Sex, 1852

California County	Total Slaves	Male Slaves	Female Slaves	Gender Unknown	Male Slaves under Age 21	Female Slaves under Age 21	Male Slaves Aged 21–45
Calaveras	17	13	4	0	4	4	7
El Dorado	12	12	0	0	1	0	9
Los Angeles	26	13	13	0	7	10	4
Mariposa	7	6	1	0	0	0	6
Napa	3	1	2	0	0	1	1
Nevada	2	0	1	1	0	0	0
Placer	3	3	0	0	0	0	3
Sacramento	10	7	3	0	2	0	5
San Diego	1	1	0	0	0	0	1
San Francisco	9	8	1	0	4	0	3
San Joaquin	32	17	15	0	5	10	10
Santa Clara	8	5	3	0	1	2	3
Solano	6	4	2	0	2	1	2
Sonoma	4	4	0	0	0	0	3
Tuolumne	10	10	0	0	2	0	8
Yuba	28	28	0	0	3	0	25
TOTAL	178	132	45	1	31	28	90

Source: State of California, California State Census, 1852.

Female Slaves Aged 21–45	Male Slaves over Age 45	Female Slaves over Age 45	Male Slaves, Age Unknown	Unknown Gender under Age 21	Total Slaveholding Households	Average Slaves per Household
0	2	0	0	0	9	1.89
0	2	0	0	0	5	2.4
3	1	0	1	0	2	13
1	0	0	0	0	3	2.3
1	0	0	0	0	3	1
1	0	0	0	1	1	2
0	0	0	0	0	2	1.5
3	0	0	0	0	8	1.25
0	0	0	0	0	1	1
1	1	0	0	0	3	3
5	2	0	0	0	12	2.67
1	1	0	0	0	6	1.33
1	0	0	0	0	5	1.2
0	1	0	0	0	3	1.3
0	0	0	0	0	3	3.33
0	0	0	0	0	6	4.67
17	10	0	1	1		

Notes

Abbreviations

BANC   Bancroft Library, University of California–Berkeley

CCHS   Contra Costa Historical Society History Center, Martinez, Calif.

CFSH   Center for Sacramento History, Sacramento, Calif.
              (formerly Sacramento Archives and Museum Collection Center)

CHS   North Baker Research Library, California Historical Society,
              San Francisco, Calif.

CSA   California State Archives, Sacramento, Calif.

CSL   California History Room, California State Library, Sacramento, Calif.

HASC   Holt-Atherton Special Collections, University of the Pacific, Stockton,
              Calif.

HEH   Henry E. Huntington Library, San Marino, Calif.

M234   Record Group 75, Microfilm Publication M234, Office of Indian Affairs,
              Letters Received, 1824–81, California Superintendency, National
              Archives and Records Administration, Washington, D.C.

PEM   Phillips Library, Peabody Essex Museum, Salem, Mass.

SHC   Southern Historical Collection, University of North Carolina–Chapel Hill

SCWHR   Seaver Center for Western History Research, Natural History Museum of
              Los Angeles

SC   State of California, *The Statutes of California*, 1849/50–1874

UCLA   Charles E. Young Research Library, Department of Special Collections,
              University of California–Los Angeles

UCSB   Donald C. Davidson Library, University of California–Santa Barbara

Introduction

1. Accounts of Shasta's kidnapping, Gomez's trial, and the child's recapture appear in *San Francisco Bulletin*, Dec. 13–18, 1856; ibid., March 30, 1857; *San Francisco Herald*, Dec. 13–17, 1856; *Sacramento Daily Union*, Dec. 17, 1856; ibid., March 31, 1857; and *Pacific*, Jan. 15, 1857. I first encountered Shasta's story in Lapp, *Blacks in Gold Rush California*, 154–56. Although contemporary newspaper accounts portrayed the incident as an outright kidnapping, Lapp was able to trace Gomez's connections to local abolitionist networks.

2. *Alta California*, Sept. 13, 1851; *Sacramento Daily Union*, Dec. 15, 1856.

3. An Act for the Government and Protection of Indians, Act of April 22, 1850, ch. 133, sec. 3, SC, at 408; *San Francisco Herald*, Dec. 16, 1856; *San Francisco Bulletin*, Dec. 13, 1856; ibid., March 30, 1857; Lamb and Lamb, "Dream of a Desert Paradise," 24–25. A copy of Wozencraft's petition for guardianship can be found in the appendix to Belknap, *California Probate Law*, civ. The Wozencrafts later moved to San Bernardino, where Shasta was photographed with the family in 1882.

4. "Significance of the Frontier in American History," in Turner, *Frontier in American History*. The "natural limits" argument is most clearly articulated in Ramsdell, "Natural Limits of Slavery Expansion." Works that emphasize the prominence of free-soil, free-labor, antislavery, and antiblack ideology in California and the Far West include Berwanger, *Frontier against Slavery*; and Almaguer, *Racial Fault Lines*, esp. 32–37.

5. See, for example, Earle, *Jacksonian Antislavery*; Holt, *Fate of Their Country*; and Morrison, *Slavery and the American West*.

6. My thinking here owes much to Almaguer's delineation of California's multiracial labor systems in *Racial Fault Lines*, as well as to Moon-Ho Jung's *Coolies and Cane*, which examines the U.S. debate over imagined "coolie" laborers whose liminal status between black and white, free and slave, and alien and immigrant disrupted familiar racial and labor binaries.

7. Here I build on the studies of scholars who have integrated Asian American history with African American history and the history of Reconstruction. My arguments about the tensions between Chinese exclusion and Reconstruction law, as well as the importance of antislavery rhetoric to framing the anti-Chinese debate, owe much to Leong, "A Distinct and Antagonistic Race"; Aarim-Heriot, *Chinese Immigrants*, esp. 84–102, 140–55, 172–214; and Jung, *Coolies and Cane*. Jung has gone the farthest in emphasizing the centrality of antislavery arguments in the campaign to restrict Chinese immigration. In focusing on Asian laborers in the Caribbean and Louisiana, Jung deliberately shifts away from familiar California-centered narratives of Asian American history to argue for Asian workers' crucial place in the national history of slavery, emancipation, and Reconstruction. This groundbreaking effort to recenter Asian American history may, however, discount the antislavery, anti-Chinese discourse emanating from California and its importance to the national coolie debate.

8. The prominence of California's role in the national push toward Chinese exclusion has been a matter of considerable disagreement among historians. As Andrew Gyory explains, the "California thesis" posits that the push for exclusion came from California's labor movement and that the state's congressional delegation led the campaign at the federal level. Restricting Chinese immigration only became a major national political issue once Democrats and Republicans coveted West Coast votes in presidential elections. In contrast, scholars who favor a "national racist consensus thesis" argue that anti-Asian stereotypes were widespread across the United States long before the California gold rush. National labor leaders seized the Chinese question to create solidarity among white workers and forced national political parties to take up exclusion. Gyory proposes that instead of responding to California or to organized labor, the "national politicians of both parties . . . seized, transformed and manipulated the issue of Chinese immigration in the quest for votes." Moreover, national politicians took up the anti-Chinese banner as a "smoke

screen" to mollify workers and distract from more pressing class inequalities of the industrial age. Gyory, *Closing the Gate*, 6–16. Here I shift the emphasis back to California and argue that the state's Reconstruction-era battles over alleged Chinese coolieism and enslaved prostitution were key to the national drive for Chinese exclusion.

9. Lamar, "From Bondage to Contract," 294, 317.

10. On slavery in the southwestern borderlands, see Ramón A. Gutiérrez, *When Jesus Came*; Brooks, *Captives and Cousins*; Barr, *Peace Came in the Form of a Woman*; and Blackhawk, *Violence over the Land*. On transnational labor migrations to the West and the unfreedoms associated with crossing vast western landscapes, see Peck, *Reinventing Free Labor*; and Sisson, "Bound for California."

11. Research on slaves and the fugitive slave law in California includes Finkelman, "Law of Slavery and Freedom"; Lapp, *Archy Lee*; Taylor, *In Search of the Racial Frontier*, 77–80; and Demaratus, *Force of a Feather*. On American Indian slavery, apprenticeship, and indenture in California, see William J. Bauer Jr., *We Were All Like Migrant Workers*, 30–57; Magliari, "Free Soil, Unfree Labor"; Magliari, "Free State Slavery"; Rawls, *Indians of California*, 81–134; and Street, *Beasts of the Field*, 39–59, 89–134. The scholarship on bound Chinese American women and sexual commerce in California includes Cheng Hirata, "Free, Indentured, Enslaved"; Tong, *Unsubmissive Women*; and Yung, *Unbound Feet*, 24–37. There is a large literature on the anti-Chinese movement and the "coolie" debate in California. Some of the most relevant works to this study are Gyory, *Closing the Gate*; Aarim-Heriot, *Chinese Immigrants*; Saxton, *Indispensable Enemy*; and McClain, *In Search of Equality*.

12. Berwanger, *Frontier against Slavery*; Berwanger, *West and Reconstruction*; West, "Reconstructing Race"; West, *Last Indian War*; Josephy, *The Civil War in the American West*; Paddison, *American Heathens*; Yarbrough, *Race and the Cherokee Nation*; Miles, *Ties That Bind*; Kidwell, *Choctaws in Oklahoma*; Mulroy, *The Seminole Freedmen*. A recent dissertation (Bottoms, "'An Aristocracy of Color'") also investigates the racial politics of Reconstruction in California, while William Deverell attends to how California functioned as a landscape of healing in the wake of the Civil War in "Convalescence and California" and "Redemptive California?"

13. Foner, *Reconstruction*, esp. 460–511; Amy Dru Stanley, *From Bondage to Contract*; Heather Cox Richardson, *Death of Reconstruction*.

14. Richards, *California Gold Rush*; Heather Cox Richardson, *West from Appomattox*; Arenson, *Great Heart of the Republic*.

15. On the Mexican prohibition of slavery, see Finkelman, "Law of Slavery and Freedom," 438. For the Wilmot Proviso, see Earle, *Jacksonian Antislavery*, 123–43; and Morrison, *Slavery and the American West*, 41–65.

16. California Constitution (1850), art. 1, sec. 18; Browne, *Report of the Debates*, 43–44; Richards, *California Gold Rush*, 62–77, 91–118; Morrison, *Slavery and the American West*, 96–115; David Alan Johnson, *Founding the Far West*, 24–40, 104, 125. The quotation is from Jessie Benton Frémont, "Great Events during the Life of Major General John C. Frémont, United States Army," 1891, p. 126, box 6, Frémont Family Papers, BANC.

17. For a discussion of the number of slaves and slaveholders present in gold rush California, see chapter 1 and the appendix to this work.

18. U.S. Census Office, *Seventh Census of the United States*, xxxvi–xxxvii; Shuck, *History of the Bench and Bar*, 253–54. The quotation is from Caleb T. Fay, "Statement of Historical Facts on California," pp. 18–19, Banc MSS C-D 78, BANC.

19. David Alan Johnson, *Founding the Far West*, 244–50.

20. Ibid.; Richards, *California Gold Rush*, 180–82.

21. Gerald Stanley, "Slavery and the Origins of the Republican Party," 3, 8–10; Winfield J. Davis, *History of Political Conventions*, 36.

22. This proslavery argument is usually associated with its most strident proponent, John C. Calhoun of South Carolina. Potter, *Impending Crisis*, 59–61; Morrison, *Slavery and the American West*, 58–61; Holt, *Fate of Their Country*, 30–35.

23. An Act Respecting Fugitives from Labor, and Slaves Brought to This State Prior to Her Admission into the Union, Act of April 15, 1852, ch. 33, SC, at 67–69. The contest over the fugitive slave law is the subject of chapter 2. For other scholarly works on the topic, see note 11 above.

24. For Sonoran migrations, see Susan Lee Johnson, *Roaring Camp*, 29–34, 59–63; Standart, "Sonoran Migration"; and Pitt, *Decline of the Californios*, 52–57. Scholarship on Chileans in the gold rush includes Susan Lee Johnson, *Roaring Camp*, 63–67; Melillo, "Strangers on Familiar Soil"; and Sisson, "Bound for California." Hawaiian contract labor in California is best outlined in Duncan, *Minority without a Champion*. On Chinese methods of financing California journeys, see chapter 1; Takaki, *Strangers from a Different Shore*, 35–36; Chan, *This Bittersweet Soil*, 25–26; and Qin, *Diplomacy of Nationalism*, 21.

25. The 1850s California struggle over "coolie" and "peon" labor is discussed in chapter 3, as well as in Susan Lee Johnson, *Roaring Camp*, 193–208, 242–51; Pitt, *Decline of the Californios*, 55–68; and Aarim-Heriot, *Chinese Immigrants*, 30–39.

26. The crisis over domestic labor, gender, and sex in the diggings is analyzed best in Susan Lee Johnson, *Roaring Camp*, 99–139.

27. Act of April 22, 1850, ch. 133, sec. 3, SC, at 408; An Act to Provide for the Appointment and Prescribe the Duties of Guardians, Act of April 19, 1850, ch. 115, sec. 5, SC, at 268–69.

28. An Act Amendatory to an Act Entitled An Act for the Government and Protection of Indians, Act of April 16, 1860, ch. 231, SC, at 196–97; Rawls, *Indians of California*, 91–105; Street, *Beasts of the Field*, 146–51.

29. On contests over the salability of women's bodies and labor—in contexts ranging from wage labor to slavery to prostitution—see Stansell, *City of Women*; Boydston, *Home and Work*; Amy Dru Stanley, *From Bondage to Contract*; Gilfoyle, *City of Eros*; Clark, "'Sacred Rights of the Weak'"; and Walters, "Erotic South."

30. On the rise of California Republicans, the collapse of the state Democratic Party, and the creation of the Union coalition, see chapter 6; Gerald Stanley, "Slavery and the Origins of the Republican Party"; Gerald Stanley, "Slavery and the Election Issue in California"; David Alan Johnson, *Founding the Far West*, 244–45, 249–51; and Chandler, "Friends in Time of Need," 323–28.

31. An Act to Amend an Act Concerning Crimes and Punishments, Act of March 18, 1863, ch. 70, SC, at 69; An Act for the Repeal of Sections Two and Three of an Act Entitled An Act for the Protection and Government of Indians [*sic*], Act of April 27,

1863, ch. 475, SC, at 743. The tensions in the Union coalition are addressed in Chandler, "Friends in Time of Need," 335–37; and Bottoms, "'An Aristocracy of Color,'" 80–83, 90–95.

32. San Francisco Regular Democratic Ticket, 1867, San Francisco Oversize Miscellaneous Collection, CHS.

33. Saxton, *Indispensable Enemy*, 80–91; Bottoms, "'An Aristocracy of Color,'" 75–127. In 1867, Democrats regained power in New Jersey and Ohio and took half of New York's legislature. On this point, see Aarim-Heriot, *Chinese Immigrants*, 107.

34. An Act to Prevent the Kidnapping and Importation of Mongolian, Chinese, and Japanese Females, for Criminal or Demoralizing Purposes, Act of March 18, 1870, ch. 230, SC, at 330; An Act to Prevent the Immigration of Chinese Criminals and to Prevent the Establishment of Coolie Slavery, Act of March 18, 1870, ch. 231, SC, at 332–33.

35. An Act Supplementary to the Acts in Relation to Immigration (March 3, 1875), ch. 141, *U.S. Statutes at Large* 18 (1875), 477. For discussions of the Page Law and its impact on Chinese women's immigration, see Peffer, *If They Don't Bring Their Women Here*, 33–37, 43–72; Chan, "Exclusion of Chinese Women," 105–9; and Tong, *Unsubmissive Women*, 47–50.

36. An Act to Execute Certain Treaty Stipulations Relating to the Chinese (May 6, 1882), ch. 126, *U.S. Statutes at Large* 22 (1882), 58–61. My argument about the interconnections between the Chinese Exclusion Act and Reconstruction policy and politics is influenced by Leong, "A Distinct and Antagonistic Race," 138–40; and Jung, *Coolies and Cane*, 37–38.

Chapter 1

1. Quinn, *The Rivals*, 66; Browne, *Report of the Debates*, 18. It is unclear whether Semple was himself a slaveholder, but census records indicate that his father, John W. Semple, owned eleven slaves. U.S. Bureau of the Census, *Third Census of the United States*, 1810, roll 9, p. 173, Burkesville, Cumberland County, Ky. For more on Robert Semple, see Warner, *Men of the California Bear Flag Revolt*, 107–23.

2. Browne, *Report of the Debates*, 148.

3. Ibid., 143, 150, 152. For the role of race in the constitutional convention, see Almaguer, *Racial Fault Lines*, 34–37; and David Alan Johnson, *Founding the Far West*, 125–30.

4. Browne, *Report of the Debates*, 338–40.

5. This analysis is influenced by the work of Tomás Almaguer and Susan Lee Johnson, who have examined the unstable nature of racial and labor categories in gold rush California. For these analyses, see Almaguer, *Racial Fault Lines*, 1–41; and Susan Lee Johnson, *Roaring Camp*, 185–234.

6. Coronel, "A Translation of the Mining Experiences of Antonio Franco Coronel," 76–78; Coronel, *Cosas de California*, 1877, pp. 143–44, Banc MSS C-D 61, BANC. On Coronel's background, see Bancroft, *Works of Hubert Howe Bancroft*, 19:768; and Woolsey, *Migrants West*, 138–59. For Augustín's age, see U.S. Bureau of the Census, *Seventh Federal Population Census*, 1850, roll 35, p. 7A, Los Angeles, Los Angeles County,

Calif. The census indicates that Coronel and his parents had six Indian servants laboring in their home.

7. Coronel, "A Translation of the Mining Experiences of Antonio Franco Coronel," 76–79, 81, 86–88, 93; Pitt, *Decline of the Californios*, 49–52; Susan Lee Johnson, *Roaring Camp*, 11–12, 30, 62, 219–20, 193–95.

8. An Act for the Government and Protection of Indians, Act of April 22, 1850, ch. 133, SC, at 408–10.

9. The literature on the mission system, secularization, the rise of the ranchos, and the hide and tallow trade in California is vast. This overview relies on Street, *Beasts of the Field*, 79–85, 89–101; Phillips, *Vineyards and Vaqueros*, 159–81; Monroy, *Thrown among Strangers*, 113–34; Pitt, *Decline of the Californios*, 7–10; Hackel, *Children of Coyote*, esp. 369–419; and Pubols, *Father of All*, 105–47, 164–89, 214–24. The quotation is from Weber, *Mexican Frontier*, 211.

10. Salvador Vallejo, quoted in Cook, *Conflict between the California Indian and White Civilization*, 305; Francisca Benicia Carrillo de Vallejo, quoted in Monroy, *Thrown among Strangers*, 153.

11. Almaguer, *Racial Fault Lines*, 48; Amador, *Californio Voices*, 218–21; Madley, "American Genocide," 36.

12. Rawls, *Indians of California*, 20–21; Phillips, "Indians in Los Angeles," 437–38; Weber, *Mexican Frontier*, 211; Pubols, *Father of All*, 220; Gillis and Magliari, *John Bidwell*, 106. Unlike Bidwell, Walter Colton, a magistrate in Monterey, issued an 1847 ordinance that allowed non-Indians to hold onto Indian workers to whom they had advanced wages. Madley, "American Genocide," 168–69.

13. Coronel, "A Translation of the Mining Experiences of Antonio Franco Coronel," 77–78; Phillips, *Vineyards and Vaqueros*, 202; Monroy, *Thrown among Strangers*, 143, 153; Wilson, *Indians of Southern California*, 51. On New Mexicans, Utes, and the captive trade in southern California and the Great Basin, see Blackhawk, *Violence over the Land*, 133–44; and Zappia, "Indigenous Borderlands."

14. Madley, "American Genocide," 36–37, 59–60; Revere, *Keel and Saddle*, 178–79; Revere, *A Tour of Duty in California*, 114.

15. Street, *Beasts of the Field*, 688n60. Michael J. González speculates that there were dozens, perhaps even hundreds, of Indian captives in the pueblo of Los Angeles alone. On this point, see *This Small City*, 124–44.

16. Coronel, *Tales of Mexican California*, 67; Pico, *Don Pío Pico's Historical Narrative*, 154–55.

17. On Sutter's captive raiding and his treatment of female captives, see Madley, "American Genocide," 37, 43; Street, *Beasts of the Field*, 104; Hurtado, *John Sutter*, 115–17; and Hurtado, *Intimate Frontiers*, 41–42.

18. *California Star*, Feb. 20, 1847; ibid., Sept. 18, 1847; Hurtado, "Controlling California's Indian Labor Force," 225–26; Madley, "American Genocide," 167–68.

19. Madley, "American Genocide," 65–69; Rawls, *Indians of California*, 119, 124–25; Rawls, "Gold Diggers," 33–37.

20. Pitt, *Decline of the Californios*, 50; Rawls, *Indians of California*, 116.

21. Simpson, *Three Weeks in the Gold Mines*, 8; Rawls, *Indians of California*, 121, 123; Hurtado, *Indian Survival*, 118.

22. Rawls, "Gold Diggers," 38–42; Madley, "American Genocide," 72–75, 81–94.

23. Case, "Reminiscences," 281, 288–89.

24. Rawls, "Gold Diggers," 38–42; Hurtado, *Indian Survival*, 107–8; Madley, "American Genocide," 92–94, 98.

25. Coronel, "A Translation of the Mining Experiences of Antonio Franco Coronel," 86–87, 92–93; Janssens, *Life and Adventures*, 137; Kelly, *Excursion to California*, 23, 33.

26. Madley, "American Genocide," 11; Lindsay, *Murder State*, 128.

27. On the aftermath of these expulsions and the effects of the gold rush on Native communities, see Rawls, *Indians of California*, 130–33, 171; Madley, "American Genocide," 67–68, 96–97; and Hurtado, *Indian Survival*, 108–11. An Act for the Government and Protection of Indians, Act of April 22, 1850, ch. 133, sec. 3, SC, at 408–10.

28. Coronel, "A Translation of the Mining Experiences of Antonio Franco Coronel," 77, 93–94.

29. Ibid., 93–94, 96n13.

30. Ibid., 77–78; Pitt, *Decline of the Californios*, 54–55; Susan Lee Johnson, *Roaring Camp*, 195; Kelly, *Excursion to California*, 23.

31. Bancroft, *Works of Hubert Howe Bancroft*, 23:113n5; Susan Lee Johnson, *Roaring Camp*, 61.

32. Susan Lee Johnson, *Roaring Camp*, 59–61. On the impact of Apache raiding on Sonora, see DeLay, *War of a Thousand Deserts*, esp. 141–64, 172–74, 194–98, 266–67.

33. Standart, "Sonoran Migration," 336–37; Susan Lee Johnson, *Roaring Camp*, 61–63; Coronel, "A Translation of the Mining Experiences of Antonio Franco Coronel," 79–80.

34. Coronel, "A Translation of the Mining Experiences of Antonio Franco Coronel," 81, 90–91; Standart, "Sonoran Migration," 335–36.

35. Pitt, *Decline of the Californios*, 54; Guinn, "Sonoran Migration," 32. For contemporary accounts of wealthy Sonorans traveling with their *peones*, see Woods, *Sixteen Months at the Gold Diggings*, 47; Meyer, *Bound for Sacramento*, 72–80; and *Alta California*, Jan. 20, 1851. For an analysis of how peonage operated in the New Mexico Territory, see Montoya, *Translating Property*, 63–73. William M. Case, an Oregonian who participated in the expulsion of Indian and Mexican miners in 1849, claimed that the majority of Mexican miners were peons. They had been imprisoned for debt in their home country and bailed out of jail by Mexican and American "speculators" who imported them to dig gold in the mines. No other evidence supports these claims, however. Case, "Reminiscences," 281, 288–89; Case, "Notes by William M. Case," 176–78.

36. Navarro, *Gold Rush Diary*, ix–xi, 1; Melillo, "Strangers on Familiar Soil," 263–64; Sisson, "Bound for California," 259–305; Sisson, "Diaspora," 47–93.

37. Melillo, "Strangers on Familiar Soil," 1–2, 9, 145–53, 231–33; Sisson, "Bound for California," 259–62; Monaghan, *Chile, Peru, and the California Gold Rush*, chapters 2, 3.

38. Melillo, "Strangers on Familiar Soil," 12–13, 132; Arnold J. Bauer, "Chilean Rural Labor," 1061–69.

39. Susan Lee Johnson, *Roaring Camp*, 64–65; Sisson, "Diaspora," 6, 16–31; Arnold J. Bauer, "Chilean Rural Labor," 1069–74.

40. Loveman, *Chile*, 120–21, 129–30; Sisson, "Diaspora," 23–35. The quotation is from Pedro Ruiz Aldea in an 1862 letter to *La Tarántula* newspaper, reprinted in Beilharz and López, *We Were 49ers*, 226–27.

41. On the nature of these contracts, see below and Sisson, "Diaspora," 47–93.

42. Sisson, "Diaspora," 69–70, 94–95. Some of these rural arrangements may have been *contratos de palabra*, informal verbal contracts. On this point, see Melillo, "Strangers on Familiar Soil," 264.

43. Kelly Sisson argues that these entrepreneurs constructed a "capitalist-peonage" contract labor system that fused older Chilean social hierarchies with the language and conventions of modern capitalist wage labor. Sisson, "Diaspora," 49–61.

44. Ibid.; Sisson, "Bound for California," 274–79, 281.

45. Navarro, *Gold Rush Diary*, 6–7.

46. Ibid., 38–40, 42, 60–62. A similar incident happened to Carlos Armstrong, whose eight *peones* contracted to work for him for sixteen months in California but then refused to do anything beyond pay back their passage money once they got to San Francisco. For Armstrong's dilemma and contract enforcement in California, see Sisson, "Diaspora," 94; and Sisson, "Bound for California," 286–87.

47. Barrows and Ingersoll, *A Memorial and Biographical History*, 368–69; Contract between Thomas Oliver Larkin and Jacob Primer Leese, Feb. 12, 1849, reprinted in Larkin, *Larkin Papers*, 138–39; Hague and Langum, *Thomas O. Larkin*, 167–68.

48. Indenture, Kanwa to Jacob Leese, March 23, 1849; Jacob Primer Leese contracts with Awye, Atu, and Ahine, Aug. 3, 1849; all in folder 11, Oversize Manuscript Collection 10, Jacob Primer Leese Papers, CHS. The latter group of documents has also been reprinted in the appendix of Lim, "Chinese in San Francisco," 109–14. Another set of contracts between Leese and Monq qui, 'Ai, and Achue, executed July 28, 1849, are items VA 160–VA 161b, in Mariano Guadalupe Vallejo Papers, HEH. A final contract between Leese and a man named Affon, dated July 28, 1849, can be found in Small Manuscript Collections Box 915, Jacob P. Leese Collection, CSL. A report in the *New York Times*, Nov. 8, 1885, suggests that Leese may have brought up to eighteen Chinese to California in 1849.

49. On the making of a Pacific World and California's place in it, see Melillo, "Strangers on Familiar Soil," 13–16, 26–93; Gulliver, "Finding the Pacific World"; Cartwright, "Pacific Passages"; and Osborne, "Pacific Eldorado." David A. Chang questions the usefulness of the term "Pacific World" for understanding gold rush California's place in nineteenth-century globalization. He argues that the term ignores indigenous peoples' concepts of history and geography and obscures Atlantic influences in the Pacific. He sees gold rush California as a complex borderland, one of many "nodes in a globalizing world," in which indigenous and nonindigenous peoples became linked together through social networks, family relationships, and colonial processes. On this point, see Chang, "Borderlands in a World at Sea," esp. 400. For the transpacific fur trade and its relationship to Chinese markets, see Gibson and Whitehead, *Yankees in Paradise*, 103–30; and Melillo, "Strangers on Familiar

Soil," 72–76. For the transformation of Chinese trade by British imperialism, see ibid., 40–41; Qin, *Diplomacy of Nationalism*, 17–18; Chan, *This Bittersweet Soil*, 22–23; and Susan Lee Johnson, *Roaring Camp*, 84.

50. Beechert, *Working in Hawaii*, 12–39; Takaki, *Pau Hana*, 3–21; Gibson and Whitehead, *Yankees in Paradise*, 156–58, 269–84; Silva, *Aloha Betrayed*, 15–44; Cartwright, "Pacific Passages," 46–63. On Chinese and Hawaiian labor migrations prior to the gold rush, see Susan Lee Johnson, *Roaring Camp*, 81–85; Chan, *This Bittersweet Soil*, 16–26; Cartwright, "Pacific Passages," 99–108; Duncan, *Minority without a Champion*; and Duncan, "Kanaka World Travelers."

51. Hurtado, *John Sutter*, 44–45; Duncan, *Minority without a Champion*, 1–15; Dillon, "Kanaka Colonies"; Lamar, "From Bondage to Contract," 309–10; Indenture, Kanwa to Jacob Leese, March 23, 1849, folder 11, Oversize Manuscript Collection 10, Jacob Primer Leese Papers, CHS.

52. Wyatt, "Alaska and Hawai'i," 570, 578; Hurtado, *John Sutter*, 44; Beechert, *Working in Hawaii*, 6–14.

53. Hurtado, *John Sutter*, 44–45; Lamar, "From Bondage to Contract," 309; Duncan, *Minority without a Champion*, 9, 11. An 1840 contract between the governor of Oahu and a Hudson's Bay Company official required that the Englishman forfeit twenty dollars for every worker who never returned to the Islands or deserted "by reason of ill treatment." Blue, "A Hudson's Bay Company Contract."

54. Hurtado, *John Sutter*, 45, 58, 115, 239; Sutter, "Discovery of Gold," 197–98.

55. Kelly, *Excursion to California*, 32–33; Haskins, *Argonauts of California*, 77–78. On Hawaiian communities in gold rush California, particularly their interaction with Native American communities, see Chang, "Borderlands in a World at Sea."

56. U.S. Bureau of the Census, *Seventh Federal Population Census*, 1850, roll 36, pp. 32B–33A, 35A–35B, Lacy['s] Bar and Manhattan Bar, Sutter County, Calif.

57. Qin, *Diplomacy of Nationalism*, 13–17; Chan, *This Bittersweet Soil*, 7–16; Chen, "Internal Origins of Chinese Emigration," 531–38.

58. Qin, *Diplomacy of Nationalism*, 17–19; Chan, *This Bittersweet Soil*, 18–20; Susan Lee Johnson, *Roaring Camp*, 83–85; Hsu, *Dreaming of Gold*, 16–31. Yong Chen argues that scholars have overestimated the degree to which overpopulation, poverty, and political chaos were push factors for Chinese immigration to California. He emphasizes that the commercial and cultural vitality of Guangdong Province, as well as its extensive involvement in international trade, prompted the region's residents to look abroad for economic opportunities. On this point, see Chen, "Internal Origins of Chinese Emigration," 522–46; and Chen, *Chinese San Francisco*, 11–23.

59. See note 48 above for full citations for the contracts between Jacob Leese and Monq qui, 'Ai, Achue, Awye, Atu, Ahine, and Affon.

60. Qin, *Diplomacy of Nationalism*, 21.

61. Bernard Peyton Jr., Contract, June 11, 1852, reproduced in Lim, "Chinese in San Francisco," 117–18. See note 48 above for full citations for the contracts between Jacob Leese and Monq qui, 'Ai, Achue, Awye, Atu, Ahine, and Affon. Entire performance clauses were common components of antebellum American labor contracts, especially in the agricultural sector. By the 1850s and 1860s, however, the rise of free-labor ideology led to the decline of entire performance as judges began to

uphold workers' right to quit and to receive partial wages for uncompleted contracts. Schmidt, *Free to Work*, 7–52.

62. *Stockton Times*, March 23, 1850; Lucett, *Rovings in the Pacific*, 363–64.

63. *Alta California*, March 25, 1851; ibid., May 16, 1851; Barth, *Bitter Strength*, 57. On the enforceability of foreign labor contracts in California, see chapter 3.

64. In 1853, a committee of Chinese merchants reported to the California assembly that some Chinese had arrived under fixed contracts in the early years of the gold rush. The practice quickly diminished, however, because "it was not found to be as profitable as was anticipated and is now abandoned." Instead, most Chinese "hired money" to finance California journeys. "Report of the Committee on Mines and Mining Interests," in State of California, *Appendix to the Journal of the Assembly*, 4th sess. (1853), 10.

65. Agreement between the English Merchant and Chinamen, 1849, reprinted in Lim, "Chinese in San Francisco," 115–16.

66. On the basic principles of the credit-ticket system, see Takaki, *Strangers from a Different Shore*, 35–36; Chan, *This Bittersweet Soil*, 25–26; and Qin, *Diplomacy of Nationalism*, 21.

67. "Report of the Committee on Mines and Mining Interests," in State of California, *Appendix to the Journal of the Assembly*, 4th sess. (1853), 10. The enforcement mechanisms that Chinese merchants used to ensure repayment under the credit-ticket system are a source of controversy among immigration scholars. Patricia Cloud and David W. Galenson argue that the Six Companies extended credit to migrants, managed their debts, and prohibited them from returning to China before they fulfilled their obligations. Cloud and Galenson, "Chinese Immigration," 26–34. Charles McClain and Yucheng Chen dispute that the Six Companies played any role in recruiting labor from abroad or enforcing debt agreements. The companies served only as mutual aid societies and fraternal organizations for their members. The idea that the Six Companies imported "coolie" workers, enforced labor contracts, and collected debts was an invention of the anti-Chinese movement in the 1860s and 1870s. McClain, "Chinese Immigration," esp. 367–72; Qin, *Diplomacy of Nationalism*, 63–77.

68. *Alta California*, March 8, 1851; Tong, *Unsubmissive Women*, 6–9; Yung, *Unbound Feet*, 33–34; Hurtado, *Intimate Frontiers*, 90–91.

69. *Alta California*, Aug. 15, 1852; *Sacramento Daily Union*, March 22, 1855.

70. Cheng Hirata, "Free, Indentured, Enslaved," 8–10, 13–21; Tong, *Unsubmissive Women*, 9–12, 42–55, 69–77, 102–7, 140–44, 154–55, 172–75; Hurtado, *Intimate Frontiers*, 91–92. A detailed discussion of Chinese women and debt bondage appears in chapter 5.

71. Knox, *A Medic Fortyniner*, 1–4; Elizabeth Washington Grist Knox to Franklin Grist, Dec. 19, 1847, folder 12, box 1, Elizabeth Washington Grist Knox Papers, #4269, SHC. Hiring out was an extremely common practice in both rural and urban Missouri. On this practice, see Burke, *On Slavery's Border*, 107–18.

72. Reuben Knox to Joseph A. Knox, Jan. 14, 1850, in Knox, *A Medic Fortyniner*, 19. Throughout the text, I refer to enslaved people by their first names only, rather than automatically giving them their masters' surnames. I have included slaves' surnames

only in cases where the documentary record indicates that they adopted or went by a particular surname.

73. Reuben Knox to Elizabeth Washington Grist Knox, Sept. 20, 1850, and May 1, 1851, in ibid., 58–59, 69. The enslaved people's ages, occupations, and locations can be found in U.S. Bureau of the Census, *Seventh Federal Population Census*, 1850, roll 35, pp. 169A, 182B, 183A, Sacramento City, Sacramento County, Calif.

74. See U.S. Census Office, *Seventh Census of the United States*, xxxvi–xxxvii, for a breakdown of California residents by their state of origin. The census, though notoriously incomplete for 1850, indicates that 24,794 Californians came from the slave states, making up roughly 36 percent of the U.S.-born population. Just under half of these, 12,109, hailed from the Border States, while another 8,645 originated in the Upper South.

75. Data drawn from my research on slaves in the 1850 federal census and 1852 state census of California appears in the appendix of this book. See Lapp, *Blacks in Gold Rush California*, 65, for his estimate of 500 to 600 enslaved people. Southern newspapers reported the departure of dozens, sometimes hundreds, of enslaved people for the diggings, suggesting that slave totals may be higher than Lapp and I have reconstructed. See, for instance, reports discussed in Richards, *California Gold Rush*, 127; and Inscoe, *Mountain Masters*, 73. For the estimate of 1,500 slaves, see James Pratt to Cornelius Cole, June 30, 1852, folder 1, box 2, Cole Family Papers, #217, UCLA.

76. On southern westward migration, the expansion of slavery, and the networks of capital and kinship that financed this movement, see Rothman, *Slave Country*, esp. 165–216; Cashin, *A Family Venture*, esp. 32–77, 84–98; Martin, *Divided Mastery*, 34–42; and Oakes, *The Ruling Race*, 69–95. Susan Lee Johnson, in *Roaring Camp*, 67–69, found that many slaveholders and slaves who migrated to California had already moved west several times with the expanding southern frontier. Census data on the origins of masters and slaves in 1852, which I have compiled in table 3 in the appendix, supports that observation.

77. Broussard, "Slavery in California Revisited," 17; George M. Murrell to Eliza F. Murrell, June 7, 1850, HM 36356; George M. Murrell to Samuel Murrell, Sept. 17, 1849, HM 36384; both in George McKinley Murrell Correspondence, HEH. On Robert McElrath and George P. Dodson, see Thomas Parks to Carlo M. De Ferrari, Sept. 11, 1969, folder 13; Thomas Parks to sister, n.d., folder 2; and George P. Dodson to Robert McElrath, March 20, 1853, folder 3; all in subcollection 2, #4464, Thomas Parks Collection of Parks and McElrath Family Papers, SHC.

78. Inscoe, *Mountain Masters*, 73; *Liberator*, Jan. 23, 1852.

79. Major gold discoveries happened in North Carolina, Virginia, Georgia, and South Carolina from the 1790s to the 1840s. On gold mining in the South, see Otis E. Young Jr., "Southern Gold Rush"; Starobin, *Industrial Slavery*, 23–24, 215–22; and Forret, "Slave Labor." Burke County cousins Samuel McDowell and Robert Dickson went to California with a party of at least seven enslaved men, whom they supervised and worked alongside in the mines. See the two men's correspondence with North Carolina relatives in folders 7–8, box 1, #221, William G. Dickson Papers, SHC; and Rohrbough, *Days of Gold*, 211–15. Thomas Lenoir Avery and Alexander

Hamilton Erwin arrived in California in 1852 with nineteen slaves whom they supervised in small gangs. Robert McElrath sent a group of four enslaved men to California and employed both his son-in-law and a hired overseer to supervise them. On Thomas Lenoir Avery, Alexander Hamilton Erwin, and Robert McElrath, see Inscoe, *Mountain Masters*, 73; and De Ferrari, "Southern Miners." The 1852 California state census recorded several large parties of masters and slaves from North Carolina. Just over 25 percent of all California slaves in 1852 (45 of 178) had last resided in North Carolina before heading west. For this data, see table 3 in the appendix.

80. On labor relations and economics in Missouri's small slaveholding households, including hiring out, see Burke, *On Slavery's Border*, esp. 93–141. For examples of Border State residents who brought only one or two slaves to the mines, see Broussard, "Slavery in California Revisited"; William D. Marmaduke to Elmira Marmaduke, March 6, 1850, MSS 1403, filed with uncataloged manuscripts, William Marmaduke Letters, CHS; and Thomas B. Eastland to wife, Dec. 31, 1849, folder 2, MSS 19 (vault), Thomas B. Eastland Papers, CHS. Walter T. Durham documented numerous instances of Tennesseans traveling west with one or two family slaves whom they worked alongside in the mines. There is evidence, however, that some Tennesseans in California pooled enslaved labor by forming joint-stock companies in which members contributed slaves as part of the capital stock. Durham, *Volunteer Forty-Niners*, 31, 33–36, 110–11, 184–90.

81. *Jackson Mississippian*, Oct. 26, 1849, Ralph Bieber Collection, HEH; Robert M. Dickson to Margaret Dickson, Dec. 10, 1852, folder 7, box 1, William G. Dickson Papers, SHC; Martin, *Divided Mastery*, 42; Burke, *On Slavery's Border*, 112–13.

82. George M. Murrell to Elisabeth R. Murrell, Oct. 15, 1849, HM 36350; George M. Murrell to John Grider, Aug. 24, 1850, HM 36345; both in George McKinley Murrell Correspondence, HEH.

83. Rheubin was just one of many enslaved men profitably hired out in domestic service. Dow, an enslaved man who traveled to California with his master, Thomas Eastland, labored as a cook in San Francisco for $150 a month. Bob, an enslaved man belonging to Missouri goldseeker William Marmaduke, brought in five dollars a day as a cook. Another enslaved man from Georgia, Ephraim, was hired out by his master to be a cook in a restaurant. For these cases, see Thomas B. Eastland to wife, Dec. 31, 1849, folder 2, Thomas B. Eastland Papers, CHS; William D. Marmaduke to Elmira Marmaduke, March 6, 1850, William Marmaduke Letters, CHS; and Degroot, "Diving for Gold in '49," 278.

84. These family members included Isaac T. Avery (cousin to Thomas Lenoir Avery); Samuel McDowell and Robert Dickson (distantly related to the Averys and Erwins through the Erwin line); and George P. Dodson (whose father-in-law was a distant relative of Samuel McDowell's father). For these family connections, see Phifer, "Saga of a Burke County Family"; Inscoe, *Mountain Masters*, 74; McDowell, *History of the McDowells*, 203; and Wheeler, *Reminiscences and Memoirs*, 85–87.

85. For a survey of slaves in the Southern Mines, see tables 2 and 4 in the appendix. See also Johnson, *Roaring Camp*, 68–69, 189–90; and Robert Givens to father, Sept. 10, 1852, Robert R. Givens Letters to Family, Banc MSS C-B Film, BANC.

86. W. P. Robinson to George P. Dodson, May 18, 1852, folder 2, subcollection 2, Thomas Parks Collection of Parks and McElrath Family Papers, SHC. This correspondence is also reprinted in De Ferrari, "Southern Miners," 301–2.

87. *Liberator*, Oct. 11, 1850; ibid., Nov. 26, 1852; *An Illustrated History of Los Angeles County*, 358–59; Cornelius Cole, "Andy Habeas Corpus Case," bound essay, vol. 3, folder 2, box 29, Cole Family Papers, UCLA.

88. Isaac T. Avery to William Waightsill Avery, Nov. 26, 1852, folder 8, box 1, #246, George Phifer Erwin Papers, SHC. Samuel McDowell returned to Burke County in 1853, leaving behind five slaves. His cousin, Robert Dickson, made frequent visits to the enslaved men's claims and reported their activities to family in North Carolina. Rohrbough, *Days of Gold*, 211–15; Albert to Anna McDowell, July 13, 1854, folder 4, box 1, #1689, Nicholas Washington Woodfin Collection, SHC.

89. Rothman, *Slave Country*, 50–54, 188–203. For example, Rheubin, the enslaved man who went to California with George Murrell, drowned in a flood on the American River in 1851. See Apostol, "'Fickel Goddess Evades Me,'" 113. Thomas Lenoir Avery and some of the twelve enslaved men he brought to the mines died of cholera. See the discussion of Avery above, and Inscoe, *Mountain Masters*, 73.

90. On the complexity of fugitivism in southern slave communities, see Franklin and Schweninger, *Runaway Slaves*, esp. 17–74; Naragon, "Communities in Motion"; and Camp, "'I Could Not Stay There.'"

91. Reuben Knox to Elizabeth Washington Grist Knox, May 1, 1851, in Knox, *A Medic Fortyniner*, 69; Elizabeth Washington Grist Knox to Reuben Knox, May 4, 1851, and July 3, 1851, folder 13, box 1, Elizabeth Washington Grist Knox Papers, SHC.

92. For information on the enslaved people's backgrounds and their methods of escape, see Elizabeth Washington Grist Knox to Franklin Grist, Dec. 19, 1847, folder 12, box 1, Elizabeth Washington Grist Knox Papers, SHC; Reuben Knox to Joseph A. Knox, Jan. 14, 1850, in Knox, *A Medic Fortyniner*, 19; and Reuben Knox to Elizabeth Washington Grist Knox, May 1, 1851, in ibid., 69.

93. Knox, *A Medic Fortyniner*, 15.

94. An Act Respecting Fugitives from Labor, and Slaves Brought to This State Prior to Her Admission into the Union, Act of April 15, 1852, ch. 33, SC, at 67–69.

Chapter 2

1. Sherman, "Sherman Was There (Part 2)," 350–56; Sherman, "Sherman Was There (Part 1)," 259–60. For Thomas Jefferson Green's biography and proslavery arguments, see Green, *Journal of the Texian Expedition*, esp. vii–xxii, 200–208. Green stayed in California after his expulsion from Rose's Bar and became a state senator from Sacramento in 1850. In an ironic turn of events, he criticized Mexican and Chilean peonage and authored the foreign miners' tax of 1850 to suppress the practice.

2. For previous interpretations of the events at Rose's Bar, see Goodwin, *Establishment of State Government*, 110–13; Berwanger, *Frontier against Slavery*, 62–63; and Pitt, *Decline of the Californios*, 57–58.

3. "Memorial from Southern States to the Legislature Seeking to Establish a Slave Colony in California," Miscellaneous Petition Reports, CSA. Emphasis in original.

California Constitution (1850), art. I, sec. 18; James Gadsden to Thomas Jefferson Green, Dec. 7, 1851, in Parish, "A Project for a California Slave Colony"; State of California, *Journal of the Assembly*, 3rd sess. (1852), 159–60. For Gadsden's slave colony, see also Finkelman, "Law of Slavery and Freedom," 437–38; and Richards, *California Gold Rush*, 126–27. Antislavery Californians who corresponded with Frederick Douglass's abolitionist journal believed that the assembly's failure to reject the memorial outright indicated support for it. *Frederick Douglass' Paper*, March 25, 1852.

4. William Marmaduke to Elmira Johns Marmaduke, March 6, 1850, William Marmaduke Letters, MSS 1403, filed with uncataloged manuscripts, CHS. The biographical data on William Marmaduke appears in a sketch that accompanies the letters.

5. On policing slave behavior in the antebellum South, see Hadden, *Slave Patrols*.

6. *Daily Republican Banner and Nashville Whig*, March 28, 1850; and *Louisville Daily Journal* (Ky.), May 9, 1849; both in Ralph Bieber Collection, HEH. Bieber compiled an extensive collection of gold rush newspaper clippings from every state. The collection is not cataloged, but the articles are organized by state and date.

7. *National Era* (Washington, D.C.), July 11, 1850, quoted in Lapp, *Blacks in Gold Rush California*, 134.

8. Ibid., 134–38; David Cosad, journal entry, Aug. 11, 1849, in "Journal of a Trip to California," MSS 453, CHS; Horace Snow to Charles Fitz, Aug. 9, 1854, in Snow, *"Dear Charlie" Letters*, 39–41. Emphasis in original.

9. Andrew Jackson to Sarah Trigg, Oct. 19, 1851, folder 32, box 1, Wyles MSS 75, Slave Documents Collection, UCSB; Durham, *Volunteer Forty-Niners*, 186. Short-term flight or truancy aimed at achieving more tolerable working conditions was also the most common type of running away in the antebellum South. Franklin and Schweninger, *Runaway Slaves*, 98–109.

10. *Charleston Courier* (S.C.), Feb. 23, 1850, Ralph Bieber Collection, HEH; *Eads v. Miller*, Dec. 18, 1849, Case #330, Court of First Instance Records, Sacramento County, file 22:02, box 2, CFSH.

11. Penningroth, *Claims of Kinfolk*, 45–78, esp. 46–52.

12. Typescript of Leonard Withington Noyes's Gold Rush reminiscences, p. 44, Leonard W. Noyes Papers, Family MSS 677, PEM; De Ferrari, "Southern Miners," 300; Amount of Boys Gold, an undated account sheet with the amount of money each slave earned in California, in folder 22, subcollection 2, Thomas Parks Collection of Parks and McElrath Family Papers, #4464, SHC. Other accounts of Sunday claims appear in Susan Lee Johnson, *Roaring Camp*, 190; Inscoe, *Mountain Masters*, 96; and Lapp, *Blacks in Gold Rush California*, 72. The North Carolina Supreme Court actually upheld slaves' entitlement to money that they had accumulated in California with their masters' permission, in *White v. Cline and White*, 52 N.C. 174 (1859).

13. Isaac Theodore Avery to James Avery, Feb. 20, 1853, quoted in Inscoe, *Mountain Masters*, 74; Albert to Charles McDowell, May 15, 1855, folder 4, box 1, Nicholas Washington Woodfin Collection, #1689, SHC.

14. Beasley, *Negro Trail Blazers*, 69–71, 117; Lapp, *Blacks in Gold Rush California*, 71–74; Susan Lee Johnson, *Roaring Camp*, 190; Durham, *Volunteer Forty-Niners*, 185–86; Haskins, *Argonauts of California*, 70.

15. Albert to Charles McDowell, May 15, 1855, folder 4, box 1, Nicholas Washington Woodfin Collection, SHC; W. P. Robinson to unidentified correspondent, Sept. 20, 1852, folder 2, subcollection 2, Thomas Parks Collection of Parks and McElrath Family Papers, SHC, also reprinted in De Ferrari, "Southern Miners," 303.

16. *People v. Lewis Kethley* (1851), case file, folder 12, Justice Court Criminal Case Files, Sacramento County, May 12–June 1851, CFSH; *An Illustrated History of Los Angeles County*, 358–59.

17. Sherman, "Sherman Was There (Part 2)," 350–56; *An Illustrated History of Los Angeles County*, 358–59; Richards, *California Gold Rush*, 57–59, 67–68; Lapp, *Blacks in Gold Rush California*, 75–76. Census records indicate that Thorn did not lose all of his bondpeople in this "stampede." In 1850, he still had ten enslaved people living in his Mariposa County home. U.S. Bureau of the Census, *Seventh Federal Population Census*, 1850, roll 35, p. 59B, Mariposa County, Calif.; Susan Lee Johnson, *Roaring Camp*, 68–69, 115.

18. James Williams, *Fugitive Slave in the Gold Rush*, 24; Beasley, *Negro Trail Blazers*, 92.

19. *Alta California*, March 31, 1851; ibid., April 1, 1851; ibid., April 2, 1851; Lapp, *Blacks in Gold Rush California*, 138–39, 143–45; *Liberator*, May 9, 1851; Albin, "Perkins Case," 218–19. The quotation is from James Pratt to Cornelius Cole, June 30, 1852, folder 1, box 2, Cole Family Papers, #217, UCLA.

20. For these prohibitions, see An Act Concerning Crimes and Punishments, Act of April 16, 1850, ch. 99, sec. 14, SC, at 230; and An Act to Regulate Proceedings in Civil Cases, in the Courts of This State, Act of April 20, 1851, ch. 5, sec. 394, SC, at 114. These laws also banned Indian testimony against whites in cases tried under the regular criminal and civil codes of California. Under cases tried under the 1850 Act for the Government and Protection of Indians (Act of April 22, 1850, ch. 133, sec. 6, SC, at 409), however, Native Americans could initiate complaints against whites before justices of the peace and testify against them. This law initially stipulated that whites could not be convicted on the basis of Indian testimony alone, but this provision was eliminated in 1855. On these important nuances of the testimony law, see Magliari, review of *Ambiguous Justice*. In 1854, the California Supreme Court extended the prohibition on black and Indian testimony in regular civil and criminal courts to Chinese. Relying on tortured ethnographic arguments, the court ruled that Chinese were both nonwhite and biologically related to American Indians and therefore had the same legal status. The case that established this precedent was *People v. Hall*, 4 Cal. 399 (1854). For California's racialized testimony laws, see Bottoms, "'An Aristocracy of Color,'" 28–74; Lapp, *Blacks in Gold Rush California*, 192–209; and Fisher, "Struggle for Negro Testimony."

21. *Placer Times*, May 27, 1850; Demaratus, *Force of a Feather*, 87.

22. An Act to Amend an Act Entitled An Act Concerning Crimes and Punishments, Act of March 18, 1863, ch. 70, SC, at 69.

23. On conceptions of contract in nineteenth-century America and contract's relationship to both slavery and free labor, see Amy Dru Stanley, *From Bondage to Contract*; Steinfeld, *Coercion, Contract, and Free Labor*; Steinfeld, *Invention of Free Labor*; and Schmidt, *Free to Work*.

24. Morris, *Southern Slavery and the Law*, 380–85; Finkelman, *Slavery and the Founders*, 57–79; Steinfeld, *Invention of Free Labor*, 141–44; Campbell, *An Empire for Slavery*, 23–25. The California practice also closely resembled the tradition of term slavery, most common in the cities of the Upper South. Under term slavery, masters wrote up manumission papers freeing their slaves at a future date if they worked faithfully for a term of years. Rockman, *Scraping By*, 60–61, 112–15.

25. Indenture contract, William H. Fairchild, William Hubbard, and Nathaniel, March 20, 1850, Indenture and Emancipation Papers, San Joaquin County, MSS 2.I38, HASC. The contract between Taylor Barton and "Negro Bob," dated Oct. 9, 1851, and the contract between Thomas Thorn and Peter Green, dated Feb. 5, 1853, are reprinted in Beasley, *Negro Trail Blazers*, 84.

26. Most of the contracts that Delilah Beasley collected and transcribed in her study of early black Californians were filed before local justices of the peace and entered into county record books. Beasley, *Negro Trail Blazers*, 84–85. Additional examples of this trend include a contract between W. J. Kyle and a slave named Andrew, Oct. 14, 1852, recorded before Judge Lorenzo Sawyer in San Joaquin County and located in Indenture and Emancipation Papers, HASC. Another between James Holman and an enslaved woman named Clanpa, filed with the Los Angeles County District Court, is reprinted in *An Illustrated History of Los Angeles County*, 360.

27. Complaint of James Brown, June 9, 1851, in *People v. Richard and Louisa [a.k.a. Lucy]*, and transcript of testimony, June 20, 1851, *People v. Lewis Kethley*, both located in the *People v. Lewis Kethley* case file, cited in note 16 above. For a similar 1860 ruling, see the case of Aaron and Nathaniel Rice discussed in chapter 6.

28. *Alta California*, April 20, 1853.

29. Emancipation papers, Richard Christmas to Jacob Christmas, March 7, 1853, Indenture and Emancipation Papers, HASC; Mansfield, *History of Butte County*, 227.

30. For the highlights of the constitutional convention's debate over black migration, see Browne, *Report of the Debates*, 43–44, 48–50, 137–52, 330–40. The quotation is from delegate W. M. Steuart, in ibid., 146.

31. Henry Tefft, quoted in ibid., 144.

32. Edward Gilbert, quoted in ibid., 150.

33. State of California, *Journal of the Senate*, 1st sess. (1849/1850), 38–39.

34. California State Assembly, Assembly Bill #145, A Bill for an Act Prohibiting the Immigration of Free Negroes and Persons of Colour to This State, April 15, 1850, Original Bill File, CSA.

35. California State Assembly, Assembly Bill #34, A Bill for an Act Relative to Free Negroes, Mulattoes, Servants, and Slaves, Jan. 28, 1850, Original Bill File, CSA. Williams's bill was similar to measures governing slavery in Illinois. In fact, the bill may have been modeled on an 1819 Illinois statute, as both have the same title and contain some identical language. For a comparison, see State of Illinois, *Revised Laws of Illinois (1833)*, 457–66. On slavery in Illinois, see Finkelman, *Slavery and the Founders*, 67–79; and Steinfeld, *Invention of Free Labor*, 141–46.

36. Goodwin, *Establishment of State Government*, 320–23; State of California, *Journal of the Assembly*, 1st sess. (1849/1850), 729; Emancipation Certificate, Elizabeth

Walthall to Edward and Martha, Oct. 30, 1854, Indenture and Emancipation Papers, HASC.

37. Berwanger, *Frontier against Slavery*, 72; State of California, *Journal of the Assembly*, 2nd sess. (1851), 1315–16, 1440; California State Assembly, unnumbered bill, A Bill for an Act Concerning Free Persons of Color, April 29, 1852, Original Bill File, CSA; State of California, *Journal of the Assembly*, 3rd sess. (1852), 95, 703–4; State of California, *Journal of the Senate*, 3rd sess. (1852), 438.

38. State of California, *Journal of the Senate*, 2nd sess. (1851), 21.

39. An Act Respecting Fugitives from Labor, and Slaves Brought to This State Prior to Her admission into the Union, Act of April 15, 1852, ch. 33, SC, at 67–69.

40. Richards, *California Gold Rush*, 62–67, 91–118. One of the best analyses of the Calhoun doctrine remains Potter, *Impending Crisis*, 59–62. The U.S. Supreme Court would, of course, make the same argument in *Dred Scott v. Sandford* in 1857.

41. In other states with antislavery constitutions, such as Illinois, slaves became free only after the legislature or judiciary explicitly decreed that all slavery was abolished within the state boundaries. Finkelman, "Law of Slavery and Freedom," 443–47; *In re Perkins*, 2 Cal. 425 (1852).

42. On the problem of slave transit and comity in free-state courts, see Finkelman, *An Imperfect Union*; and Finkelman, "Law of Slavery and Freedom," 445–550; as well as Fehrenbacher, *Dred Scott Case*, 50–61.

43. Lapp, *Blacks in Gold Rush California*, 8–9.

44. *Bean v. Charles*, Sept. 19, 1849, Sacramento Court of First Magistrate Records, Civil Case #122, file 22:02, box 2, CFSH; *New Orleans Picayune*, Nov. 30, 1849.

45. *Alta California*, Feb. 16, 1850.

46. Fugitive Slave Law of 1850 (Sept. 18, 1850), ch. 60, U.S. *Statutes at Large* 9 (1850), 462–65; Potter, *Impending Crisis*, 130–31; Fehrenbacher, *Slaveholding Republic*, 231–52.

47. Limited evidence suggests that some Missouri and Kentucky slaves sought asylum in California by attaching themselves to westbound wagon trains. See, for instance, Asa Cyrus Call, April 23, 1850, in Asa Cyrus Call Journal, MSS 301, CHS; and *Liberator*, Aug. 6, 1852. These instances were rare, however, as none of California's fugitive slave cases involved people who had fled across state lines.

48. *Alta California*, March 31, 1851; ibid., April 1, 1851; ibid., April 2, 1851; Lapp, *Blacks in Gold Rush California*, 139; *Liberator*, May 9, 1851.

49. Lapp, *Blacks in Gold Rush California*, 139.

50. Historians have long assumed that the 1852 California fugitive slave law was the first effort to pass a fugitive slave measure. My research here reveals, however, that the initial push for a fugitive slave law came in 1851. California State Assembly, Assembly Bill #168, An Act Respecting Persons Escaping from the Service of Their Masters, April 10, 1851, Original Bill File, CSA; State of California, *Journal of the Assembly*, 2nd sess. (1851), 1569. On Saunders's party affiliation and birthplace, see *Alta California*, Jan. 8, 1851; and *Sacramento Transcript*, Feb. 1, 1851.

51. Finkelman, "Law of Slavery and Freedom," 451.

52. Assembly Bill #168 (1851), Original Bill File, CSA.

53. Finkelman, "Law of Slavery and Freedom," 452–53.

54. Ibid., 451–52; State of California, *Journal of the Assembly*, 2nd sess. (1851), 1711–15; State of California, *Journal of the Senate*, 2nd sess. (1851), 49, 463. Four of the thirty assemblymen were absent during the vote. A year later, Thomas Van Buren helped David C. Broderick contest the 1852 version of the bill.

55. Hittell, *History of California*, 3:806; Richards, *California Gold Rush*, 131–32; Greenberg, *Manifest Manhood*, 31.

56. Act of April 15, 1852, ch. 33, SC, at 67–69; *Alta California*, Feb. 8, 1852. For moderate critiques of the bill and demand for a sunset clause, see *Sacramento Daily Union*, Feb. 6, 1852.

57. State of California, *Journal of the Assembly*, 3rd sess. (1852), 146–47.

58. State of California, *Journal of the Senate*, 3rd sess. (1852), 237, 257–60, 268–72, 274–85; *Alta California*, April 9, 1852; ibid., April 10, 1852.

59. U.S. Bureau of the Census, *Seventh Federal Population Census*, 1850, roll 36, p. 7A, Solano County, Calif. The federal census of 1850 reveals that James Estell brought fourteen enslaved people from Kentucky and Missouri. The census taker noted that the slaves had "contracted to work in this state and then be free after two years." On Estell's involvement with the bill, as well as the passage of the amendment concerning reclaimed slaves and the final vote, see State of California, *Journal of the Senate*, 3rd sess. (1852), 237, 257, 262, 275–76, 285–86; *Alta California*, April 10, 1852; and Finkelman, "Law of Slavery and Freedom," 452–53. The final compromise version of the bill may even have attracted some free-soil stalwarts. Thomas Van Buren, a free-soiler who tried to help Broderick obstruct the bill with motions to adjourn, voted for it in the end.

60. *California Christian Advocate*, Aug. 15, 1852, reproduced in scrapbook #1, box 38, Cole Family Papers, UCLA; Complaint of plaintiffs in *Robert Perkins, Carter Perkins, and Sandy Jones v. [Albert] Green Perkins*, June 7, 1852, box 27, in ibid.; *In re Perkins*, 2 Cal. 455–57 (1852). The most detailed secondary account of the Perkins case appears in Albin, "Perkins Case."

61. Cornelius Cole, undated brief in the Perkins case presented before Judge Aldrich, pp. 64, 86–88, located in box 27, Cole Family Papers, UCLA.

62. Cornelius Cole, "Andy Habeas Corpus Case," bound essay, vol. 3, folder 2, box 29, Cole Family Papers, UCLA; Cole, *Memoirs*, 95. Cole mistakenly referred to Sandy Jones as "Andy" in his reminiscences.

63. Chief Justice Hugh C. Murray of Missouri and Justice Alexander Anderson of Tennessee, both with ties to the Democratic Party, were the only justices present at the hearing. Albin, "Perkins Case," 224–25; Shuck, *Bench and Bar in California*, 86–87.

64. *In re Perkins*, 2 Cal. 438–39, 453–67, 459 (1852); Finkelman, "Law of Slavery and Freedom," 454–57; Albin, "Perkins Case," 225–26. Fortunately for the enslaved men, they managed to escape from their master's agents once they reached Panama.

65. Richards, *California Gold Rush*, 129.

66. *Alta California*, March 30, 1854.

67. *Liberator*, Nov. 26, 1852; Caleb T. Fay, "Statement of Historical Facts on California," pp. 18–21, Banc MSS C-D 78, BANC.

68. *Liberator*, Nov. 26, 1852; Susan Lee Johnson, *Roaring Camp*, 67–68, 191; Jolly, *Gold Spring Diary*, 125–39.

69. State of California, *Journal of the Assembly*, 4th sess. (1853), 343, 394–95, 417, 420; State of California, *Journal of the Senate*, 4th sess. (1853), 346–49; An Act to Amend an Act Respecting Fugitives from Labor and Slaves Brought to This State Prior to Her Admission into the Union, Act of April 15, 1853, ch. 67, SC, at 94; *Alta California*, April 16, 1853. The assemblyman who proposed extension was Benjamin Franklin Myres of Placer County.

70. *Alta California*, April 1, 1854; ibid., April 21, 1854; *Sacramento Daily Union*, May 4, 1854; David A. Williams, *David C. Broderick*, 94n26; Hittell, *History of California*, 4:151; Senate Joint Resolution in Relation to the Nebraska Bill, May 10, 1854, SC, at 223–24.

71. *Alta California*, March 20, 1854; State of California, *Journal of the Assembly*, 5th sess. (1854), 240–41.

72. *Alta California*, March 20, 1854; State of California, *Journal of the Assembly*, 5th sess. (1854), 254–57; State of California, *Journal of the Senate*, 5th sess. (1854), 411; An Act Amendatory to an Act to Amend an Act Respecting Fugitives from Labor and Slaves Brought to This State Prior to Her Admission into the Union, Act of April 13, 1854, ch. 22, SC, at 30.

73. *Alta California*, April 14, 1854.

74. By 1860, people born in the slave states had declined to just around 20 percent of the U.S.-born population of California, down from 36 percent in 1850. U.S. Census Office, *Seventh Census of the United States*, xxxvi–xxxvii; U.S. Census Office, *Population of the United States in 1860*, 34.

75. Winfield J. Davis, *History of Political Conventions*, 30–31; David A. Williams, *David C. Broderick*, 89–102, 107–9; *Alta California*, July 29, 1854.

76. Hurt, "Rise and Fall of the 'Know Nothings,'" 24–36, 41–42; Richards, *California Gold Rush*, 176–78, 187–88.

77. David A. Williams, *David C. Broderick*, 103–6; *Alta California*, May 7, 1855.

78. The case eventually became *Ex Parte Archy*, 9 Cal. 147 (1858). Accounts of the case include Lapp, *Archy Lee*; William E. Franklin, "Archy Case"; and Finkelman, "Law of Slavery and Freedom," 457–62.

79. Wagstaff, *Life of David S. Terry*, 146; Buchanan, *David S. Terry*, 93–94; Uelmen, "Know Nothing Justices," 98, 103–5. For more on the political views of the supreme court justices, see Lapp, *Archy Lee*, 12–13; Finkelman, "Law of Slavery and Freedom," 459; and William E. Franklin, "Archy Case," 153.

80. *Ex Parte Archy*, 9 Cal. 147–56, 165–71 (1858). Here I rely heavily on the analyses in William E. Franklin, "Archy Case," 139–42, 147–51; and Finkelman, "Law of Slavery and Freedom," 459–63.

81. For diverse criticisms of the ruling, see *Sacramento Daily Union*, Feb. 16, 1858; ibid., Feb. 18, 1858; Lapp, *Archy Lee*, 14–16; and William E. Franklin, "Archy Case," 151–53. *San Joaquin Republican*, quoted in *Sacramento Daily Union*, Feb. 16, 1858; Thomas B. Pate to "Dear Dabney," April 4, 1858, folder 56, box 4, Charles William Dabney Papers, #1412, SHC.

82. For the birth of California's Republican Party, consult Gerald Stanley, "Slavery and the Origins of the Republican Party"; Gerald Stanley, "Racism and the Early Republican Party"; and Chandler, "Friends in Time of Need."

83. Lapp, *Archy Lee*, 4–5; Writ of Habeas Corpus for Archy Lee, Jan. 7, 1858, Criminal Case #52, 22:02, box 1:5, Court of First Instance Records, Sacramento County, CFSH.

84. *Alta California*, April 8, 1858; Lapp, *Archy Lee*, 40–62.

85. These failed measures included Assembly Bill #26, An Act Concerning the Recapture of Slaves Escaping from the Service of Their Owners and Masters While Traveling through or Sojourning in This State, reprinted in *Sacramento Daily Union*, Jan. 19, 1858; and Assembly Bill #395, An Act to Restrict and Prevent the Immigration to and Residence in This State of Negroes and Mulattoes, reprinted in *Sacramento Daily Union*, March 30, 1858. For the legislative journey of the bills, protests against them, and efforts to defeat them, see State of California, *Journal of the Assembly*, 9th sess. (1858), 84, 108, 489, 500, 523–25; State of California, *Journal of the Senate*, 9th sess. (1858), 623, 661; Chandler, "Friends in Time of Need," 322; *San Francisco Bulletin*, Jan. 19–20, 1858; *Sacramento Daily Union*, March 27, 1858; and ibid., March 30, 1858.

86. David Alan Johnson, *Founding the Far West*, 249–50; David A. Williams, *David C. Broderick*, 171–82, 189–94, 207–9, 215–44; Richards, *California Gold Rush*, 202–7, 214, 217–21. The quotations from Broderick are from ibid., 218, 220.

Chapter 3

1. State of California, *Appendix to the Journal of the Assembly*, 3rd sess. (1852), 831, 834–35.

2. No historian has systematically compared antipeon and anticoolie campaigns in gold rush California. Many scholars have, however, investigated these campaigns separately, sometimes as part of broader studies of race and labor in nineteenth-century California. Discussions of antipeon rhetoric and violence against Latino miners include Pitt, *Decline of the Californios*, 50–68; Peterson, "Foreign Miners' Tax," 265–72; Peterson, "Anti-Mexican Nativism," 310–11; and Michael J. González, "'My Brother's Keeper,'" 126–27. On the coolie question during the gold rush, consult Aarim-Heriot, *Chinese Immigrants*, 30–42; Barth, *Bitter Strength*, 129–56; and Pfaelzer, *Driven Out*, 24–48. For works that treat both questions, see Susan Lee Johnson, *Roaring Camp*, 193–218, 242–51; and Almaguer, *Racial Fault Lines*, 69–73, 153–82.

3. For glimpses of the diverse population of the Mokelumne area and the ethnic conflicts there, see Gudde, *California Gold Camps*, 220–21; and Susan Lee Johnson, *Roaring Camp*, 171, 208.

4. *Alta California*, July 26, 1849.

5. On the negroization of Latinos in California, consult Michael J. González, "'My Brother's Keeper,'" 126–27.

6. Green, *Journal of the Texian Expedition*, 204–5; Henry, *Campaign Sketches*, 134, 304.

7. Thomas B. Eastland to Wife, Sept. 11, 1849, MSS 19 (vault), Thomas B. Eastland Papers, CHS. Emphasis in original. For similar condemnation of peonage in New Mexico, see Montoya, *Translating Property*, 63–68.

8. For a discussion of expulsion campaigns against rancheros and their Indian workers, see chapter 1, and Madley, "American Genocide," 83–94. The quotation is from Case, "Reminiscences," 288.

9. Case, "Notes by William M. Case," 176–78; Case, "Reminiscences," 281, 288–90.

10. John Hovey, "Historical Account," p. 3, HM 4384, HEH; Ayers, *Gold and Sunshine*, 46–47, 61–62; Limbaugh and Fuller, *Calaveras Gold*, 114–17. An account of the Chilean War also appears in Susan Lee Johnson, *Roaring Camp*, 196–207, though Johnson emphasizes racial conflict rather than a dispute over unfree labor as the cause of the strife.

11. Browne, *Report of the Debates*, 138.

12. Ibid., 143.

13. For the debates over federal mineral lands and the status of foreigners working on them, see State of California, *Journal of the Assembly*, 1st sess. (1849/50), 802–17; and *Congressional Globe*, 31st Cong., 1st sess., 1850, appendix, 1362–73.

14. An Act for the Better Regulation of the Mines and the Government of Foreign Miners, Act of April 13, 1850, ch. 97, SC, at 221–23; *Alta California*, April 5, 1850. The bill in its final form would call for a twenty-dollar monthly tax.

15. Larkin, "Statistics: California," 377.

16. John Hovey, "Historical Account," pp. 7–10, HM 4384, HEH. Emphasis in original.

17. Larkin, "Statistics: California," 377; *Placer Times*, May 26, 1849; ibid., June 2, 1849.

18. State of California, *Journal of the Assembly*, 1st sess. (1849/50), 809.

19. Ibid., 803–6. Emphasis in original. For a similar critique aimed at Chilean employers, see *Placer Times*, April 28, 1849.

20. *Alta California*, April 5, 1850.

21. Ibid. Scholars have debated Green's intent in proposing the foreign miners' tax. Leonard Pitt argues that Green envisioned a system of "taxation and indenture" designed to "exploit alien caste laborers" by funneling their earnings into the state treasury and making their labor available to Americans. Pitt, "Beginnings of Nativism," 28–29; Pitt, *Decline of the Californios*, 58–61. Richard H. Peterson contends, however, that legislators always intended the bill as an expulsion measure because the tax was so high and enforced mainly against Spanish speakers. Peterson, "Foreign Miners' Tax," 265–72. Here I suggest that the bill had both outcomes in mind. It could draw money from the wealthiest foreign employers and force the rest to quit the mines and leave their peons behind for Americans to employ.

22. State of California, *Journal of the Assembly*, 1st sess. (1849/50), 803.

23. Navarro, "California in 1849," 115.

24. The quotation appears in Pitt, *Decline of the Californios*, 56. On fears of a Mexican invasion in the mines, see Michael J. González, "'My Brother's Keeper,'" 120–24.

25. State of California, *Journal of the Assembly*, 1st sess. (1849/50), 809–10.

26. Ibid., 1013–18; Pitt, *Decline of the Californios*, 58.

27. *Congressional Globe*, 31st Cong., 1st sess., 1850, appendix, 1362–63; Frémont, *Expeditions of John Charles Frémont*, 214–15. Frémont's plan differed from those recommended by the California Assembly in that he proposed charging miners a nominal fee and limiting the size of the claims they could stake. Susan Lee Johnson notes that this plan was unpopular in the Southern Mines, where gold diggers opposed

any formal system of land leasing and fee collection. Susan Lee Johnson, *Roaring Camp*, 262.

28. *Congressional Globe*, 31st Cong., 1st sess., 1850, appendix, 1365–67; *Sacramento Transcript*, Nov. 12, 1850.

29. *Congressional Globe*, 31st Cong., 1st sess., 1850, appendix, 1368.

30. Paul, *Mining Frontiers*, 168–75.

31. State of California, *Journal of the Assembly*, 1st sess. (1849/50), 1147, 1165; State of California, *Journal of the Senate*, 1st sess. (1849/50), 257–58; Act of April 13, 1850, ch. 97, SC, at 221–23.

32. Peterson, "Anti-Mexican Nativism," 310–11.

33. State of California, *Journal of the Senate*, 2nd sess. (1851), appendix M, no. 2, pp. 660–61; Pitt, *Decline of the Californios*, 62; Pitt, "Beginnings of Nativism," 29. A detailed account of the events in Sonora, taken from multiple sources, appears in Susan Lee Johnson, *Roaring Camp*, 211–15.

34. Peterson, *Manifest Destiny*, 64.

35. Ibid., 64, 66.

36. *The People, ex. rel. The Attorney General v. Naglee*, 1 Cal. 232 (1850).

37. Pitt, *Decline of the Californios*, 66; An Act to Repeal an Act for the Better Regulation of the Mines, and the Government of Foreign Miners, Act of March 14, 1851, ch. 108, SC, at 424.

38. Pitt, *Decline of the Californios*, 63–64, 67; Peterson, *Manifest Destiny*, 58; Susan Lee Johnson, *Roaring Camp*, 217–18.

39. *Alta California*, March 7, 1851.

40. On late nineteenth- and early twentieth-century U.S. controversies over Mexican immigration, contract labor, and peonage, see David G. Gutiérrez, *Walls and Mirrors*, 39–68; Guérin-Gonzales, *Mexican Workers*, 25–47; González and Fernández, *A Century of Chicano History*, 75–90; and Reisler, "Always the Laborer."

41. *Sacramento Daily Union*, April 14, 1852. Emphasis in original.

42. Jung, *Coolies and Cane*, 13–14. On the origins of coolies, see also Aarim-Heriot, *Chinese Immigrants*, 30–31; and Gyory, *Closing the Gate*, 32–33.

43. Jung, *Coolies and Cane*, 4–5, 9, 13–33.

44. Aarim-Heriot, *Chinese Immigrants*, 30, 36.

45. Susan Lee Johnson, *Roaring Camp*, 243–44.

46. Ibid., 242.

47. Rohrbough, *Days of Gold*, 197–206; Paul, *California Gold*, 116–46. The quotation is from *Alta California*, Feb. 14, 1851.

48. Susan Lee Johnson, *Roaring Camp*, 237–74, esp. 241.

49. A discussion of how miners fused anti-Chinese and anticapitalist sentiment in the Southern Mines appears in ibid., 246–51.

50. Senate Bill #63, A Bill to Enforce Contracts and Obligations to Perform Work and Labor, March 6, 1852, California Senate, Original Bill File, CSA; Shuck, *History of the Bench and Bar*, 590–93. The quotation is from *San Joaquin Republican*, Sept. 1, 1852.

51. *Alta California*, March 21, 1852; Shuck, *History of the Bench and Bar*, 411–12; David A. Williams, *David C. Broderick*, 46–47; State of California, *Journal of the Assembly*, 3rd sess. (1852), 159; Barth, *Bitter Strength*, 136–37.

52. Senate Bill #63 (1852), Original Bill File, CSA; *Alta California*, March 21, 1852.

53. State of California, *Journal of the Senate*, 3rd sess. (1852), 192; State of California, *Journal of the Assembly*, 3rd sess. (1852), 348–53.

54. *Alta California*, May 15, 1852; Alfred Jackson, *Diary of a Forty-Niner*, 222–23; Pfaelzer, *Driven Out*, 33.

55. *Sacramento Daily Union*, April 14, 1852; State of California, *Journal of the Senate*, 3rd sess. (1852), 672. For additional denunciations of Hawaiian workers along with coolies and peons, see *Alta California*, July 26, 1849; ibid., April 5, 1850; ibid., June 23, 1853; and State of California, *Journal of the Assembly*, 1st sess. (1849/50), 809.

56. *Sacramento Transcript*, Sept. 21, 1850; *Alta California*, July 3, 1852; ibid., Dec. 7, 1854; *Sacramento Daily Union*, Oct. 7, 1852.

57. State of California, *Journal of the Senate*, 3rd sess. (1852), 305–7, 669–75, 731–37; David A. Williams, *David C. Broderick*, 46–47; *Analysis of the Chinese Question*; State of California, *Journal of the Assembly*, 3rd sess. (1852), 829–35; Barth, *Bitter Strength*, 138–42. On Roach's later strong support for the Chivalry faction, see Richards, *California Gold Rush*, 217.

58. *Analysis of the Chinese Question*, 2–3. For a similar argument, see State of California, *Journal of the Senate*, 3rd sess. (1852), 734–35.

59. *Alta California*, March 10, 1852. On wage rates in the mines, see Paul, *California Gold*, 349.

60. State of California, *Journal of the Senate*, 3rd sess. (1852), 673.

61. State of California, *Journal of the Assembly*, 3rd sess. (1852), 831; *Analysis of the Chinese Question*, 2–3.

62. A senate committee that investigated "Asiatic immigration" made a similar assertion. State of California, *Journal of the Senate*, 3rd sess. (1852), 673, 735.

63. The accusation that Chinese employers held workers' families as hostages or slaves probably grew out of a misunderstanding of the credit-ticket system that brought most Chinese to California. Family members sometimes agreed to stand as securities for credit-ticket migrants' debts to Chinese merchants, but they were not under the absolute control of these creditors. For divergent scholarly interpretations of this issue, see Barth, *Bitter Strength*, 86; and Cloud and Galenson, "Chinese Immigration," 34–35.

64. *Alta California*, March 10, 1852; State of California, *Journal of the Senate*, 3rd sess. (1852), 674.

65. State of California, *Journal of the Senate*, 3rd sess. (1852), 735.

66. Ibid., 669–70, 671, 674; *Alta California*, March 10, 1852.

67. State of California, *Journal of the Assembly*, 3rd sess. (1852), 831.

68. State of California, *Journal of the Senate*, 3rd sess. (1852), 674, 733–34, 736.

69. *Alta California*, May 16, 1851; State of California, *Journal of the Senate*, 3rd sess. (1852), 736.

70. State of California, *Journal of the Senate*, 3rd sess. (1852), 669, 672–73, 735.

71. *Alta California*, April 14, 1852.

72. Ibid.; David A. Williams, *David C. Broderick*, 46–47; State of California, *Journal of the Senate*, 3rd sess. (1852), 303–4, 306–7; Senate Bill #140, A Bill for an Act to

Prevent "Coolie" Labor in the Mines, and to Prevent Involuntary Servitude, Except for Crime, April 12, 1852, California Senate, Original Bill File, CSA.

73. Aarim-Heriot, *Chinese Immigrants*, 34–37; State of California, *Appendix to the Journal of the Assembly*, 3rd sess. (1852), 831, 834; An Act to Provide for the Protection of Foreigners, and to Define Their Liabilities and Privileges, Act of May 4, 1852, ch. 37, SC, at 84–87.

74. In 1853, a group of Chinese merchants claimed that high taxation, combined with violence against Chinese miners, prompted them to write home and discourage their countrymen from traveling to California. State of California, *Appendix to the Journal of the Assembly*, 4th sess. (1853), doc. 28, pp. 8–10. Chinese immigration sank to only 4,720 people in 1853 but rose to more than 16,000 arrivals in 1854. Aarim-Heriot, *Chinese Immigrants*, 43.

75. Pfaelzer, *Driven Out*, 31; Susan Lee Johnson, *Roaring Camp*, 248; Paul, "Origin of the Chinese Issue," 194.

76. McClain, *In Search of Equality*, 16–20, 24–25.

77. *Analysis of the Chinese Question*, 6–7.

78. Ibid., 13.

79. *Alta California*, May 4, 1852.

Chapter 4

1. Benjamin D. Wilson to Margaret H. Wilson, July 13, 1856, WN 1754; Margaret H. Wilson to Benjamin D. Wilson, Aug. 14, 1856, WN 1070; and Benjamin D. Wilson to Margaret H. Wilson, Oct. 23, 1856, WN 1761; all in Benjamin Davis Wilson Collection, HEH. For biographical information about the Wilson family, see Woolsey, *Migrants West*, 29–44; and Hyde, *Empires, Nations, and Families*, 75–83.

2. J. Earl to Benjamin D. Wilson, April 30, 1857, WN 248, Benjamin Davis Wilson Collection, HEH; An Act for the Government and Protection of Indians, Act of April 22, 1850, ch. 133, sec. 3, SC, at 408.

3. Petition of Esther Hereford, April 11, 1857, *In the Matter of the Guardianship of Emily and Maria, Negroes*, Probate Case #66, Los Angeles County Probate Records, Los Angeles Area Court Records Collection, HEH; An Act to Provide for the Appointment and Prescribe the Duties of Guardians, Act of April 19, 1850, ch. 115, sec. 5–6, SC, at 269.

4. On domestic labor in the gold rush and its racial, gender, and class dimensions, see Susan Lee Johnson, *Roaring Camp*, esp. 99–139.

5. An Act for the Government and Protection of Indians, Act of April 22, 1850, ch. 133, sec. 3, SC, at 408; Assembly Bill #34, "A Bill for an Act Relative to Free Negroes, Mulattoes, Servants, and Slaves," Jan. 28, 1850, California State Assembly, Original Bill File, CSA; Act of April 19, 1850, ch. 115, SC, at 268–69.

6. The legal treatment of Indian and black wards in California both paralleled and departed from evolving family law in other parts of the nation. Michael Grossberg contends that nineteenth-century U.S. courts gradually moved away from patriarchal and hierarchical conceptions of family that emphasized men's property rights in and untrammeled mastery over their wives and children. They came, instead, to

embrace a republican model of family that emphasized consent, contract, voluntarism, and the "best interests" of dependent family members, especially children. Ironically, this emphasis on children's welfare also justified coercive state programs—including the involuntary apprenticeship of poor children—aimed at removing minors from "unfit" parents. Grossberg, *Governing the Hearth*, esp. 3–30, 234–85. Peter Bardaglio documents a different evolution of family law in the U.S. South. There, judges placed a premium on upholding slavery and white supremacy. They proved much more reluctant to undermine the power of white adult men over their household dependents, whether wives, children, or slaves. Bardaglio, *Reconstructing the Household*, esp. xi–xviii, 3–36, 79–112. In some ways, California legal officials' stance on the wardship of Indian and black children fit with understandings of the republican family. Judges often awarded guardianship to white petitioners, against the claims of Native or African American families, on the grounds that wardship would serve the best interests of the children. At the same time, the stalwart defense of white guardians' rights to their nonwhite wards resembles the patriarchal concepts of family that persisted in the antebellum South and that were critical to the slave economy.

7. Early efforts to establish a system of Indian apprenticeship include Assembly Bill #143, An Act for the Government and Protection of Indians, March 19, 1853; and Assembly Bill #49, An Act for the Government and Protection of Indians, Jan. 23, 1854; both in California State Assembly, Original Bill File, CSA. In 1858, the legislature passed a general apprenticeship law, An Act to Provide for Binding Minors as Apprentices, Clerks, and Servants, Act of April 10, 1858, ch. 182, SC, at 134–37, which those in favor of Indian and black apprenticeship tried to amend the following year with Senate Bill #224, An Act to Amend an Act Entitled An Act to Provide for the Binding of Minors, as Apprentices, Clerks, and Servants, Approved April 10, 1858, March 24, 1859, California State Senate, Original Bill File, CSA. The final, successful Indian apprenticeship bill was An Act Amendatory to an Act Entitled An Act for the Government and Protection of Indians, Act of April 16, 1860, ch. 231, SC, at 196–97.

8. Browne, *Report of the Debates*, 139.

9. Ibid., 141.

10. Act of April 22, 1850, ch. 133, sec. 3, SC, at 408.

11. Assembly Bill #34 (1850), Original Bill File, CSA; Act of April 19, 1850, ch. 115, SC, at 268–69.

12. Phillips, *Indians and Indian Agents*, esp. 6–15, 57–77, 155–82; Madley, "American Genocide," 198–210, 212–321; Lindsay, *Murder State*, 271–77.

13. The two bills included the successful Act of April 22, 1850, ch. 133, SC, at 408–10; and the unsuccessful Senate Bill #54, An Act Relative to the Protection, Punishment, and Government of Indians, March 16, 1850, California State Senate, Original Bill File, CSA. For analyses of the labor policies in the Act for the Government and Protection of Indians, see Magliari, "Free Soil, Unfree Labor," 351–56; Magliari, "Free State Slavery"; Madley, "American Genocide," 188–97; Street, *Beasts of the Field*, 118–21; Rawls, *Indians of California*, 86–90; Lindsay, *Murder State*, 248–62; and Hurtado, *Indian Survival*, 128–31.

14. Senate Bill #54 (1850), Original Bill File, CSA; Gillis and Magliari, *John Bidwell*, 249–53; Hurtado, *Indian Survival*, 128–29.

15. Hurtado, *Indian Survival*, 129; Gillis and Magliari, *John Bidwell*, 253. The original text of Brown's bill appears in Assembly Bill #129, A Bill Entitled An Act for the Government and Protection of Indians, April 13, 1850, California State Assembly, Original Bill File, CSA.

16. State of California, *Journal of the Senate*, 1st sess. (1849/50), 366–67; Lindsay, *Murder State*, 147–48. The final version of Brown's bill became Act of April 22, 1850, ch. 133, SC, at 408–10.

17. Assembly Bill #34 (1850), Original Bill File, CSA.

18. State of California, *Journal of the Assembly*, 1st sess. (1849/1850), 729.

19. On laws regarding parental rights, guardianship, and custody in nineteenth-century America, as well as evolving attitudes about parents' suitability to retain their children, see Grossberg, *Governing the Hearth*, 234–85, esp. 263–68; and Bardaglio, *Reconstructing the Household*, 79–112.

20. Act of April 19, 1850, ch. 115, sec. 1 and 5, SC, at 268–69.

21. Testimony of Sarah Snyder, Jeremiah Henry, George Hendry, and F. Harris, in *People v. George Hendry*, May 23, 1853, folder 16, Justice Court Criminal Case Files, Sacramento County, CFSH; *Sacramento Daily Union*, May 25, 1853; ibid., Sept. 14, 1854; ibid., July 16, 1853; *People v. George Hendry*, June 1853, Case #210, Sacramento County District Court, Criminal Files, CFSH.

22. Transcription of proceedings, Nov. 26, 1853, Justice Court of Santa Barbara Docket, 1850–55, p. 182, Banc MSS C-F 151, BANC.

23. Indenture of Timotea, n.d., filed in the case of *M. G. Vallejo v. Nicholas Kerreger* [sic], June 22, 1852, Case #199 (Civil), Sonoma County Justice Court Records, CSA.

24. *In the Matter of the Estate and Guardianship of Refugia, an Indian Girl, Minor*, April 15, 1852, Old Probate Case #66, New Case #74-16915, roll #1491212, Santa Clara County Probate Court, Genealogical Society of Utah Microfilm Collection, CSA; *In the Matter of the Guardianship of Chapo, an Indian*, Aug. 24, 1857, Probate Case #75, Los Angeles County Probate Records, Los Angeles Area Court Records Collection, HEH.

25. *In the Matter of the Guardianship of Santiago Barton, a Minor*, June 1, 1858, Probate Case #101; and *In the Matter of the Guardianship of Joseph Benton, a Minor*, Nov. 30, 1860, Probate Case #316; both in Los Angeles County Probate Records, Los Angeles Area Court Records Collection, HEH.

26. Affidavit of Felix Gallardo against Juan Mendos, Dec. 2, 1851, cataloged as *Gallardo v. Mendos*, Case #123 (Civil), Sonoma County Justice Court Records, CSA.

27. Affidavit of M. G. Vallejo, June 22, 1852, in *M. G. Vallejo v. Nicholas Kerreger* [sic], CSA.

28. *C. J. Couts v. Francisco, an Indian Boy*, May 6, 1858, CT-204, Cave Johnson Couts Papers, HEH.

29. Complaint of José Arguello and warrant for the arrest of Jesús Dominguez, June 15, 1860, CT-193 (37–38); and Complaint of Patrick O'Neil, Sept. 11, 1860, CT-193–41; both in Cave Johnson Couts Papers, HEH.

30. Hezier and Almquist, *The Other Californians*, 40–41. *People v. Juan Berryessa*, Dec. 13, 1852, doc. 1, box E13, Court of Sessions, Contra Costa County; Damascus

Berryessa and Magill [sic] Berryessa, Dec. 7, 1854, Court of Sessions, Solano County, doc. 8, in "Fragments #1," box CC244; and *People v. La Komopaw and Mompet, Indians,* June 15, 1850, District Court Records, Contra Costa County, uncataloged Contra Costa cases; all CCHS. Arrigoni, "None of Which Required a War," 64–88.

31. Peter Campbell to Commissioner of Indian Affairs (Orlando Brown), June 1, 1851, roll 32, ID#C672, M234; *Alta California,* July 17, 1851.

32. John Quincy Adams Stanley to Cave Johnson Couts, Dec. 22, 1865, CT-2118–1, Cave Johnson Couts Papers, HEH.

33. Cave Johnson Couts to John Quincy Adams Stanley, Dec. 26, 1865, CT-2118–2, ibid. Emphasis in original.

34. Petition for indenture of José Antonio, Aug. 13, 1866, CT-207, ibid. My account of the custody battle over Reyes relies heavily on Michael Magliari's research in "Free Soil, Unfree Labor," esp. 384–86. I am deeply indebted to Professor Magliari for sharing an early manuscript of the article with me and helping me to navigate the vast collection of Couts's papers at the Huntington Library.

35. *San Francisco Bulletin,* Nov. 11, 1857; *Alta California,* Nov. 10, 1857.

36. I compiled statistics regarding the number of slaves aged twenty-one or younger from census data, which appears in tables 2 and 4 in the appendix of this work. Of the 203 probable slaves in the 1850 federal census of California, 53 were under age twenty-one, making up approximately 26 percent of the enslaved population; 60 of the 178 probable slaves listed in the 1852 California State Census were under age twenty-one, making up just under 34 percent of all enslaved people.

37. Richards, *California Gold Rush,* 54–58. Thorn's troubles are outlined in ibid., as well as in chapter 2.

38. U.S. Census Office, *Seventh Census of the United States,* 982; State of California, California State Census, 1852, roll 2, p. 29. On the early African American community in Los Angeles, see Guillow, "Origins of Race Relations," 182–214; Flamming, *Bound for Freedom,* 19–24; and Lapp, *Blacks in Gold Rush California,* 118–25. For slavery in Utah Territory and the San Bernardino Mormon colony, see Demaratus, *Force of a Feather;* and Rich, "True Policy for Utah."

39. Guillow, "Origins of Race Relations," 189–97; Lapp, *Blacks in Gold Rush California,* 122–23; Richards, *California Gold Rush,* 129–30; Ellison, "Movement for State Division"; Woolsey, "Politics of a Lost Cause"; Glenna Matthews, *The Golden State in the Civil War,* 183–84.

40. Petition of Esther Hereford, April 11, 1857, *In the Matter of the Guardianship of Emily and Maria, Negroes,* Probate Case #66, Los Angeles County Probate Records, Los Angeles Area Court Records Collection, HEH.

41. Petition of J. McCatrick and order of the court, Nov. 5. 1855, *In the Matter of the Guardianship of Tom (a Negro Boy),* Case #2 1/2, Los Angeles Alcalde/County Court Records, 1850–60, Probate, box 8, SCWHR; U.S. Bureau of the Census, *Eighth Federal Population Census,* 1860, roll 59, p. 348, Los Angeles, Los Angeles County, Calif.

42. These constructions of enslaved mothers likely drew from stereotyped images of female slaves as Jezebels, elucidated by White, in *Ar'n't I a Woman?,* 27–46.

43. Petition of John Rowland, undated, and Petition of Charlotte Rowland, May 23, 1856, *In the Matter of the Guardianship of Rose, a Minor Negro*, Probate Case #45, Los Angeles County Probate Records, Los Angeles Area Court Records Collection, HEH. Biographical material about the Rowland family can be found in Rowland, *John Rowland*, esp. 13–28.

44. *In the Matter of the Guardianship of Cassady, a Minor Negro Girl*, July 7, 1858, Probate Case #106, Los Angeles County Probate Records, Los Angeles Area Court Records Collection, HEH.

45. On the assault case against Evertsen, see Woolsey, *Migrants West*, 46–47. Petition of John Evertsen, Sept. 13, 1850, *In the Matter of the Guardianship of Lucy, a Mulatto Child*, case #11 1/2, Los Angeles Alcalde/County Court Records, 1850–60, Probate, box 8, SCWHR.

46. Petition of John Nichols, undated; Petition of Benjamin Davis Wilson, July 2, 1851; and Petition of John Evertsen, July 20, 1851; all located in Los Angeles Alcalde/County Court Records, 1850–60, Probate, box 8, SCWHR. "Southern California: Los Angeles County, Miscellany," vol. 43, p. 28, Hayes Scraps, BANC; U.S. Bureau of the Census, *Eighth Federal Population Census*, 1860, roll 59, p. 419, Los Angeles, Los Angeles County, Calif.

47. A detailed examination of the case of Biddy Mason, Hannah, and the children appears in Demaratus, *Force of a Feather*, 67–90, 109–20.

48. The quotations and summary of the case are taken from the full transcription of Hayes's opinion, entitled "Suit for Freedom," which appeared in the *Sacramento Daily Democratic State Journal* on Feb. 19, 1856. I worked from a copy of the article in "Southern California: Los Angeles County, Miscellany," vol. 43, pp. 519–27, Hayes Scraps, BANC.

49. "Suit for Freedom"; Beasley, *Negro Trail Blazers*, 88–89.

50. Assembly Bill #143 (1853), Original Bill File, CSA.

51. *Alta California*, April 9, 1853; Bell, *Reminiscences of a Ranger*, 275.

52. State of California, *Journal of the Assembly*, 4th sess. (1853), 295, 394, 407.

53. Assembly Bill #49 (1854), Original Bill File, CSA; State of California, *Journal of the Assembly*, 5th sess. (1854), 118, 245.

54. Street, *Beasts of the Field*, 145–51; Magliari, "Free State Slavery"; Chandler and Quinn, "Emma Is a Good Girl"; Bailey, "Indian Life," 13–14, 17–18.

55. Firsthand descriptions of violent encounters between whites and Native peoples in the northwestern counties can be found in "Testimony Taken before the Joint Special Committee on the Mendocino Indian War," in State of California, *Appendix to the Journal of the Senate*, 11th sess. (1860), 13–75. The most recent analyses of the warfare in California's northwestern counties include Madley, "California's Yuki Indians"; and Lindsay, *Murder State*, esp. 179–222. Chapters 4 and 5 of Madley's dissertation, "American Genocide," also recount the creation of militias and dozens of "Indian-hunting" expeditions around the state. Other secondary accounts of the northwestern conflicts include Carranco and Beard, *Genocide and Vendetta*; Baumgardner, *Killing for Land*; and William J. Bauer Jr., *We Were All Like Migrant Workers*, 30–57.

56. J. Ross Browne to J. W. Denver, Jan. 14, 1858, roll 36, ID#B411; and J. Ross Browne to J. Thompson, Oct. 16, 1858, roll 36, ID#B629; both M234.

57. "Annual Report of the Quartermaster and Adjutant General," in State of California, *Appendix to the Journal of the Assembly*, 11th sess. (1860), 9–10.

58. Ellison documents each of these campaigns and their demise in "Movement for State Division." He disputes the idea that state division was aimed at introducing slavery into southern California. Instead, he attributes the movement to southern Californians' desires for greater self-governance and lower taxes. But most contemporary commentators, as well as most nineteenth-century historians, linked state division to slavery. On this point, see ibid., 137–39.

59. Grossberg, *Governing the Hearth*, 259–68; Schmidt, *Free to Work*, 61–63.

60. *Alta California*, March 13, 1852; ibid., March 9, 1855; State of California, *Journal of the Assembly*, 8th sess. (1857), 522. For an overview of the state's apprenticeship laws in the nineteenth century, see Eaves, *History of California Labor Legislation*, 287–94.

61. State of California, *Journal of the Senate*, 9th sess. (1858), 29–30.

62. Act of April 10, 1858, ch. 182, SC, at 134–37. On the practice of involuntary apprenticeship, common across the United States in the nineteenth century, see Grossberg, *Governing the Hearth*, 263–68; Rockman, *Scraping By*, 107–8; and Zipf, *Labor of Innocents*, esp. 8–39.

63. Act of April 10, 1858, ch. 182, SC, at 134–37; *Past and Present of Alameda County*, 514–17.

64. Senate Bill #224 (1859), Original Bill File, CSA.

65. Ibid. The implications of the bill are also laid out in *San Francisco Bulletin*, March 25, 1859; and *Sacramento Daily Union*, March 25, 1859. On Thom's background and his role in the state division movement, see *Press Reference Library*, 347; *Sacramento Daily Union*, Feb. 22, 1859; and ibid., March 25, 1859. Thom's proposal to exclude black children from the educational benefits of apprenticeship had precedents in other states. Kentucky, Missouri, and Indiana phased out educational requirements in their general apprenticeship laws to deny black children training and schooling, and free black apprentices had little access to education under Deep South laws. Grossberg, *Governing the Hearth*, 266; Bardaglio, *Reconstructing the Household*, 104.

66. *Sacramento Daily Union*, March 25, 1859.

67. Senate Bill #224 (1859), Original Bill File, CSA; State of California, *Journal of the Senate*, 10th sess. (1859), 556, 706; *Sacramento Daily Union*, April 12, 1859.

68. Ellison, "Movement for State Division," 130–37; *Press Reference Library*, 347.

69. *Sacramento Daily Union*, July 31, 1860.

70. "Minority Report of the Special Joint Committee on the Mendocino War," in State of California, *Appendix to the Journal of the Senate*, 11th sess. (1860), 11–12; Lindsay, *Murder State*, 235–36; *Sacramento Daily Union*, July 31, 1860; Act of April 16, 1860, ch. 231, SC, at 196–97. For Burson's original bill, amendments to it, and its final passage, see Johnston-Dodds, *Early California Laws*, 31–39; State of California, *Journal of the Assembly*, 11th sess. (1860), 469; and State of California, *Journal of the Senate*, 11th sess. (1860), 599.

71. *Sacramento Daily Union*, July 31, 1860.

Chapter 5

1. *San Francisco Bulletin*, Aug. 19, 1863.

2. On indentured Australian women, see *Alta California*, Feb. 2, 1850; and Robert Effinger to "Brother Mike," March 1, 1850, Robert Patterson Effinger Papers, CHS. On indentured Latin American women, see Barnhart, *Fair but Frail*, 43–44; and Pillors, "Criminalization of Prostitution," 93–95. On Pacific Islander women, see *Alta California*, Dec. 21–27, 1850; and *Ex Parte The Queen of the Bay et al.*, 1 Cal. 157 (1850).

3. The social, political, cultural, and legal dilemmas posed by women's waged work outside the home in the nineteenth-century United States are delineated in Stansell, *City of Women*; Boydston, *Home and Work*; and Amy Dru Stanley, *From Bondage to Contract*. On questions of women's marketability in the world of urban sexual commerce, see Amy Dru Stanley, *From Bondage to Contract*, 218–63; Stansell, *City of Women*, 171–92; and Gilfoyle, *City of Eros*.

4. Denunciations of the marketability of enslaved women's bodies and sexuality, as well as the destruction of slave households and the violation of black men's rights that it entailed, played a central role in the antislavery critique of the slave South. For analyses of American abolitionists' treatment of these issues, see Amy Dru Stanley, *From Bondage to Contract*, 23–35; Clark, "'Sacred Rights of the Weak,'" 482–84; Walters, "Erotic South"; and Walters, *Antislavery Appeal*, 70–87. On similar critiques that emerged within the Republican Party, consult Pierson, *Free Hearts*, 133–38, 173–87.

5. Young and Murphy, "Out of the Past," 354–58; Egli, *No Rooms of Their Own*, 47–50.

6. Young and Murphy, "Out of the Past," 357–58; Egli, *No Rooms of Their Own*, 49–50. For a similar Wailacki captivity narrative, drawn from oral histories, see William J. Bauer Jr., *We Were All Like Migrant Workers*, 30–31.

7. For captive trades in New Mexico and Texas, see Brooks, *Captives and Cousins*; Blackhawk, *Violence over the Land*; Ramón A. Gutiérrez, *When Jesus Came*, esp. 176–90; Barr, "From Captives to Slaves"; and Barr, *Peace Came*.

8. Bouvier, *Women and the Conquest of California*, 97–99, 101–14; Street, *Beasts of the Field*, 76–77, 104; Cook, *Conflict between the California Indian and White Civilization*, 74–80. Sutter's relationship to captive women and children is discussed in chapter 1 as well as in Hurtado, *John Sutter*, 115–17; and Hurtado, *Intimate Frontiers*, 41–42. A firsthand Californio account of trading in captive Native girls is Pico, *Don Pío Pico's Historical Narrative*, 155. On the traffic in Paiute captives, see Blackhawk, *Violence over the Land*, 133–44; and Phillips, *Vineyards and Vaqueros*, 201–3.

9. Robert White to Thomas J. Henley, Aug. 9, 1855, enclosed in Thomas J. Henley to George Manypenny, Aug. 18, 1855, roll 34, ID#H1018, M234; *People of California v. Marcus Vaca*, 1854/55, Criminal Case #486, Sacramento County Court of Sessions Records, CFSH; *Sacramento Daily Union*, Sept. 13, 1854; ibid., Sept. 14, 1854. For another discussion of "Spanish" kidnappers of Indian women and children, see *Alta California*, Nov. 8, 1854.

10. Robert White to Thomas J. Henley, Aug. 20, 1855, enclosed in Thomas J. Henley to George Manypenny, Sept. 18, 1855, roll 34, ID#H1025, M234; Asbill and Shawley, *Last of the West*, 31–44.

11. San Diego Justice of the Peace, Indenture of Sasaria, Jan. 25, 1854, CT-2615, Cave Johnson Couts Papers, HEH; Heizer and Almquist, *The Other Californians*, 54–56; Magliari, "Free State Slavery," 170–71, 175–76.

12. Baumgardner, *Killing for Land*, 32–33; J. J. Jackson, "Bridge Gulch Massacre," 7–14; Cox, *Annals of Trinity County*, 100–103, 232n102.

13. J. J. Jackson, "Bridge Gulch Massacre," 14; Cox, *Annals of Trinity County*, 112, 114.

14. Indenture of Charles and Kate, Nov. 13, 1861, reel 170, frame 606, Robert Fleming Heizer Papers, MSS 78/17c, subseries 6:3, miscellaneous subject files, "Indian Slaves and Indentured Servants," BANC; Carpenter, "Among the Diggers," 390–91; A. O. Carpenter, Articles of Apprenticeship, Sept. 24, 1861, HM 16778, HEH. Statistics on the number of captive children in white households can be found in Street, *Beasts of the Field*, 148. According to William J. Bauer Jr., Helen Carpenter's Indian apprentices voluntarily bound themselves to her husband, Aurelius, to avoid removal to the Mendocino Reservation. William J. Bauer Jr., *We Were All Like Migrant Workers*, 70. On the role of bound Indian children, male and female, as domestic laborers in white households, see also Magliari, "Free State Slavery," esp. 175–84; and Chandler and Quinn, "Emma Is a Good Girl."

15. *Mendocino Herald*, March 7, 1862, quoted in Chandler, "Failure of Reform," 292.

16. *Marysville Appeal*, Dec. 7, 1861; Rawls, *Indians of California*, 98–99.

17. Irvine, *History of Humboldt County*, 70; *Sacramento Daily Union*, Jan. 15, 1858. On interracial households in Trinity County, see Hurtado, "'Hardly a Farmhouse,'" 266–68. For discussions of the rape and forced concubinage of California Native women and girls, see Hurtado, *Indian Survival*, 180–82; Hurtado, *Intimate Frontiers*, 88–89; and Lindsay, *Murder State*, 155, 219–21.

18. *Red Bluff Beacon*, Nov. 4, 1857; *Sacramento Daily Union*, May 30, 1859. A similar incident, involving a white man named Bland who kidnapped a Yuki woman from her people, occurred in 1859. Tassin, "Chronicles of Camp Wright," 31.

19. *Sacramento Daily Union*, July 31, 1860.

20. On abolitionist representations of enslaved black women, see Amy Dru Stanley, *From Bondage to Contract*, 23–35.

21. For an example of how discourses about manhood and control over female dependents, rooted in republican ideology, shaped gender and race relations in the slave South, see McCurry, *Masters of Small Worlds*, esp. 56–91. Amy Dru Stanley explores how similar understandings of manhood and independence informed struggles over women's waged work outside the home in the postbellum North and the postemancipation South. For this discussion, see Amy Dru Stanley, *From Bondage to Contract*, 138–74. In the antebellum United States, men of color, particularly enslaved African American men, were often excluded from this way of conceptualizing manhood rights. One of the things that marked enslaved black men as slaves was their lack of legal entitlement to the bodies, labor, and reproduction of their female

kin. For an analysis of discourses about enslaved men's rights to female kin and the way that they influenced abolitionist critiques, see ibid., 23–35.

22. Hurtado, *Indian Survival*, 172–73; Susan Lee Johnson, *Roaring Camp*, 130–31; Pascoe, *Relations of Rescue*, 56–59; Smits, "'Squaw Drudge,'" 281–306.

23. Oliver M. Wozencraft to Luke Lea, Oct. 14, 1851, roll 32, ID#W652, M234; "Indian Tribes in California," an undated 1851 article from *Daily True Standard* (San Francisco), vol. 1, HM 51846, J. G. Marvin Scrapbooks, HEH.

24. The *Trinity Journal* article was reprinted in *Sacramento Daily Union*, March 4, 1858.

25. *Marysville Appeal*, Aug. 20, 1861, reprinted in *San Francisco Bulletin*, Aug. 21, 1861. Bret Harte's editorial originally appeared in the Uniontown *Northern Californian* where he briefly worked as an assistant editor. It was reprinted in *Alta California*, July 13, 1859. On Harte's Republican connections and his articles about Indian affairs, see Scharnhorst, *Bret Harte*, 12–14, 17–18, 33. Harte was eventually run out of Uniontown when he wrote a condemnatory exposé of the Indian Island Massacre of February 1860, in which local whites indiscriminately murdered as many as 250 Wiyot, Eel, and Mad River Indians on an island in the Humboldt Bay. Madley, "American Genocide," 416–18.

26. *Sacramento Daily Union*, Oct. 19, 1857.

27. Phillips, *Indians and Indian Agents*, esp. 109–90; Hurtado, *Indian Survival*, 125–64; Carranco and Beard, *Genocide and Vendetta*, 55–83. Contemporary accusations that U.S. officials failed to contain Native peoples appear in "Testimony Taken before the Joint Special Committee on the Mendocino Indian War," in State of California, *Appendix to the Journal of the Senate*, 11th sess. (1860), esp. 65–68.

28. *San Francisco Bulletin*, Sept. 13, 1856; *Sacramento Daily Union*, Oct. 19, 1857.

29. Hislop, *Nome Lackee Indian Reservation*, 95.

30. John Markle to James Denver, March 13, 1859, roll 37, ID#M604, M234.

31. On the late nineteenth-century use of the phrase "squaw man" in the United States and Canada, see Smits, "'Squaw Men'"; Carter, *Capturing Women*, 184–85; and McManus, *The Line Which Separates*, 76, 92–93, 160–61. The term "squaw man" may actually have originated in California. The *Oxford English Dictionary* records the earliest use of the term in an 1866 report by Charles Maltby, California's superintendent of Indian affairs. Newspaper research reveals, however, that the term appeared in the *Humboldt Times* as early as 1855. The article was reprinted in *Alta California*, Jan. 21, 1855. The term appears in dozens of northwestern California newspaper articles from the late 1850s and early 1860s, and several other California Indian agents used it in their reports before Maltby adopted it. See, for instance, George Hanson to William Dole, June 19, 1862, roll 38, ID#H495, M234; and George Hanson to William Dole, Sept. 7, 1863, in U.S. Congress, 38th Cong., 1st sess., *House Ex. Doc. no. 1*, pp. 207–8.

32. *Red Bluff Beacon*, Oct. 28, 1857; *San Francisco Bulletin*, April 4, 1862, reprinted in Robert F. Heizer, *Destruction of California Indians*, 303; *Humboldt Times*, June 12, 1858; ibid., Dec. 10, 1859; H. P. Heintzelman to Thomas J. Henley, July 1, 1858, in Office of Indian Affairs, *Report of the Commissioner of Indian Affairs*, 1858, 287.

33. *Red Bluff Beacon*, June 23, 1858; Pitelka, "Mendocino," 145; Lindsay, *Murder State*, 297–98.

34. *Red Bluff Beacon*, Feb. 10, 1858.

35. Trinity Journal, quoted in *Red Bluff Beacon*, Aug. 18, 1858.

36. *Humboldt Times*, Aug. 7, 1858; ibid., Sept. 18, 1858; Hurtado, *Indian Survival*, 176.

37. *Red Bluff Beacon*, May 26, 1858; ibid., June 16, 1858. Lindsay also recounts these anti–squaw man campaigns in *Murder State*, 297–98.

38. *Red Bluff Beacon*, Feb. 10, 1858; An Act Regulating Marriages, Act of April 22, 1850, ch. 140, sec. 3, SC, at 424; *Humboldt Times*, March 20, 1858; *San Francisco Bulletin*, Jan. 26, 1858; State of California, *Journal of the Senate*, 9th sess. (1858), 124, 185–86, 289.

39. State of California, *Journal of the Senate*, 13th sess. (1862), 528.

40. For analyses of western antimiscegenation laws in California and the American West, see Pascoe, *What Comes Naturally*, 77–108, 150–59.

41. *Humboldt Times*, March 20, 1858; *Shasta Herald*, reprinted in *Humboldt Times*, Dec. 31, 1859.

42. Mary Barham, Habeas Corpus, Oct. 30, 1861, Case #49, Mendocino County Records, District and County Courts, Civil and Criminal Cases, CSA.

43. C. S. Williams, Habeas Corpus, April 22, 1862, Case #72, Mendocino County Records, District and County Courts, Civil and Criminal Cases, CSA.

44. Lt. W. P. Carlin to Maj. W. W. Marshall, Feb. 6, 1860, enclosed in J. Y. McDuffie to A. B. Greenwood, Feb. 18, 1860, roll 37, ID#M202, M234.

45. Trinity Journal, March 2, 1861.

46. My argument is influenced by studies of Chinese America that explore how discourses about gender and the status of women shaped the debate over Chinese immigration, including Leong, "A Distinct and Antagonistic Race"; Peffer, *If They Don't Bring Their Women*; and Aarim-Heriot, *Chinese Immigrants*.

47. Cheng Hirata, "Free, Indentured, Enslaved," 8–11; Tong, *Unsubmissive Women*, 6–12.

48. Pascoe, *Relations of Rescue*, 93–94; Augustus Ward Loomis, "Chinese in California," 1876, MSS C-E 158, BANC; *San Francisco Bulletin*, April 2, 1869. For discussions of *mui tsai*, see Tong, *Unsubmissive Women*, 40, 143; and Yung, *Unbound Feet*, 2, 37–41.

49. My interpretation of how this system of debt servitude may have worked comes from extensive newspaper research. For articles that discuss prostitutes' debt bondage and the role that family debts played in the system, see *Sacramento Daily Union*, Oct. 10, 1856; ibid., Feb. 13, 1857; ibid., Nov. 30, 1857; ibid., Dec. 4, 1857; ibid., Dec. 20, 1857; ibid., Dec. 23, 1857; *San Francisco Bulletin*, July 22, 1857; ibid., Oct. 21, 1858; ibid., Dec. 10, 1858; ibid., Dec. 17, 1858; ibid., Sept. 27, 1859; and *Alta California*, Oct. 16, 1857.

50. There are four known extant copies of such transactions, the earliest from 1873 and the latest from the 1890s. This one appears in Otis Gibson, *Chinese in America*, 139. The others appear in ibid., 138–40; and Cheng Hirata, "Free, Indentured, Enslaved," 15–16.

51. *Alta California*, Oct. 19, 1857; *Mariposa News*, quoted in *San Francisco Bulletin*, Dec. 14, 1860.

52. *Sacramento Daily Union*, Feb. 5, 1859.

53. *San Francisco Bulletin*, Sept. 17, 1857; ibid., July 18, 1857.

54. *Alta California*, May 14, 1858.

55. *California Police Gazette*, April 14, 1860; ibid., Sept. 25, 1869.

56. Peffer, *If They Don't Bring Their Women*, 102; *Alta California*, July 23, 1855; *Trinity Journal*, March 2, 1861.

57. Yung, *Unbound Feet*, 31.

58. Tong, *Unsubmissive Women*, 171–76. Hundreds of these cases appeared before the California courts from the 1850s to the 1870s. For some representative examples, see *California Police Gazette*, June 11, 1859; *Sacramento Daily Union*, Dec. 23–24, 1857; ibid., June 3–4, 1859; *San Francisco Bulletin*, June 3, 1863; *In the Matter of Ah Quee*, Feb. 24, 1871, Case #716, 21:69, box 6, Sacramento County Court, Criminal Files, CFSH; *The People v. Yow How and Yen Uck*, Jan. 8, 1876, Case #1174, 21:70, box 12, Sacramento County Court, Criminal Files, CFSH; and *Ex Parte Good Toy*, May 18, 1876, Case #1229, 21:70, box 12, Sacramento County Court, Criminal Files, CFSH.

59. *Sacramento Daily Union*, Sept. 17–18, 1857; ibid., Nov. 13, 1857; ibid., Aug. 18, 1859; *Alta California*, Nov. 12, 1857. Newspaper accounts sometimes reported Ma Ho's name as Be Ho or Me How.

60. *Sacramento Daily Union*, Nov. 4–5, 1859; ibid., Nov. 7, 1859; ibid., Nov. 18, 1859; *Sacramento Bee*, Nov. 4, 1859; ibid., Nov. 7, 1859.

61. *Sacramento Daily Union*, Nov. 4, 1859; ibid., Nov. 17, 1859.

62. Ibid., Nov. 18, 1859.

63. Ibid.

64. Ibid., Nov. 17, 1859; Petition of Chu Quong, Nov. 5, 1859, in *In re Quin Ti*, folder 4, box 4, "unidentified 1859 cases," Sacramento County District Court, Criminal Files, CFSH.

65. *Sacramento Daily Union*, Nov. 17–18, 1859.

66. Ibid., Nov. 18, 1859; ibid., Nov. 21, 1859; *Sacramento Bee*, Nov. 19, 1859.

67. *People v. Chu Quong*, 15 Cal. 332 (1860); *Sacramento Daily Union*, Feb. 9, 1860; "Register and Descriptive List of Convicts under Sentence of Imprisonment in the State Prison of California," Corrections, Governor's Office, San Quentin Prison Registers, 1851–67, pp. 157–58, CSA.

68. Testimony of Ah Moon, in Ah Chung [aka Ah Chon], Application for Pardon, Oct. 31, 1860, WPA File #1348, CSA.

69. Ah Chung [aka Ah Chon], Application for Pardon, Oct. 31, 1860, WPA File #1348, CSA; State of California, *Journal of the Assembly*, 12th sess. (1861), 115; *California Police Gazette*, Nov. 17, 1860.

Chapter 6

1. *San Francisco Bulletin*, Oct. 28, 1865; Winfield J. Davis, *History of Political Conventions*, 206. For the decline of the Chivalry Democrats, the founding of the Union Party, and the repeal of anti–black testimony laws, see ibid., 159–92; Chandler, "Friends in Time of Need," 324–29; and Bottoms, "'An Aristocracy of Color,'" 51–62.

2. On the complexity of Reconstruction, in the North and the South, see Montgomery, *Beyond Equality*; Foner, *Reconstruction*; Amy Dru Stanley, *From Bondage to Contract*; Heather Cox Richardson, *Death of Reconstruction*; and Schmidt, *Free to Work*,

among many others. Older works that explore Reconstruction in the American West and California are Moody, "Civil War and Reconstruction"; Gerald Stanley, "Civil War Politics"; Chandler, "Press and Civil Liberties"; and Berwanger, West and Reconstruction. A wealth of new scholarship on the Civil War and Reconstruction in the West has emerged in the last decade. These newer works include Arenson, Great Heart of the Republic; Bottoms, "'An Aristocracy of Color'"; Deverell, "Convalescence and California"; Heather Cox Richardson, West from Appomattox; Taylor, In Search of the Racial Frontier, esp. 71–94, 103–29; West, "Reconstructing Race"; West, Last Indian War; Paddison, American Heathens; and Glenna Matthews, The Golden State in the Civil War.

3. San Francisco Bulletin, Aug. 20, 1860. Data from the 1860 census suggests that Aaron and Nathaniel Rice belonged to an entire family of enslaved people whom William Rice transported to California. U.S. Bureau of the Census, Eighth Federal Population Census, 1860, roll 61, p. 88, Napa Township, Napa County, Calif. Researcher Delilah Beasley lists Aaron Rice as one of several enslaved men who escaped a Napa County farm with the aid of California's leading white abolitionist, Rev. Thomas Starr King. Beasley, Negro Trail Blazers, 91. As an African American, Aaron Rice could file a complaint against a white resident but could not give testimony against him or her in open court.

4. The three other cases are the Mathews fugitive slave case of 1859, related in Lapp, Blacks in Gold Rush California, 154–56; the 1861 case of John Turner, reported in Sacramento Daily Union, Jan. 25, 1861; and an 1864 custody battle over an enslaved girl named Adda in Sacramento County, which can be found in People v. Gammon/In the Matter of the Guardianship of Adda [aka Edith], Case #737, 17:04, box 30, Sacramento County Probate Court Records, CFSH.

5. Chandler, "Friends in Time of Need," 320–25; Gerald Stanley, "Civil War Politics," 119.

6. Pacific Appeal, April 5, 1862; "Petition for Legal Recognition of Black Californians," MSS 169A, CHS.

7. State of California, Journal of the Assembly, 13th sess. (1862), 254; Sacramento Daily Union, March 26, 1862.

8. Chandler, "Friends in Time of Need," 327; Sacramento Daily Union, March 26, 1862.

9. An Act Concerning Crimes and Punishments, Act of April 16, 1850, ch. 99, sec. 14, SC, at 230; An Act to Regulate Proceedings in Civil Cases, in the Courts of This State, Act of April 20, 1851, ch. 5, sec. 394, SC, at 114. In cases tried under the special provisions of the 1850 Act for the Government and Protection of Indians (Act of April 22, 1850, ch. 133, sec. 6, SC, at 409), Indians could testify and bring complaints against whites. The California Supreme Court decision that established the exclusion of Chinese testimony was People v. Hall, 4 Cal. 399 (1854).

10. San Francisco Bulletin, March 17, 1862; Sacramento Daily Union, March 26, 1862.

11. Charles Maclay, "Speech before the Assembly for a Bill to Permit 'Inferior Races' to Testify in Court," April 1862, MC 164, Charles Maclay Papers, HEH.

12. Bottoms, "'An Aristocracy of Color,'" 60.

13. Pacific Appeal, May 3, 1862.

14. Winfield J. Davis, *History of Political Conventions*, 182–92; Chandler, "Friends in Time of Need," 328–29; Gerald Stanley, "Civil War Politics," 121; *Pacific Appeal*, Jan. 31, 1863. In California, the Union Party was not merely a renamed Republican Party as it was elsewhere. It was a genuine (though short-lived) fusion between Republicans and northern-born, free-soil Democrats. Chandler, "Friends in Time of Need," especially 319n1.

15. *Sacramento Daily Union*, March 5, 1863.

16. Ibid.

17. An Act to Amend an Act Concerning Crimes and Punishments, Act of March 18, 1863, ch. 70, SC, at 69; Wunder, "Chinese in Trouble," 39. Despite many challenges in the state courts, the ban on Indian and Chinese testimony persisted until 1872. That year, the legislature overhauled the state's statutes and simply left the prohibition out of the new political code. On this change, see Bottoms, "'An Aristocracy of Color,'" 68.

18. *Pacific Appeal*, March 7, 1863; Senate Resolution no. 1, Jan. 26, 1863, SC, at 793; *San Francisco Bulletin*, Jan. 12, 1863.

19. Chandler, "Friends in Time of Need," 328; Winfield J. Davis, *History of Political Conventions*, 197–99; *San Francisco Bulletin*, Jan. 12, 1863.

20. *Sacramento Daily Union*, Dec. 19, 1865; Senate Resolution no. 1, Dec. 20, 1865, SC, at 896. By the time California legislators approved the amendment, it had already been ratified by the requisite number of states.

21. Saxton, *Indispensable Enemy*, 80–91; Bottoms, "'An Aristocracy of Color,'" 75–127; San Francisco Regular Democratic Ticket for 1867, San Francisco Oversize Miscellaneous Collection, CHS.

22. *Mendocino Herald*, April 10, 1863; Carpenter, "Among the Diggers," 398–99. "Rosa" is the name that Carpenter gave the girl when she recalled her death thirty years later.

23. An Act Amendatory to an Act Entitled An Act for the Government and Protection of Indians, Act of April 16, 1860, ch. 231, SC, at 196–97. On violence and the mass killing of Indians in northwestern California during the Civil War era, see Madley, "California's Yuki Indians"; and Madley, "American Genocide," 425–85.

24. On the ways in which the 1860 amendment encouraged and expanded Indian slave trafficking in a different part of northern California—Colusa County—see Magliari, "Free State Slavery."

25. Street, *Beasts of the Field*, 704n32. Street found that 308 of 782 people enumerated in the 1860 census for Calpella Township, Mendocino County, were apprenticed Indians. Estimates of the number of apprenticed Indians vary widely because census takers enumerated Indian populations erratically and often did not record their apprenticeship status. Some historians estimate that 3,000 to 4,000 people suffered apprenticeship, while others put the number at well over 4,000. For a discussion of these numbers, see Rawls, *Indians of California*, 96.

26. Act of April 16, 1860, ch. 231, sec. 1, SC, at 196.

27. *Mendocino Herald*, April 4, 1862; *Sacramento Daily Union*, Sept. 18, 1862; George Hanson to Charles Mix, July 23, 1861, roll 38, ID#H245, M234. For an analysis of the rise of California's Indian-fighting militias, the atrocities they perpetrated, and

captive taking in northwestern California, see Madley, "American Genocide," chapters 4–6, esp. 435–38, 447–49.

28. *Humboldt Times*, July 20, 1861; Elijah Renshaw Potter Reminiscences, MSS C-D 5136, BANC; George Hanson to William Dole, April 25, 1863, roll 39, ID#H183, M234; *Mendocino Herald*, April 10, 1863.

29. *Humboldt Times*, Jan. 12, 1861; ibid., June 12, 1861; ibid., Oct. 19, 1861; ibid., Oct. 26, 1861; ibid., Nov. 9, 1861; ibid., Nov. 16, 1861. James Beith to William Huestis, Jan. 12, 1862; and James Beith to Hugh Clauson, Jan. 24, 1862; both in James Beith Letterbook, 1854–67, MSS 70/116c, BANC. Emphasis in original. Dissent against Indian apprenticeship may not have been widespread everywhere in northwestern California. Linda Pitelka argues that most whites in overwhelmingly Democratic Mendocino County supported apprenticeship. Pitelka, "Mendocino," 42–43.

30. *San Francisco Bulletin*, June 11, 1861; *Columbia Times*, Jan. 10, 1861; *Marysville Appeal*, Jan. 4, 1861; Hislop, *Nome Lackee Indian Reservation*, 33–52.

31. *San Francisco Bulletin*, June 11, 1861; *Marysville Appeal*, June 1, 1861, reprinted in *San Francisco Bulletin*, June 3, 1861; "History of Lake County," 247–50.

32. George Hanson to William P. Dole, July 15, 1861, in Office of Indian Affairs, *Report of the Commissioner of Indian Affairs*, 1861, 149–50; George Hanson to William P. Dole, Oct. 10, 1862, in Office of Indian Affairs, *Report of the Commissioner of Indian Affairs*, 1862, 315. George Hanson to Charles Mix, July 23, 1861, roll 38, ID#H245; and George Hanson to William P. Dole, July 15, 1861, roll 38, ID#H246; both M234.

33. George Hanson to William P. Dole, Oct. 10, 1862, in Office of Indian Affairs, *Report of the Commissioner of Indian Affairs*, 1862, 315; *San Francisco Bulletin*, Oct. 21, 1861; *Humboldt Times*, Nov. 2, 1861.

34. *Siddons v. Woodman*, Case #106 (1862), Mendocino County Court Records, District and County Courts, Civil and Criminal Cases, CSA; *Mendocino Herald*, April 4, 1862.

35. *Mendocino Herald*, May 2, 1862.

36. *Marysville Appeal*, quoted in *Sacramento Daily Union*, Oct. 18, 1861; *Mendocino Herald*, July 4, 1862.

37. George Hanson to William P. Dole, Oct. 10, 1862, in Office of Indian Affairs, *Report of the Commissioner of Indian Affairs*, 1862, 315.

38. *Mendocino Herald*, April 4, 1862; ibid., May 2, 1862; Carpenter, "Among the Diggers," 390, 398–99.

39. *San Francisco Bulletin*, March 7, 1862; ibid., April 17, 1862. Assembly Bill #463, An Act to Repeal an Act Amendatory of an Act Entitled An Act for the Government and Protection of Indians, April 15, 1862; and Assembly Bill #464, An Act to Amend an Act for the Government and Protection of Indians, April 15, 1862; both in California State Assembly, Original Bill File, CSA. State of California, *Journal of the Assembly*, 13th sess. (1862), 323. For a discussion of vagrancy laws in the eastern United States, consult Amy Dru Stanley, *From Bondage to Contract*, 98–137; and Schmidt, *Free to Work*, 53–81.

40. *Sacramento Daily Union*, May 5, 1862; ibid., May 9, 1862; ibid., May, 12, 1862; Assembly Bill #464 (1862), Original Bill File, CSA; *San Francisco Bulletin*, May 10, 1862.

41. State of California, *Journal of the Assembly*, 14th sess. (1863), 642; State of California, *Journal of the Senate*, 14th sess. (1863), 534; An Act for the Repeal of Sections Two and Three of an Act Entitled An Act for the Protection and Government of Indians [sic], Act of April 27, 1863, ch. 475, SC, at 743.

42. Heizer and Almquist, *The Other Californians*, 58. For examples of similar arguments, see Street, *Beasts of the Field*, 150–51; and Gillis and Magliari, *John Bidwell*, 251. Not until 1865 would a Republican-leaning California Supreme Court outlaw the whipping of Indian convicts as cruel and unusual punishment. For this decision, see *People v. Juan Antonio*, 27 Cal. 404 (1865).

43. Act of April 27, 1863, ch. 475, SC, at 743; An Act for the Government and Protection of Indians, Act of April 22, 1850, ch. 133, sec. 14, 16, 20, SC, at 409–10.

44. This data was compiled by Lindsay, in *Murder State*, 267–68.

45. *The People v. John McGill*, May 6, 1864, Case #156; and *The People v. Robert Hildreth*, Aug. 9, 1865, Case #211; both in Mendocino County Records, District and County Courts, Civil and Criminal Cases, CSA. *California Police Gazette*, Aug. 26, 1865.

46. Elijah Steele to William P. Dole, Oct. 30, 1863, roll 39, ID#S199, M234; Office of Indian Affairs, *Report of the Commissioner of Indian Affairs*, 1867, 121. For the contests over labor on the Round Valley Reservation during Reconstruction, see William J. Bauer Jr., *We Were All Like Migrant Workers*, 58–79, esp. 68–69.

47. Office of Indian Affairs, *Report of the Commissioner of Indian Affairs*, 1867, 134; *Alta California*, June 8, 1874.

48. *Yreka Semi-Weekly Union*, Sept. 28, 1864, reprinted in Robert F. Heizer, *They Were Only Diggers*, 94–95; *Colusa Sun*, May 26, 1866. Discussions of Bidwell's political career and his relations with Native laborers can be found in Gillis and Magliari, *John Bidwell*, 249–53; Street, *Beasts of the Field*, 151–53; and Rawls, *Indians of California*, 94–95.

49. *Colusa Sun*, May 26, 1866.

50. For an overview of the political struggle over the Chinese question during the 1860s, see also Chandler, "'Anti-Coolie Rabies.'"

51. Chan, *This Bittersweet Soil*, 52–66; Chan, "Chinese Livelihood in Rural California"; Chiu, *Chinese Labor in California*, 29; Saxton, *Indispensable Enemy*, 3–10, 72–80.

52. Jung, *Coolies and Cane*, 33–38; An Act to Prohibit the "Coolie Trade" by American Citizens in American Vessels (Feb. 19, 1862), ch. 27, *U.S. Statutes at Large* 12 (1862), 340.

53. An Act to Protect Free White Labor against Competition with Chinese Coolie Labor, and to Discourage the Immigration of Chinese into the State of California, Act of April 26, 1862, ch. 339, SC, at 462–65; McClain, *In Search of Equality*, 25–29; Aarim-Heriot, *Chinese Immigrants*, 67–68.

54. On these oppositions, see Aarim-Heriot, *Chinese Immigrants*, 67.

55. Healy and Poon Chew, *Statement for Non-exclusion*, 18–24; *Sacramento Daily Union*, March 27, 1862.

56. *Sacramento Daily Union*, March 26, 1862; *San Francisco Bulletin*, March 18, 1862.

57. *Sacramento Daily Union*, March 26–27, 1862; *San Francisco Bulletin*, April 9, 1862.

58. For Stanford's take on the Chinese question, see Aarim-Heriot, *Chinese Immigrants*, 68–69, 72. Background on the Lin Sing case appears in ibid., 72; and McClain, *In Search of Equality*, 26–29.

59. *Lin Sing v. Washburn*, 20 Cal. 539–40, 547–49 (1862); McClain, *In Search of Equality*, 26–29.

60. *Lin Sing v. Washburn*, 20 Cal. 554–59 (1862); Gerald Stanley, "Frank Pixley."

61. *Lin Sing v. Washburn*, 20 Cal. 577–80 (1862).

62. *Sacramento Daily Union*, March 26, 1862.

63. Amy Dru Stanley, *From Bondage to Contract*, 44–59, 175–263; DuBois, *Feminism and Suffrage*; Edwards, *Gendered Strife and Confusion*. On white women's political movements in California during the nineteenth century, see Schuele, "None Could Deny."

64. George Hanson to William Dole, Oct. 10, 1862, in Office of Indian Affairs, *Report of the Commissioner of Indian Affairs*, 1862, 311; George Hanson to William Dole, July 15, 1861, in Office of Indian Affairs, *Report of the Commissioner of Indian Affairs*, 1861, 148.

65. George Hanson to Abraham Lincoln, June 4, 1863, roll 39, ID#P45, M234. Khal Ross Schneider analyzes Hanson's interest in suppressing interracial sex in "Citizen Lives," 40–42.

66. Albert L. Hurtado discusses the associations between squaw men and secessionism in *Indian Survival*, 176–77. The high number of southerners and Missourians in northwestern California, as well as the prevalence of secessionist sentiment, is documented in Pitelka, "Mendocino," 70, 74–77; and Tassin, "Chronicles of Camp Wright," 171–72. George Hanson to William Dole, Nov. 14, 1864, roll 39, ID#H1022, M234; Brewer, *Up and Down California*, 546.

67. George Hanson to William Dole, Sept. 7, 1863, in Office of Indian Affairs, *Report of the Commissioner of Indian Affairs*, 1863, 89.

68. George Hanson to William Dole, Dec. 3, 1861, and March 1, 1862, roll 38, ID#H340 and ID#H392, M234.

69. George Hanson to William Melendy, May 25, 1864, enclosed in George Hanson to William Dole, Nov. 14, 1864, roll 39, ID#H1022, M234.

70. *Mendocino Herald*, Aug. 28, 1863; *Henry J. Abbot v. C. D. Douglass and W. P. Melinda [aka Melendy]*, Sept. 9, 1865, Case #255, Mendocino County Records, District and County Courts, Civil and Criminal Cases, CSA. George Hanson to William Dole, Nov. 14, 1864, roll 39, ID#H1022; E. Steele to William Dole, Jan. 26, 1864, roll 39, ID#S240; and William P. Melendy to D. N. Cooley, June 2, 1867, roll 42, ID#M541; all M234.

71. Tassin, "Chronicles of Camp Wright," 172–73; *Henry J. Abbot v. C. D. Douglass and W. P. Melinda [aka Melendy]*, Sept. 9, 1865, Case #255, Mendocino County Records, District and County Courts, Civil and Criminal Cases, CSA. William P. Melendy to William Dole, Nov. 7, 1864; and George Hanson to William Dole, Nov. 14, 1864, roll 39, ID#H1022; both M234. Melendy's letter was enclosed in Hanson's letter to Dole.

72. A. S. Downer to Commissioner of Indian Affairs (Lewis V. Bogley), July 11, 1867, ID#D524; and A. S. Downer to O. H. Browning, Nov. 1, 1867, ID#I566; both roll 42, M234. Pitelka, "Mendocino," 45–46.

73. Assembly Bill #247, An Act to Prohibit the Sale of Chinese Persons of Either Sex, March 15, 1860, California State Assembly, Original Bill File, CSA; State of California, *Journal of the Assembly*, 11th sess. (1860), 408, 445; *Trinity Journal*, March 2, 1861; *San Francisco Bulletin*, March 19, 1866.

74. For the initial bill, see *California Police Gazette*, Jan. 20, 1866. The revised version became An Act for the Suppression of Chinese Houses of Ill Fame, Act of March 31, 1866, ch. 505, SC, at 641–42. The act was probably meant to reinforce a recent San Francisco municipal ordinance that called for the removal of "Chinese women of ill-fame" from particular districts of the city. For a discussion of both of these laws, see Tong, *Unsubmissive Women*, 118.

75. *Sacramento Daily Union*, March 20, 1866; *San Francisco Bulletin*, March 19, 1866; ibid., March 21, 1866.

76. *California Police Gazette*, Sept. 8, 1866; *Golden Era*, June 3, 1866; *Sacramento Daily Union*, June 1, 1866; *San Francisco Bulletin*, June 1, 1866.

77. *San Francisco Bulletin*, June 23, 1866; *California Police Gazette*, June 9, 1866; ibid., Sept. 8, 1866.

78. *Alta California*, Sept. 1, 1867; ibid., Dec. 22, 1867. The legislature later amended the law, in 1874, to strike out the word "Chinese," thus making it a general antiprostitution measure. Legislators may have made this change to comply with the Fourteenth Amendment. An Act to Amend an Act Entitled An Act for the Suppression of Chinese Houses of Ill Fame, Act of Feb. 7, 1874, ch. 76, SC, at 84.

Chapter 7

1. *Ex Parte Ah Fook* Case File, WPA #10716 (1874), Supreme Court of California Case Files, CSA. Ah Fook's testimony appears on pp. 84–87 of the handwritten case file. Ah Fung's testimony appears on pp. 40–42. An Act to Prevent the Kidnapping and Importation of Mongolian, Chinese, and Japanese Females, for Criminal or Demoralizing Purposes, Act of March 18, 1870, ch. 230, SC, at 330–32.

2. An Act to Prevent the Importation of Chinese Criminals and to Prevent the Establishment of Coolie Slavery, Act of March 18, 1870, ch. 231, SC, at 332–33.

3. Here my emphasis on the intertwined nature of anti-Chinese and antislavery/anti–slave trade arguments is influenced by Leong, "A Distinct and Antagonistic Race"; and Jung, *Coolies and Cane*. In locating the antislavery impulse of exclusion primarily in California, however, I depart from Jung, who argues for shifting the focus of Asian American history away from the West Coast. My California-centric interpretation of exclusion also differs substantially from that of Gyory in *Closing the Gate*, which emphasizes that national politicians, from both major parties and across all regions, took up the anti-Chinese cause to garner votes when victory in national elections could be won by razor-thin margins. Here I suggest that California's national legislators played a particularly crucial role in the national debate by providing models of anti-Chinese legislation that, in linking Chinese immigration to slavery, evaded Reconstruction civil rights laws. Finally, in emphasizing the centrality of alleged Chinese slavery and unfreedom to the exclusion debate, I also depart from Joshua Paddison's recent interpretation in *American Heathens*. Paddison locates the origins of exclusion in evolving religious debates about Chinese immigrants' aptitude for Christianization and their ability to assimilate into a polity in which Christian manhood, rather than race, became the key prerequisite for citizenship.

4. Chandler, "Friends in Time of Need," 336.

5. Aarim-Heriot, *Chinese Immigrants*, 104–5; Chandler, "Friends in Time of Need," 337; Saxton, *Indispensable Enemy*, 67–78; Chan, *This Bittersweet Soil*, 26–28.

6. Winfield J. Davis, *History of Political Conventions*, 241–42; Saxton, *Indispensable Enemy*, 80–91; Paddison, *American Heathens*, 20–22.

7. *San Francisco Bulletin*, March 13, 1867.

8. *Sacramento Daily Union*, July 12, 1867.

9. Bottoms, "'An Aristocracy of Color,'" 112.

10. Ibid., 113; Berwanger, *West and Reconstruction*, 120–21, 209–10. Three other free states—New Jersey, Ohio, and Oregon—initially ratified the Fourteenth Amendment in 1866 but rescinded ratification in 1868. Epps, *Democracy Reborn*, 252–53.

11. Winfield J. Davis, *History of Political Conventions*, 290; Haight, *Speech of Governor Haight*, 5.

12. Casserly, *Speech of Hon. Eugene Casserly*, 2, 9.

13. *Sacramento Daily Union*, July 12, 1867; *Mountain Democrat*, Aug. 7, 1869; State of California, *Journal of the Assembly*, 18th sess. (1869/70), 55–56.

14. Winfield J. Davis, *History of Political Conventions*, 293; Berwanger, *West and Reconstruction*, 177.

15. *San Francisco Bulletin*, Jan. 28, 1870. California, Oregon, Maryland, Kentucky, Tennessee, and Delaware were the only states that never ratified the Fifteenth Amendment in the 1860s or 1870s. John Mabry Matthews, *Legislative and Judicial History*, 68–75; Berwanger, *West and Reconstruction*, 183.

16. McClain, *In Search of Equality*, 31–42; Bottoms, "'An Aristocracy of Color,'" 62–65, 94–95; Aarim-Heriot, *Chinese Immigrants*, 84–92, 140–43.

17. Burlingame Treaty (July 28, 1868), Art. 5–6, U.S. Statutes at Large 16 (1868), 740; McClain, *In Search of Equality*, 30–31; Aarim-Heriot, *Chinese Immigrants*, 109–12; Schrecker, "'For the Equality of Men.'"

18. Act of March 18, 1870, ch. 230, SC, at 330–32. For other discussions of the bill, see Chan, "Exclusion of Chinese Women," 95–109; and Peffer, *If They Don't Bring Their Women*, 32–42. The act was initially proposed by John S. Hager. On Hager's background, see Shuck, *History of the Bench and Bar*, 447–49.

19. Act of March 18, 1870, ch. 230, SC, at 330–32.

20. Ibid., ch. 231, SC, at 332–33.

21. *Sacramento Daily Union*, March 1, 1870; *San Francisco Bulletin*, March 1, 1870.

22. *Alta California*, March 4, 1870.

23. *Sacramento Daily Union*, March 11, 1870.

24. Ibid., March 1, 1870.

25. Ibid.

26. For cases involving Chinese women examined or deported under the law before 1874, see *San Francisco Chronicle*, June 15, 1870; ibid., June 16, 1870; *Alta California*, Aug. 13, 1873; ibid., Aug. 27, 1873; *San Francisco Bulletin*, Oct. 1, 1873; ibid., Feb. 13, 1874; and ibid., April 21, 1874. There is no evidence that California's commissioner of immigration ever detained Chinese men suspected of being coolies.

27. Abrams, "Polygamy," 690; Winfield J. Davis, *History of Political Conventions*, 293, 308.

28. Aarim-Heriot, *Chinese Immigrants*, 172–74, 181–82; Gyory, *Closing the Gate*, 72–75.

29. Abrams, "Polygamy," 691; Peffer, *If They Don't Bring Their Women*, 33–37.

30. *Congressional Record*, 43rd Cong., 1st sess., 1874, 4534–35, 4537.

31. *Sacramento Daily Union*, July 26, 1875.

32. *Ex Parte Ah Fook Case File*, WPA #10716 (1874), Supreme Court of California Case Files, pp. 84–87, CSA. Arguments and decisions in the California District Court and the California Supreme Court can be found in this case file as well as in *Ex Parte Ah Fook*, 49 Cal. 402 (1874), which is analyzed in McClain, *In Search of Equality*, 54–63.

33. *Slaughter-House Cases*, 83 U.S. 101 (1873). On Field's importance in postwar jurisprudence, see Kens, *Justice Stephen Field*; and Swisher, *Stephen J. Field*. In the *Slaughter-House Cases*, New Orleans butchers sought to overturn a Louisiana state law that created a corporation to monopolize the slaughter of animals in the city. The butchers alleged that the law violated the equal protection clause of the Fourteenth Amendment because it abridged their "right of free labor," that is, their right to pursue a lawful trade without the state's interference. The U.S. Supreme Court found against the butchers in a 5–4 decision. The majority opinion declared that the equal protection clause applied primarily to former slaves and, even then, only protected a limited number of federal citizenship rights such as the ability to run for federal office or to travel abroad. Field rejected this narrow interpretation.

34. *In re Ah Fong*, 1 Federal Cases 213 (C.C.D. Cal. 1874) (No. 102), 216–17; *Chy Lung v. Freeman*, 92 U.S. 275 (1876); McClain, *In Search of Equality*, 58–63.

35. *San Francisco Bulletin*, Sept. 25, 1874; ibid., Dec. 26, 1874.

36. *Sacramento Daily Union*, Nov. 17, 1874; ibid., Dec. 17, 1874; *Alta California*, Dec. 17, 1874.

37. Ulysses S. Grant, "Sixth Annual Message," Dec. 7, 1874, in James D. Richardson, *Compilation of Messages*, 7:4242; Aarim-Heriot, *Chinese Immigrants*, 173–76.

38. An Act Supplementary to the Acts in Relation to Immigration (March 3, 1875), ch. 141, *U.S. Statutes at Large* 18 (1875), 477; Abrams, "Polygamy," 696.

39. An Act Supplementary to the Acts in Relation to Immigration (March 3, 1875), ch. 141, *U.S. Statutes at Large* 18 (1875), 477.

40. *Appendix to the Congressional Record*, 43rd Cong., 2nd sess., 1875, 41, 43, 44.

41. Aarim-Heriot, *Chinese Immigrants*, 177; *Sacramento Daily Union*, July 26, 1875.

42. Dawson, *Republican Campaign Text-Book for 1884*, 92. Emphasis in original.

43. Zhao, *Remaking Chinese America*, 10.

44. Peffer, *If They Don't Bring Their Women*, 8–9, 43–56.

45. Smalley, *A History of the Republican Party*, 116.

46. Gyory, *Closing the Gate*, 95–97, 169–70; Aarim-Heriot, *Chinese Immigrants*, 190–92; California Constitution (1879), art. 19, sec. 2, 4. Most of the anti-Chinese legislation in the 1879 constitution was nullified by state and federal courts on the grounds that it violated the U.S. Constitution. McClain, *In Search of Equality*, 79–97.

47. Horace Davis, *Chinese Immigration*, 15.

48. Rutherford B. Hayes, "Veto Message," March 1, 1879, in James D. Richardson, *Compilation of Messages*, 6:4468–69. See also Aarim-Heriot, *Chinese Immigrants*, 197–204, on the Fifteen Passenger Bill and Hayes's veto.

49. *Republican Campaign Text-Book for 1880*, 187.

50. Treaty of Immigration between the United States and China (Nov. 17, 1880), U.S. *Statutes at Large* 22 (1883), 826–27; Gyory, *Closing the Gate*, 212–16; Aarim-Heriot, *Chinese Immigrants*, 204–5.

51. *Congressional Record*, 47th Cong., 1st sess., 1882, 1482.

52. Page had introduced a very similar exclusion bill in the House but withdrew it in favor of Miller's Senate bill. Ibid., 1899, 1932–33, 1935, 1936, 1973.

53. Ibid., 1983, 1520, 2183.

54. Ibid., 1517.

55. Ibid., 1641.

56. Ibid., 1979. For similar arguments, see ibid., 1636, 1980.

57. Ibid., 1634, 1933.

58. For arguments in favor of reducing the length of the Exclusion Act, see Gyory, *Closing the Gate*, 233–34.

59. An Act to Execute Certain Treaty Stipulations Relating to the Chinese (May 6, 1882), ch. 126, U.S. *Statutes at Large* 22 (1882), 58–61; Aarim-Heriot, *Chinese Immigrants*, 210–14; Gyory, *Closing the Gate*, 238–39. Arthur initially vetoed the bill because he felt that the original twenty-year exclusion violated the 1880 treaty with China. That treaty allowed the United States to suspend and regulate the immigration of Chinese laborers but not to prohibit it permanently and completely.

60. Lee, *At America's Gates*, 43–44.

61. On Chinese legal challenges to the Exclusion Act, see ibid., esp. 1–5, 111–45, 189–220; and Salyer, *Laws Harsh as Tigers*.

62. Aarim-Heriot, *Chinese Immigrants*, 221–28; Lee, *At America's Gates*, 44–46.

Conclusion

1. Gilbert, *Illustrated Atlas and History of Yolo County*, 84–85. According to Gilbert's biographical sketch, Campbell accumulated nearly 3,000 acres of land, valued at $20 per acre, and between $5,000 and $10,000 worth of livestock by 1879. An article in the *Nevada State Journal*, Sept. 6, 1884, placed Basil Campbell's total wealth at $100,000. On Campbell's landownership, wealth, political activities, and death, see U.S. Bureau of the Census, "Census of Productions of Agriculture," 1870, roll 19, p. 9; *Woodland Daily Democrat*, Jan. 9, 1896; *Great Registers, 1866–1898*, roll 138, register #3740, CSL; and Beasley, *Negro Trail Blazers*, 71.

2. *In the Matter of the Estate of Basil Campbell, Deceased*, 12 Cal. App. 718 (1910); Gilbert, *Illustrated Atlas and History of Yolo County*, 84–85; Beasley, *Negro Trail Blazers*, 71.

3. *In the Matter of the Estate of Basil Campbell, Deceased*, 12 Cal. App. 718 (1910). In a subsequent decision, reported at the end of ibid., the California Supreme Court upheld the ruling of the lower courts. Only one justice dissented from the decision, calling the invalidation of slave marriages "repugnant to humanity."

Appendix

1. For the difficulties and pitfalls of using the 1850s California censuses, consult Harris, "California Census of 1852."

Bibliography

Archival Sources

Berkeley, Calif.
Bancroft Library, University of California
    Antonio Francisco Coronel, *Cosas de California,* 1877
    Augustus Ward Loomis, "The Chinese in California," 1876
    Caleb T. Fay, "Statement of Historical Facts on California for the Bancroft Library," 1878
    Elijah Renshaw Potter Reminiscences
    Frémont Family Papers, c. 1839–1927
    Hayes Scraps, 1847–75
    James Beith Letterbook, 1854–67
    Justice Court of Santa Barbara, Docket, 1850–55
    Robert Fleming Heizer Papers, 1851–1980
    Robert R. Givens Letters to Family, 1849–59

Chapel Hill, N.C.
Southern Historical Collection, University of North Carolina–Chapel Hill
    Charles William Dabney Papers
    Elizabeth Washington Grist Knox Papers
    George Phifer Erwin Papers
    Nicholas Washington Woodfin Collection
    Thomas Parks Collection of Parks and McElrath Family Papers
    William G. Dickson Papers

Los Angeles, Calif.
Charles E. Young Research Library, Department of Special Collections, University of California–Los Angeles
    Cole Family Papers
Seaver Center for Western History Research, Natural History Museum of Los Angeles
    Los Angeles Alcalde/County Court Records, 1850–60

Martinez, Calif.
Contra Costa Historical Society History Center
    Court of Sessions Records, Contra Costa County

District Court Records, Contra Costa County
"Fragments #1"

Sacramento, Calif.
California History Room, California State Library
  Great Registers, 1866–1898, microfilm, 185 rolls. Reproduced in *California, Voter Registers*, 1866–1898 (on-line database). Provo, Utah: Ancestry.com. Operations, 2011. Accessed through Ancestry.com.
  Jacob P. Leese Collection
California State Archives
  Ah Chung (aka Ah Chon), Application for Pardon, 1860
  California State Assembly, Original Bill File
  California State Senate, Original Bill File
  Genealogical Society of Utah Microfilm Collection
  Mendocino County Records, District and County Courts, Civil and Criminal Cases
  Miscellaneous Petition Reports, 1852
  San Quentin Prison Registers, 1851–67
  Sonoma County Justice Court Records
  Supreme Court of California Case Files
Center for Sacramento History (formerly Sacramento Archives and Museum Collection Center)
  Court of First Instance Records, Sacramento County
  Justice Court Criminal Case Files, Sacramento County
  Sacramento County Court, Criminal Files
  Sacramento County Court of Sessions Records
  Sacramento County District Court, Criminal Files
  Sacramento County Probate Court Records
  Sacramento Court of First Magistrate Records

Salem, Mass.
Phillips Library, Peabody Essex Museum
  Leonard W. Noyes Papers

San Francisco, Calif.
North Baker Research Library, California Historical Society
  Asa Cyrus Call Journal
  David Cosad, "Journal of a Trip to California," 1849
  Jacob Primer Leese Papers
  "Petition for Legal Recognition of Black Californians," c. February 1862
  Robert Patterson Effinger Papers, 1849–50
  San Francisco Oversize Miscellaneous Collection
  Thomas B. Eastland Papers
  William Marmaduke Letters

San Marino, Calif.

Henry E. Huntington Library

A. O. Carpenter, Articles of Apprenticeship, 1861

Benjamin Davis Wilson Collection, 1836–1941

Cave Johnson Couts Papers, 1832–1951

Charles Maclay Papers, 1841–1922

George McKinley Murrell Correspondence, 1849–54

J. G. Marvin Scrapbooks

John Hovey, "Historical Account of the Troubles between the Chilian and American Miners in the Calaveras Mining District, Commencing Dec. 6, 1849, and Ending Jan. 4, 1850"

Los Angeles County Probate Records, Los Angeles Area Court Records Collection

Mariano Guadalupe Vallejo Papers, 1833–88

Ralph Bieber Collection

Santa Barbara, Calif.

Donald C. Davidson Library, University of California–Santa Barbara

Slave Documents Collection

Stockton, Calif.

Holt-Atherton Special Collections, University of the Pacific

Indenture and Emancipation Papers, San Joaquin County

Washington, D.C.

National Archives and Records Administration

Record Group 29, Microfilm Publication M252

U.S. Bureau of the Census, Third Census of the United States, 1810

Record Group 29, Microfilm Publication M432

U.S. Bureau of the Census, Seventh Federal Population Census, 1850

Record Group 29, Microfilm Publication M653

U.S. Bureau of the Census, Eighth Federal Population Census, 1860

Record Group 75, Microfilm Publication M234

Office of Indian Affairs, Letters Received, 1824–81, California Superintendency

Government Documents

Federal Documents

Appendix to the Congressional Record.

Congressional Globe.

Congressional Record.

Office of Indian Affairs. *Report of the Commissioner of Indian Affairs, 1858.* Washington, D.C.: William A. Harris, 1858.

————. *Report of the Commissioner of Indian Affairs, 1861.* Washington, D.C.: Government Printing Office, 1861.

————. *Report of the Commissioner of Indian Affairs, 1862.* Washington, D.C.: Government Printing Office, 1863.

————. *Report of the Commissioner of Indian Affairs, 1863.* Washington, D.C.: Government Printing Office, 1864.

————. *Report of the Commissioner of Indian Affairs, 1867.* Washington, D.C.: Government Printing Office, 1868.

U.S. Bureau of the Census. "Census of Productions of Agriculture," 1870. Reproduced in *Selected U.S. Federal Census Non-Population Schedules, 1850–1880* (online database). Provo, Utah: Ancestry.com Operations, 2010. Accessed through Ancestry.com.

U.S. Census Office. *Population of the United States in 1860.* Washington, D.C.: Government Printing Office, 1864.

————. *Seventh Census of the United States: 1850.* Washington, D.C.: Robert Armstrong, 1853.

U.S. Congress. 38th Cong., 1st sess., *House Executive Document No. 1.*

U.S. *Statutes at Large.*

State Documents

State of California. *California State Census, 1852.* Accessed through Ancestry.com.

————. *Appendix to the Journal of the Assembly, 1852–53.*

————. *Appendix to the Journal of the Senate, 1860.*

————. *Journal of the Assembly, 1849/50–1870.*

————. *Journal of the Senate, 1849/50–1870.*

————. *The Statutes of California, 1849/50–1874.*

State of Illinois. *The Revised Laws of Illinois.* Vandalia, Ill.: Greiner and Sherman, 1833.

Court Cases
California Supreme Court Cases

Ex Parte Ah Fook, 49 Cal. 402.

Ex Parte The Queen of the Bay et al., 1 Cal. 157 (1850).

In re Archy/Ex Parte Archy, 9 Cal. 147 (1858).

In re Perkins, 2 Cal. 424 (1852).

Lin Sing v. Washburn, 20 Cal. 534 (1862).

People v. Hall, 4 Cal. 399 (1854).

People v. Juan Antonio, 27 Cal. 404 (1865).

People, ex. rel. The Attorney General v. Naglee, 1 Cal. 232 (1850).

U.S. Supreme Court Cases

Chy Lung v. Freeman, 92 U.S. 275 (875).

Slaughter-House Cases, 83 U.S. 101 (1873).

Miscellaneous Court Cases

In re Ah Fong, 1 Federal Cases 213 (C.C.D. Cal 1874) (No. 102).
In the Matter of the Estate of Basil Campbell, Deceased, 12 Cal. App. 718 (1910).
White v. Cline and White, 52 N.C. 174 (1859).

Newspapers

Alta California (San Francisco)
California Police Gazette (San Francisco)
California Star (Yerba Buena/San Francisco)
Columbia (Calif.) Times
Colusa (Calif.) Sun
Frederick Douglass' Paper (Rochester, N.Y.)
Golden Era (San Francisco)
Humboldt Times (Eureka, Calif.)
Liberator (Boston)
Marysville (Calif.) Appeal
Mendocino Herald (Ukiah, Calif.)
Mountain Democrat (Placerville, Calif.)
Nevada State Journal (Reno)
New Orleans Picayune
New York Times

Pacific (San Francisco)
Pacific Appeal (San Francisco)
Placer Times (Sacramento)
Red Bluff (Calif.) Beacon
Sacramento Bee
Sacramento Daily Union
Sacramento Transcript
San Francisco Bulletin
San Francisco Chronicle
San Francisco Herald
San Joaquin Republican (Stockton, Calif.)
Stockton (Calif.) Times
Trinity Journal (Weaverville, Calif.)
Woodland (Calif.) Daily Democrat

Published Primary Sources

Amador, José María. Californio Voices: The Oral Memoirs of José María Amador and Lorenzo Asisara. Edited and translated by Gregorio Mora-Torres. Denton: University of North Texas Press, 2005.

An Analysis of the Chinese Question: Consisting of a Special Message of the Governor, and, in Reply Thereto, Two Letters of the Chinamen, and a Memorial of the Citizens of San Francisco. San Francisco: Office of the San Francisco Herald, 1852.

Asbill, Frank, and Argle Shawley. The Last of the West. New York: Carlton Press, 1975.

Ayers, James J. Gold and Sunshine: Reminiscences of Early California. Boston: Gorham Press, 1922.

Bailey, Henry Clay. "Indian Life in Sacramento Valley." Quarterly of the San Bernardino County Museum Association 7, no. 1 (Fall 1959): 1–18.

Belknap, D. P. California Probate Law and Practice. San Francisco: Sterett and Butler, 1858.

Bell, Horace. Reminiscences of a Ranger, or Early Times in Southern California. Los Angeles: Yarnell, Caystile, and Mathies, 1881.

Blue, George Verne, ed. "A Hudson's Bay Company Contract for Hawaiian Labor." Quarterly of the Oregon Historical Society 25, no. 1 (March 1924): 72–75.

Brewer, William H. *Up and Down California in 1860–1864: The Journal of William H. Brewer, Professor of Agriculture in the Sheffield Scientific School from 1864 to 1903.* Edited by Francis P. Farquhar. Berkeley: University of California Press, 1966.

Browne, J. Ross. *Report of the Debates in the Convention of California on the Formation of the State Constitution in September and October 1849.* Washington, D.C.: John T. Towers, 1850.

Carpenter, Helen M. "Among the Diggers of Thirty Years Ago, Part II." *Overland Monthly and Out West Magazine* 21, no. 124 (April 1893): 389–99.

Case, William M. "Notes by William M. Case." Edited by H. S. Lyman. *Quarterly of the Oregon Historical Society* 2, no. 2 (June 1901): 168–79.

———. "Reminiscences of Wm. M. Case." Edited by H. S. Lyman. *Quarterly of the Oregon Historical Society* 1, no. 3 (1900): 269–95.

Casserly, Eugene. *Speech of Hon. Eugene Casserly, on the Fifteenth Amendment, and the Labor Question, Delivered in San Francisco, California, July 28, 1869.* N.p.: 1869.

Cole, Cornelius. *Memoirs of Cornelius Cole: Ex-senator of the United States from California.* New York: McLoughlin Brothers, 1908.

Coronel, Antonio Francisco. *Tales of Mexican California: Cosas de California.* Edited by Doyce B. Nunis Jr. and translated by Diane Avalle-Arce. Santa Barbara, Calif.: Bellerophon Books, 1994.

———. "A Translation of the Mining Experiences of Antonio Franco Coronel, as Described in His Memoir 'Cosas de California.'" In Richard Henry Morefield, *The Mexican Adaptation in American California, 1846–1875,* 76–96. 1955; reprint, San Francisco: R and E Research Associates, 1971.

Cox, Isaac. *The Annals of Trinity County.* 1858; reprint, Eugene, Ore.: John Henry Nash, 1940.

Davis, Horace. *Chinese Immigration: Speech of Hon. Horace Davis, of California, in the House of Representatives.* Washington, D.C.: N.p., 1878.

Dawson, George Francis, ed. *The Republican Campaign Text-Book for 1884.* New York: Republican National Committee, 1884.

Degroot, Henry. "Diving for Gold in '49." *Overland Monthly and Out West Magazine* 13, no. 3 (September 1874): 273–80.

Frémont, John C. *The Expeditions of John Charles Frémont.* Vol. 3. Edited by Mary Lee Spence. Chicago: University of Illinois Press, 1984.

Gibson, Rev. Otis. *The Chinese in America.* Cincinnati: Hitchcock and Walden, 1877.

Green, Thomas Jefferson. *Journal of the Texian Expedition against Mier.* Edited by Sam W. Haynes. Austin: W. Thomas Taylor, 1993.

Haight, Henry H. *Speech of Governor Haight, at the Democratic State Convention at Sacramento, June 29, 1869.* San Francisco: San Francisco Daily Examiner, 1869.

Haskins, Charles Warren. *The Argonauts of California.* New York: Fords, Howard, and Hulbert, 1890.

Heizer, Robert F., ed. *The Destruction of California Indians.* Santa Barbara: Peregrine Smith, 1974.

———, ed. *They Were Only Diggers: A Collection of Articles from California Newspapers, 1851–1866, on Indian White Relations.* Ramona, Calif.: Ballena Press, 1974.

Henry, W. S. *Campaign Sketches of the War with Mexico*. New York: Harper, 1847.

Jackson, Alfred. *The Diary of a Forty-Niner*. Edited by Chauncey L. Canfield. Boston: Houghton Mifflin, 1920.

Janssens, Agustín. *The Life and Adventures in California of Don Agustín Janssens, 1834–1856*. Edited by William H. Ellison and Francis Price and translated by Francis Price. San Marino, Calif.: Huntington Library, 1953.

Jolly, John. *Gold Spring Diary: The Journal of John Jolly, and Including a Brief History of Stephen Spencer Hill, Fugitive from Labor*. Edited by Carlo De Ferrari. Sonora, Calif.: Tuolumne County Historical Society, 1966.

Kelly, William. *An Excursion to California, over the Prairie, Rocky Mountains, and Great Sierra Nevada*. Vol. 2. London: Chapman and Hall, 1851.

Knox, Reuben. *A Medic Fortyniner: Life and Letters of Dr. Reuben Knox, 1849–1851*. Edited by Charles W. Turner. N.p.: McClure Press, 1974.

Larkin, Thomas O. *The Larkin Papers: Personal, Business, and Official Correspondence of Thomas Oliver Larkin, Merchant and United States Consul in California*. Vol. 8. Edited by George P. Hammond. Berkeley: University of California Press, 1951–64.

———. "Statistics: California." *American Quarterly Register and Magazine* 3, no. 2 (December 1849): 377–85.

Lucett, Edward. *Rovings in the Pacific from 1838–1849*. Vol. 2. London: Longman, Brown, Green, and Longmans, 1851.

Meyer, Carl. *Bound for Sacramento: Travel-Pictures of a Returned Wanderer*. Translated by Ruth Frey Axe. Claremont, Calif.: Saunders Studio Press, 1938.

Navarro, Ramón Gil. "California in 1849." In *We Were 49ers! Chilean Accounts of the California Gold Rush*, edited and translated by Edwin A. Beilharz and Carlos U. López, 103–49. Pasadena, Calif.: Ward Ritchie Press, 1976.

———. *The Gold Rush Diary of Ramón Gil Navarro*. Edited and translated by María del Carmen Ferreyra and David S. Reher. Lincoln: University of Nebraska Press, 2000.

Pico, Pío. *Don Pío Pico's Historical Narrative*. Edited by Martin Cole and Henry Welcome and translated by Arthur P. Botello. Glendale, Calif.: Arthur Clark, 1973.

The Republican Campaign Text-Book for 1880. Washington, D.C.: Republican National Convention, 1880.

Revere, Joseph Warren. *Keel and Saddle: A Retrospect of Forty Years of Military and Naval Service*. Boston: James R. Osgood, 1872.

———. *A Tour of Duty in California*. Boston: C. S. Francis, 1849.

Richardson, James D., ed. *A Compilation of Messages and Papers of the Presidents*. 10 vols. New York: National Bureau of Literature, 1897.

Sherman, Edwin Allen. "Sherman Was There: The Recollections of Major Edwin A. Sherman (Part 1)." Edited by Allen B. Sherman. *California Historical Society Quarterly* 23, no. 3 (September 1944): 259–81.

———. "Sherman Was There: The Recollections of Major Edwin A. Sherman (Part 2)." Edited by Allen B. Sherman. *California Historical Society Quarterly* 23, no. 4 (December 1944): 349–71.

Simpson, Henry I. *Three Weeks in the Gold Mines; Or Adventures with the Gold Diggers of California in August, 1848*. New York: Joyce, 1848.

Snow, Horace. *"Dear Charlie" Letters: Recording the Everyday Life of a Young 1854 Gold Miner as Set Forth by Your Friend, Horace Snow*. Fresno, Calif.: Mariposa County Historical Society, 1979.

Sutter, John A. "The Discovery of Gold in California." *Hutchings' California Magazine* 2 (November 1857): 194–203.

Tassin, A. G. "The Chronicles of Camp Wright, Part I." *Overland Monthly and Out West Magazine* 10, no. 55 (July 1887): 24–32.

Williams, James. *Fugitive Slave in the Gold Rush: The Life and Adventures of James Williams*. Lincoln: University of Nebraska Press, 2002.

Wilson, Benjamin D. *The Indians of Southern California in 1852*. Edited by John Walton Caughey and introduction by Albert L. Hurtado. Lincoln, Nebr.: Bison Books, 1995.

Woods, Daniel B. *Sixteen Months at the Gold Diggings*. New York: Harper, 1851.

Young, Lucy, and Edith V. A. Murphy. "Out of the Past: A True Indian Story." *California Historical Quarterly* 20, no. 4 (December 1941): 349–64.

Secondary Sources

Aarim-Heriot, Najia. *Chinese Immigrants, African Americans, and Racial Anxiety in the United States, 1848–1882*. Urbana: University of Illinois Press, 2003.

Abrams, Kerry. "Polygamy, Prostitution, and the Federalization of Immigration Law." *Columbia Law Review* 105, no. 3 (April 2005): 641–715.

Albin, Ray R. "The Perkins Case: The Ordeal of Three Slaves in Gold Rush California." *California History* 67 (1988): 215–27.

Almaguer, Tomás. *Racial Fault Lines: The Historical Origins of White Supremacy in California*. Berkeley: University of California Press, 1994.

Apostol, Jane. "'The Fickel Goddess Evades Me': The Gold Rush Letters of a Kentucky Gentleman." *Register of the Kentucky Historical Society* 79, no. 2 (1981): 99–121.

Arenson, Adam I. *The Great Heart of the Republic: St. Louis and the Cultural Civil War*. Cambridge: Harvard University Press, 2011.

Bancroft, Hubert Howe. *The Works of Hubert Howe Bancroft*. 39 vols. San Francisco: A. L. Bancroft, 1885.

Bardaglio, Peter W. *Reconstructing the Household: Families, Sex, and the Law in the Nineteenth-Century South*. Chapel Hill: University of North Carolina Press, 1995.

Barnhart, Jacqueline Baker. *The Fair but Frail: Prostitution in San Francisco, 1849–1900*. Reno: University of Nevada Press, 1986.

Barr, Juliana. "From Captives to Slaves: Commodifying Indian Women in the Borderlands." *Journal of American History* 92, no. 1 (June 2005): 19–46.

———. *Peace Came in the Form of a Woman: Indians and Spaniards in the Texas Borderlands*. Chapel Hill: University of North Carolina Press, 2007.

Barrows, Henry D., and Luther A. Ingersoll, eds. *A Memorial and Biographical History of the Coast Counties of Central California*. Chicago: Lewis, 1893.

Barth, Gunther. *Bitter Strength: A History of the Chinese in the United States, 1850–1870*. Cambridge: Harvard University Press, 1964.

Bauer, Arnold J. "Chilean Rural Labor in the Nineteenth Century." *American Historical Review* 76, no. 4 (October 1971): 1059–83.

Bauer, William J., Jr. *We Were All Like Migrant Workers Here: Work, Community, and Memory on California's Round Valley Reservation, 1850–1941.* Chapel Hill: University of North Carolina Press, 2009.

Baumgardner, Frank M., III. *Killing for Land in Early California: Indian Blood at Round Valley, Founding the Nome Cult Farm.* New York: Algora, 2005.

Beasley, Delilah. *The Negro Trail Blazers of California.* Los Angeles: N.p., 1919.

Beechert, Edward D. *Working in Hawaii: A Labor History.* Honolulu: University of Hawaii Press, 1985.

Beilharz, Edwin A., and Carlos U. López, eds. *We Were 49ers! Chilean Accounts of the California Gold Rush.* Pasadena, Calif.: Ward Ritchie Press, 1976.

Berwanger, Eugene. *The Frontier against Slavery: Western Anti-Negro Prejudice and the Slavery Extension Controversy.* Urbana: University of Illinois Press, 1967.

———. *The West and Reconstruction.* Urbana: University of Illinois Press, 1981.

Blackhawk, Ned. *Violence over the Land: Indians and Empires in the Early American West.* Cambridge: Harvard University Press, 2006.

Bouvier, Virginia Marie. *Women and the Conquest of California, 1542–1840: Codes of Silence.* Tucson: University of Arizona Press, 2001.

Boydston, Jeanne. *Home and Work: Housework, Wages, and the Ideology of Labor in the Early Republic.* New York: Oxford University Press, 1990.

Brooks, James F. *Captives and Cousins: Slavery, Kinship, and Community in the Southwest Borderlands.* Chapel Hill: University of North Carolina Press, 2002.

Broussard, Albert S. "Slavery in California Revisited: The Fate of a Kentucky Slave in Gold Rush California." *Pacific Historian* 29, no. 1 (Spring 1985): 17–21.

Buchanan, A. Russell. *David S. Terry of California: Dueling Judge.* San Marino, Calif.: Huntington Library, 1956.

Burke, Diane Mutti. *On Slavery's Border: Missouri's Small-Slaveholding Households, 1815–1875.* Athens: University of Georgia Press, 2010.

Camp, Stephanie M. H. "'I Could Not Stay There': Enslaved Women, Truancy, and the Geography of Everyday Forms of Resistance in the Antebellum Plantation South." *Slavery and Abolition* 23, no. 3 (December 2002): 1–20.

Campbell, Randolph B. *An Empire for Slavery: The Peculiar Institution in Texas, 1821–1865.* Baton Rouge: Louisiana State University Press, 1989.

Carranco, Lynwood, and Estle Beard. *Genocide and Vendetta: The Round Valley Indian Wars of Northern California.* Norman: University of Oklahoma Press, 1981.

Carter, Sarah. *Capturing Women: The Manipulation of Cultural Imagery in Canada's Prairie West.* Montreal: McGill-Queen's University Press, 1997.

Cashin, Joan E. *A Family Venture: Men and Women on the Southern Frontier.* New York: Oxford University Press, 1991.

Chan, Sucheng. "Chinese Livelihood in Rural California: The Impact of Economic Change, 1860–1880." *Pacific Historical Review* 53, no. 3 (August 1984): 273–307.

———. "The Exclusion of Chinese Women, 1870–1943." In *Entry Denied: Exclusion and the Chinese Community in America, 1882–1943,* edited by Sucheng Chan, 94–146. Philadelphia: Temple University Press, 1994.

————. *This Bittersweet Soil: The Chinese in California Agriculture, 1860–1910.* Berkeley: University of California Press, 1986.

Chandler, Robert J. "'Anti-Coolie Rabies': The Chinese Issue in California Politics in the 1860s." *Pacific Historian* 28, no. 1 (Spring 1984): 29–42.

————. "The Failure of Reform: White Attitudes and Indian Response in California during the Civil War Era." *Pacific Historian* 24, no. 3 (Fall 1980): 284–94.

————. "Friends in Time of Need: Republicans and Black Civil Rights in California during the Civil War." *Arizona and the West* 24, no. 4 (Winter 1982): 319–40.

Chandler, Robert J., and Ronald J. Quinn. "Emma Is a Good Girl." *Californians* 8, no. 5 (January/February 1991): 34–37.

Chang, David A. "Borderlands in a World at Sea: Concow Indians, Native Hawaiians, and South Chinese in Indigenous, Global, and National Spaces." *Journal of American History* 98, no. 2 (September 2011): 384–403.

Chen, Yong. *Chinese San Francisco, 1850–1943: A Trans-Pacific Community.* Stanford: Stanford University Press, 2000.

————. "The Internal Origins of Chinese Emigration to California Reconsidered." *Western Historical Quarterly* 28, no. 4 (Winter 1997): 521–46.

Cheng Hirata, Lucie. "Free, Indentured, Enslaved: Chinese Prostitutes in Nineteenth-Century America." *Signs* 5, no. 11 (Autumn 1979): 3–29.

Chiu, Ping. *Chinese Labor in California, 1850–1880: An Economic Study.* Madison: State Historical Society of Wisconsin, 1963.

Clark, Elizabeth B. "'The Sacred Rights of the Weak': Pain, Sympathy, and the Culture of Individual Rights in Antebellum America." *Journal of American History* 82, no. 2 (September 1993): 463–93.

Cloud, Patricia, and David W. Galenson. "Chinese Immigration and Contract Labor in the Late Nineteenth Century." *Explorations in Economic History* 24, no. 1 (January 1987): 22–42.

Cook, Sherburne F. *The Conflict between the California Indian and White Civilization.* Berkeley: University of California Press, 1976.

Davis, Winfield J. *History of Political Conventions in California, 1849–1882.* Sacramento: California State Library, 1893.

De Ferrari, Carlo M., ed. "Southern Miners in the Diggings: Gold Rush Letters Written from the Placer Mines of Lower Wood's Creek and Jacksonville." *Chispa: The Quarterly of the Tuolumne County Historical Society* 9, no. 2 (October 1969): 300–304.

DeLay, Brian. *War of a Thousand Deserts: Indian Raids and the U.S.-Mexican War.* New Haven: Yale University Press, 2008.

Demaratus, DeEtta. *The Force of a Feather: The Search for a Lost Story of Slavery and Freedom.* Salt Lake City: University of Utah Press, 2002.

Deverell, William. "Convalescence and California: The Civil War Comes West." *Southern California Quarterly* 90, no. 1 (Spring 2008): 1–26.

————. "Redemptive California? Re-thinking the Post–Civil War." *Rethinking History* 11, no. 1 (March 2007): 61–78.

Dillon, Richard H. "Kanaka Colonies in California." *Pacific Historical Review* 24, no. 1 (February 1955): 17–23.

DuBois, Ellen Carol. *Feminism and Suffrage: The Emergence of an Independent Women's Movement in America, 1848–1869*. Ithaca: Cornell University Press, 1978.

Duncan, Janice K. "Kanaka World Travelers and Fur Company Employees, 1785–1860." *Hawaiian Journal of History* 7 (1973): 93–111.

———. *Minority without a Champion: Kanakas on the Pacific Coast, 1788–1840*. Portland: Oregon Historical Society, 1972.

Durham, Walter T. *Volunteer Forty-Niners: Tennesseans and the California Gold Rush*. Nashville, Tenn.: Vanderbilt University Press, 1997.

Earle, Jonathan H. *Jacksonian Antislavery and the Politics of Free Soil, 1824–1854*. Chapel Hill: University of North Carolina Press, 2004.

Eaves, Lucile. *A History of California Labor Legislation, with an Introductory Sketch of the California Labor Movement*. Berkeley: University of California Press, 1910.

Edwards, Laura F. *Gendered Strife and Confusion: The Political Culture of Reconstruction*. Chicago: University of Illinois Press, 1997.

Egli, Ida Rae, ed. *No Rooms of Their Own: Women Writers of Early California, 1849–1869*. Berkeley: Heyday Books, 1992.

Ellison, William Henry. "The Movement for State Division in California, 1849–1860." *Southwestern Historical Quarterly* 17, no. 2 (April 1914): 101–39.

Epps, Garrett. *Democracy Reborn: The Fourteenth Amendment and the Fight for Civil Rights in Post–Civil War America*. New York: Henry Holt, 2006.

Fehrenbacher, Don E. *The Dred Scott Case: Its Significance in American Law and Politics*. New York: Oxford University Press, 1978.

———. *The Slaveholding Republic: An Account of the United States Government's Relations to Slavery*. Completed and edited by Ward M. McAfee. New York: Oxford University Press, 2001.

Finkelman, Paul. *An Imperfect Union: Slavery, Federalism, and Comity*. Chapel Hill: University of North Carolina Press, 1981.

———. "The Law of Slavery and Freedom in California, 1848–1860." *California Western Law Review* 17, no. 3 (1981): 437–64.

———. *Slavery and the Founders: Race and Liberty in the Age of Jefferson*. Armonk, N.Y.: M. E. Sharpe, 1996.

Fisher, James A. "The Struggle for Negro Testimony in California, 1851–1863." *Southern California Quarterly* 51, no. 4 (December 1969): 313–24.

Flamming, Douglas. *Bound for Freedom: Black Los Angeles in Jim Crow America*. Berkeley: University of California Press, 2005.

Foner, Eric. *Reconstruction: America's Unfinished Revolution, 1863–1877*. New York: Harper and Row, 1988.

Forret, Jeff. "Slave Labor in North Carolina's Antebellum Gold Mines." *North Carolina Historical Review* 76, no. 2 (April 1999): 135–62.

Franklin, John Hope, and Loren Schweninger. *Runaway Slaves: Rebels on the Plantation*. New York: Oxford University Press, 1999.

Franklin, William E. "The Archy Case: The California Supreme Court Refuses to Free a Slave." *Pacific Historical Review* 32, no. 2 (May 1963): 137–54.

Gibson, Arrell Morgan, and John S. Whitehead. *Yankees in Paradise: The Pacific Basin Frontier*. Albuquerque: University of New Mexico Press, 1993.

Gilbert, Frank T. *The Illustrated Atlas and History of Yolo County, California*. San Francisco: DePue, 1879.

Gilfoyle, Timothy. *City of Eros: New York City, Prostitution, and the Commercialization of Sex, 1790–1920*. New York: W. W. Norton, 1992.

Gillis, Michael J., and Michael F. Magliari. *John Bidwell and California: The Life and Writings of a Pioneer, 1841–1900*. Spokane: Arthur H. Clark, 2003.

González, Gilbert G., and Raul A. Fernández. *A Century of Chicano History: Empire, Nations, and Migration*. New York: Routledge, 2003.

González, Michael J. "'My Brother's Keeper': Mexicans and the Hunt for Prosperity in California, 1848–2000." In *Riches for All: The California Gold Rush and the World*, edited by Kenneth N. Owens, 118–41. Lincoln: University of Nebraska Press, 2002.

———. *This Small City Will Be a Mexican Paradise: Exploring the Origins of Mexican Culture in Los Angeles, 1821–1846*. Albuquerque: University of New Mexico Press, 2005.

Goodwin, Cardinal. *The Establishment of State Government in California*. New York: Macmillan, 1914.

Greenberg, Amy S. *Manifest Manhood and the Antebellum American Empire*. Cambridge: Cambridge University Press, 2005.

Grossberg, Michael. *Governing the Hearth: Law and the Family in Nineteenth-Century America*. Chapel Hill: University of North Carolina Press, 1985.

Gudde, Erwin G. *California Gold Camps: A Geographical and Historical Dictionary of Camps, Towns, and Localities Where Gold Was Found and Mined; Wayside Stations and Trading Centers*. Edited by Elisabeth K. Gudde. Berkeley: University of California Press, 1975.

Guérin-Gonzales, Camille. *Mexican Workers and American Dreams: Immigration, Repatriation, and California Farm Labor, 1900–1939*. Brunswick, N.J.: Rutgers University Press, 1994.

Guinn, J. M. "The Sonoran Migration." *Historical Society of Southern California Annual Publications* 8 (1909–11): 31–36.

Gulliver, Katrina. "Finding the Pacific World." *Journal of World History* 22, no. 1 (March 2011): 83–100.

Gutiérrez, David G. *Walls and Mirrors: Mexican Americans, Mexican Immigrants, and the Politics of Ethnicity*. Berkeley: University of California Press, 1995.

Gutiérrez, Ramón A. *When Jesus Came, the Corn Mothers Went Away: Marriage, Sexuality, and Power in New Mexico, 1500–1846*. Stanford, Calif.: Stanford University Press, 1991.

Gyory, Andrew. *Closing the Gate: Race, Politics, and the Chinese Exclusion Act*. Chapel Hill: University of North Carolina Press, 1998.

Hackel, Steven W. *Children of Coyote, Missionaries of Saint Francis: Indian-Spanish Relations in Colonial California, 1769–1850*. Chapel Hill: University of North Carolina Press, 2005.

Hadden, Sally E. *Slave Patrols: Law and Violence in Virginia and the Carolinas*. Cambridge: Harvard University Press, 2001.

Hague, Harlan, and David J. Langum. *Thomas O. Larkin: A Life of Patriotism and Profit in Old California*. Norman: University of Oklahoma Press, 1990.

Harris, Dennis E. "The California Census of 1852: A Note of Caution and Encouragement." *Pacific Historian* 28, no. 2 (Summer 1984): 58–64.

Healy, Patrick, and Ng Poon Chew. *A Statement for Non-exclusion*. San Francisco: N.p., 1905.

Heizer, Robert F., and Alan F. Almquist. *The Other Californians: Prejudice and Discrimination under Spain, Mexico, and the United States to 1920*. Berkeley: University of California Press, 1971.

Hislop, Donald Lindsay. *The Nome Lackee Indian Reservation, 1854–1870*. Chico: Association for Northern California Records and Research, 1978.

"History of Lake County, California." In *History of Napa and Lake Counties, California*. San Francisco: Slocum and Brown, 1881.

Hittell, Theodore. *History of California*. 4 vols. San Francisco: N. J. Stone, 1898.

Holt, Michael F. *The Fate of Their Country: Politicians, Slavery Extension, and the Coming of the Civil War*. New York: Hill and Wang, 2004.

Hsu, Madeline Yuan-yin. *Dreaming of Gold, Dreaming of Home: Transnationalism and Migration between the United States and China, 1882–1943*. Stanford, Calif.: Stanford University Press, 2000.

Hurt, Payton. "The Rise and Fall of the 'Know Nothings' in California." *California Historical Society Quarterly* 9, no. 1 (March 1930): 9–46.

Hurtado, Albert L. "Controlling California's Indian Labor Force: Federal Administration of California Indian Affairs during the Mexican War." *Southern California Quarterly* 61 (1979): 217–38.

———. "'Hardly a Farmhouse—A Kitchen without Them': Indian and White Households on the California Borderland Frontier in 1860." *Western Historical Quarterly* 13, no. 3 (July 1982): 245–70.

———. *Indian Survival on the California Frontier*. New Haven: Yale University Press, 1988.

———. *Intimate Frontiers: Sex, Gender, and Culture in Old California*. Albuquerque: University of New Mexico Press, 1999.

———. *John Sutter: A Life on the North American Frontier*. Norman: University of Oklahoma Press, 2006.

Hyde, Anne F. *Empires, Nations, and Families: A History of the North American West, 1800–1860*. Lincoln: University of Nebraska Press, 2011.

An Illustrated History of Los Angeles County, California. Chicago: Lewis, 1889.

Inscoe, John C. *Mountain Masters: Slavery and the Sectional Crisis in Western North Carolina*. Knoxville: University of Tennessee Press, 1989.

Irvine, Leigh Hadley. *History of Humboldt County, California*. Los Angeles: Historic Record Company, 1915.

Jackson, J. J. "Bridge Gulch Massacre." In *Trinity: The Yearbook of the Trinity County Historical Society*, edited by Edward Mello, 7–14. Weaverville, Calif.: Trinity County Historical Society, 1956.

Johnson, David Alan. *Founding the Far West: California, Oregon, and Nevada, 1840–1890*. Berkeley: University of California Press, 1992.

Johnson, Susan Lee. *Roaring Camp: The Social World of the California Gold Rush*. New York: W. W. Norton, 2000.

Johnston-Dodds, Kimberly. *Early California Laws and Policies Related to California Indians.* Sacramento: California State Research Bureau of the California State Library, 2002.

Josephy, Alvin M., Jr. *The Civil War in the American West.* New York: Knopf, 1992.

Jung, Moon-Ho. *Coolies and Cane: Race, Labor, and Sugar in the Age of Emancipation.* Baltimore: Johns Hopkins University Press, 2006.

Kens, Paul. *Justice Stephen Field: Shaping Liberty from the Gold Rush to the Gilded Age.* Lawrence: University Press of Kansas, 1997.

Kidwell, Clara Sue. *The Choctaws in Oklahoma: From Tribe to Nation, 1855–1970.* Norman: University of Oklahoma Press, 2007.

Lamar, Howard. "From Bondage to Contract: Ethnic Labor in the American West, 1600–1890." In *The Countryside in the Age of Capitalist Transformation: Essays in the Social History of Rural America,* edited by Steven Hahn and Jonathan Prude, 293–324. Chapel Hill: University of North Carolina Press, 1985.

Lamb, Taze, and Jesse Lamb. "Dream of a Desert Paradise." *Desert Magazine* 2, no. 8 (June 1939): 22–27.

Lapp, Rudolph. *Archy Lee: A California Fugitive Slave Case.* 1969; reprint, Berkeley, Calif.: Heyday Books, 2008.

———. *Blacks in Gold Rush California.* New Haven: Yale University Press, 1977.

Lee, Erika. *At America's Gates: Chinese Immigration during the Exclusion Era, 1882–1943.* Chapel Hill: University of North Carolina Press, 2003.

Leong, Karen J. "A Distinct and Antagonistic Race: Constructions of Chinese Manhood in the Exclusionist Debates, 1869–1878." In *Across the Great Divide: Cultures of Manhood in the American West,* edited by Matthew Basso, Laura McCall, and Dee Garceau, 131–48. New York: Routledge, 2001.

Limbaugh, Ronald H., and Willard P. Fuller Jr. *Calaveras Gold: The Impact of Mining on a Mother Lode County.* Reno: University of Nevada Press, 2004.

Lindsay, Brendan C. *Murder State: California's Native American Genocide.* Lincoln: University of Nebraska Press, 2012.

Loveman, Brian. *Chile: The Legacy of Hispanic Capitalism.* New York: Oxford University Press, 2001.

Madley, Benjamin Logan. "California's Yuki Indians: Defining Genocide in Native American History." *Western Historical Quarterly* 39, no. 3 (Autumn 2008): 303–32.

Magliari, Michael F. "Free Soil, Unfree Labor: Cave Johnson Couts and the Binding of Indian Workers in California, 1850–1867." *Pacific Historical Review* 73, no. 3 (August 2004): 349–90.

———. "Free State Slavery: Bound Indian Labor and Slave Trafficking in California's Sacramento Valley, 1850–1864." *Pacific Historical Review* 81, no. 2 (May 2012): 155–92.

———. Review of *Ambiguous Justice: Native Americans and the Law in Southern California, 1848–1890,* by Vanessa Ann Gunther. *Pacific Historical Review* 77, no. 2 (May 2008): 321–22.

Mansfield, George C. *History of Butte County California.* Los Angeles: Historic Record Company, 1918.

Martin, Jonathan D. *Divided Mastery: Slave Hiring in the American South*. Cambridge: Harvard University Press, 2004.

Matthews, Glenna. *The Golden State in the Civil War: Thomas Starr King, the Republican Party, and the Birth of Modern California*. New York: Cambridge University Press, 2012.

Matthews, John Mabry. *Legislative and Judicial History of the Fifteenth Amendment*. Baltimore: Johns Hopkins University Press, 1909.

McClain, Charles J., Jr. "Chinese Immigration: A Comment on Cloud and Galenson." *Explorations in Economic History* 27, no. 3 (July 1990): 363–78.

———. *In Search of Equality: The Chinese Struggle against Discrimination in Nineteenth-Century America*. Berkeley: University of California Press, 1994.

McCurry, Stephanie. *Masters of Small Worlds: Yeoman Households, Gender Relations, and the Political Culture of the Antebellum South Carolina Low Country*. New York: Oxford University Press, 1995.

McDowell, John Hugh. *History of the McDowells, Erwins, Irwins, and Connections*. Memphis, Tenn.: C. B. Johnston, 1918.

McManus, Sheila. *The Line Which Separates: Race, Gender, and the Making of the Alberta-Montana Borderlands*. Lincoln: University of Nebraska Press, 2005.

Miles, Tiya. *Ties That Bind: The Story of an Afro-Cherokee Family in Slavery and Freedom*. Berkeley: University of California Press, 2005.

Monaghan, Jay. *Chile, Peru, and the California Gold Rush of 1849*. Berkeley: University of California Press, 1973.

Monroy, Douglas. *Thrown among Strangers: The Making of Mexican Culture in Frontier California*. Berkeley: University of California Press, 1990.

Montgomery, David. *Beyond Equality: Labor and the Radical Republicans, 1862–1872*. New York: Vintage Books, 1972.

Montoya, María E. *Translating Property: The Maxwell Land Grant and the Conflict over Land in the American West, 1840–1900*. Lawrence: University Press of Kansas, 2002.

Morris, Thomas D. *Southern Slavery and the Law, 1619–1860*. Chapel Hill: University of North Carolina Press, 1996.

Morrison, Michael A. *Slavery and the American West: The Eclipse of Manifest Destiny and the Coming of the Civil War*. Chapel Hill: University of North Carolina Press, 1997.

Mulroy, Kevin. *The Seminole Freedmen: A History*. Norman: University of Oklahoma Press, 2007.

Naragon, Michael D. "Communities in Motion: Drapetomania, Work, and the Development of African-American Slave Cultures." *Slavery and Abolition* 15, no. 3 (1994): 63–87.

Oakes, James. *The Ruling Race: A History of American Slaveholders*. New York: Vintage, 1992.

Osborne, Thomas J. "Pacific Eldorado: Rethinking Greater California's Past." *California History* 87, no. 1 (Winter 2009): 26–45.

Paddison, Joshua. *American Heathens: Religion, Race, and Reconstruction in California*. Berkeley: University of California Press, 2012.

Parish, John C. "A Project for a California Slave Colony in 1851." *Huntington Library Bulletin* 8 (October 1935): 171–75.

Pascoe, Peggy. *Relations of Rescue: The Search for Female Moral Authority in the American West, 1874–1939*. New York: Oxford University Press, 1990.

————. *What Comes Naturally: Miscegenation and the Making of Race in America.* New York: Oxford University Press, 2009.

Past and Present of Alameda County. Vol. 2. Chicago: S. J. Clarke, 1914.

Paul, Rodman W. *California Gold: The Beginning of Mining in the Far West.* Cambridge: Harvard University Press, 1947.

————. *Mining Frontiers of the Far West, 1848–1880.* Edited by Elliott West. Albuquerque: University of New Mexico Press, 2001.

————. "The Origin of the Chinese Issue in California." *Mississippi Valley Historical Review* 25, no. 2 (September 1938): 181–96.

Peck, Gunther. *Reinventing Free Labor: Padrones and Immigrant Workers in the North American West, 1880–1930.* Cambridge: Cambridge University Press, 2000.

Peffer, George Anthony. *If They Don't Bring Their Women Here: Chinese Female Immigration before Exclusion.* Urbana: University of Illinois Press, 1999.

Penningroth, Dylan C. *The Claims of Kinfolk: African American Property and Community in the Nineteenth-Century South.* Chapel Hill: University of North Carolina Press, 2003.

Peterson, Richard H. "Anti-Mexican Nativism in California, 1848–1853: A Study of Cultural Conflict." *Southern California Quarterly* 62, no. 4 (Winter 1980): 309–27.

————. "The Foreign Miners' Tax of 1850 and Mexicans in California: Exploitation or Expulsion?" *Pacific Historian* 20, no. 3 (Fall 1976): 265–72.

————. *Manifest Destiny in the Mines: A Cultural Interpretation of Anti-Mexican Nativism, 1848–1853.* San Francisco: R and E Research Associates, 1975.

Pfaelzer, Jean. *Driven Out: The Forgotten War against Chinese Americans.* New York: Random House, 2007.

Phifer, Edward W. "Saga of a Burke County Family, Conclusion." *North Carolina Historical Review* 39, no. 3 (July 1962): 305–42.

Phillips, George Harwood. *Indians and Indian Agents: The Origins of the Reservation System in California, 1849–1852.* Norman: University of Oklahoma Press, 1997.

————. "Indians in Los Angeles, 1781–1875: Economic Integration, Social Disintegration." *Pacific Historical Review* 49, no. 3 (August 1980): 427–51.

————. *Vineyards and Vaqueros: Indian Labor and the Economic Expansion of Southern California, 1771–1877.* Norman, Okla.: Arthur H. Clark, 2010.

Pierson, Michael D. *Free Hearts and Free Homes: Gender and American Antislavery Politics.* Chapel Hill: University of North Carolina Press, 2003.

Pitt, Leonard. "The Beginnings of Nativism in California." *Pacific Historical Review* 30, no. 1 (February 1961): 23–38.

————. *The Decline of the Californios: A Social History of the Spanish-Speaking Californians, 1846–1890.* Berkeley: University of California Press, 1970.

Potter, David M. *The Impending Crisis: 1848–1861.* New York: Harper and Row, 1976.

Press Reference Library: Notables of the West. Vol. 2. New York: International News Service, 1915.

Pubols, Louise. *The Father of All: The de la Guerra Family, Power, and Patriarchy in Mexican California.* Berkeley: University of California Press, 2009.

Qin, Yucheng. *The Diplomacy of Nationalism: The Six Companies and China's Policy toward Exclusion.* Honolulu: University of Hawaii Press, 2009.

Quinn, Arthur. *The Rivals: William Gwin, David Broderick, and the Birth of California*. New York: Crown, 1994.

Ramsdell, Charles W. "The Natural Limits of Slavery Expansion." *Mississippi Valley Historical Review* 16, no. 2 (September 1929): 151–71.

Rawls, James J. "Gold Diggers: Indian Miners in the California Gold Rush." *California Historical Quarterly* 55, no. 1 (Spring 1979): 28–45.

———. *Indians of California: The Changing Image*. Norman: University of Oklahoma Press, 1984.

Reisler, Mark. "Always the Laborer, Never the Citizen: Anglo Perceptions of the Mexican Immigrant during the 1920s." *Pacific Historical Review* 45, no. 2 (May 1976): 231–54.

Rich, Christopher B., Jr. "The True Policy for Utah: Servitude, Slavery, and 'An Act in Relation to Service.'" *Utah Historical Quarterly* 80, no. 1 (Winter 2012): 54–74.

Richards, Leonard L. *The California Gold Rush and the Coming of the Civil War*. New York: Alfred A. Knopf, 2007.

Richardson, Heather Cox. *The Death of Reconstruction: Race, Labor, and Politics in the Post–Civil War North*. Cambridge: Harvard University Press, 2001.

———. *West from Appomattox: The Reconstruction of America after the Civil War*. New Haven: Yale University Press, 2007.

Rockman, Seth. *Scraping By: Wage Labor, Slavery, and Survival in Early Baltimore*. Baltimore: Johns Hopkins University Press, 2009.

Rohrbough, Malcolm J. *Days of Gold: The California Gold Rush and the American Nation*. Berkeley: University of California Press, 1997.

Rothman, Adam. *Slave Country: American Expansion and the Origins of the Deep South*. Cambridge: Harvard University Press, 2005.

Rowland, Donald E. *John Rowland and William Workman: Southern California Pioneers of 1841*. Spokane, Wash.: Arthur H. Clark, 1999.

Salyer, Lucy E. *Laws Harsh as Tigers: Chinese Immigrants and the Shaping of Modern Immigration Law*. Chapel Hill: University of North Carolina Press, 1995.

Saxton, Alexander. *The Indispensable Enemy: Labor and the Anti-Chinese Movement in California*. Berkeley: University of California Press, 1971.

Scharnhorst, Gary. *Bret Harte: Opening the American Literary West*. Norman: University of Oklahoma Press, 2000.

Schmidt, James D. *Free to Work: Labor Law, Emancipation, and Reconstruction, 1850–1880*. Athens: University of Georgia Press, 1998.

Schrecker, John. "'For the Equality of Men—For the Equality of Nations': Anson Burlingame and China's First Embassy to the United States, 1868." *Journal of American–East Asian Relations* 17, no. 1 (Spring 2010): 9–34.

Schuele, Donna E. "None Could Deny the Eloquence of This Lady: Women, Law, and Government in California, 1850–1890." In *Taming the Elephant: Politics, Government, and Law in Pioneer California*, edited by John F. Burns and Richard J. Orsi, 169–98. Berkeley: University of California Press, 2003.

Shuck, Oscar T. *Bench and Bar in California: History, Anecdotes, Reminiscences*. San Francisco: Occident, 1889.

———. *History of the Bench and Bar in California.* Los Angeles: Commercial Printing House, 1901.

Silva, Noenoe K. *Aloha Betrayed: Native Hawaiian Resistance to American Colonialism.* Durham, N.C.: Duke University Press, 2004.

Sisson, Kelly J. "Bound for California: Chilean Contract Laborers and *Patrones* in the California Gold Rush, 1848–1852." *Southern California Historical Quarterly* 90, no. 3 (September 2008): 259–305.

Smalley, Eugene V. *A History of the Republican Party.* St. Paul, Minn.: E. V. Smalley, 1896.

Smits, David D. "The 'Squaw Drudge': A Prime Index of Savagism." *Ethnohistory* 29, no. 4 (Autumn 1982): 281–306.

———. "'Squaw Men,' 'Half-Breeds,' and Amalgamators: Late Nineteenth-Century Anglo-American Attitudes toward Indian-White Race-Mixing." *American Indian Culture and Research Journal* 15, no. 3 (1991): 38–57.

Standart, Sister M. Colette. "The Sonoran Migration to California, 1848–1856: A Study in Prejudice." *Southern California Quarterly* 58, no. 3 (Fall 1976): 333–57.

Stanley, Amy Dru. *From Bondage to Contract: Wage Labor, Marriage, and the Market in the Age of Slave Emancipation.* Cambridge: Cambridge University Press, 1998.

Stanley, Gerald. "Civil War Politics in California." *Southern California Quarterly* 64, no. 2 (Summer 1982): 115–32.

———. "Frank Pixley and the Heathen Chinese." *Phylon* 40, no. 3 (Fall 1979): 224–28.

———. "Racism and the Early Republican Party: The 1856 Presidential Election in California." *Pacific Historical Review* 43, no. 2 (May 1974): 171–87.

———. "Slavery and the Election Issue in California, 1860." *Mid-America* 62, no. 1 (Spring 1980): 35–46.

———. "Slavery and the Origins of the Republican Party in California." *Southern California Quarterly* 60, no. 1 (Spring 1978): 1–16.

Stansell, Christine. *City of Women: Sex and Class in New York, 1789–1860.* Urbana: University of Illinois Press, 1986.

Starobin, Robert S. *Industrial Slavery in the Old South.* New York: Oxford University Press, 1970.

Steinfeld, Robert J. *Coercion, Contract, and Free Labor in the Nineteenth Century.* Cambridge: Cambridge University Press, 2001.

———. *The Invention of Free Labor: The Employment Relation in English and American Law and Culture, 1350–1870.* Chapel Hill: University of North Carolina Press, 1991.

Street, Richard Steven. *Beasts of the Field: A Narrative History of California Farmworkers, 1769–1913.* Stanford, Calif.: Stanford University Press, 2004.

Swisher, Carl. *Stephen J. Field, Craftsman of the Law.* Hamden, Conn.: Archon Books, 1963.

Takaki, Ronald. *Pau Hana: Plantation Life and Labor in Hawaii, 1835–1920.* Honolulu: University of Hawaii Press, 1983.

———. *Strangers from a Different Shore: A History of Asian Americans.* New York: Penguin, 1989.

Taylor, Quintard. *In Search of the Racial Frontier: African Americans in the American West, 1528–1990.* New York: W. W. Norton, 1998.

Tong, Benson. *Unsubmissive Women: Chinese Prostitutes in Nineteenth-Century San Francisco*. Norman: University of Oklahoma Press, 1994.

Turner, Frederick Jackson. *The Frontier in American History*. 1920; reprint, New York: Dover, 1996.

Uelmen, Gerald F. "The Know Nothing Justices on the California Supreme Court." *Western Legal History* 2, no. 1 (Winter/Spring 1989): 89–106.

Wagstaff, A. E. *Life of David S. Terry: Presenting an Authentic, Impartial, and Vivid History of His Eventful Life and Tragic Death*. San Francisco: Continental Publishing, 1892.

Walters, Ronald G. *The Antislavery Appeal: American Abolitionism after 1830*. Baltimore: Johns Hopkins University Press, 1976.

———. "The Erotic South: Civilization and Sexuality in American Abolitionism." *American Quarterly* 25, no. 2 (1973): 177–201.

Warner, Barbara R. *The Men of the California Bear Flag Revolt and Their Heritage*. Spokane, Wash.: Arthur H. Clark, 1996.

Weber, David J. *Foreigners in Their Native Land: Historical Roots of the Mexican Americans*. Albuquerque: University of New Mexico Press, 1973.

———. *The Mexican Frontier, 1821–1846: The American Southwest under Mexico*. Albuquerque: University of New Mexico Press, 1982.

West, Elliott. *The Last Indian War: The Nez Perce Story*. New York: Oxford University Press, 2009.

———. "Reconstructing Race." *Western Historical Quarterly* 34, no. 1 (Spring 2003): 7–26.

Wheeler, John H. *Reminiscences and Memoirs of North Carolina and Eminent North Carolinians*. Columbus, Ohio: Columbus Print Works, 1884.

White, Deborah Gray. *Ar'n't I a Woman? Female Slaves in the Plantation South*. New York: W. W. Norton, 1985.

Williams, David A. *David C. Broderick: A Political Portrait*. San Marino, Calif.: Huntington Library, 1969.

Woolsey, Ronald C. *Migrants West: Toward the Southern California Frontier*. Claremont, Calif.: Grizzly Bear Publishing, 1996.

———. "The Politics of a Lost Cause: 'Seceshers' and Democrats in Southern California during the Civil War." *California History* 69, no. 4 (1990–91): 372–83.

Wunder, John R. "Chinese in Trouble: Criminal Law and Race on the Trans–Mississippi West Frontier." *Western Historical Quarterly* 17, no. 1 (January 1986): 25–41.

Wyatt, Victoria. "Alaska and Hawai'i." In *Oxford History of the American West*, edited by Clyde A. Milner, Carol A. O'Connor, and Martha A. Sandweiss, 565–602. New York: Oxford University Press, 1994.

Yarbrough, Faye. *Race and the Cherokee Nation: Sovereignty in the Nineteenth Century*. Philadelphia: University of Pennsylvania Press, 2008.

Young, Otis E., Jr. "The Southern Gold Rush: Contributions to California and the West." *Southern California Quarterly* 62, no. 2 (Summer 1980): 127–41.

Yung, Judy. *Unbound Feet: A Social History of Chinese Women in San Francisco*. Berkeley: University of California Press, 1995.

Zappia, Natale A. "Indigenous Borderlands: Livestock, Captivity, and Power in the Far West." *Pacific Historical Review* 81, no. 2 (May 2012): 193–220.

Zhao, Xiaojian. *Remaking Chinese America: Immigration, Family, and Community, 1940–1965*. New Brunswick, N.J.: Rutgers University Press, 2002.

Zipf, Karin L. *Labor of Innocents: Forced Apprenticeship in North Carolina, 1715–1919*. Baton Rouge: Louisiana State University Press, 2005.

Unpublished Material

Arrigoni, Aimee. "None of Which Required a War to Be Defeated: Indian People of Contra Costa, 1850–1870." M.A. thesis, California State University, 2004.

Bottoms, Donald Michael, Jr. "'An Aristocracy of Color': Race and Reconstruction in Post–Gold Rush California." Ph.D. diss., University of California, 2005.

Cartwright, Bradley Jay. "Pacific Passages: American Encounters with the Pacific and Its People, 1815–1855." Ph.D. diss., University of Colorado, 2006.

Chandler, Robert J. "The Press and Civil Liberties in California during the Civil War." Ph.D. diss., University of California, Riverside, 1978.

Guillow, Lawrence. "The Origins of Race Relations in Los Angeles, 1820–1880: A Multi-Ethnic Study." Ph.D. diss., Arizona State University, 1996.

Lim, Roger T. "The Chinese in San Francisco and the Mining Region of California, 1848–1858." M.A. thesis, Dominican College of San Rafael, 1979.

Madley, Benjamin Logan. "American Genocide: The California Indian Catastrophe, 1846–1873." Ph.D. diss., Yale University, 2009.

Melillo, Edward Dallam. "Strangers on Familiar Soil: Chile and the Making of California, 1848–1930." Ph.D. diss., Yale University, 2006.

Moody, William Penn. "The Civil War and Reconstruction in California Politics." Ph.D. diss., University of California, Los Angeles, 1950.

Pillors, Brenda. "The Criminalization of Prostitution in the U.S.: The Case of San Francisco, 1854–1919." Ph.D. diss., University of California, Berkeley, 1982.

Pitelka, Linda. "Mendocino: Race Relations in a Northern California County, 1850–1949." Ph.D. diss., University of Massachusetts, 1994.

Schneider, Khal Ross. "Citizen Lives: California Indian Country, 1855–1940." Ph.D. diss., University of California, Berkeley, 2006.

Sisson, Kelly Joan. "Diaspora, *Deseos*, and Dead Gringos." Undergraduate honors thesis, Stanford University, 2003.

Index

Note: Acts of law are Californian unless otherwise denoted with "(U.S.)"

legislation; Children; Domestic
work; Free African Americans in
California; Gold rush; Guardianship;
Slavery; Suffrage; Women

Ah Chon, 171

Ah Fook, 206, 215, 219, 222, 286 (n. 1)

Ah Fung, 206, 215, 219, 222, 286 (n. 1)

Ah Ho, 164

Ahine (Chinese contract worker), 34

Ah Jim, 166

Ah Toy, 38, 162

'Ai (Chinese contract worker), 34, 35

Ali'i (Hawaiian ruling class), 32

Almquist, Alan, 189

Alta California, 73–74, 76, 94, 132–33;
Chinese immigrants and, 37, 98, 101,
102–3, 104, 108; Chinese prostitution
and, 164, 165–66, 167, 216

Amanda (slave mother), 128

American Party, 75, 76

American River, 22, 23, 33, 85, 100, 259
(n. 89)

American West, myths of freedom in, 3,
4, 5–6, 7, 233–34

Anderson, Peter, 174, 177, 182

Anti-Chinese discourse, 95–98, 248
(n. 7); Chinese bound prostitutes
and, 161–68, 170, 175–76, 203–4;
Chinese Police Tax and, 195–98,
208; coolie labor and, 95–106, 162,
175, 179, 193, 196–97, 208, 209, 218,
223, 256 (n. 67); legislative debate in
California, during Civil War, 192–98

Anti-Chinese immigration laws: in
California, 5, 14, 204, 205, 208–17, 251
(n. 34), 287 (nn. 18, 26); California
influencing national, 5, 14, 215, 217–
18, 220–22, 248–49 (n. 8); Chinese
bound prostitutes and, 12, 203–4,
248–49 (n. 8), 251 (n. 34), 287 (n. 18);
examination of Chinese immigrant
women and, 206, 215, 217, 219, 221,
222–23, 287 (n. 26); federal anticoolie
laws, 194–95; federal laws, 5, 14, 207,
218, 220–30, 286 (n. 3), 289 (nn. 52,

59); foreign miners' tax and, 106–8;
framed as anticoolie labor, 13, 14, 39,
207, 221, 223–24, 226–27, 248–49
(n. 8); framed as antislavery laws, 3,
5, 12, 13–14, 206–7, 209–10, 214–17,
218, 220–24, 226, 229, 248 (n. 7), 248–
49 (n. 8), 286 (n. 3); Reconstruction
in California and, 3, 5, 13, 206–7,
229–30, 248 (n. 7), 248–49 (n. 8), 286
(n. 3). See also California legislation;
Chinese Exclusion Act of 1882; Page
Law of 1875

Antislavery Constitution of California:
admission to Union and, 1, 4,
7–8, 48, 65; apprenticeship law
and, 112–13, 186; attempts to limit
immigration of blacks and, 15–16,
61, 86; constitutional convention of
1849 and, 15–16, 39, 46, 47, 50, 60–61,
112; fugitive slave law of 1852 and, 9,
46, 70–71, 73–74, 76–77, 79; slavery in
California and, 60, 63, 64, 65, 66, 67,
263 (n. 41); southern-born whites in
California and, 42, 49, 61

Apache Indians, 25

Apprenticeship: African American
children and, 134–35, 136, 137–38,
275 (n. 65); attempts for formal laws
for African Americans, 11–12, 112–13,
115–17, 124–25, 131–40; constitutional
convention of 1849 and, 112–13;
court cases and, 159–60, 187–88,
190, 201–2; formal laws for Native
Americans, 11–12, 111–13, 116–17,
131–40, 148–49, 271 (n. 7); Native
Americans and, 148–50, 159–60,
175, 183–92, 199–202, 271 (n. 7), 277
(n. 14), 282 (nn. 23, 25), 283 (n. 29);
repeal of laws, 185–90, 199–200, 205,
284 (nn. 41–42); slavery, compared
with, 132–33, 134, 137–38, 139, 140,
185–86, 192; southern California
legislators and, 11–12, 132, 133, 134–
35, 136–38; warfare in northwestern
California, 1850s and 1860s, and,

Importation of Mongolian, Chinese, and Japanese Females, for Criminal or Demoralizing Purposes, 206, 207, 215, 217, 251 (n. 34), 286 (n. 1), 287 (nn. 18, 26); Act to Prohibit the Sale of Chinese Persons of Either Sex, 202–3; Act to Protect Free White Labor against Competition with Chinese Coolie Labor, and to Discourage the Immigration of Chinese into the State of California, 195–97; anticoolieism and, 13, 14, 39, 80–82, 101, 103–6, 108, 195–98, 216–17, 223–24, 288 (n. 46); antimiscegenation laws and, 156–59; antipeonage and, 80–82, 86–94, 259 (n. 1), 267–68 (n. 27); antiprostitution and woman trafficking, 14, 144, 175–76, 202–4, 205, 208, 215, 219–20, 221, 251 (n. 34), 286 (nn. 1, 74, 78); attempts for southern California statehood, 135, 137, 138, 275 (n. 58); attempts to allow "coolie" contract labor, 95, 97, 98–101, 102–3, 104–5, 107; attempts to limit immigration of blacks, 15–16, 49, 61–63, 78, 86, 112, 263 (n. 37), 266 (n. 85); Bill to Enforce Contracts to Perform Work and Labor, 98–99; Bill to Enforce the Observance of Contracts, 99; Chinese Police Tax, 195–98, 208; Committee on Mines and Mining Interests and, 80, 102; constitution, 1879, 223–24, 288 (n. 46); Criminal and Civil Practice Act, 181; dismantling of proslavery legislation, 13, 79, 174–75, 177–82, 193, 205, 250–51 (n. 31); Emancipation Proclamation (1863) and, 181–82; Fifteenth Amendment and, 13, 210–11, 213, 287 (n. 15); Fourteenth Amendment and, 5, 13, 14, 182, 207, 210, 284 (n. 78), 287 (n. 10); guardianship laws, 11–12, 114–15, 116–17, 130, 250 (nn. 27–28), 272 (n. 15); prohibition of nonwhite

testimony in court and, 56, 67, 72, 174, 175, 176, 177–82, 188, 193, 205, 214, 261 (nn. 20, 22), 281 (n. 3), 282 (n. 17); proposed slave colony and, 48–49, 99, 259–60 (n. 3); Thirteenth Amendment and, 182. *See also* Act for the Government and Protection of Indians of 1850; Anti-Chinese immigration laws; Apprenticeship; California; Foreign miners' tax; Fugitive slave law of 1852

California Police Gazette, 167, 190

California Supreme Court, 94, 171, 197, 219, 284 (n. 42); fugitive slave law of 1852 and, 9, 46, 64, 70, 71, 76, 77–78, 264 (nn. 63–64); prohibition of nonwhite testimony in court and, 179, 181, 261 (n. 20), 281 (n. 9); slavery and, 233, 289 (n. 3)

Californios: domestic servants and, 11, 110, 111, 113, 251–52 (n. 6); guardianship and, 11, 119, 121–23; Native Americans and, 18–24, 114, 147–48, 149; rancho system of labor and, 18–24, 85, 110, 114, 147, 252 (n. 12)

Calloway, John, 67

Campbell, Basil, 231–34, 289 (n. 1)

Campbell, Peter, 119, 121, 122–23

Carigen, Nicholas, 121

Carillo, Ramón, 18

Carnes, Henry, 119

Carpenter, Helen, 149, 188, 277 (n. 14), 282 (n. 22)

Carrillo de Vallejo, Francisca Benicia, 20

Cassady (slave child), 127–28

Casserly, Eugene, 211

Catholic missions in California, 19, 147

Children: enslaved women "lacking virtue" to have custody of, 127, 128, 129, 273 (n. 42); kidnapping parties for Native American children, 20–21, 184, 186–88, 190; labor and sexual exploitation of, 111–12; Native Americans and African Americans

Daylor, William, 23

Debt bondage, 17; Chinese immigrants during gold rush and, 10, 34, 36, 37–38; Hawaiians and Native Americans and, 33, 110; Latinos and, 24, 26, 28, 83, 110; prostitution and, 38–39, 163–64

Democratic Party: antiblack suffrage and, 207–8; anti-Chinese immigration laws and, 14, 214–17; apprenticeship law and, 139, 140, 183, 185, 189; Chinese immigrants and, 177, 207–8; after Civil War, 13, 182, 198, 209–11, 213, 217, 251 (n. 33); coolie labor and, 96, 98, 100–102, 103–5, 175, 179, 198, 209–13, 214, 215–16; prohibition of nonwhite testimony in court and, 177, 178; slavery and, 61, 64, 68, 69, 70, 74–75, 76, 77, 78, 174, 177, 181–82; splitting of, 12–13, 73, 74, 75, 78–79, 180; woman trafficking and, 142, 158, 203, 204. *See also* Chivalry Democrats

Democratic State Convention of 1869, 213

Dick (Paiute Indian youth), 117, 118

Dimmick, Kimball, 112–13, 127

Dodson, George P., 41

Domestic work: African American slave children and, 11–12, 109–11, 112–13, 115–16, 117, 124–25, 138–39; African American slaves and, 40, 41, 42, 110, 142, 258 (n. 83); Californios and, 11, 110, 111, 113, 251–52 (n. 6); Chinese immigrants and, 34, 163; constitutional convention of 1849 and, 112–13; Native American children as wards for, 1–2, 11–12, 20–21, 109, 110–11, 113, 114, 117–18, 121–22, 132, 138–39, 182–83, 184, 277 (n. 14); Native Americans captured for labor and sexual exploitation, 21, 110–11, 142, 147–51, 159–61, 277 (n. 18); shortage of laborers for, 10–11, 42, 110, 125, 133, 147

Dominguez, Jesús, 122

Dorsey, Civility, 128

Dorsey, Hilliard, 128

Douglas, Stephen A., 74

Dow (slave), 84, 258 (n. 83)

Downey, John, 171, 172

Dred Scott v. Sandford, 76, 263 (n. 40)

Dryden, William G., 119–21, 127, 128

Dwinelle, John, 197

Eads, Thomas, 52

Eastland, Thomas B., 84, 258 (n. 83)

Emancipation Proclamation (1863), 12, 174, 181–82, 189

Enforcement Act of 1870. *See* Civil Rights Act of 1870

Erwin, Alexander Hamilton, 42, 44, 257–58 (n. 79)

Estell, James, 70, 264 (n. 59)

Evertsen, John, 128, 129, 130

Evertsen, Laura, 128

Farrell, William, 121–22

Fay, Caleb, 178, 179, 188, 189

Field, Stephen J., 219–20, 288 (n. 33)

Fifteen Passenger Bill, 224

Fifteenth Amendment, 13, 182, 210–11, 213, 215, 287 (n. 15)

Foner, Eric, 6

Foreign miners' tax, 113, 179, 197; passing of, 93; proposal of, 80, 87, 89–90, 259 (n. 1), 267 (nn. 14, 21); repeal of, 94, 97, 268 (n. 37); revival of, 106–7, 194, 270 (nn. 73–74)

Fourteenth Amendment, 5, 13, 14, 182, 207, 210, 214, 215, 219, 284 (n. 78), 287 (n. 10), 288 (n. 33)

Francisca (Indian ward), 121

Frank (slave), 66–67

Free African Americans in California, 45, 86, 231, 289 (n. 1); abolitionists, 1, 55–57, 67, 70, 247 (n. 1); danger of reenslavement, 70, 71–72, 176; emancipation and, 174, 177–78, 219, 288 (n. 33); population in California,

slavery by whites, 164–67, 198, 199, 207, 248–49 (n. 8); court cases for women involved in, 144, 168–72; critics of, 142–43, 144, 198, 199; gold rush and, 141–42; legal attempts to break up, 175–76, 202–4, 207; *tongs* (Chinese secret societies) and, 38–39, 162–63

—Chinese immigrants and, 3, 12, 141, 162–73, 198, 199, 202, 209, 213, 220; Fourteenth Amendment and, 219; in San Francisco, 38–39, 141–42, 203–4, 221, 286 (n. 74).
See also under Anti-Chinese immigration laws; California legislation

Purdy, John, 55

Quin Ti, 169–72

Rancho system of labor, 18–24, 85, 110, 114, 147, 192, 252 (n. 12)
Rawls, James, 22
Reading, Pierson B., 22, 23
Reconstruction, 6–7; anti-Chinese immigration laws and, 3, 5, 13, 206–7, 229–30, 248 (n. 7), 248–49 (n. 8), 286 (n. 3); in California, 13–14, 175, 205, 206–17; California influencing national trends, 5, 206–7, 286 (n. 3); U.S. Congress and, 213–15, 223
Reconstruction Amendments, 213.
See also Fifteenth Amendment; Fourteenth Amendment; Thirteenth Amendment
Red Bluff Beacon, 156–57
Reed, John, 120
Refugia (Indian ward), 119
Republican Party: antislavery and, 9, 56, 78, 177, 178, 207–8; Chinese exclusion and, 5, 14, 179, 220–30; Chinese immigrants and, 192–98, 202–4, 207–8, 210, 216–17; Native American affairs and, 153, 154, 183, 200–202; Native American apprenticeship

law and, 136, 185–92; prohibition of nonwhite testimony in court and, 178–79; Reconstruction and, 175, 210–11, 213, 217–18; rise to power in California, 3, 9, 12–13, 77, 79, 140, 174, 177, 179–80, 189, 205; woman trafficking and, 13, 142, 175, 198, 199, 200–204
Reservations, 185; agricultural labor and, 191, 192; establishment of in California, 113–14, 153–55, 175, 183, 190–91; "squaw men" and, 200, 201, 202
Revere, Joseph Warren, 21
Reyes (Indian ward), 123–24, 273 (n. 34)
Rheubin (slave), 41, 42, 258 (n. 83), 259 (n. 89)
Rice, Aaron, 176, 281 (n. 3)
Rice, Nathaniel, 176, 281 (n. 3)
Rice, William, 176
Richards, Leonard L., 7, 71
Richardson, Heather Cox, 6, 7
Roach, Philip A., 101, 102, 103, 104
Rogers, Abraham, 145
Rosa (Indian apprentice), 182–83, 188, 282 (n. 22)
Rose (slave child), 127–28
Rose's Bar, 47, 48, 55, 84, 86, 259 (n. 1)
Round Valley Reservation, 146, 191, 200, 201
Rowland, Charlotte, 127–28
Rowland, John, 127–28

Sacramento Daily Union, 137–38, 139, 140, 151, 153, 154, 165, 169, 170
Sally (slave mother), 128
San Francisco: apprenticeship law and, 1, 135; Chinese immigrants and, 36, 37, 197, 206, 219; Chinese prostitution and, 38–39, 141–42, 203–4, 221, 286 (n. 74); slavery and, 56, 59, 67, 72, 124
San Francisco Bulletin, 141, 142, 154, 165, 186, 220
San Joaquin Republican, 77
San Joaquin River, 18

Varney, Jack, 51, 54

Wailacki Indians, 148
Walthall, Elizabeth, 63
Walthall, Madison, 63
Water monopolies, 98
Wheeler, G. Wyatt, 231, 233
Wheeler, John W., 231, 233
Whig Party, 8–9, 68, 69, 75, 77, 96, 98, 99, 100, 105, 135
Williams, C. S., 159–60
Williams, James, 55
Williams, John F., 62, 115–16, 124–25, 262 (n. 35)
Williams, Mary, 124, 125
Wilmot, David, 64
Wilmot Proviso (1846), 7, 64
Wilson, Benjamin Davis, 109–10, 126, 129
Wilson, Margaret Hereford, 109
Wintu Indians, 149
Women: abolitionist concerns about labor and sexual exploitation of, 142, 151, 276 (n. 4), 277–78 (n. 21); African American freedwomen, 198–99; African American slaves, 45, 128–29, 142, 276 (n. 4); Chinese immigrants not prostitutes, 163, 164, 165–67, 206–7, 215, 219, 222–23; enslaved women "lacking virtue" to have custody of children and, 127, 128, 129, 273 (n. 42); labor and sexual exploitation of, 10–11, 12, 38–39, 142; Native American, captured for labor and sexual exploitation, 12, 21, 142, 143, 144–56, 157–61, 199, 200–201, 277 (n. 18); Native American, as unsuited to have custody of children, 125, 129, 132; white view of Chinese, 103, 141, 143–44, 161, 162, 164–68, 170, 172, 198, 202, 203, 204, 213, 218; white, on reservations, 201; women's rights, 199. See also under Anti-Chinese immigration laws; Prostitution
Woodman, George, 187, 188
Workingmen's Party of California (WPC), 223–24
Wozencraft, Oliver, 1–2, 248 (n. 3)

Yaqui Indians, 25
Yberra, José, 122
Yee-Kwan, 164
Young, Lucy. See T'tcetsa
Yuba River, 47, 100
Yuki Indians, 1–2, 11, 184–85, 187, 277 (n. 18)

CPSIA information can be obtained at www.ICGtesting.com
Printed in the USA
LVOW08s0259211016

509504LV00008B/12/P